kimi ni todoke

From Me to You

Sawako "Sadako" Kuronuma is the perfect heroine... *for a horror movie.* With her jet-black hair, sinister smile and silent demeanor, she's always had trouble fitting in. But her whole life changes when she befriends the most popular boy in class, Shota Kazehaya.

Ever since the near-kiss incident on the school trip, Sawako and Kazehaya have become distant. With Ayane warming to Kento's affections and Chizuru devastated that her friendship with Ryu is beyond repair, does the change of season mean a change of heart?

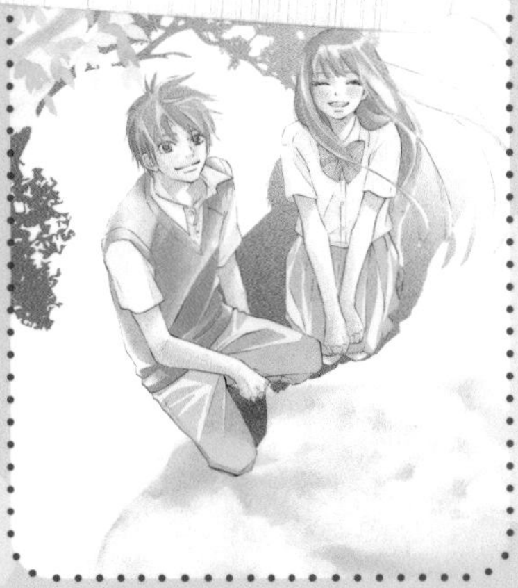

Can love trump a cursed life?

15 Karuho Shiina

www.shojobeat.com

$9.99 USA $12.99 CAN £6.99 UK

This book reads from right to left.

VIZ media

RATED T FOR TEEN

ratings.viz.com

ISBN-13: 978-1-4215-4919-4

50999

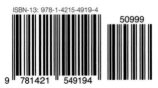

9 781421 549194

Surprise!

You may be reading the wrong way!

It's true: In keeping with the original Japanese comic format, this book reads from right to left—so action, sound effects, and word balloons are completely reversed. This preserves the orientation of the original artwork—plus, it's fun! Check out the diagram shown here to get the hang of things, and then turn to the other side of the book to get started!

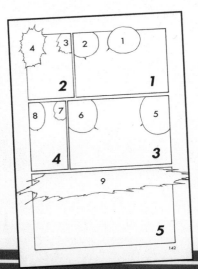

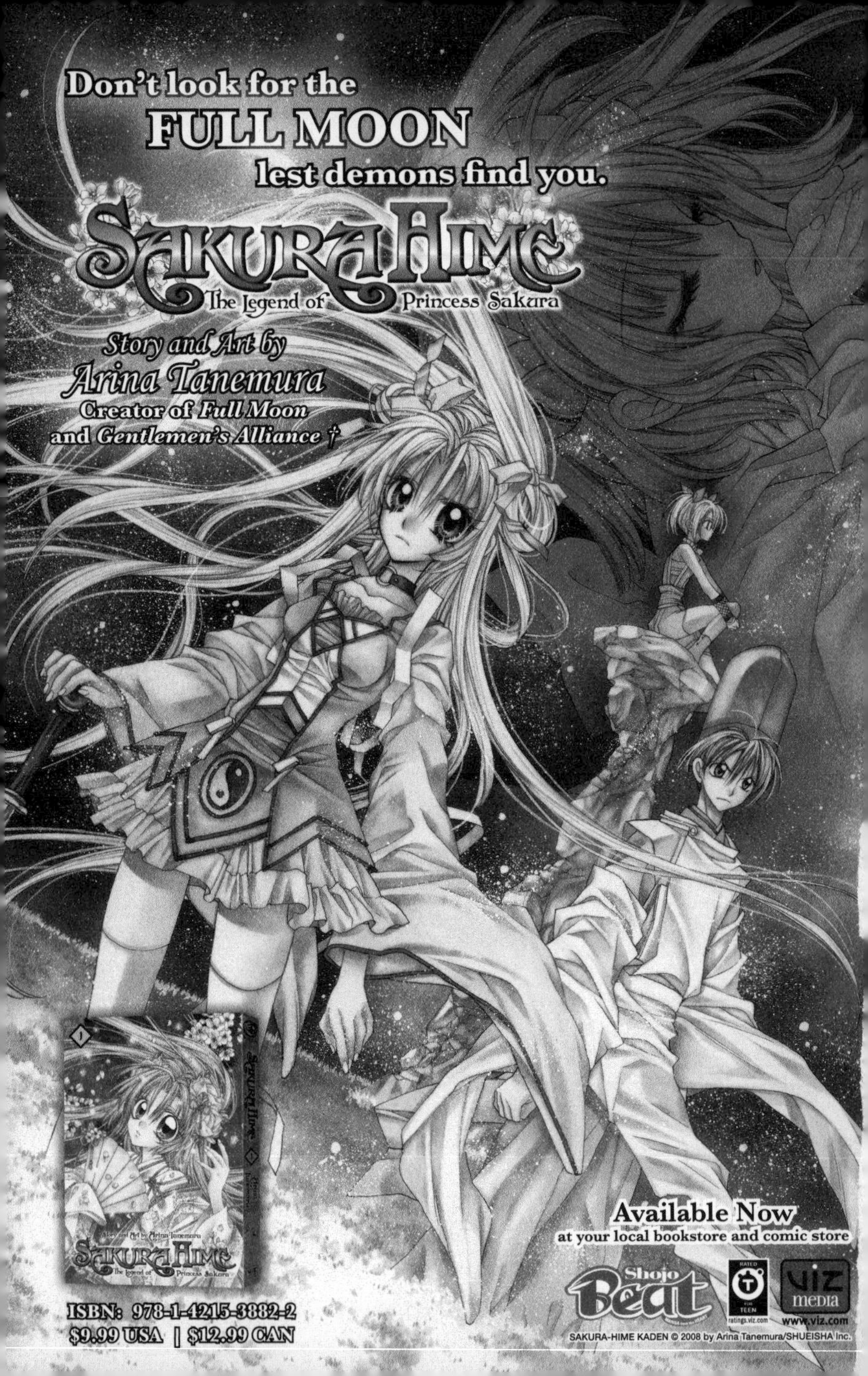
Don't look for the
FULL MOON
lest demons find you.
SAKURA HIME
The Legend of Princess Sakura
Story and Art by
Arina Tanemura
Creator of Full Moon
and Gentlemen's Alliance †
Available Now
at your local bookstore and comic store
ISBN: 978-1-4215-3882-2
$9.99 USA | $12.99 CAN
Shojo Beat
RATED T TEEN
ratings.viz.com
VIZ media
www.viz.com
SAKURA-HIME KADEN © 2008 by Arina Tanemura/SHUEISHA Inc.

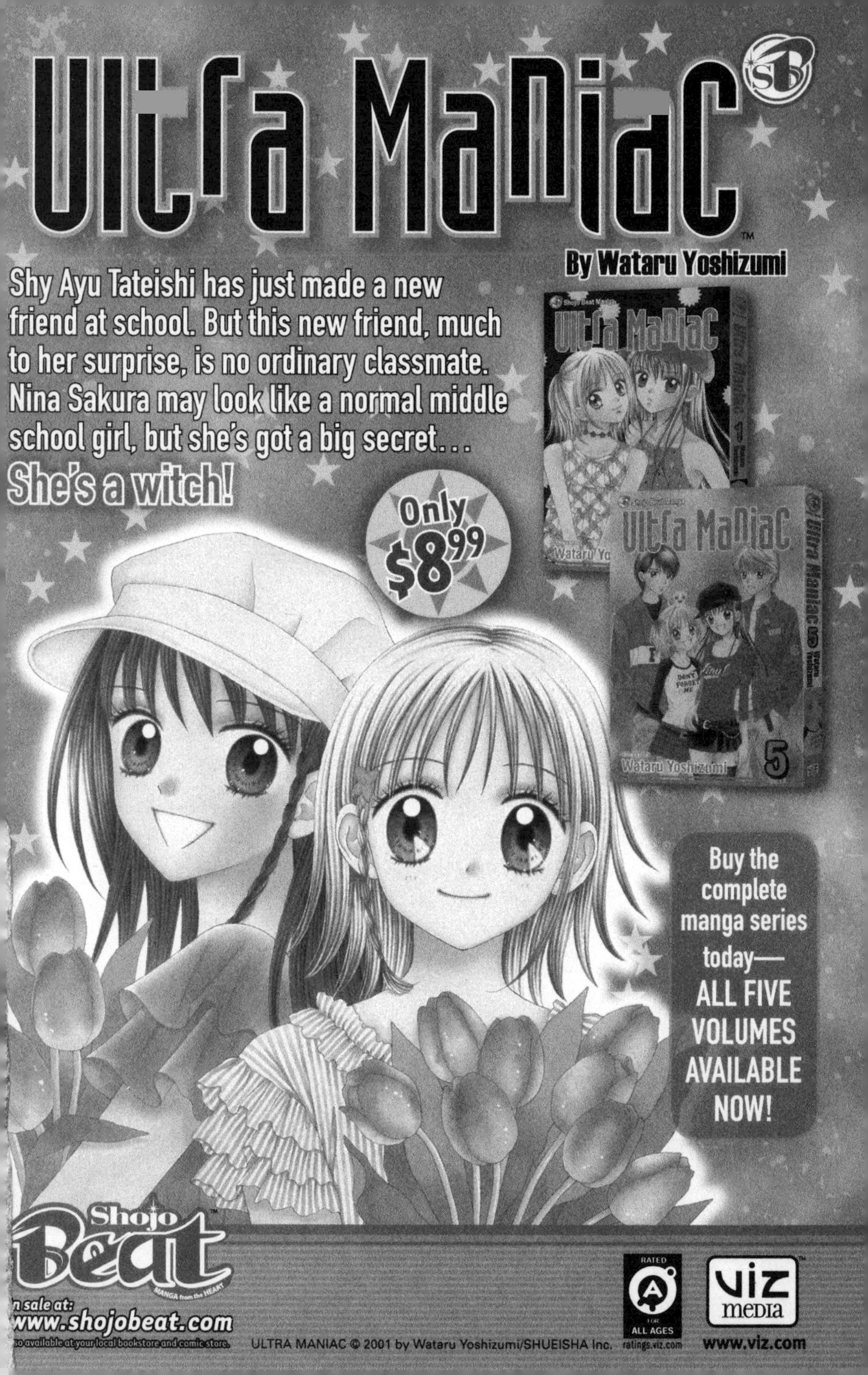
Ultra Maniac
By Wataru Yoshizumi
Shy Ayu Tateishi has just made a new friend at school. But this new friend, much to her surprise, is no ordinary classmate. Nina Sakura may look like a normal middle school girl, but she's got a big secret...
She's a witch!
Only $8.99
Ultra Maniac
Wataru Yoshizumi
5
Buy the complete manga series today—
ALL FIVE VOLUMES AVAILABLE NOW!
Shojo Beat
MANGA from the HEART
n sale at:
www.shojobeat.com
so available at your local bookstore and comic store.
ULTRA MANIAC © 2001 by Wataru Yoshizumi/SHUEISHA Inc.
RATED A FOR ALL AGES
ratings.viz.com
viz media
www.viz.com

Kimi ni Todoke
VOL. 15

Shojo Beat Edition

STORY AND ART BY
KARUHO SHIINA

Translation/Ari Yasuda, HC Language Solutions, Inc.
Touch-up Art & Lettering/Vanessa Satone
Design/Nozomi Akashi
Editor/Hope Donovan

KIMI NI TODOKE © 2005 by Karuho Shiina
All rights reserved. First published in Japan in 2005 by SHUEISHA Inc.,
Tokyo. English translation rights arranged by SHUEISHA Inc.

Printed in the U.S.A.

Published by VIZ Media, LLC
P.O. Box 77010
San Francisco, CA 94107

10 9 8 7 6 5 4 3 2 1
First printing, November 2012

www.viz.com

www.shojobeat.com

This is volume 15! Time flies! I thought
about drawing kid Chizu and Ryu on the
cover, but realized that might confuse
readers who don't know what's coming in
the graphic novel. So I drew them normal
on the cover and as kids on the title page of
Episode 63. Every single day I was working
on that chapter, I thought about rice balls.
I'd be holding one, thinking, "This is the
best food ever." You can stuff them with
veggies or fish, they're good hot or cold, and
they're even delicious with just salt and no
filling. They really are the best food ever!

--Karuho Shiina

Karuho Shiina was born and raised in
Hokkaido, Japan. Though *Kimi ni Todoke*
is only her second series following many
one-shot stories, it has already racked
up accolades from various "Best Manga
of the Year" lists. Winner of the 2008
Kodansha Manga Award for the shojo
category, *Kimi ni Todoke* also placed fifth
in the first-ever Manga Taisho (Cartoon
Grand Prize) contest in 2008. In Japan, an
animated TV series debuted in October
2009, and a live-action film was released
in 2010.

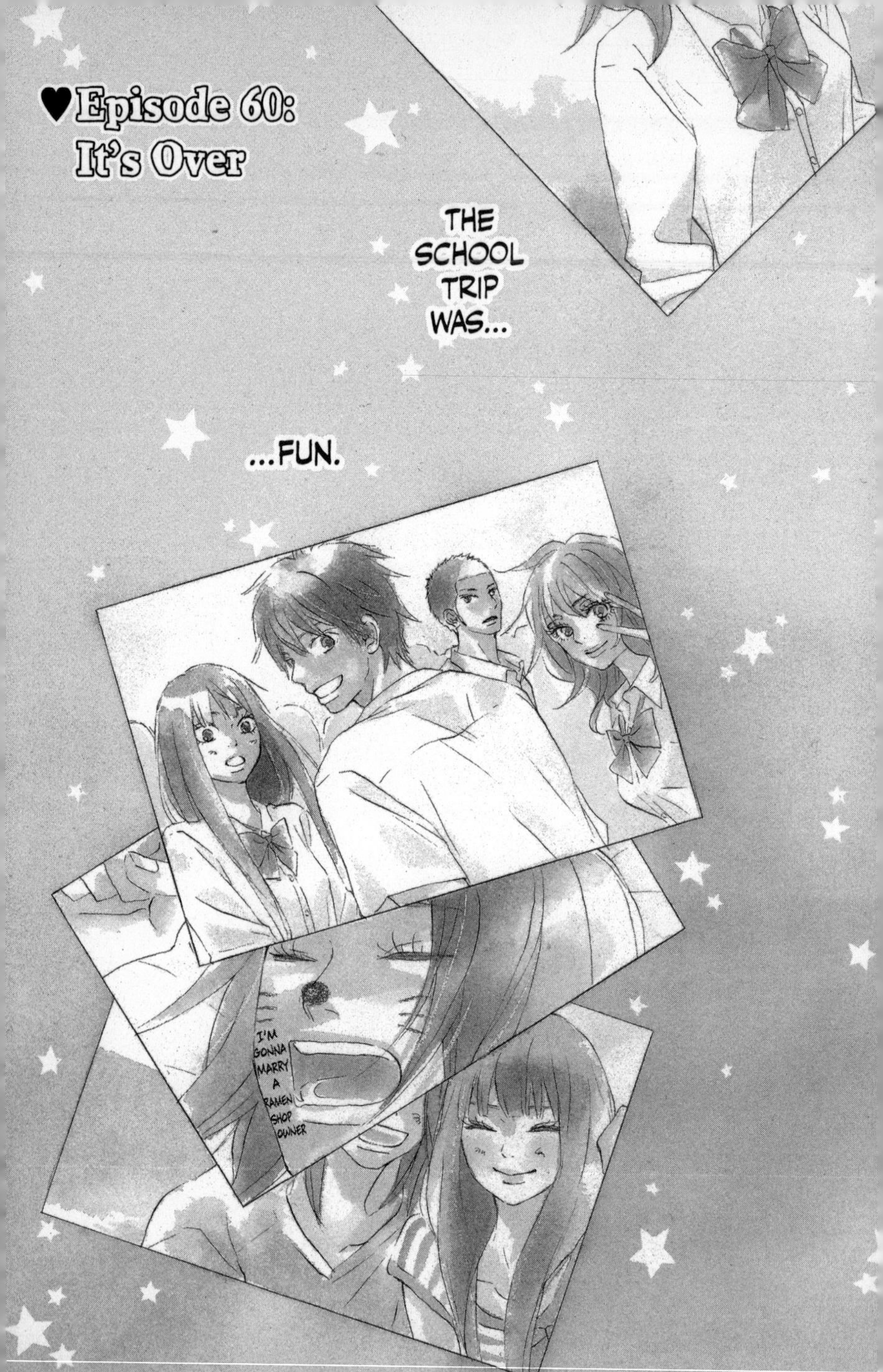
♥Episode 60: It's Over
THE SCHOOL TRIP WAS...
...FUN.
I'M GONNA MARRY A RAMEN SHOP OWNER

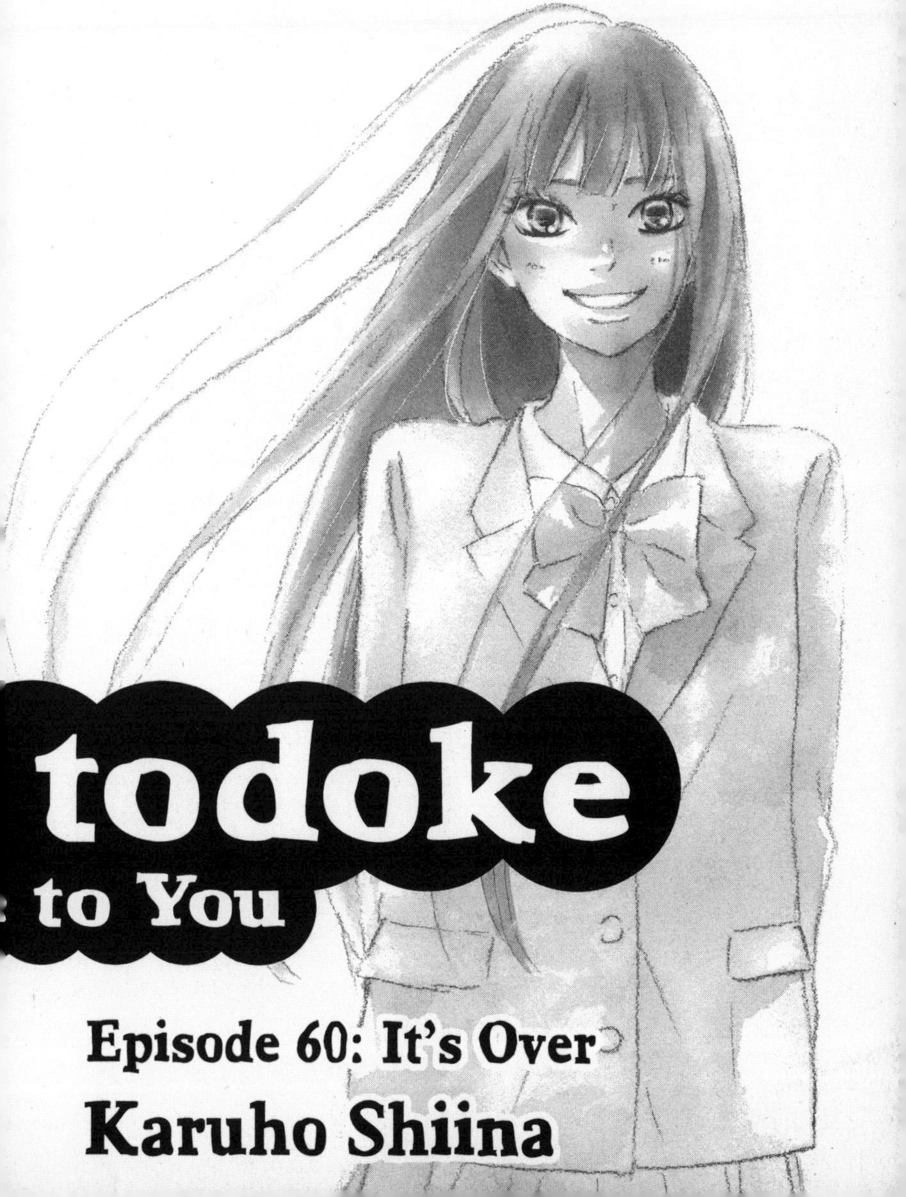
todoke
to You
Episode 60: It's Over
Karuho Shiina

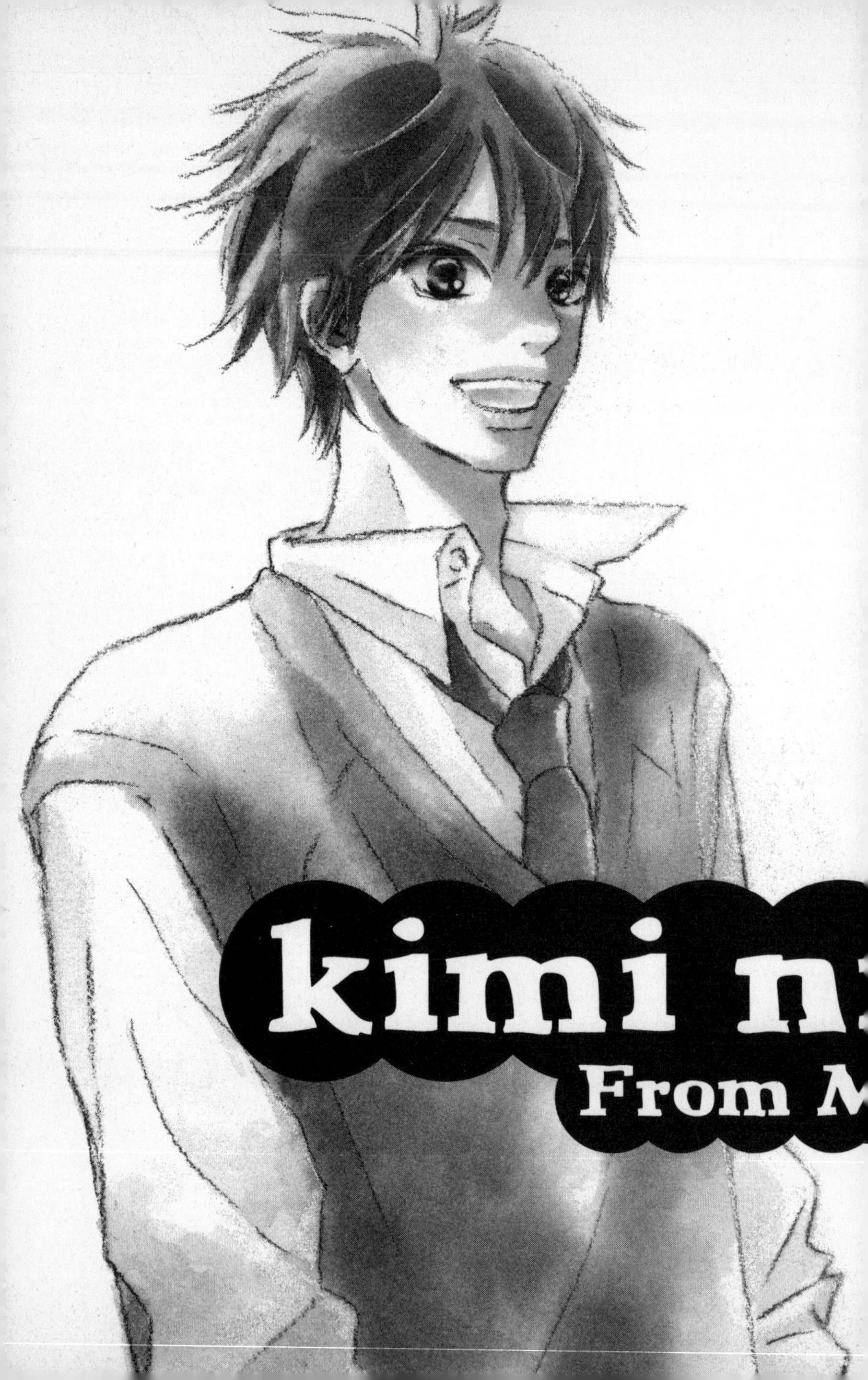
kimi n
From M

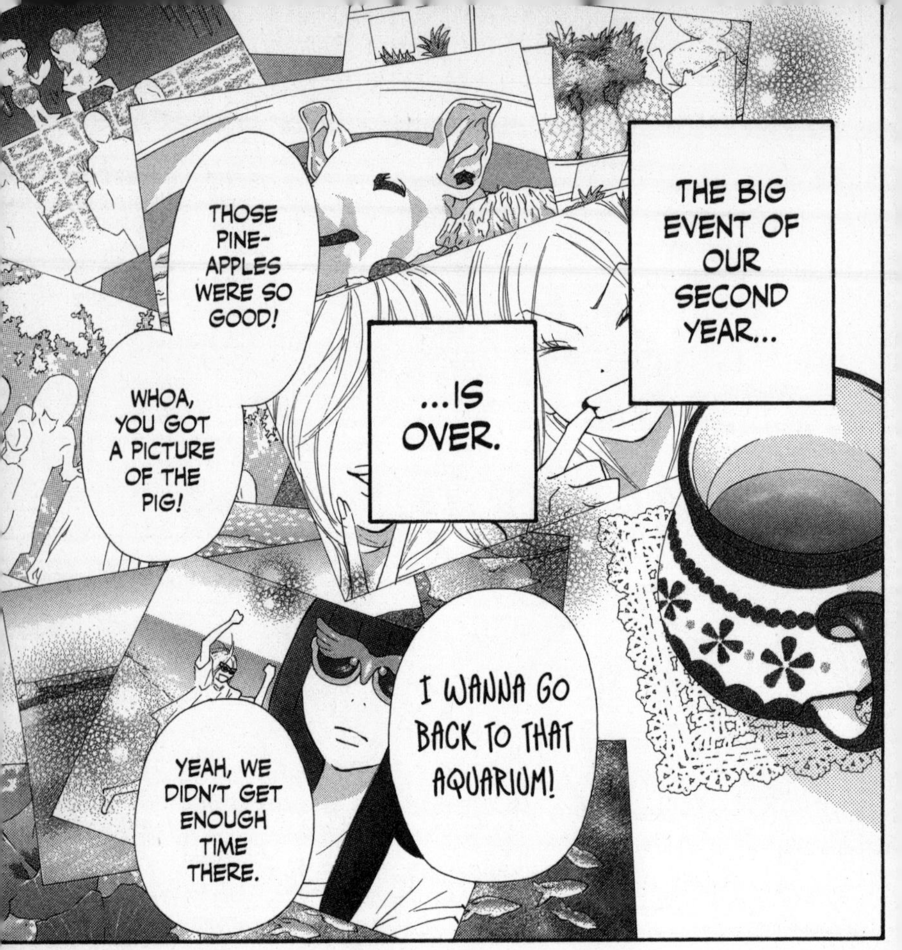
THE BIG EVENT OF OUR SECOND YEAR...
...IS OVER.
THOSE PINE-APPLES WERE SO GOOD!
WHOA, YOU GOT A PICTURE OF THE PIG!
I WANNA GO BACK TO THAT AQUARIUM!
YEAH, WE DIDN'T GET ENOUGH TIME THERE.

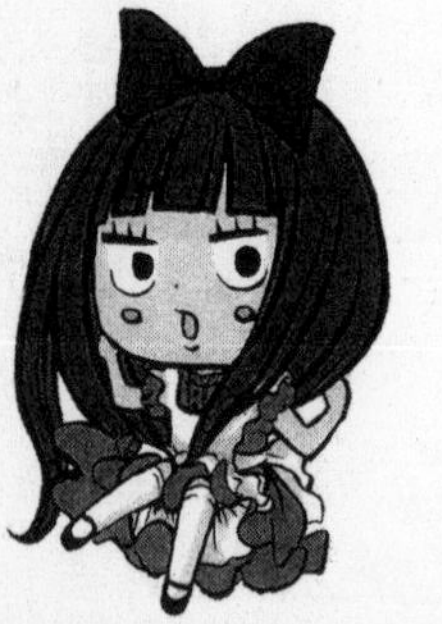

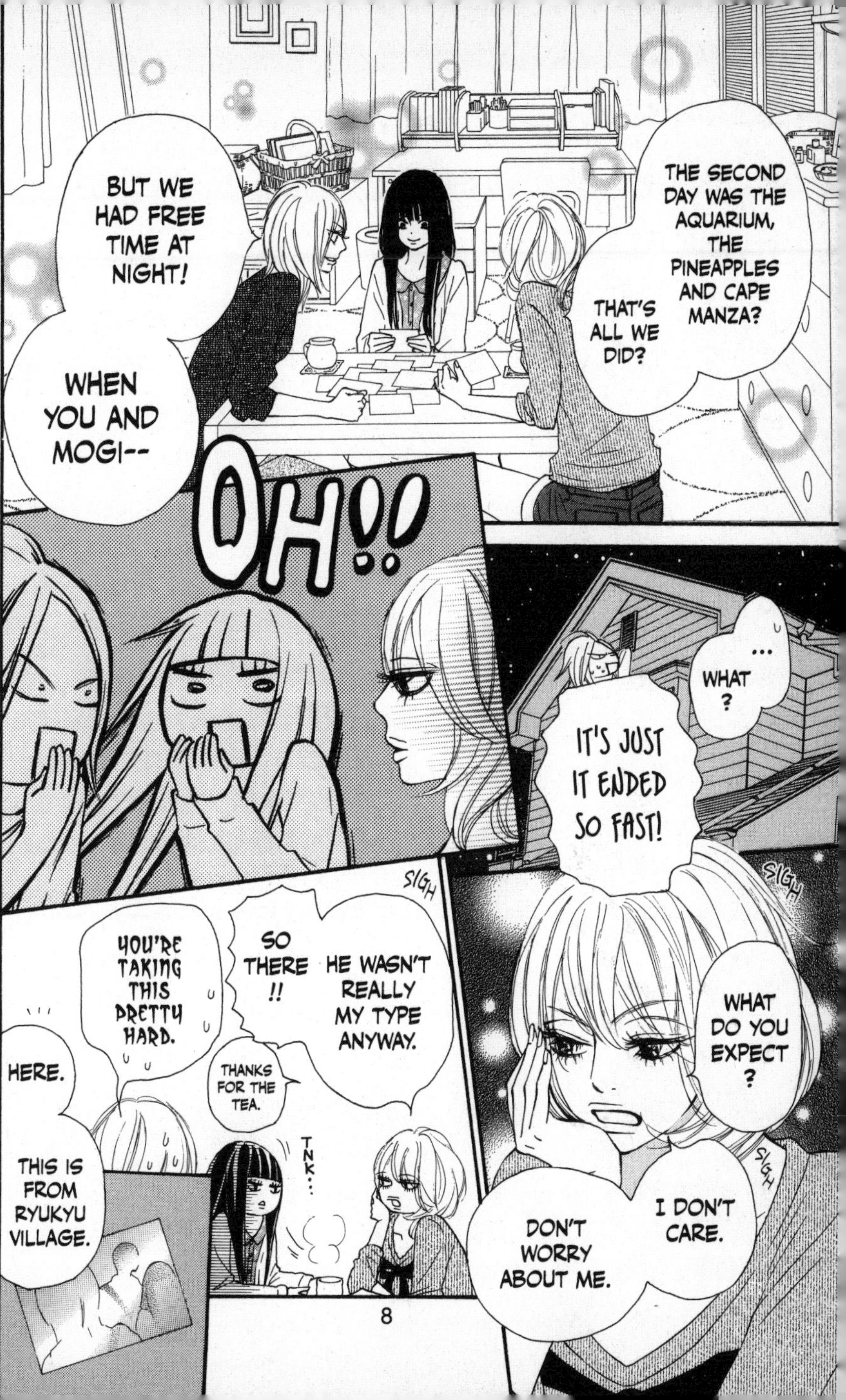
THE SECOND DAY WAS THE AQUARIUM, THE PINEAPPLES AND CAPE MANZA?
THAT'S ALL WE DID?
BUT WE HAD FREE TIME AT NIGHT!
WHEN YOU AND MOGI--
...WHAT?
IT'S JUST IT ENDED SO FAST!
OH!!
SIGH
WHAT DO YOU EXPECT?
I DON'T CARE.
DON'T WORRY ABOUT ME.
SIGH
SIGH
HE WASN'T REALLY MY TYPE ANYWAY.
SO THERE!!
YOU'RE TAKING THIS PRETTY HARD.
THANKS FOR THE TEA.
TNK...
HERE.
THIS IS FROM RYUKYU VILLAGE.

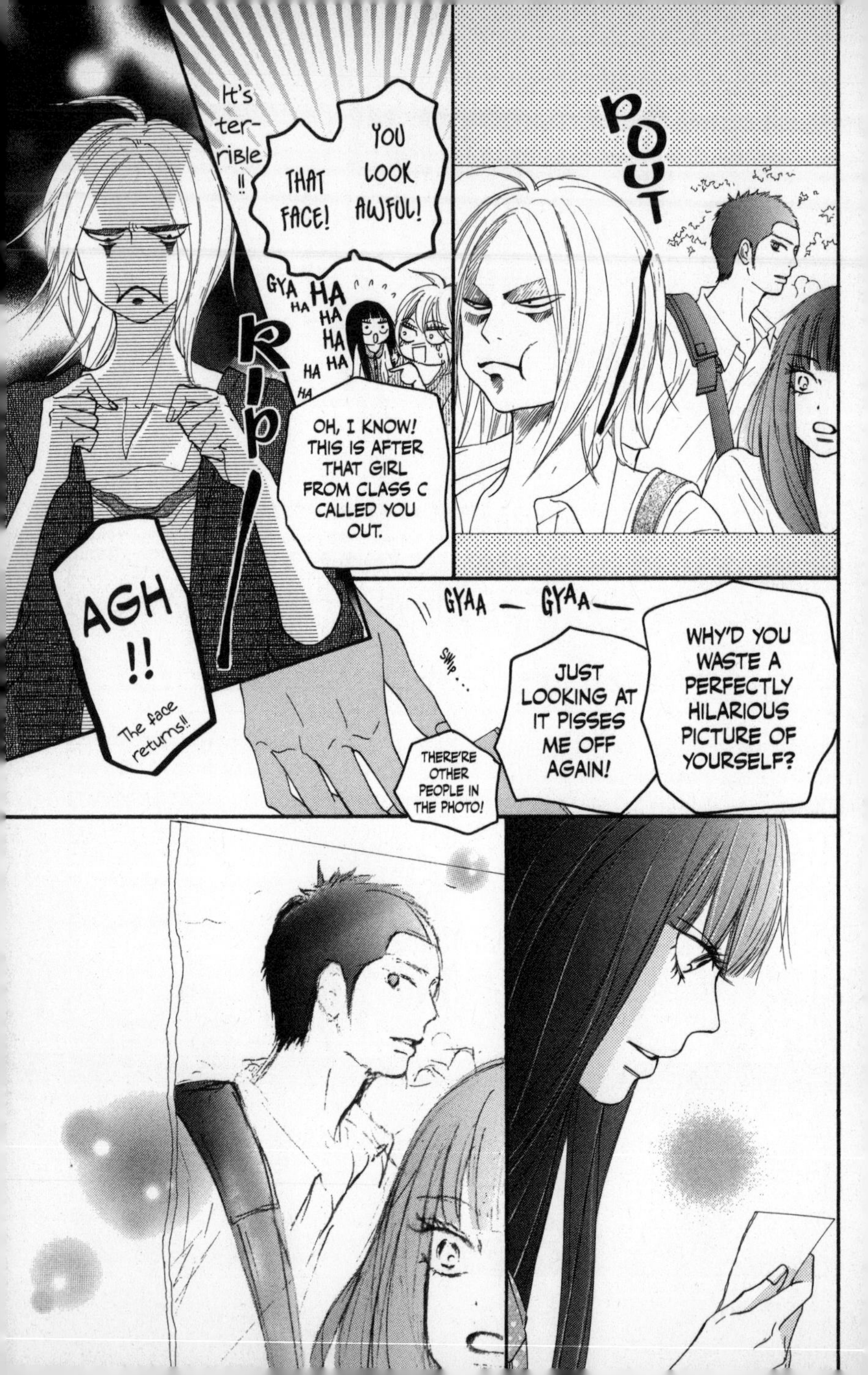
POUT
YOU LOOK AWFUL! THAT FACE!
It's terrible!!
GYAHA HA HA HA HA HA HA HA
OH, I KNOW! THIS IS AFTER THAT GIRL FROM CLASS C CALLED YOU OUT.
RIP!
AGH!!
The face returns!!
GYAA — GYAA —
WHY'D YOU WASTE A PERFECTLY HILARIOUS PICTURE OF YOURSELF?
JUST LOOKING AT IT PISSES ME OFF AGAIN!
SWIP...
THERE'RE OTHER PEOPLE IN THE PHOTO!

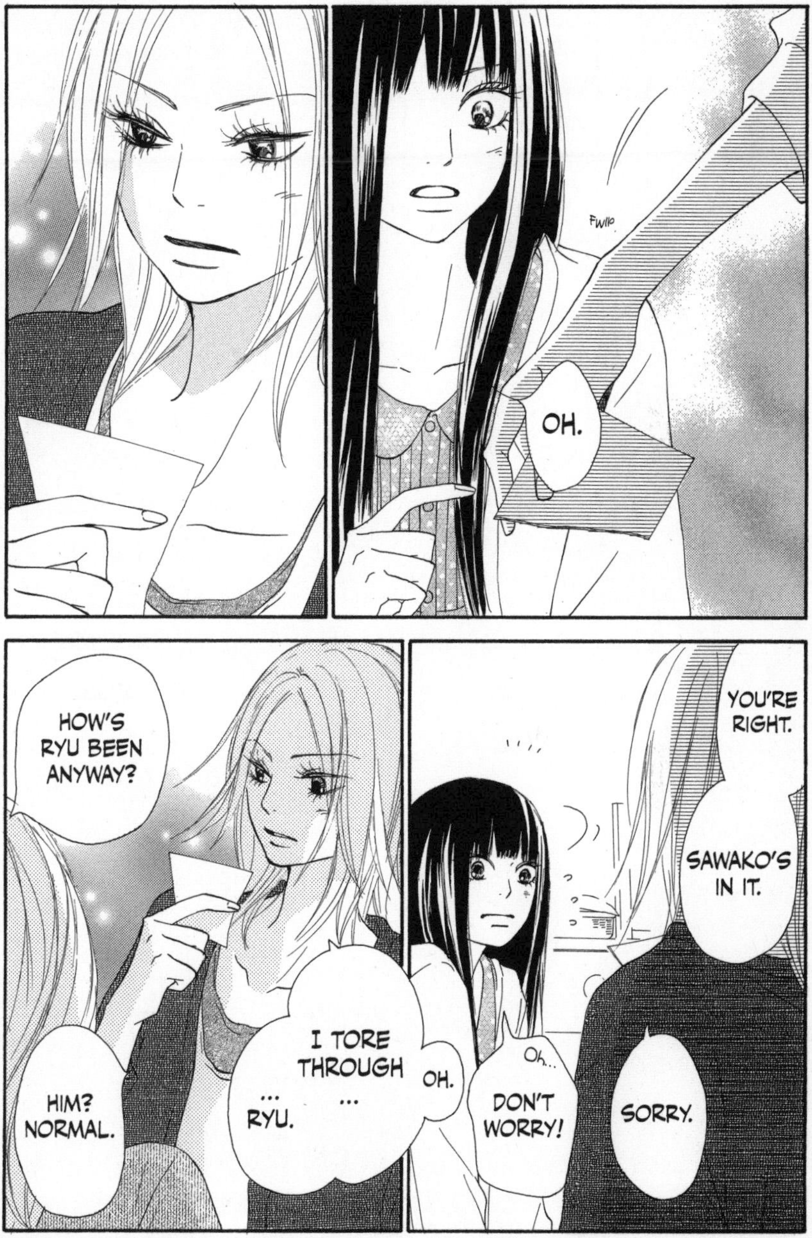
FWIP
OH.
YOU'RE RIGHT.
SAWAKO'S IN IT.
SORRY.
Oh...
DON'T WORRY!
OH.
HOW'S RYU BEEN ANYWAY?
I TORE THROUGH ...
... RYU.
HIM? NORMAL.

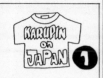

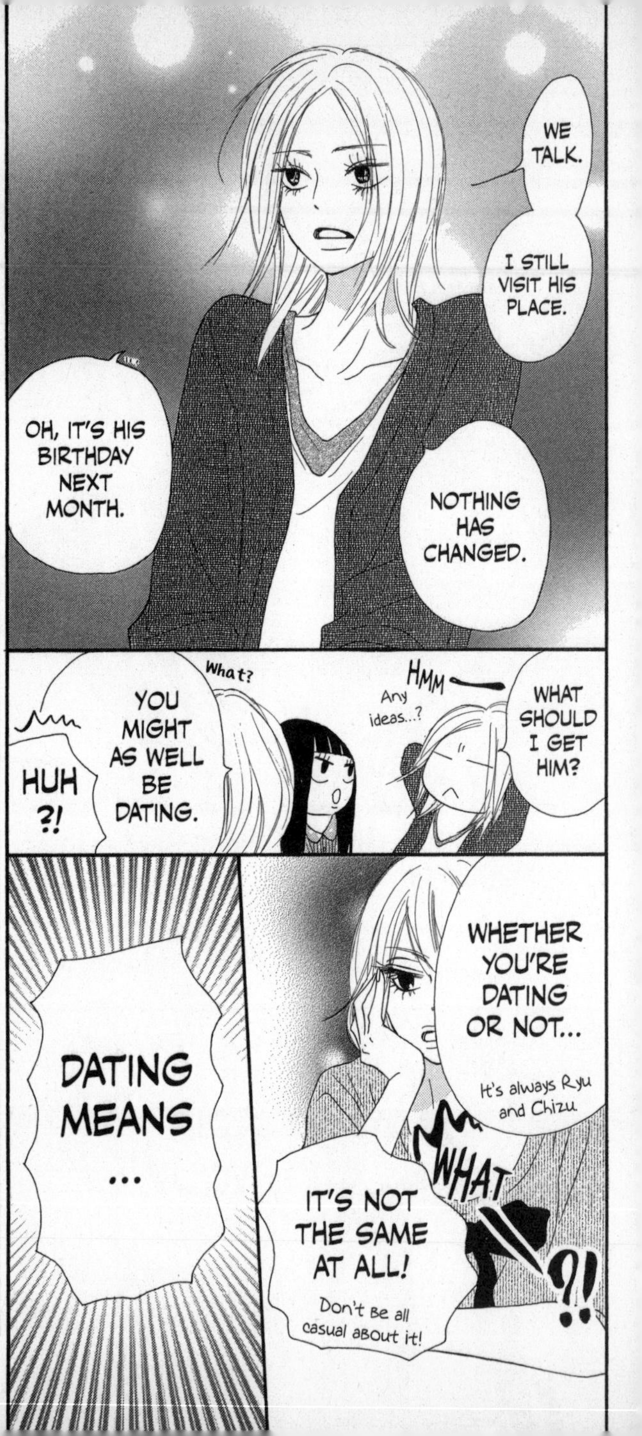
WE TALK.
I STILL VISIT HIS PLACE.
NOTHING HAS CHANGED.
OH, IT'S HIS BIRTHDAY NEXT MONTH.
WHAT SHOULD I GET HIM?
HMM—
Any ideas...?
What?
YOU MIGHT AS WELL BE DATING.
HUH ?!
WHETHER YOU'RE DATING OR NOT...
It's always Ryu and Chizu.
WHAT
?!!
IT'S NOT THE SAME AT ALL!
Don't be all casual about it!
DATING MEANS ...

KARUPIN on JAPAN 1

Hello! How are you?

This is Shiina. This is volume 15.

Ever since I wrote in volume 14 that the story was "reaching its climax," people have started asking me if it'll end soon. What I meant was I feel like it's ending... But sorry, the story itself will still take a while to finish. Sorry! Really sorry!

I feel bad for those of you who got excited about the impending conclusion. Sorry to announce this in the first sidebar. ✧

Thank you to those of you who keep reading all the way to the end. Please, keep reading.

What kind of intro is this?

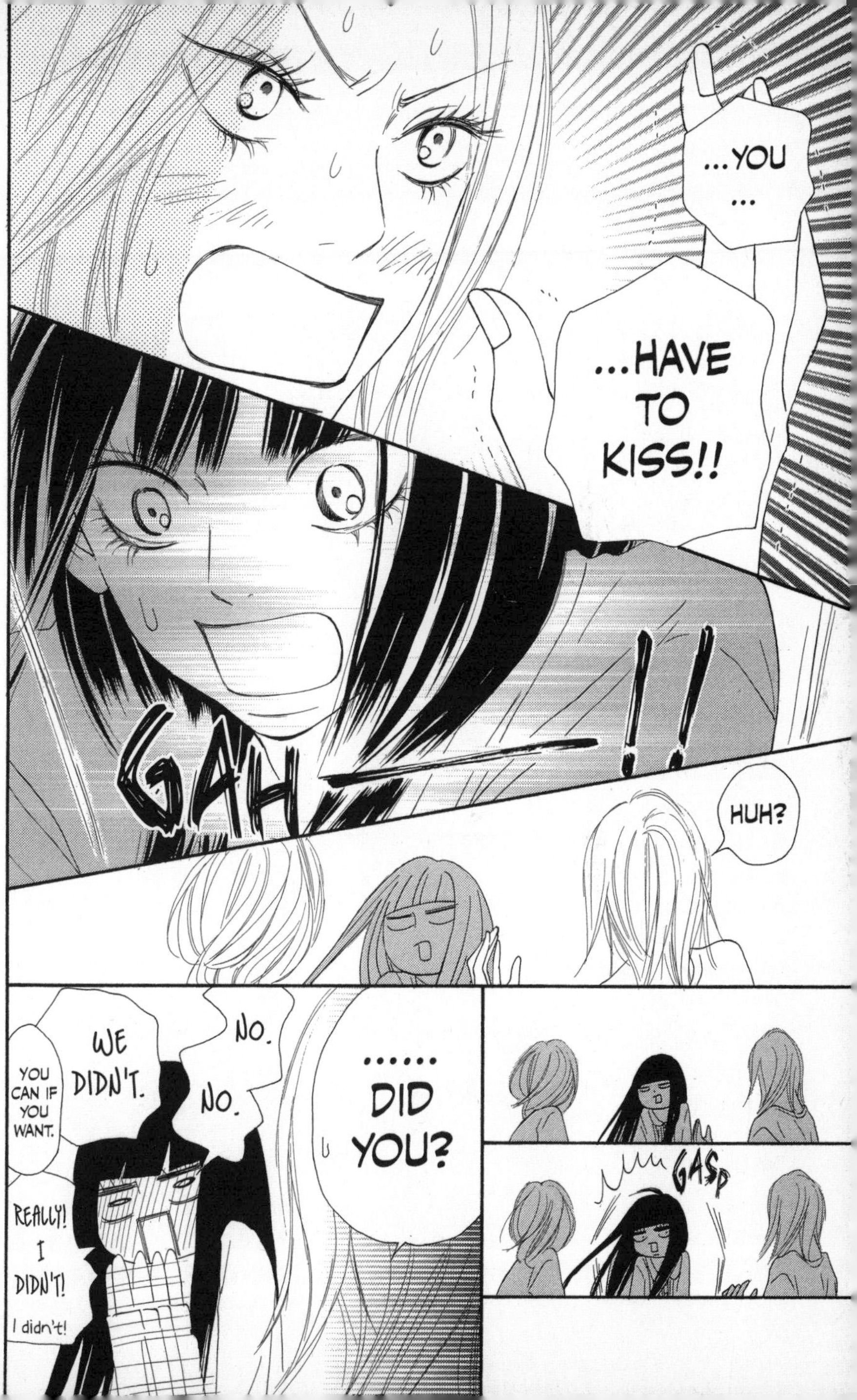
...YOU ...
...HAVE TO KISS!!
GAH—!!
HUH?
GASP
...... DID YOU?
NO.
NO.
WE DIDN'T.
YOU CAN IF YOU WANT.
REALLY! I DIDN'T!
I didn't!

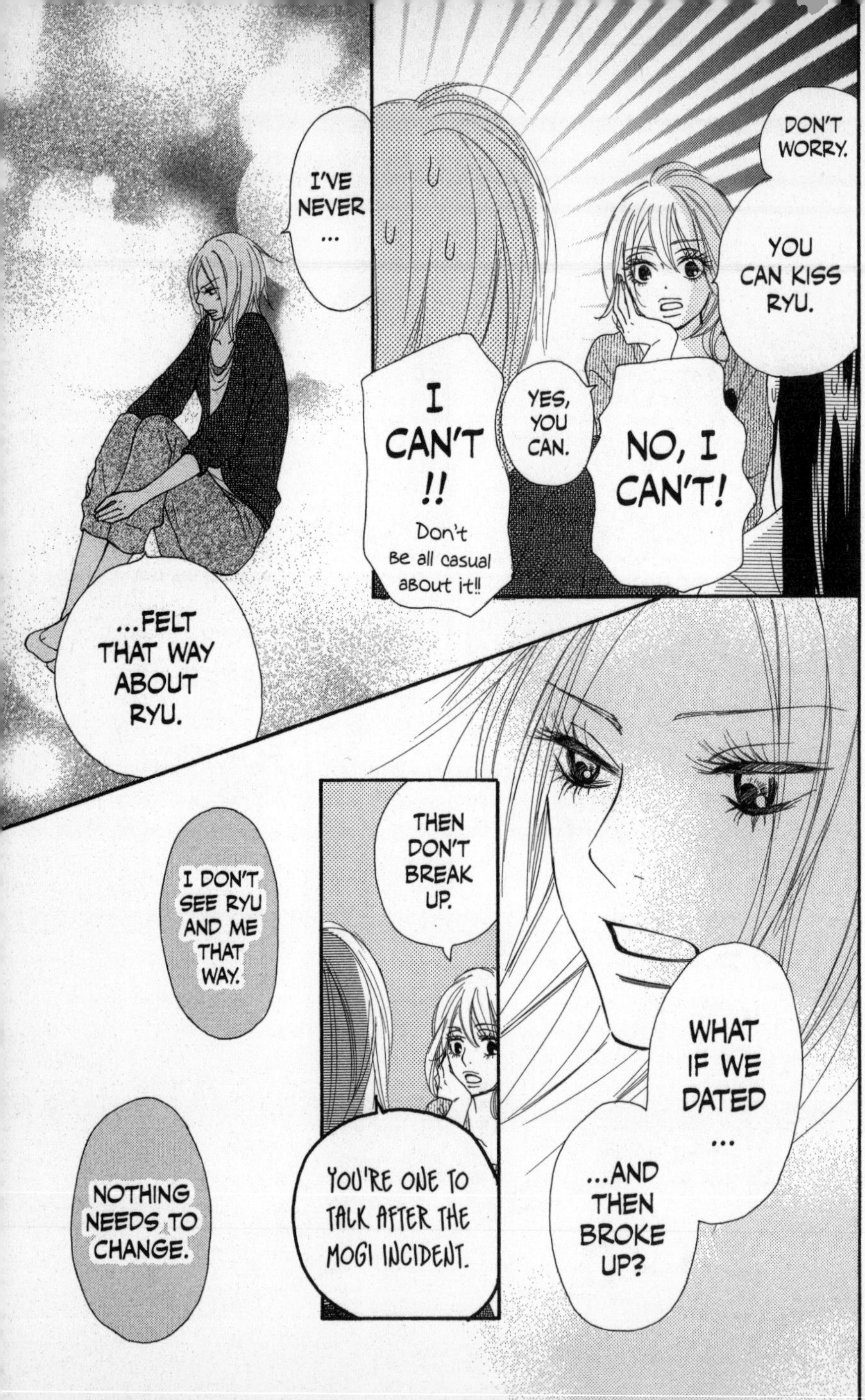
DON'T WORRY.
YOU CAN KISS RYU.
NO, I CAN'T!
YES, YOU CAN.
I CAN'T!!
Don't be all casual about it!!
I'VE NEVER ...
...FELT THAT WAY ABOUT RYU.
WHAT IF WE DATED ...
...AND THEN BROKE UP?
THEN DON'T BREAK UP.
YOU'RE ONE TO TALK AFTER THE MOGI INCIDENT.
I DON'T SEE RYU AND ME THAT WAY.
NOTHING NEEDS TO CHANGE.

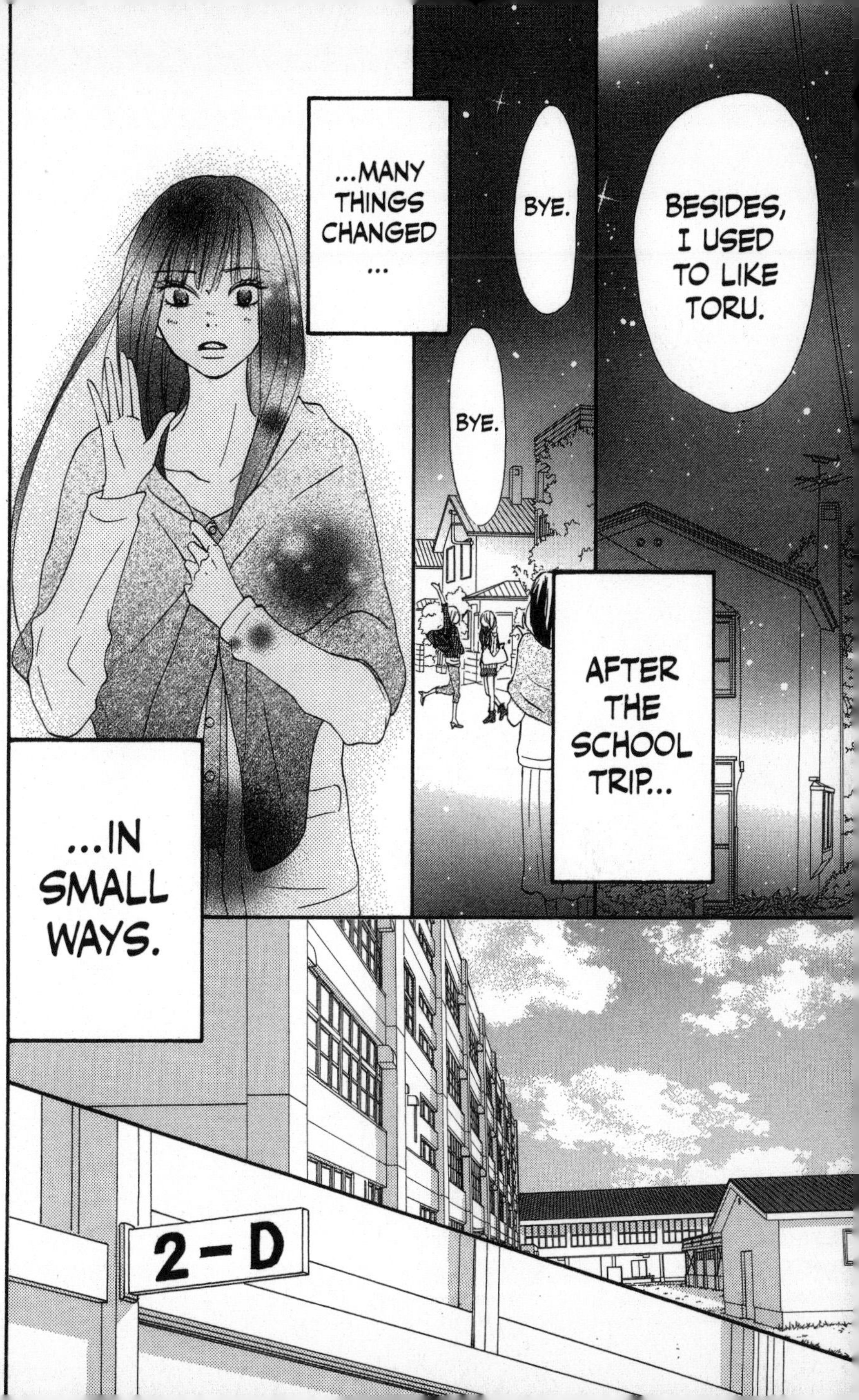
BESIDES, I USED TO LIKE TORU.
BYE.
BYE.
AFTER THE SCHOOL TRIP...
...MANY THINGS CHANGED ...
...IN SMALL WAYS.
2-D

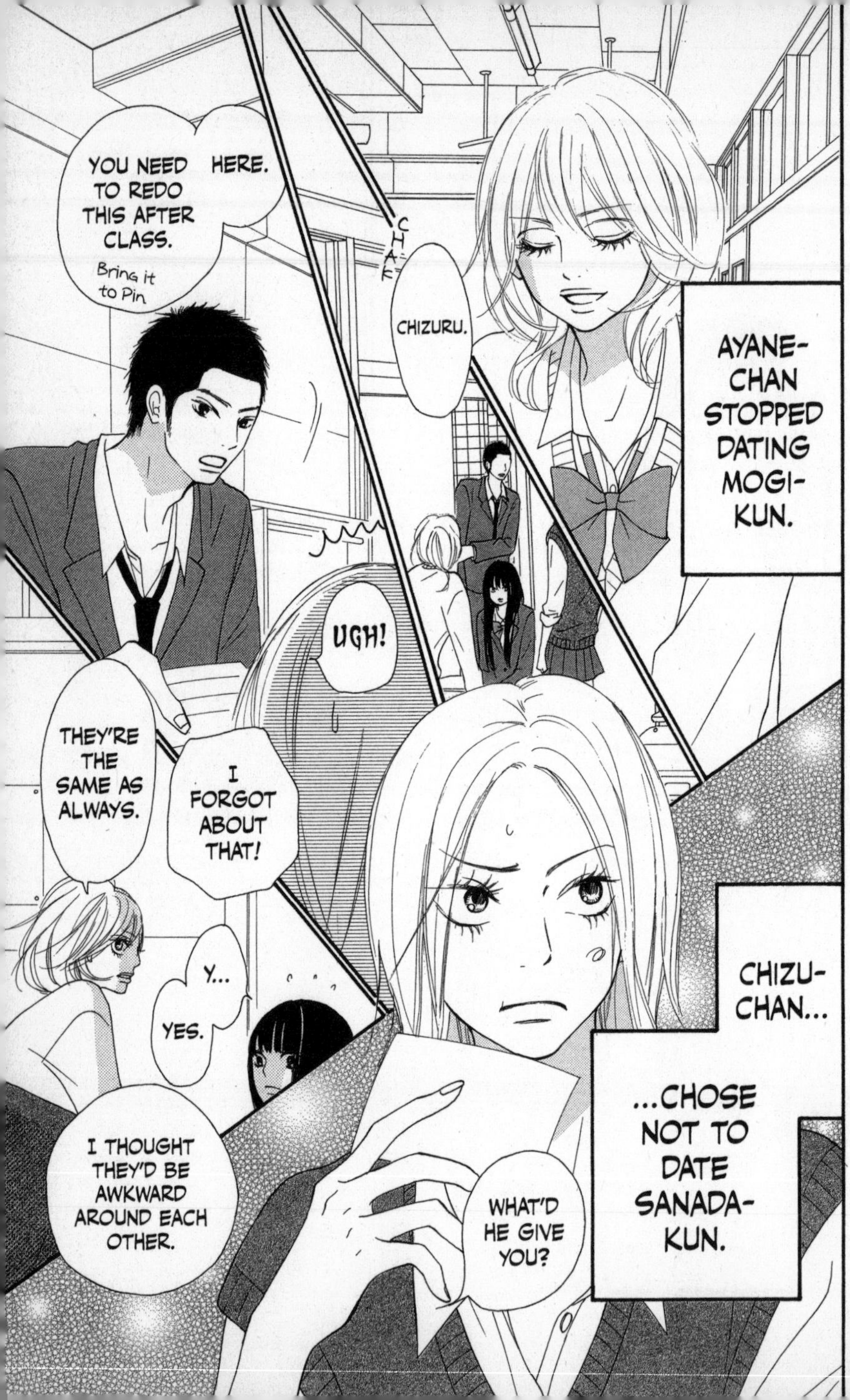
AYANE-CHAN STOPPED DATING MOGI-KUN.
CHIZURU.
CHAK
HERE.
YOU NEED TO REDO THIS AFTER CLASS.
Bring it to Pin
UGH!
CHIZU-CHAN...
...CHOSE NOT TO DATE SANADA-KUN.
WHAT'D HE GIVE YOU?
I FORGOT ABOUT THAT!
THEY'RE THE SAME AS ALWAYS.
Y...
YES.
I THOUGHT THEY'D BE AWKWARD AROUND EACH OTHER.

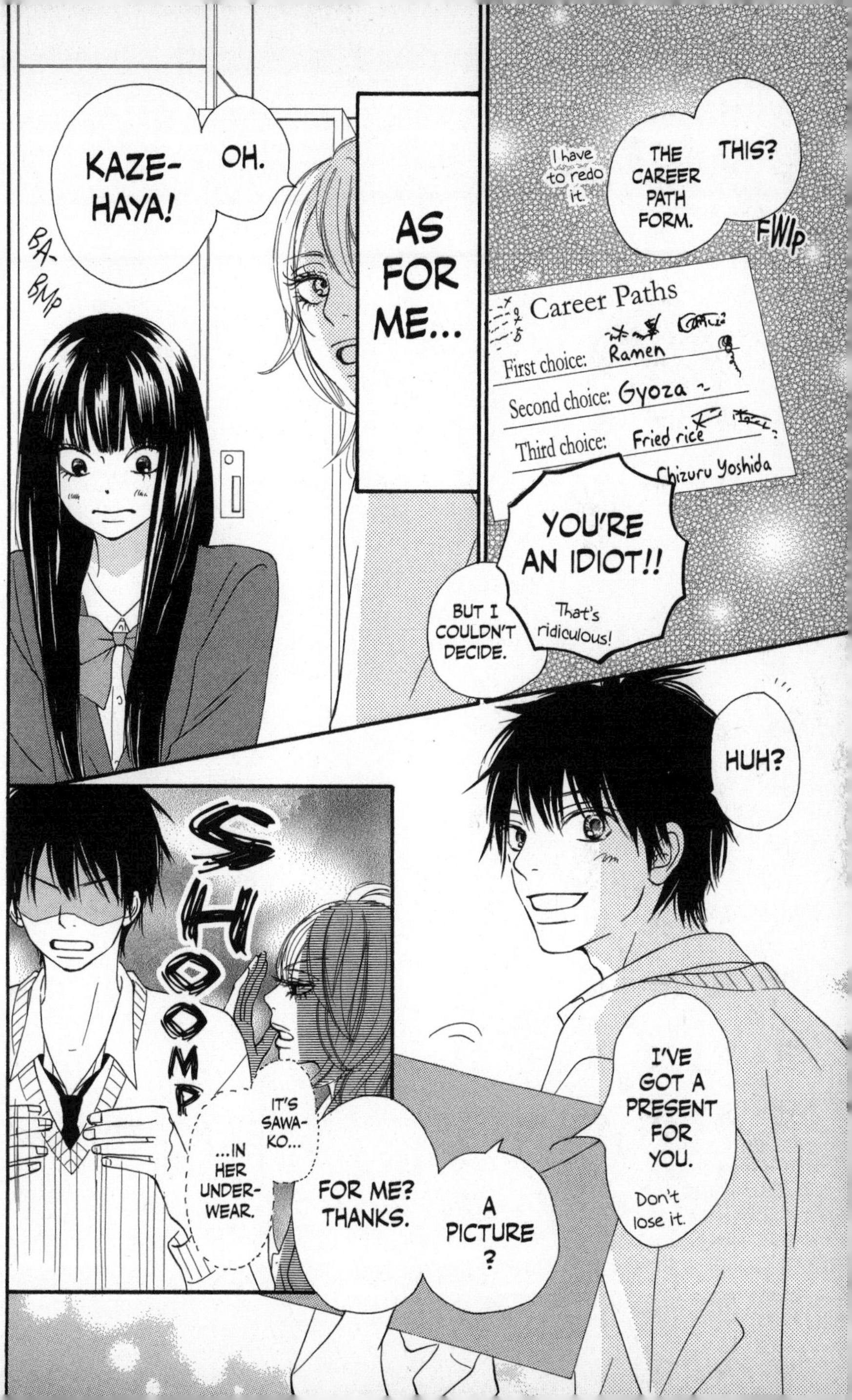
THIS?
THE CAREER PATH FORM.
I have to redo it.
FWIP
Career Paths
First choice: Ramen
Second choice: Gyoza
Third choice: Fried rice
Chizuru Yoshida
YOU'RE AN IDIOT!!
That's ridiculous!
BUT I COULDN'T DECIDE.
AS FOR ME...
OH.
KAZE-HAYA!
BA-BMP
HUH?
I'VE GOT A PRESENT FOR YOU.
Don't lose it.
A PICTURE?
FOR ME? THANKS.
SHOOMP
IT'S SAWAKO...
...IN HER UNDER-WEAR.

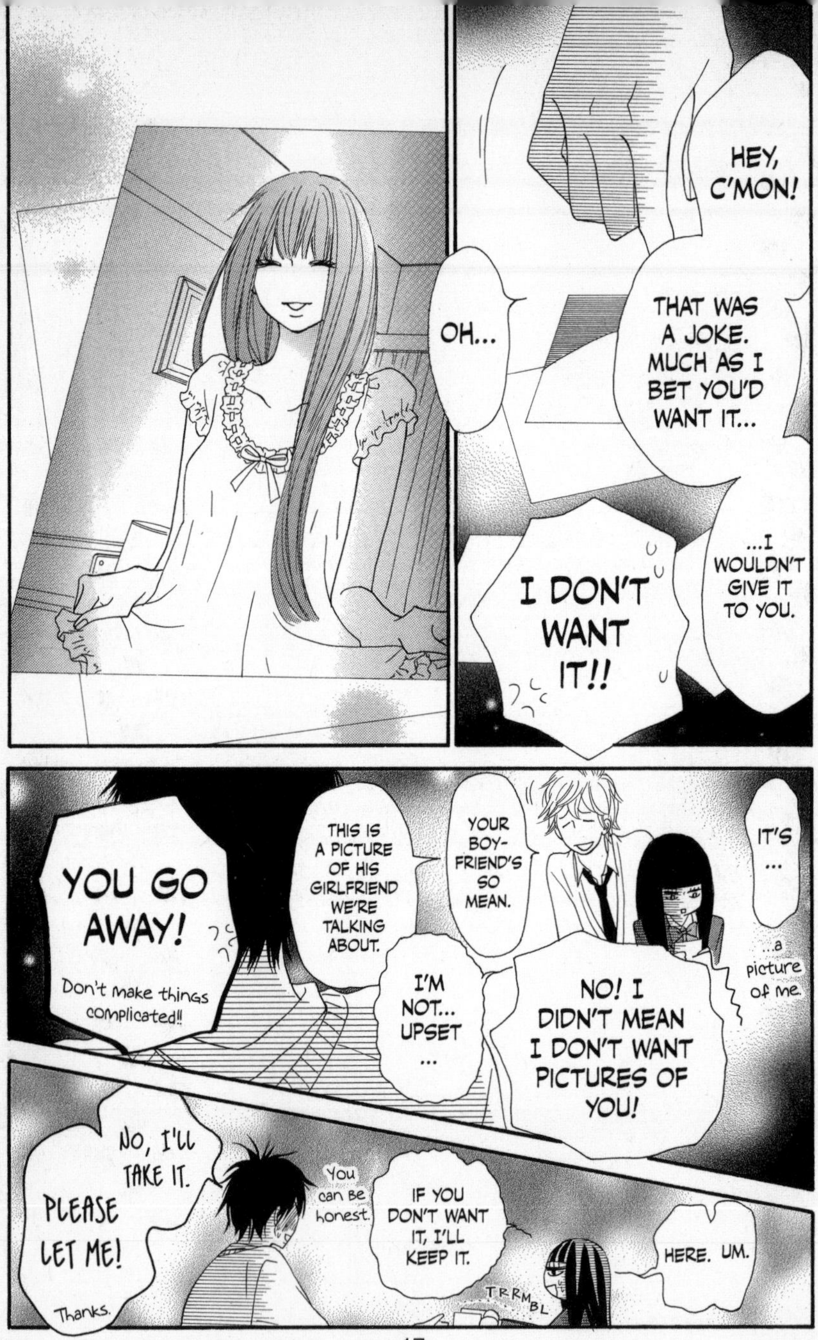
HEY, C'MON!
THAT WAS A JOKE. MUCH AS I BET YOU'D WANT IT...
OH...
...I WOULDN'T GIVE IT TO YOU.
I DON'T WANT IT!!
IT'S ...
...a picture of me.
YOUR BOY-FRIEND'S SO MEAN.
NO! I DIDN'T MEAN I DON'T WANT PICTURES OF YOU!
THIS IS A PICTURE OF HIS GIRLFRIEND WE'RE TALKING ABOUT.
I'M NOT... UPSET ...
YOU GO AWAY!
Don't make things complicated!!
HERE. UM.
TRRMBL
IF YOU DON'T WANT IT, I'LL KEEP IT.
You can be honest.
NO, I'LL TAKE IT.
PLEASE LET ME!
Thanks.

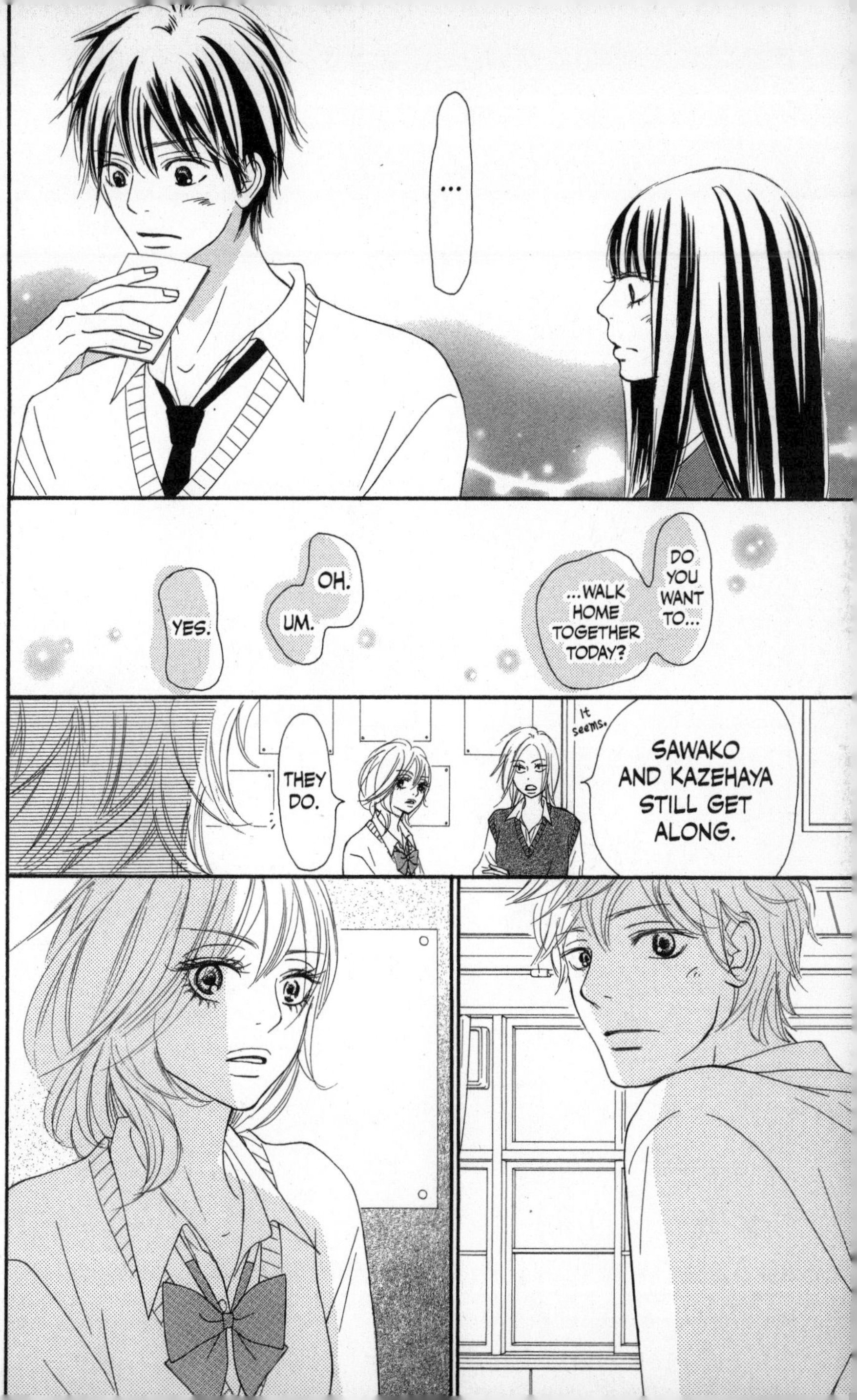
...
DO YOU WANT TO...
...WALK HOME TOGETHER TODAY?
OH.
UM.
YES.
SAWAKO AND KAZEHAYA STILL GET ALONG.
It seems.
THEY DO.

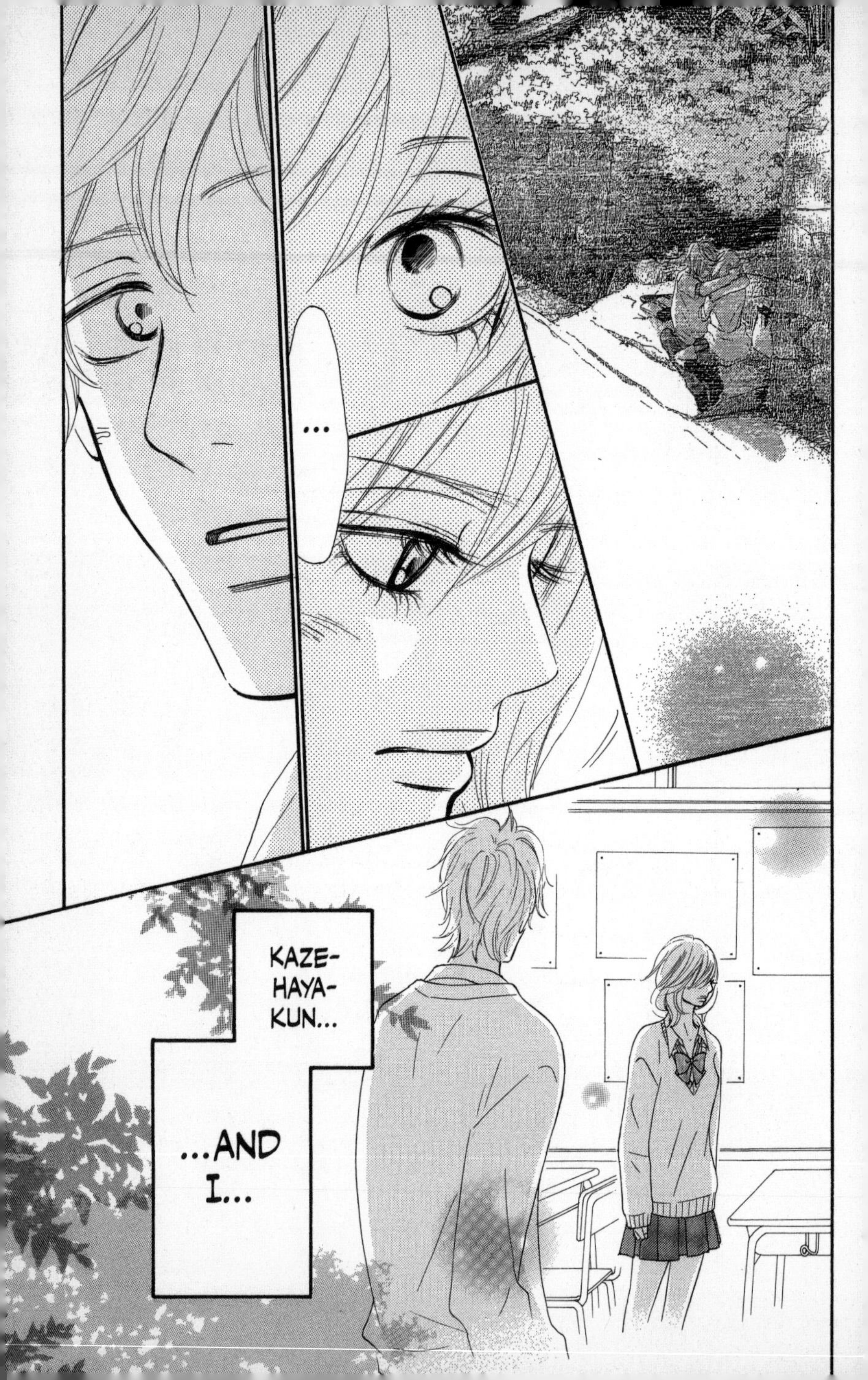
...
KAZE-HAYA-KUN...
...AND I...

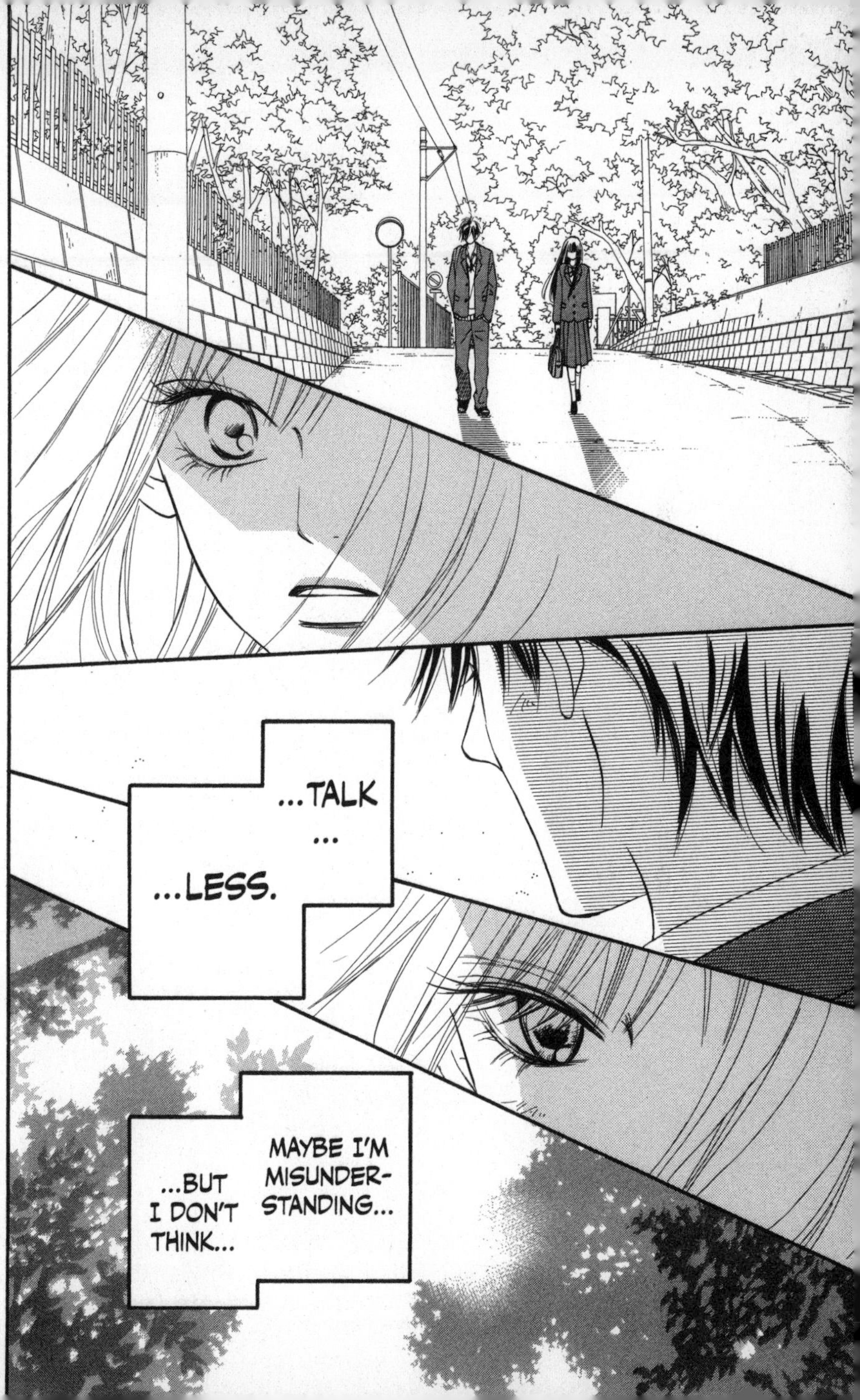
...TALK ... ...LESS.
MAYBE I'M MISUNDER-STANDING...
...BUT I DON'T THINK...

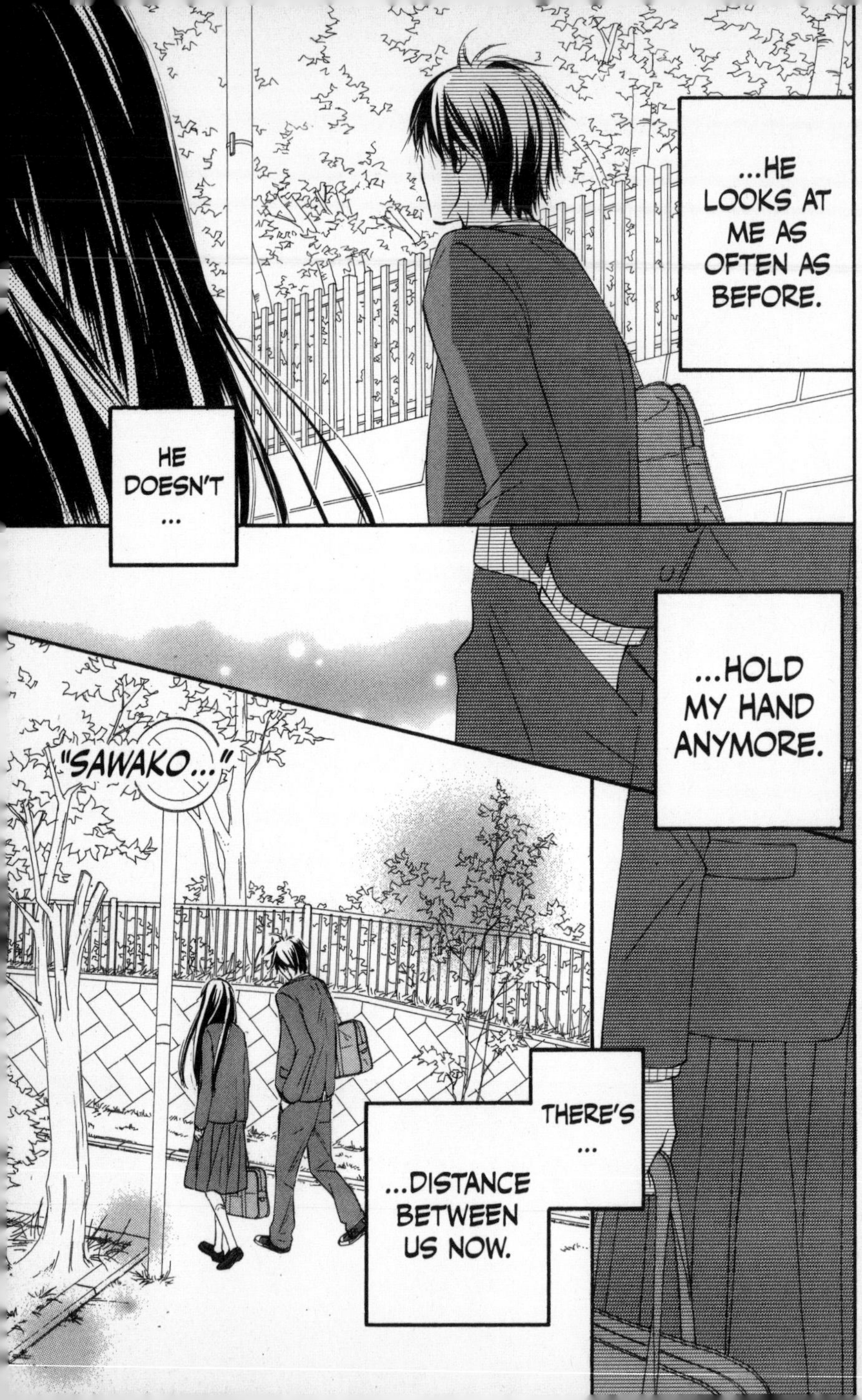
...HE LOOKS AT ME AS OFTEN AS BEFORE.
HE DOESN'T ...
...HOLD MY HAND ANYMORE.
"SAWAKO..."
THERE'S ...
...DISTANCE BETWEEN US NOW.

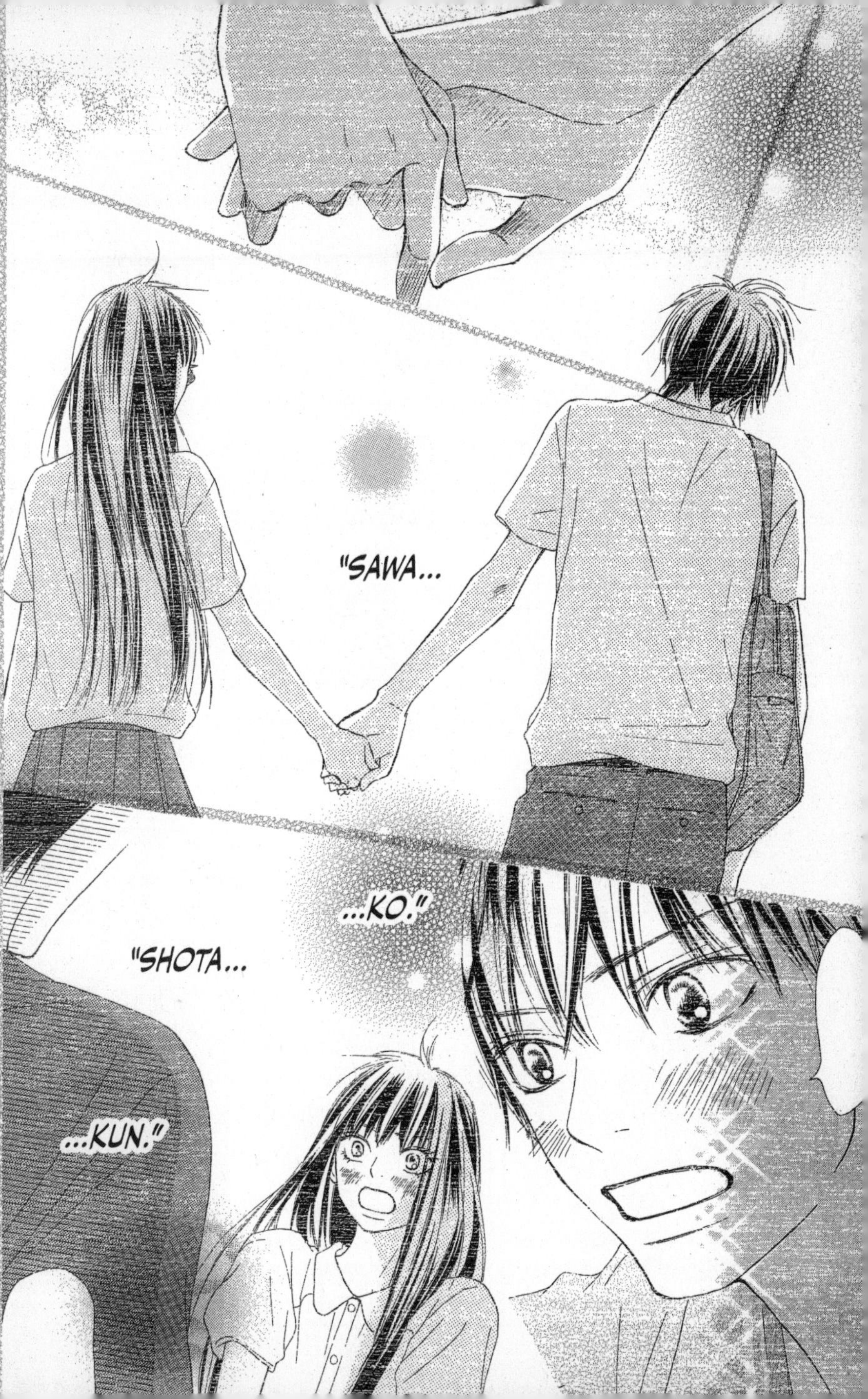
"SAWA...
...KO."
"SHOTA...
...KUN."

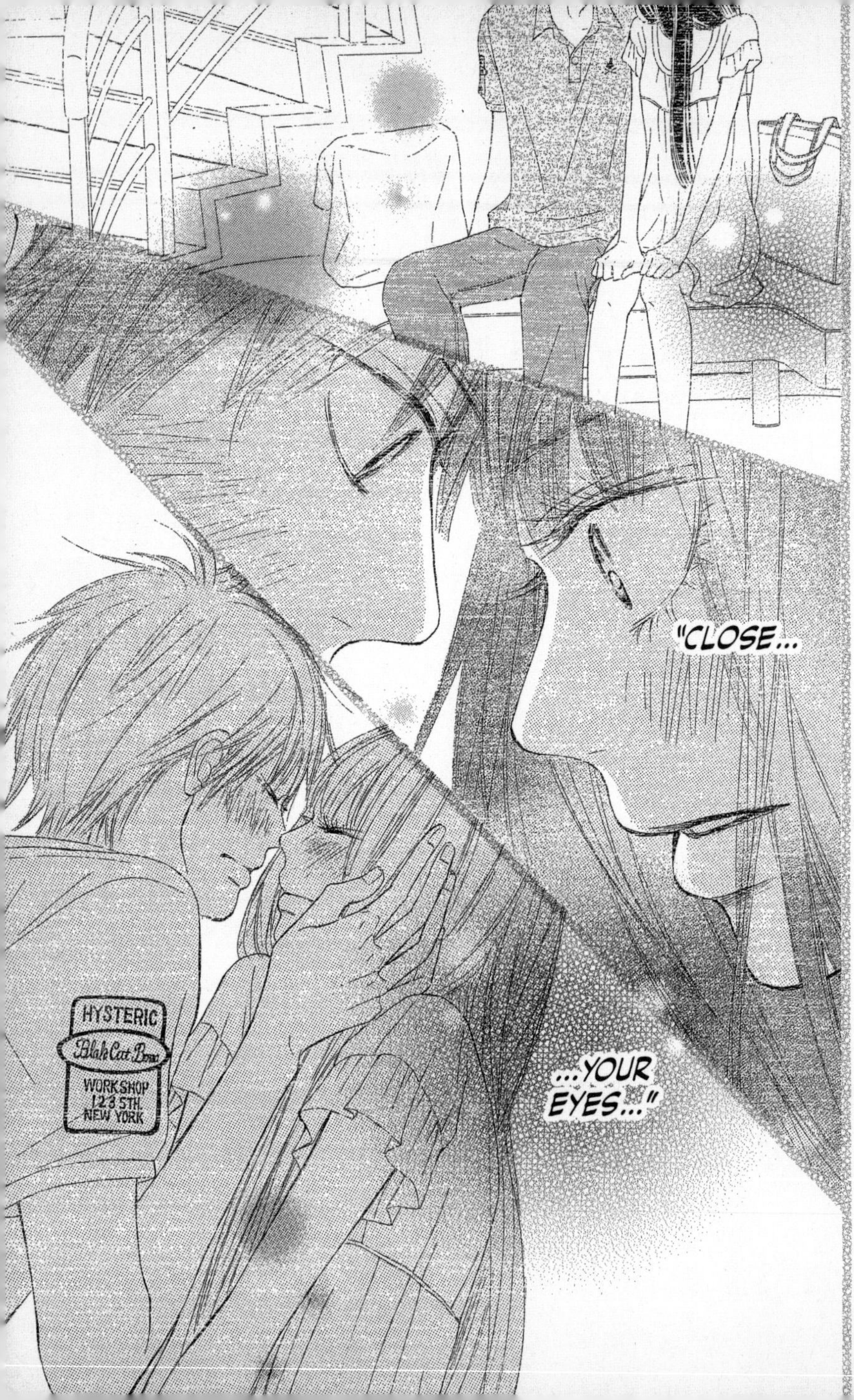
"CLOSE...
...YOUR EYES..."
HYSTERIC
WORKSHOP 123 5TH NEW YORK

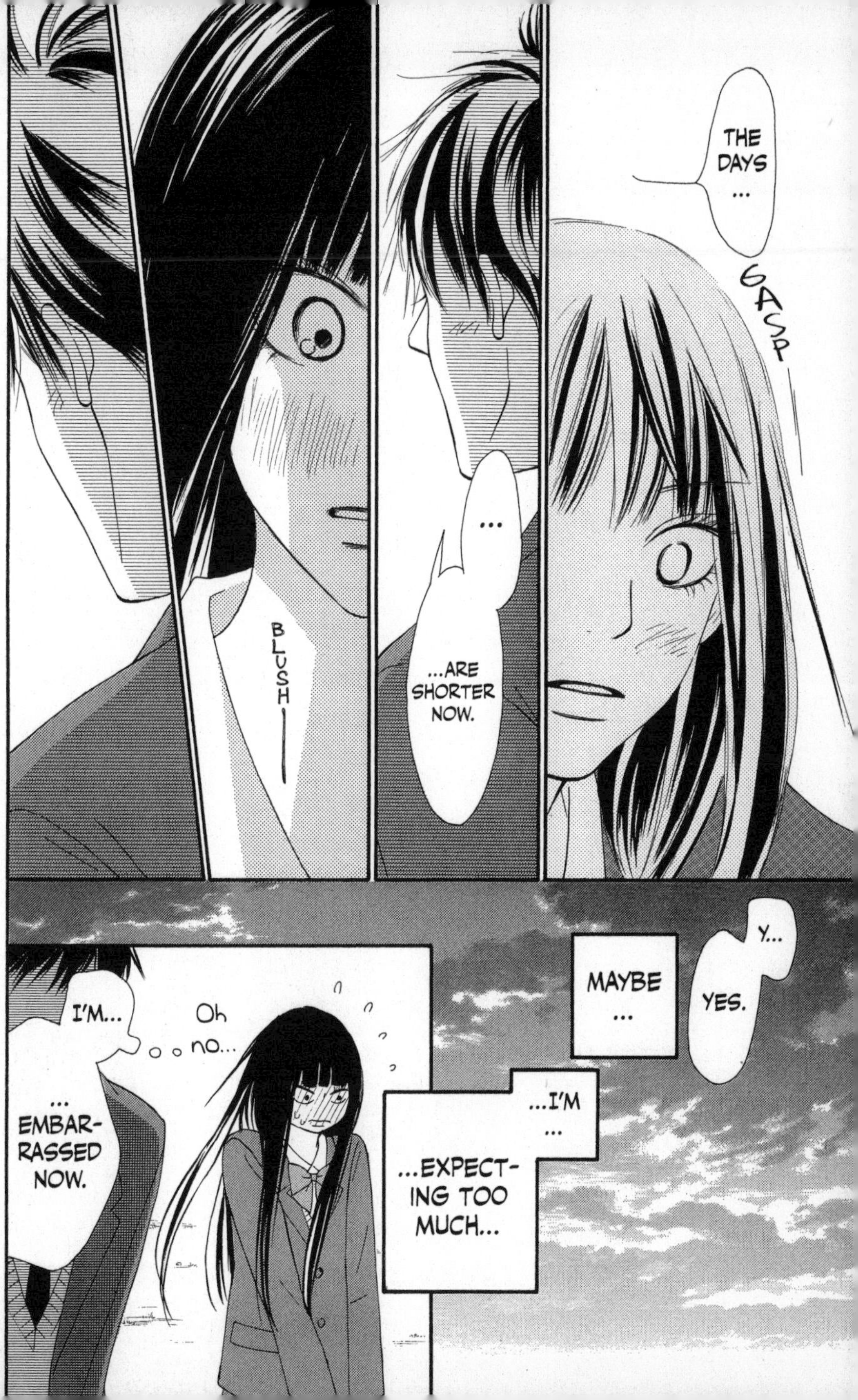
THE DAYS ...
GASP
... ...ARE SHORTER NOW.
BLUSH
Y... YES.
MAYBE ...
...I'M ...
...EXPECTING TOO MUCH...
Oh no...
I'M... ... EMBARRASSED NOW.

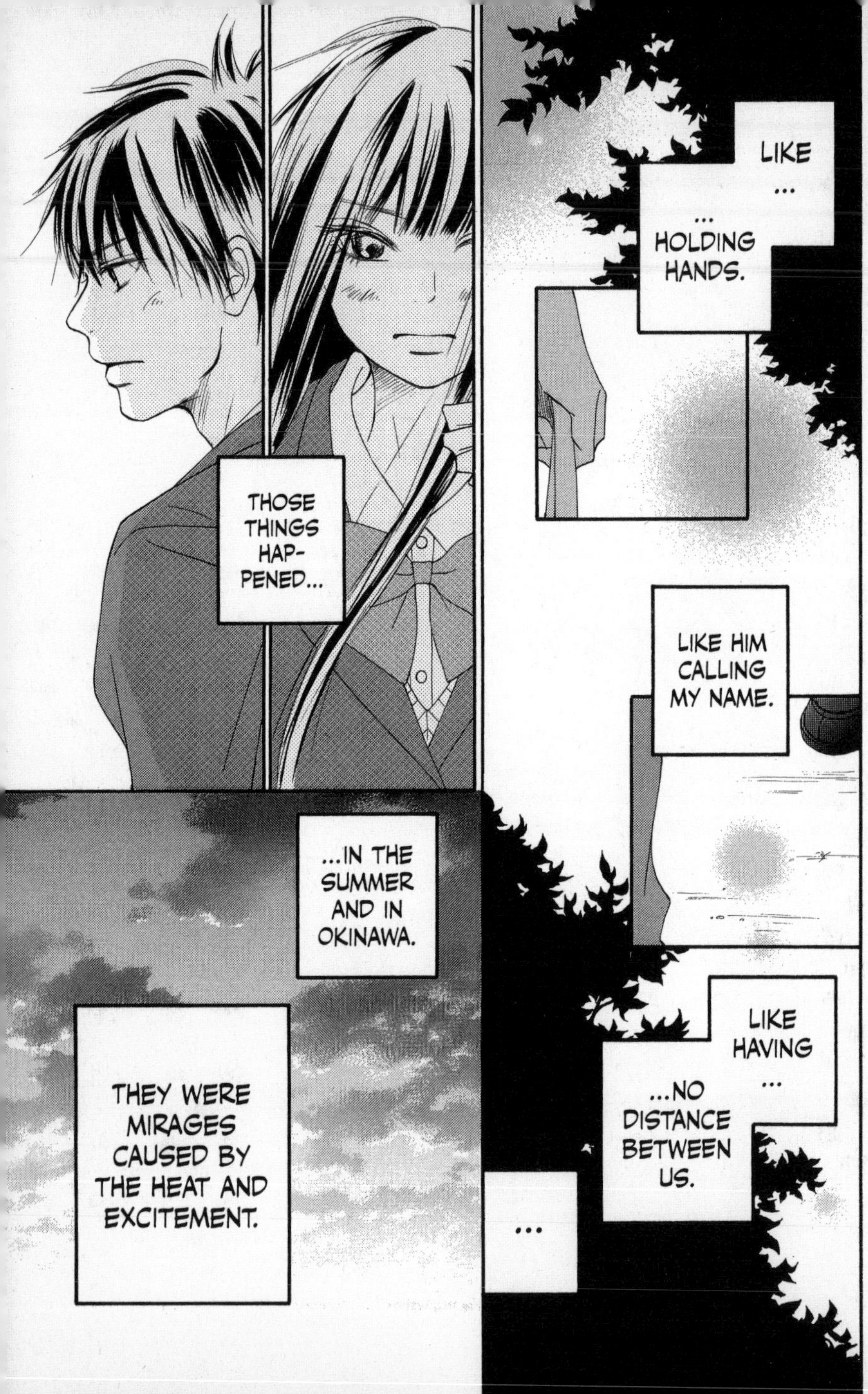
LIKE ... ... HOLDING HANDS.
LIKE HIM CALLING MY NAME.
LIKE HAVING ... ...NO DISTANCE BETWEEN US.
...
THOSE THINGS HAP-PENED...
...IN THE SUMMER AND IN OKINAWA.
THEY WERE MIRAGES CAUSED BY THE HEAT AND EXCITEMENT.

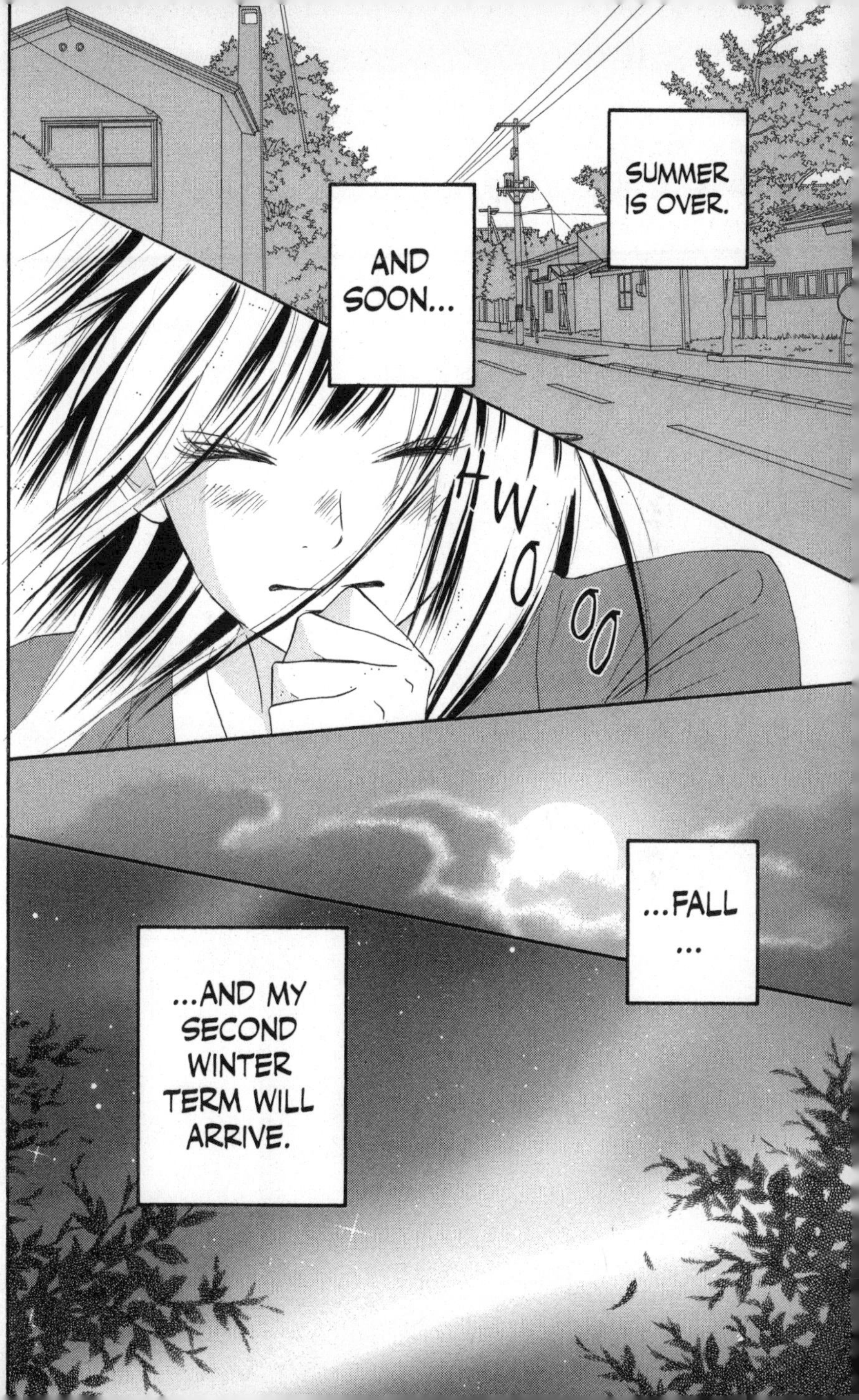
SUMMER IS OVER.
AND SOON...
HWOOO
...FALL ...
...AND MY SECOND WINTER TERM WILL ARRIVE.

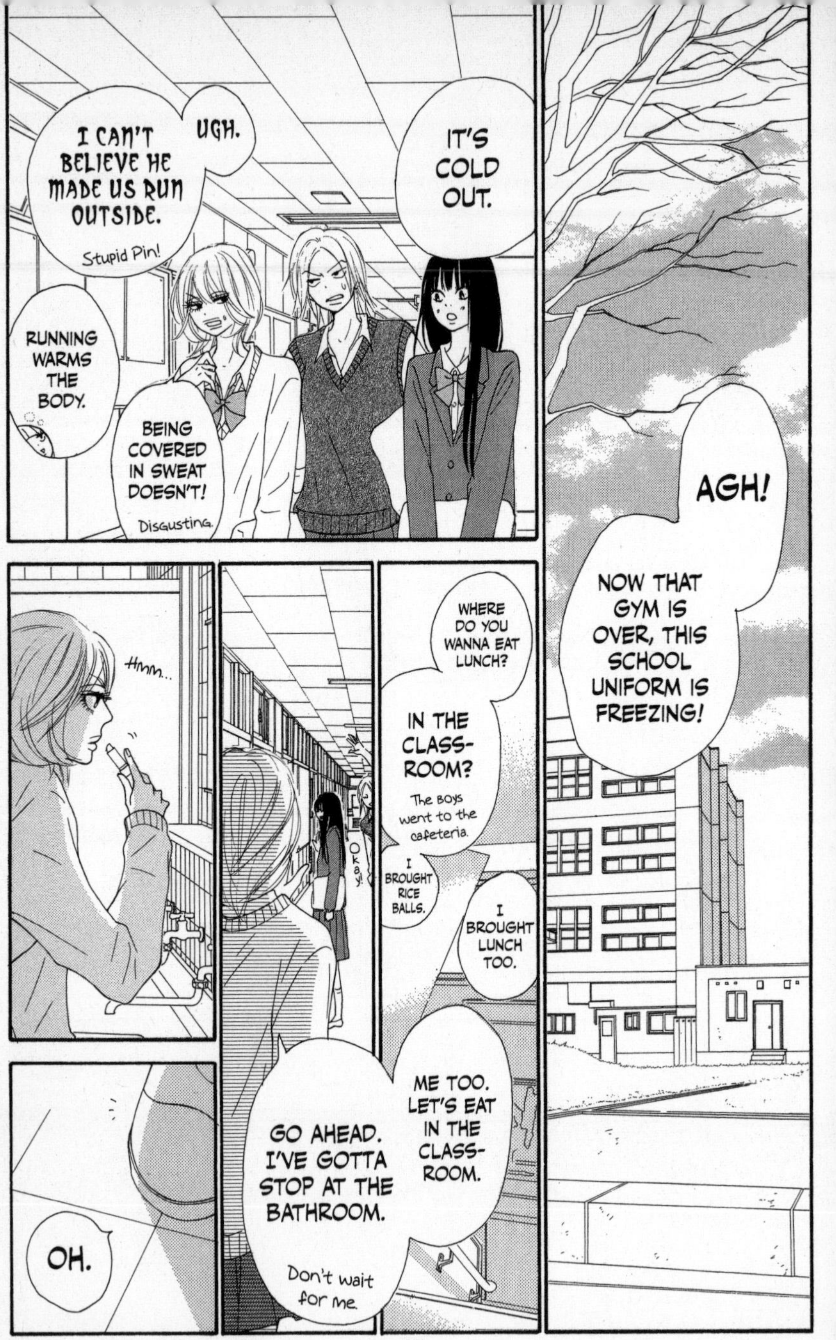
AGH!
NOW THAT GYM IS OVER, THIS SCHOOL UNIFORM IS FREEZING!
IT'S COLD OUT.
UGH.
I CAN'T BELIEVE HE MADE US RUN OUTSIDE.
Stupid Pin!
RUNNING WARMS THE BODY.
BEING COVERED IN SWEAT DOESN'T!
Disgusting.
WHERE DO YOU WANNA EAT LUNCH?
IN THE CLASS-ROOM?
The boys went to the cafeteria.
Okay!
I BROUGHT RICE BALLS.
I BROUGHT LUNCH TOO.
ME TOO. LET'S EAT IN THE CLASS-ROOM.
GO AHEAD. I'VE GOTTA STOP AT THE BATHROOM.
Don't wait for me.
Hmm...
OH.

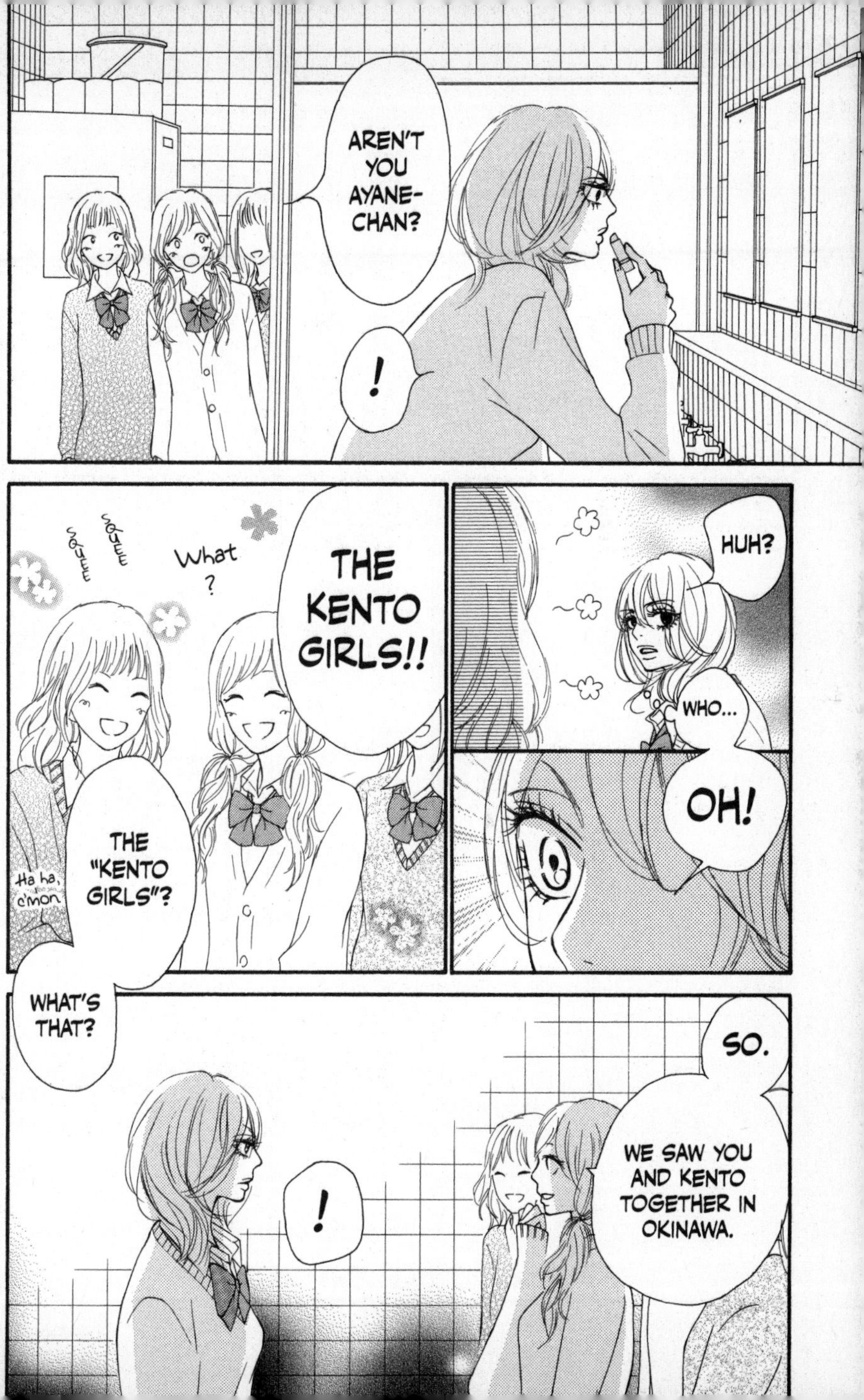
AREN'T YOU AYANE-CHAN?
!
HUH?
WHO...
OH!
THE KENTO GIRLS!!
What ?
SQUEE
SQUEE
THE "KENTO GIRLS"?
Ha ha, c'mon
WHAT'S THAT?
SO.
WE SAW YOU AND KENTO TOGETHER IN OKINAWA.
!

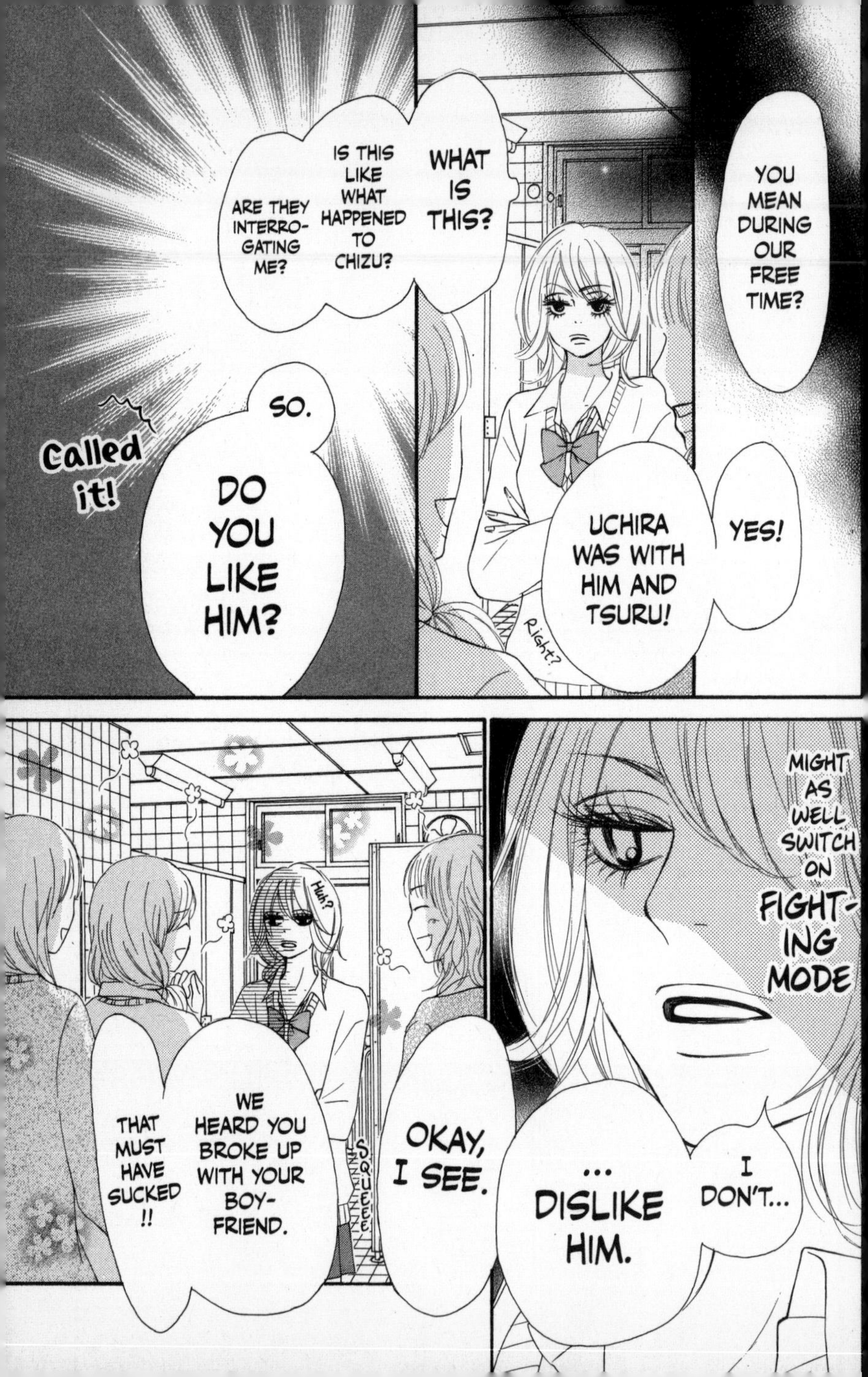

YOU MEAN DURING OUR FREE TIME?
YES!
UCHIRA WAS WITH HIM AND TSURU!
Right?
WHAT IS THIS?
IS THIS LIKE WHAT HAPPENED TO CHIZU?
ARE THEY INTERROGATING ME?
SO.
DO YOU LIKE HIM?
Called it!
MIGHT AS WELL SWITCH ON FIGHTING MODE
I DON'T...
... DISLIKE HIM.
OKAY, I SEE.
SQUEEE
WE HEARD YOU BROKE UP WITH YOUR BOYFRIEND.
THAT MUST HAVE SUCKED !!
Huh?

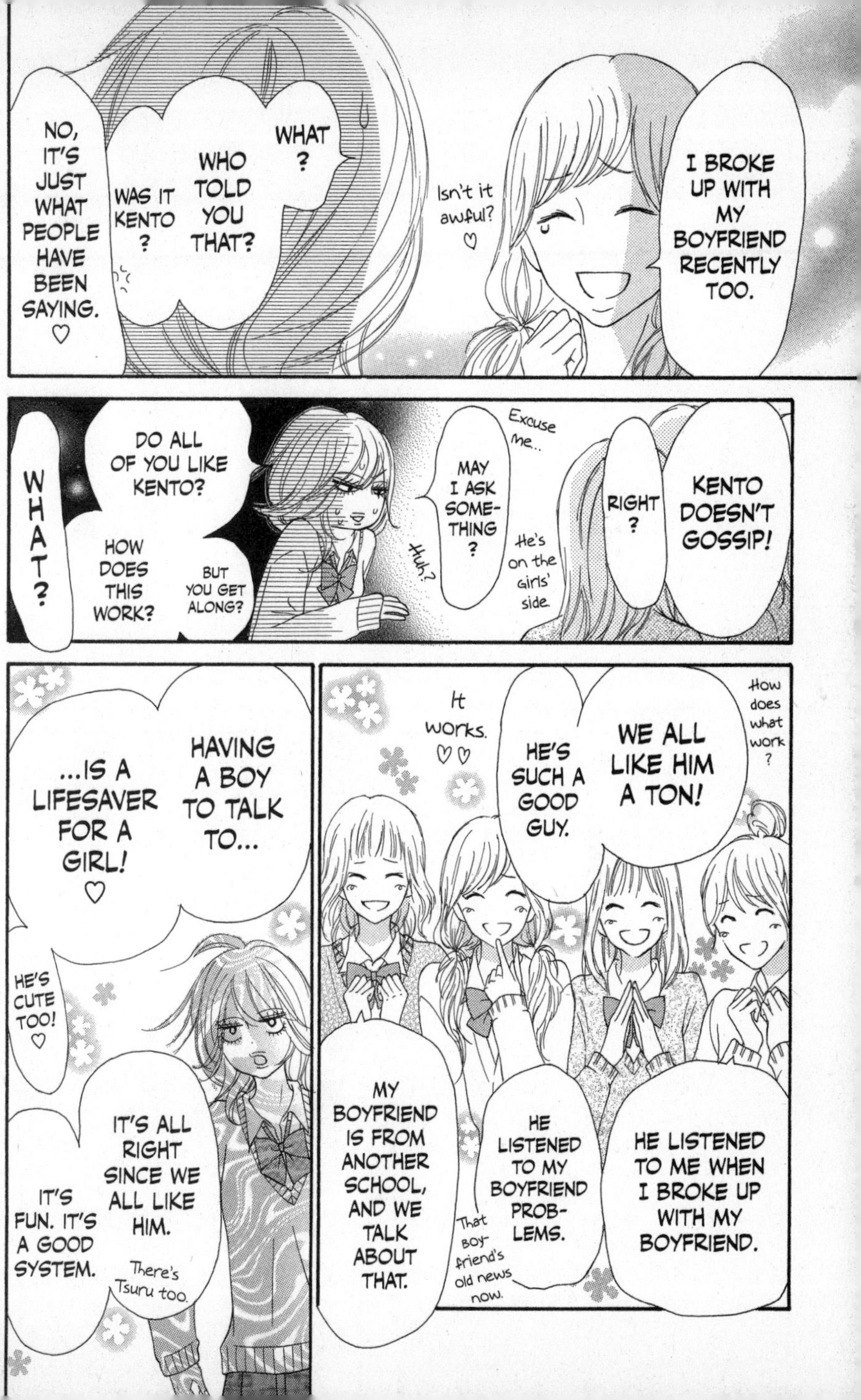
I BROKE UP WITH MY BOYFRIEND RECENTLY TOO.
Isn't it awful? ♡
WHAT?
WHO TOLD YOU THAT?
WAS IT KENTO?
NO, IT'S JUST WHAT PEOPLE HAVE BEEN SAYING. ♡
KENTO DOESN'T GOSSIP!
RIGHT?
He's on the girls' side.
Excuse me...
MAY I ASK SOME-THING?
Huh?
DO ALL OF YOU LIKE KENTO?
BUT YOU GET ALONG?
HOW DOES THIS WORK?
WHAT?
How does what work?
WE ALL LIKE HIM A TON!
HE'S SUCH A GOOD GUY.
It works. ♡♡
HE LISTENED TO ME WHEN I BROKE UP WITH MY BOYFRIEND.
That boy-friend's old news now.
HE LISTENED TO MY BOYFRIEND PROB-LEMS.
MY BOYFRIEND IS FROM ANOTHER SCHOOL, AND WE TALK ABOUT THAT.
HAVING A BOY TO TALK TO...
...IS A LIFESAVER FOR A GIRL! ♡
HE'S CUTE TOO! ♡
IT'S ALL RIGHT SINCE WE ALL LIKE HIM.
There's Tsuru too.
IT'S FUN. IT'S A GOOD SYSTEM.

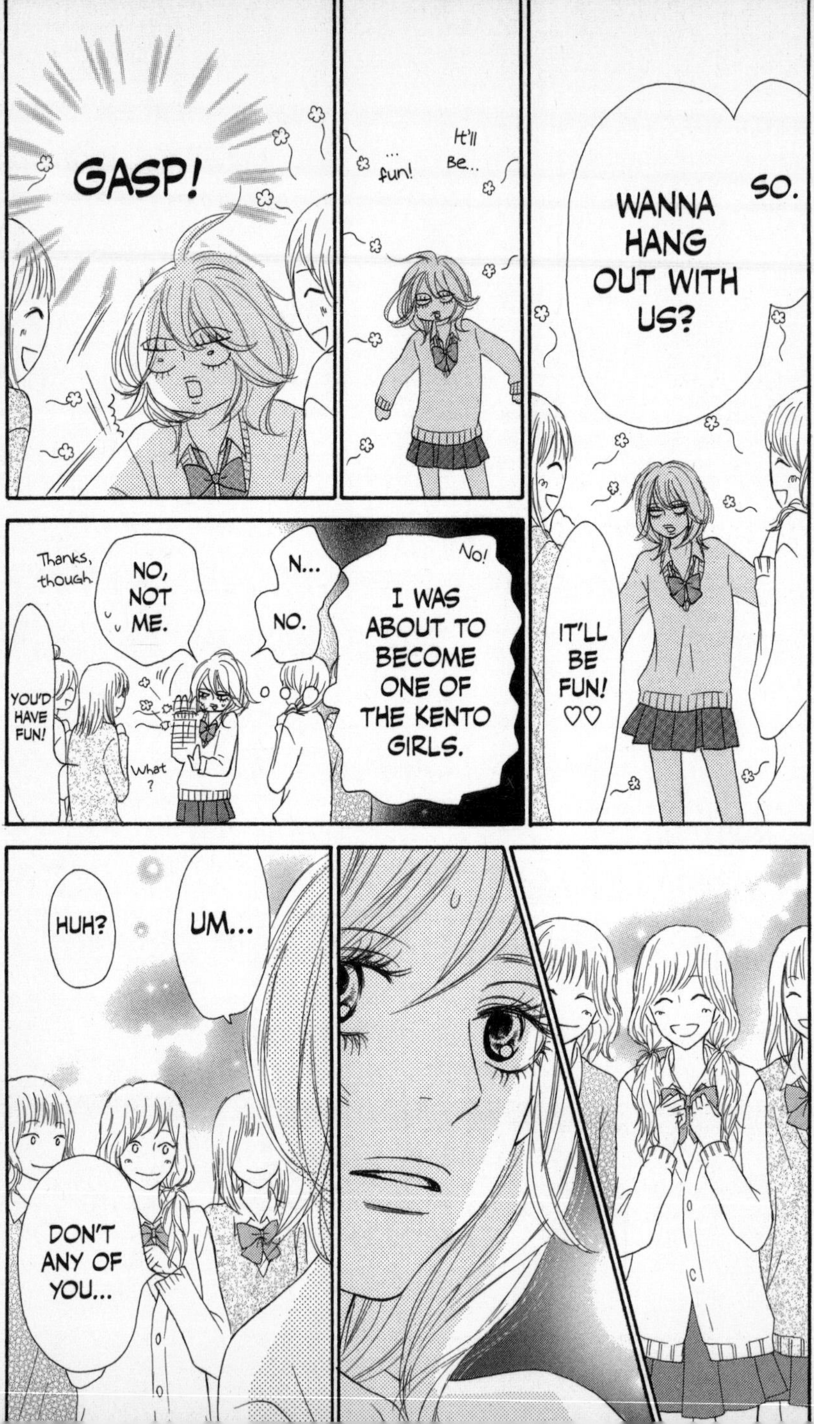
SO.
WANNA HANG OUT WITH US?
IT'LL BE FUN! ♡♡
It'll Be...
... fun!
GASP!
No!
I WAS ABOUT TO BECOME ONE OF THE KENTO GIRLS.
N... NO.
NO, NOT ME.
Thanks, though.
YOU'D HAVE FUN!
What?
UM...
HUH?
DON'T ANY OF YOU...

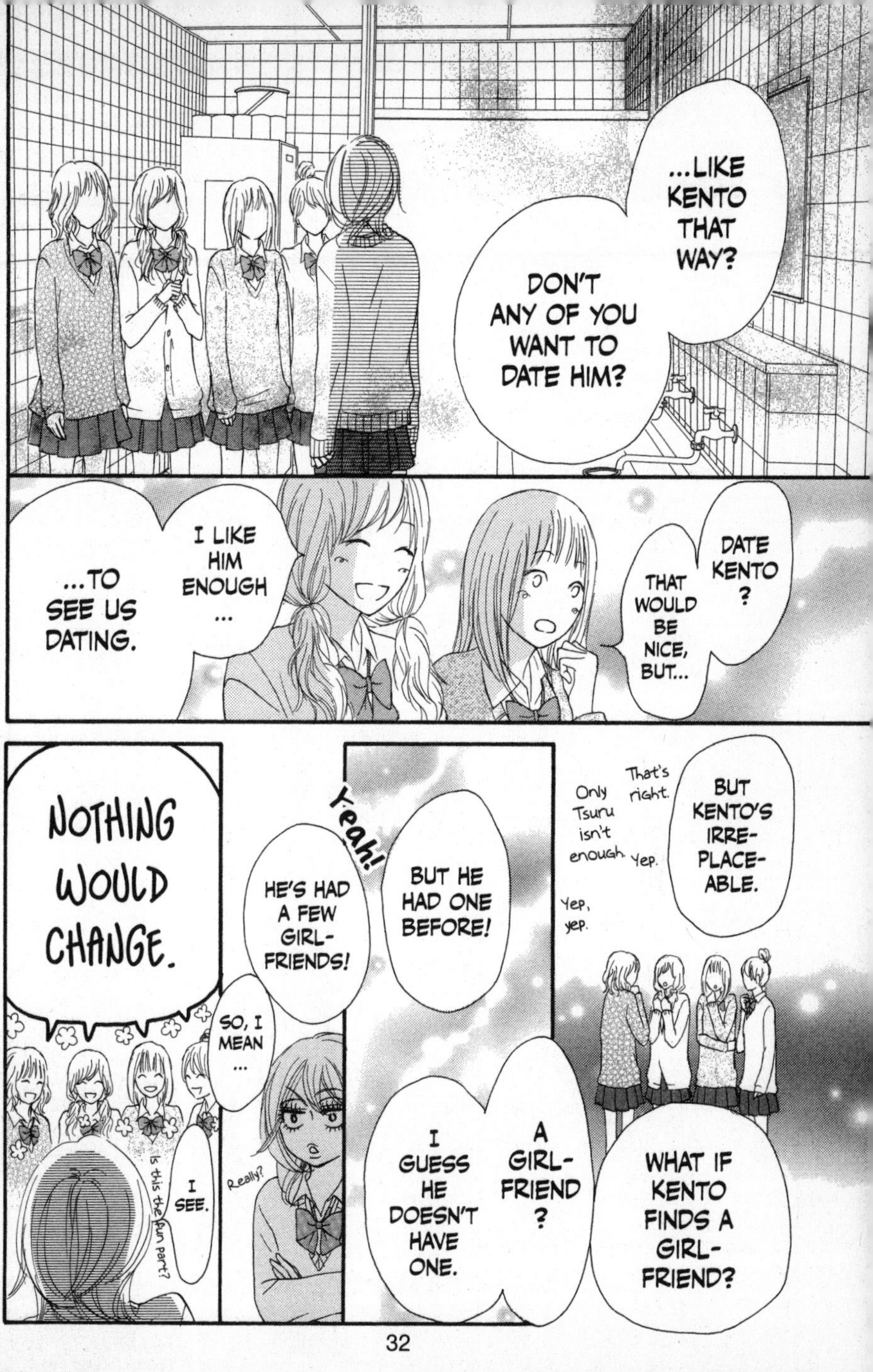
...LIKE KENTO THAT WAY?
DON'T ANY OF YOU WANT TO DATE HIM?
DATE KENTO?
THAT WOULD BE NICE, BUT...
I LIKE HIM ENOUGH...
...TO SEE US DATING.
BUT KENTO'S IRRE-PLACE-ABLE.
That's right.
Only Tsuru isn't enough.
Yep.
Yep, yep.
WHAT IF KENTO FINDS A GIRL-FRIEND?
A GIRL-FRIEND?
I GUESS HE DOESN'T HAVE ONE.
BUT HE HAD ONE BEFORE!
Yeah!
HE'S HAD A FEW GIRL-FRIENDS!
Really?
NOTHING WOULD CHANGE.
SO, I MEAN...
I SEE.
Is this the fun part?

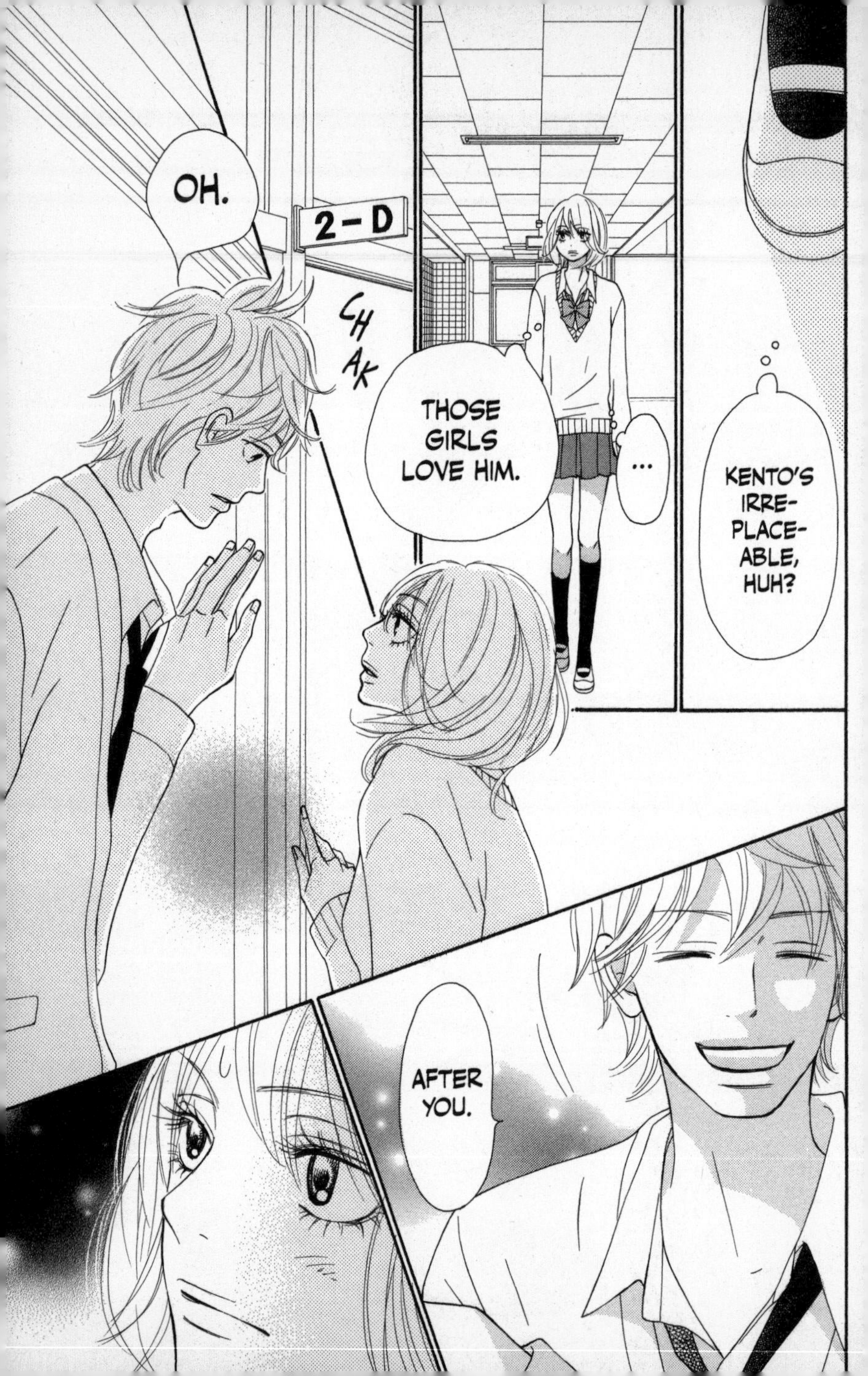
KENTO'S IRRE-PLACE-ABLE, HUH?
...
OH.
2-D
CHAK
THOSE GIRLS LOVE HIM.
AFTER YOU.

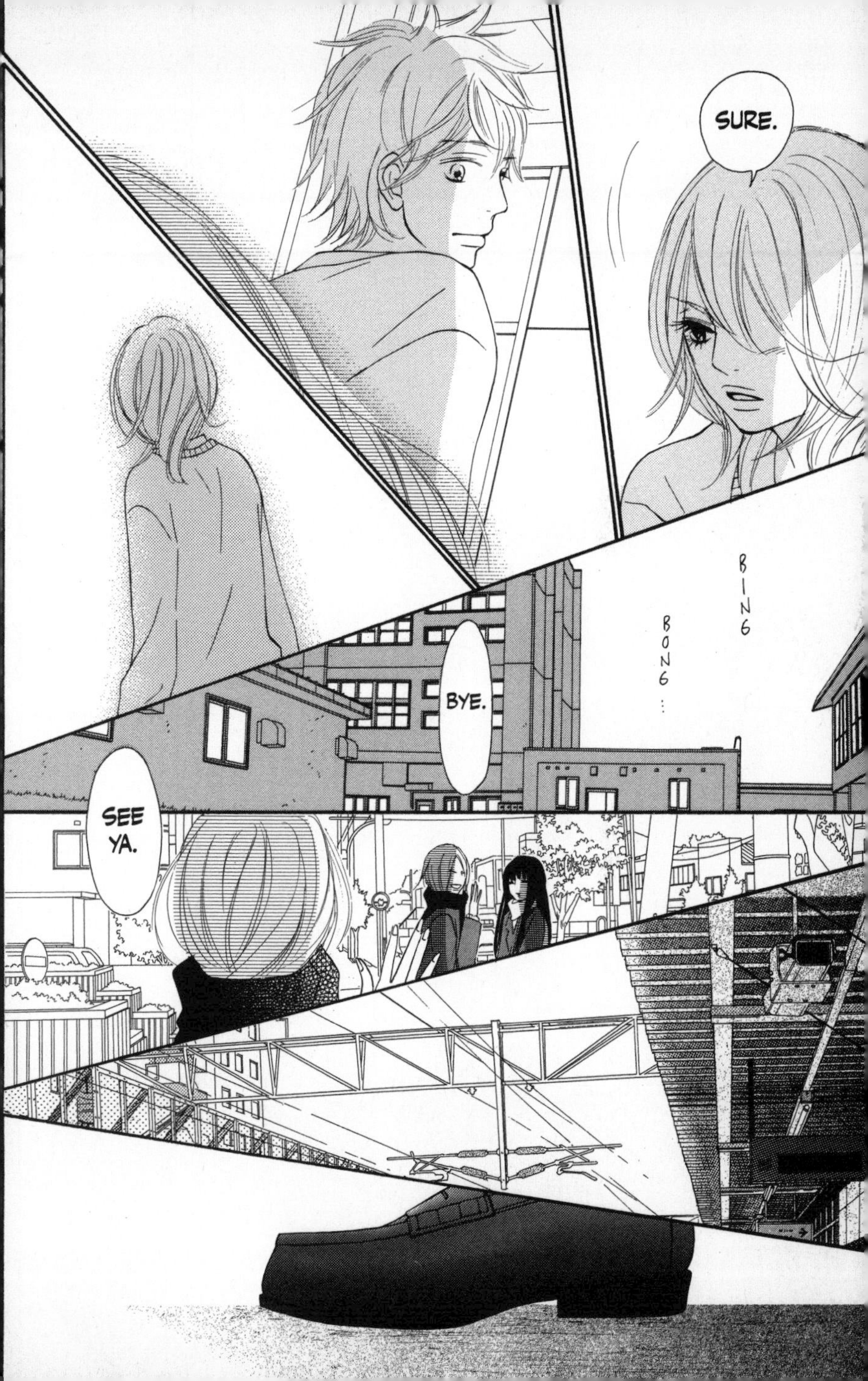
SURE.
BING
BONG ...
BYE.
SEE YA.

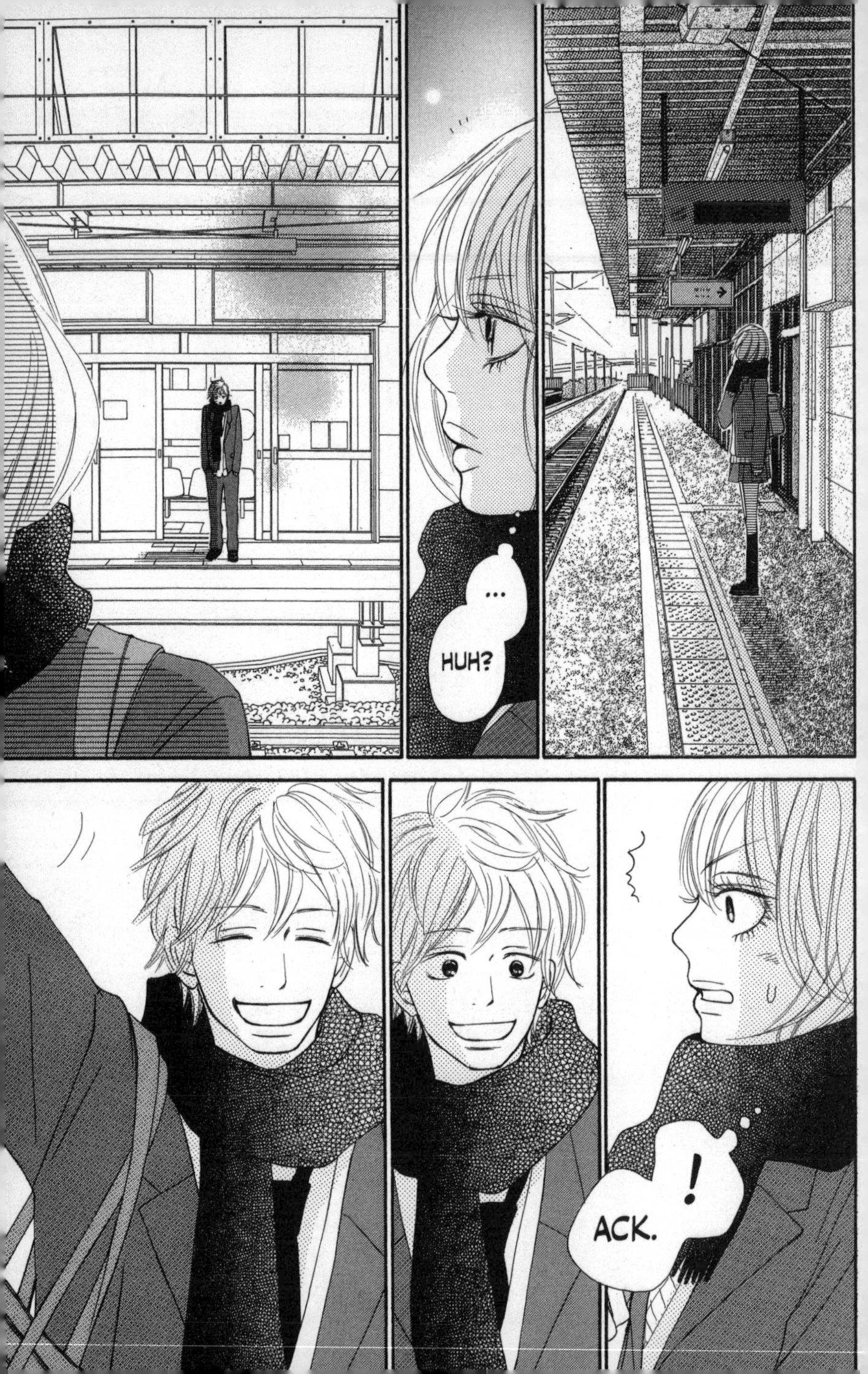
...
HUH?
!
ACK.

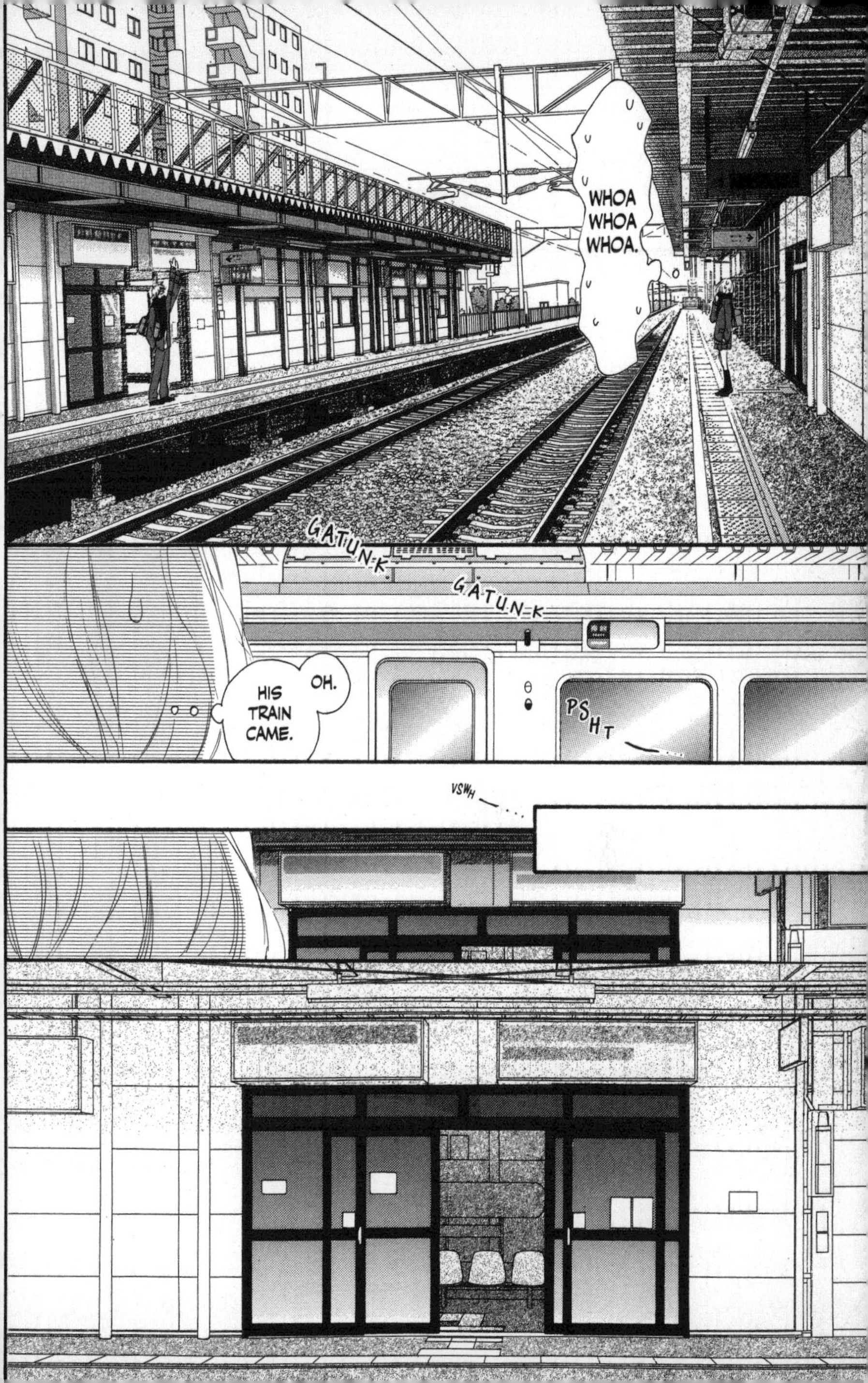
WHOA WHOA WHOA.
GATUNK
GATUNK
OH.
HIS TRAIN CAME.
PSHT
VSWH

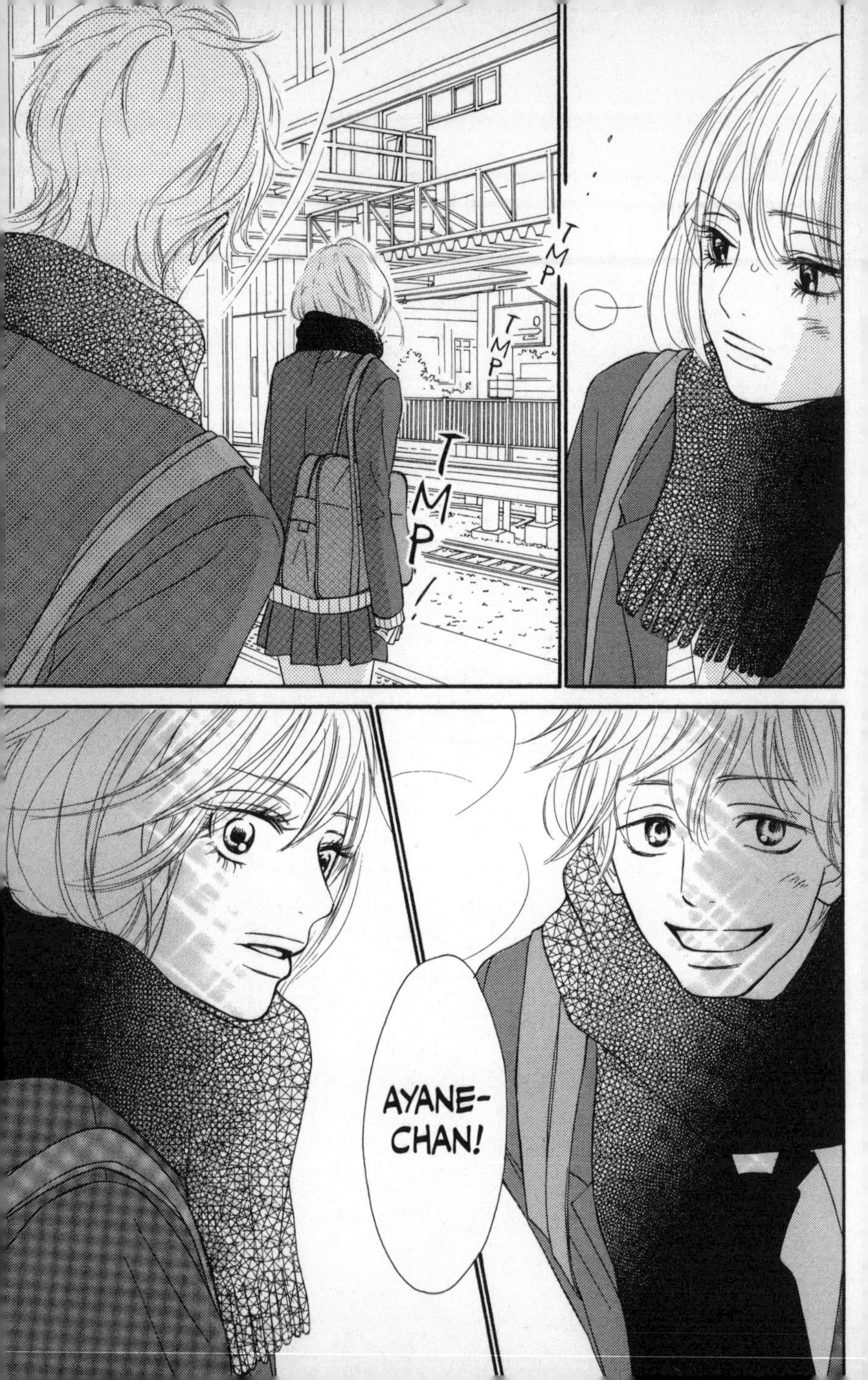
TMP
TMP
TMP!
AYANE-CHAN!

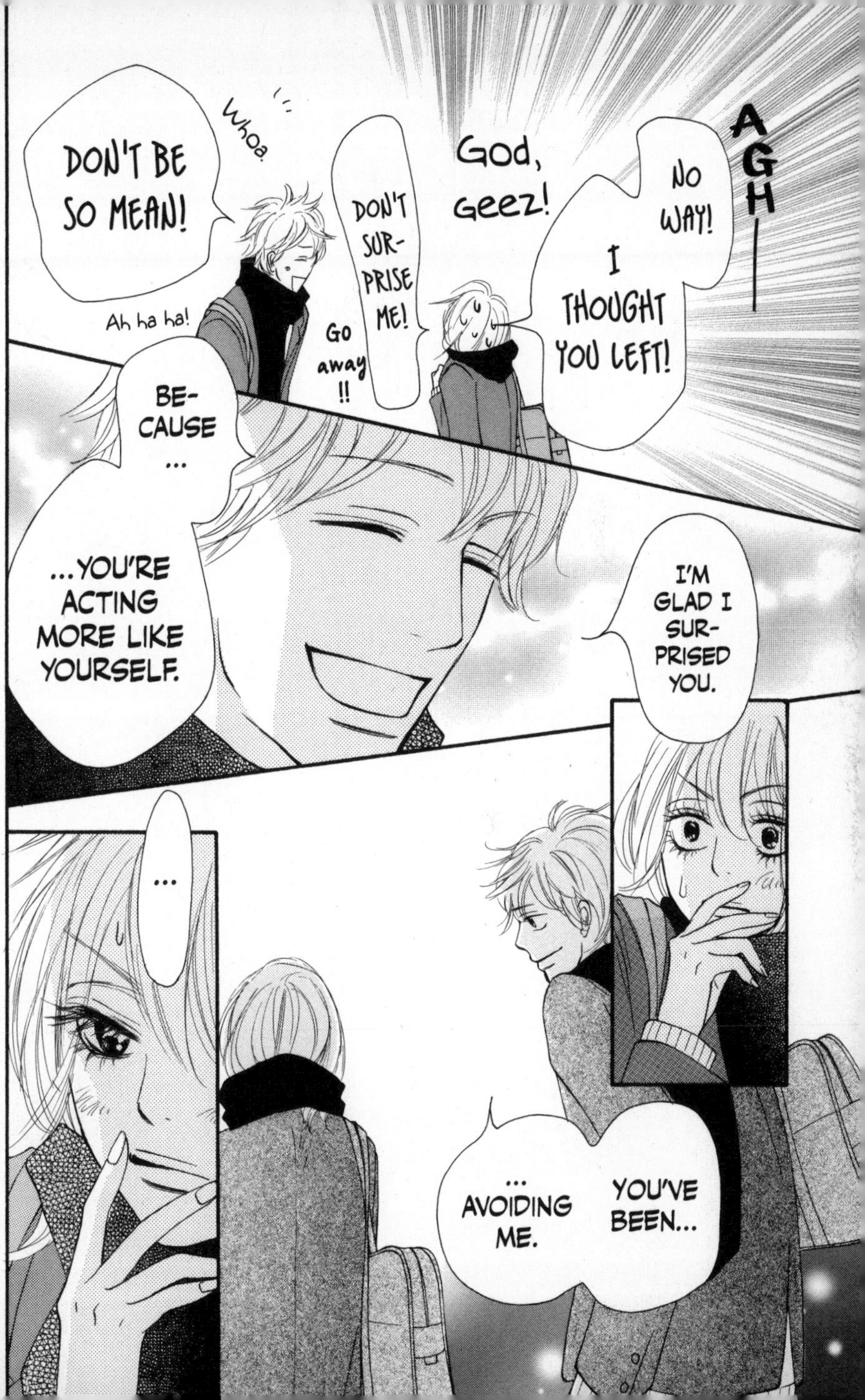
AGH—
NO WAY! I THOUGHT YOU LEFT!
God, Geez!
DON'T SUR-PRISE ME!
Go away!!
Whoa
DON'T BE SO MEAN!
Ah ha ha!
I'M GLAD I SUR-PRISED YOU.
BE-CAUSE...
...YOU'RE ACTING MORE LIKE YOURSELF.
YOU'VE BEEN...
... AVOIDING ME.
...

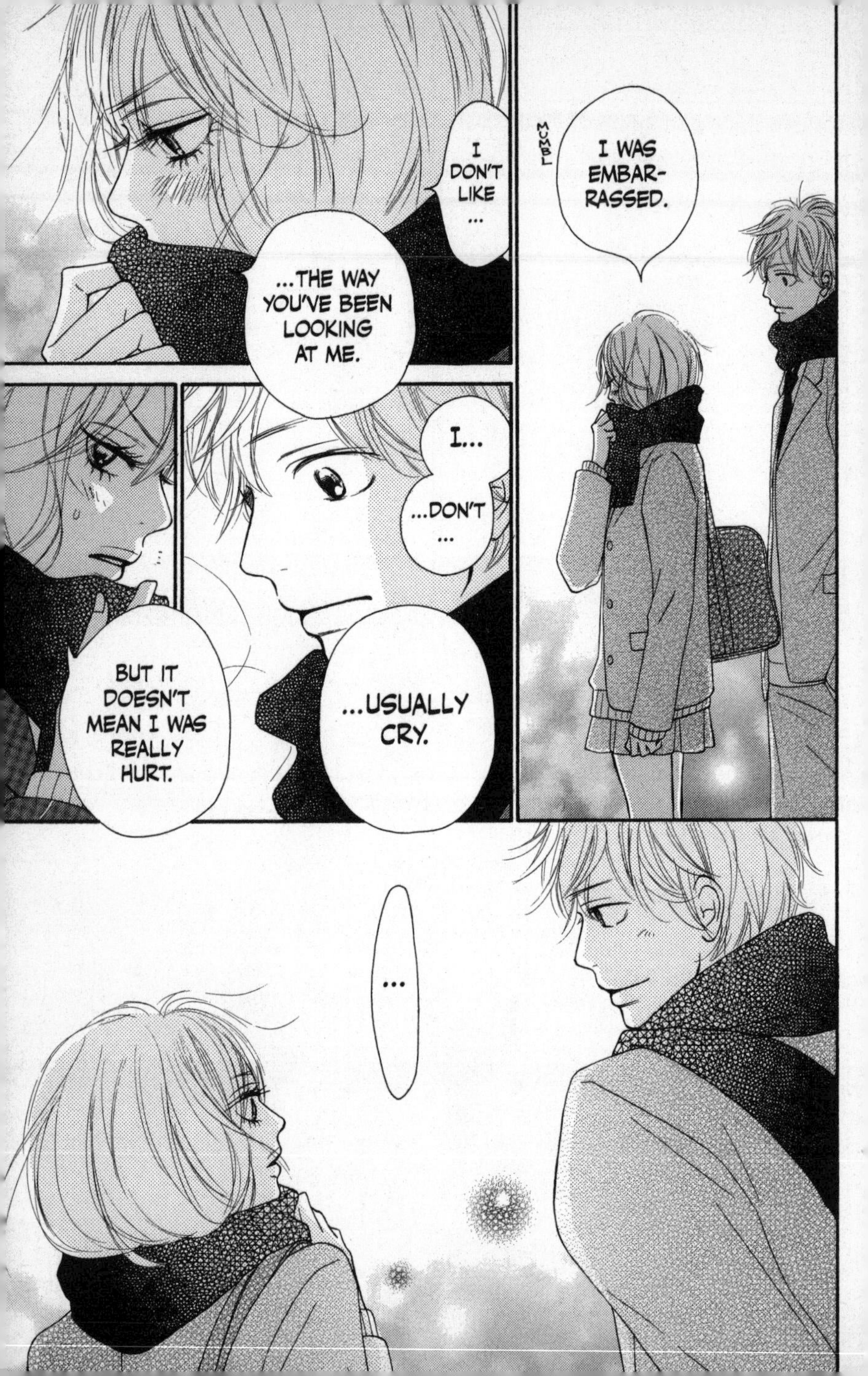
MUMBL
I WAS EMBAR-RASSED.
I DON'T LIKE ...
...THE WAY YOU'VE BEEN LOOKING AT ME.
I...
...DON'T ...
...USUALLY CRY.
BUT IT DOESN'T MEAN I WAS REALLY HURT.
...

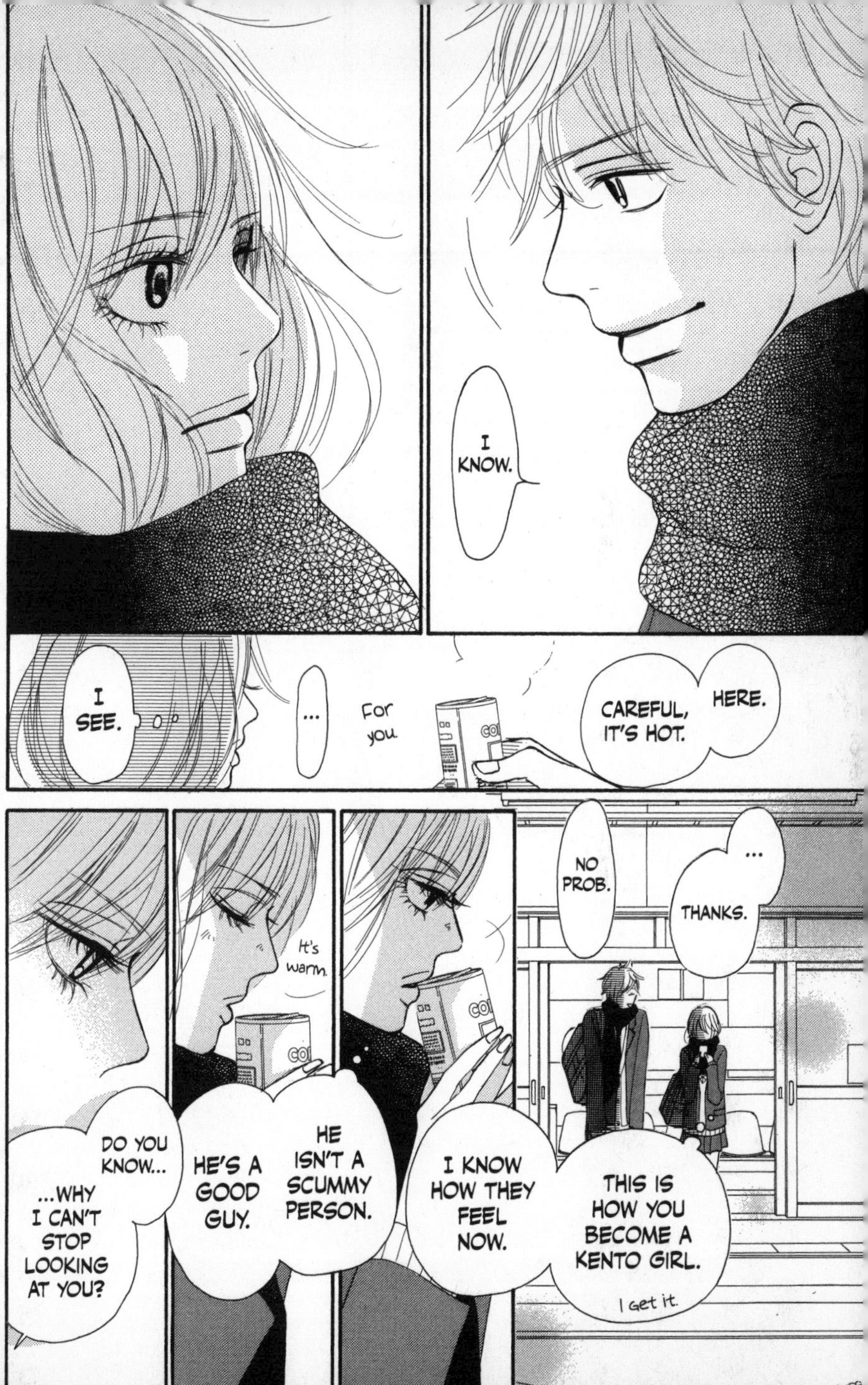
I KNOW.
HERE.
CAREFUL, IT'S HOT.
For you
...
I SEE.
...
THANKS.
NO PROB.
THIS IS HOW YOU BECOME A KENTO GIRL.
I get it.
I KNOW HOW THEY FEEL NOW.
It's warm.
HE ISN'T A SCUMMY PERSON.
HE'S A GOOD GUY.
DO YOU KNOW...
...WHY I CAN'T STOP LOOKING AT YOU?

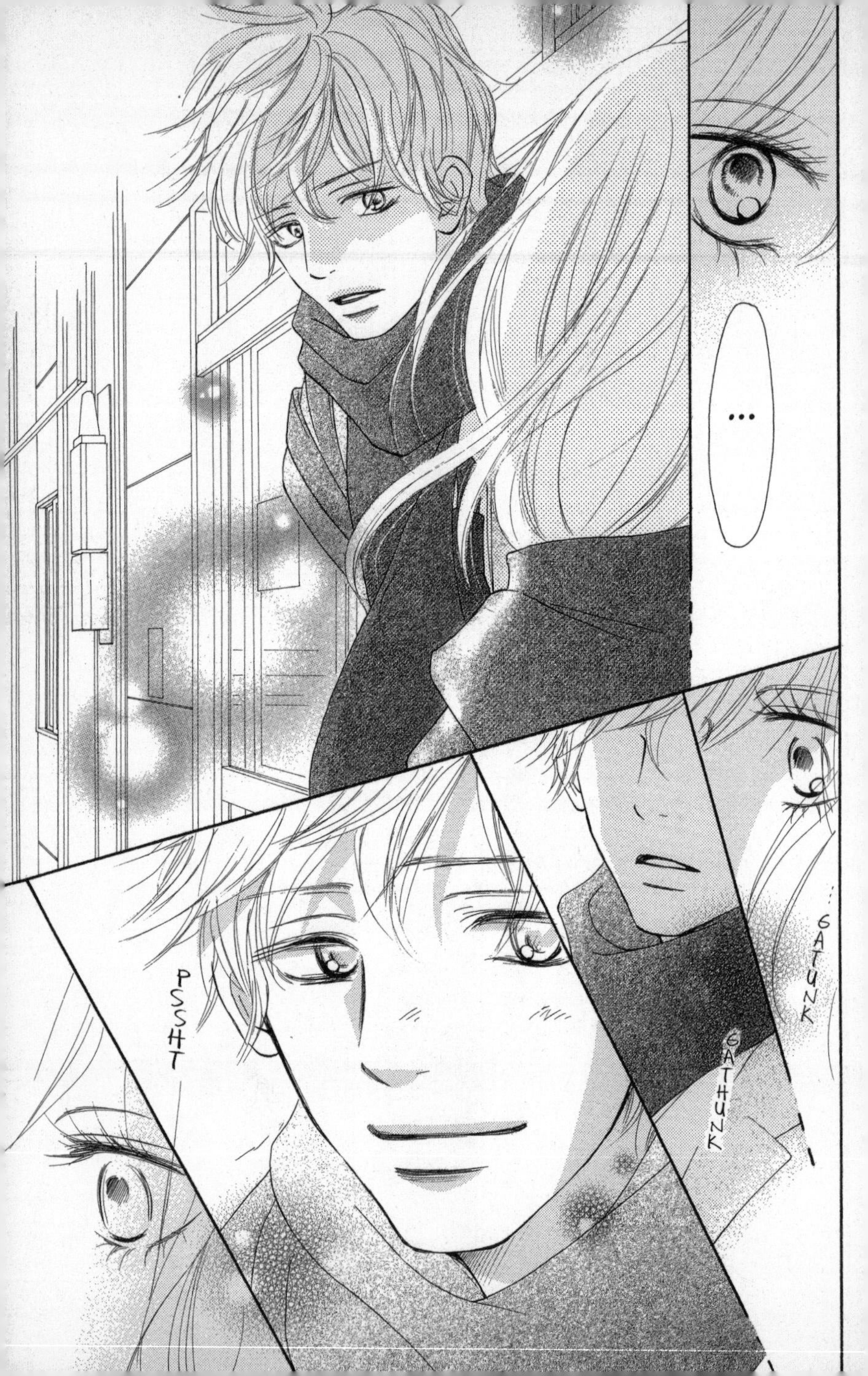
...
...GATUNK
GATHUNK
PSSHT

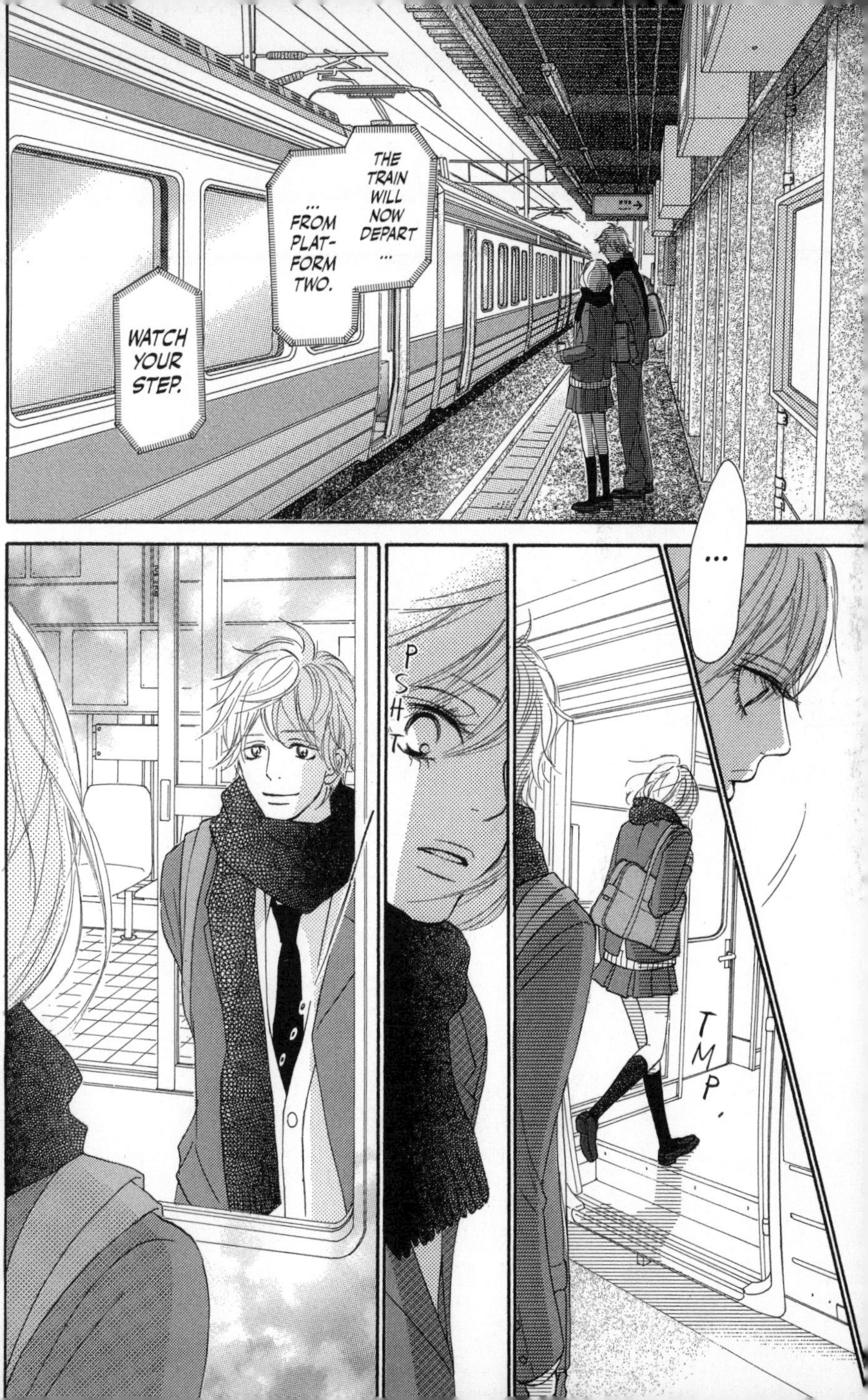
THE TRAIN WILL NOW DEPART ...
... FROM PLATFORM TWO.
WATCH YOUR STEP.
...
TMP.
PSHT

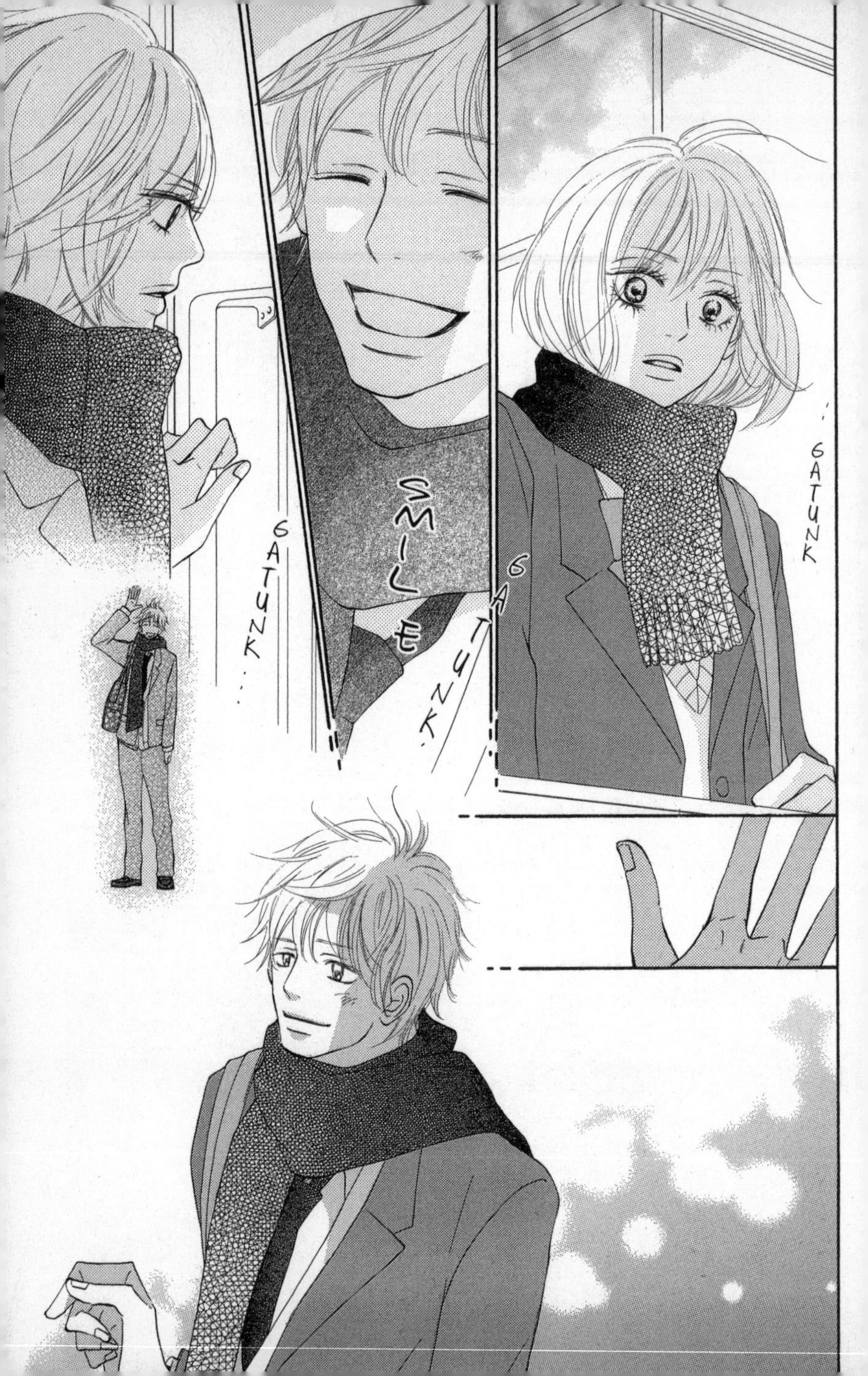
...GATUNK
GATUNK...
SMILE
GATUNK...

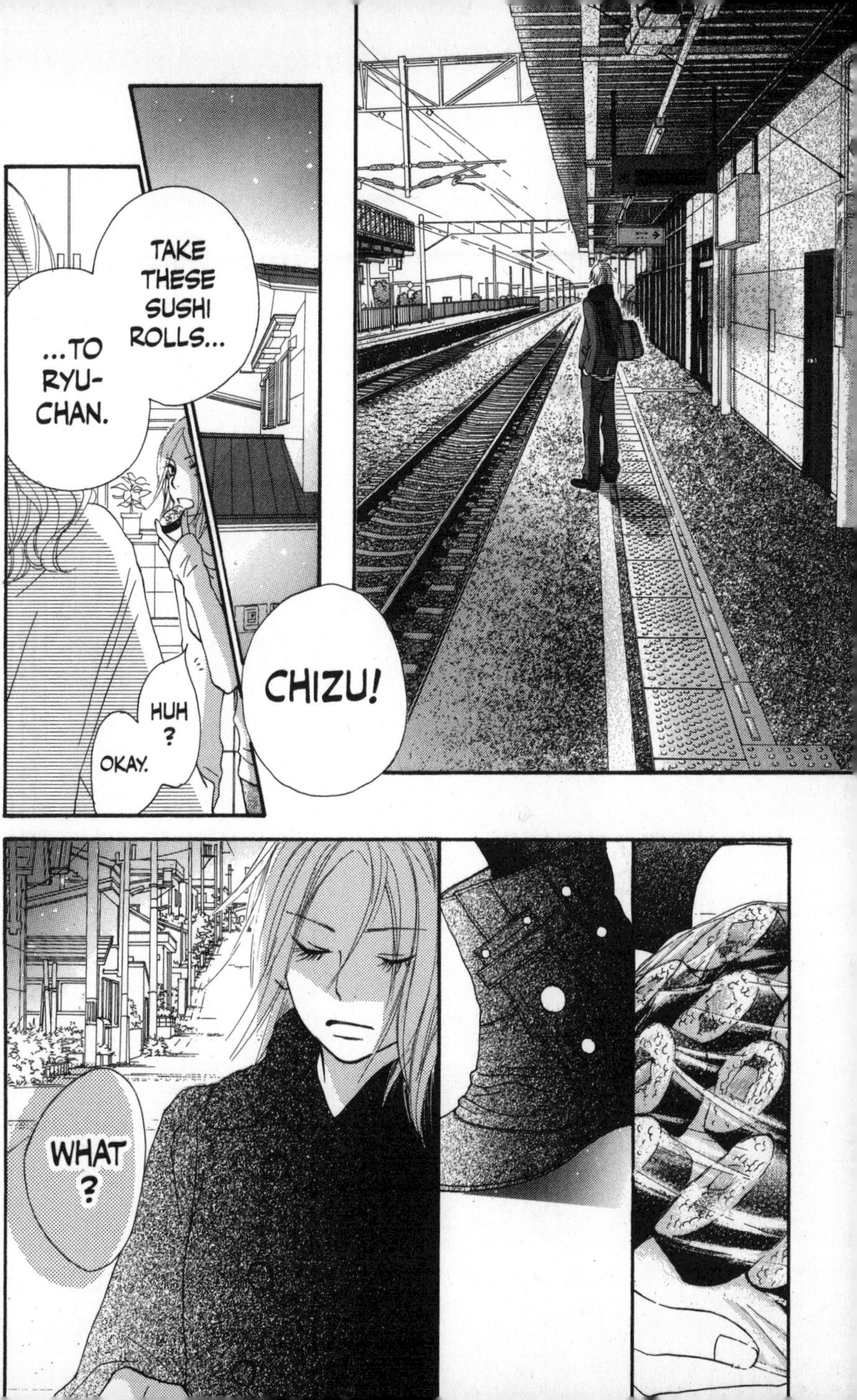
CHIZU!
TAKE THESE SUSHI ROLLS...
...TO RYU-CHAN.
HUH?
OKAY.
WHAT?

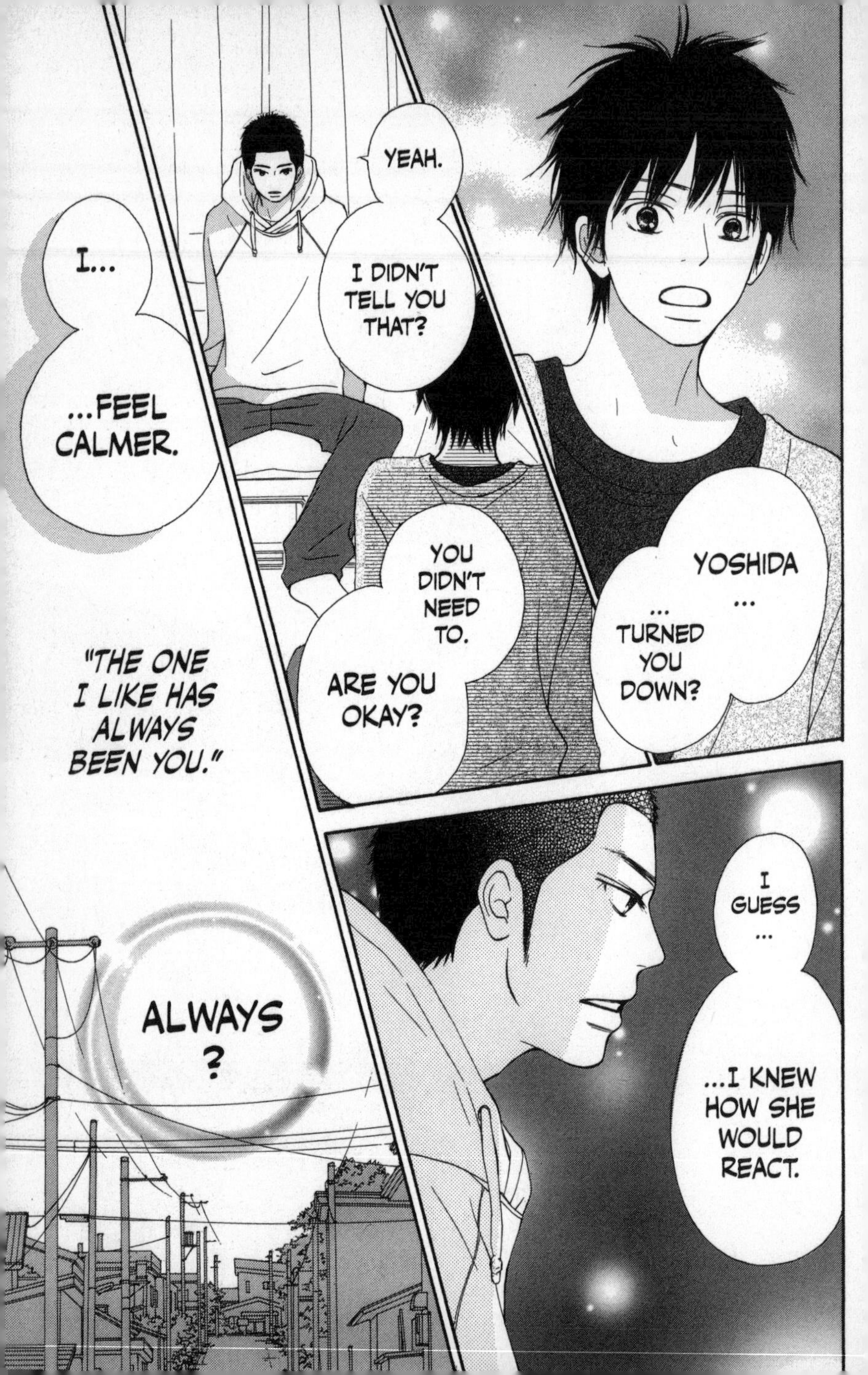

YOSHIDA ... ... TURNED YOU DOWN?
YEAH.
I DIDN'T TELL YOU THAT?
YOU DIDN'T NEED TO.
ARE YOU OKAY?
I GUESS ...
...I KNEW HOW SHE WOULD REACT.
I...
...FEEL CALMER.
"THE ONE I LIKE HAS ALWAYS BEEN YOU."
ALWAYS ?

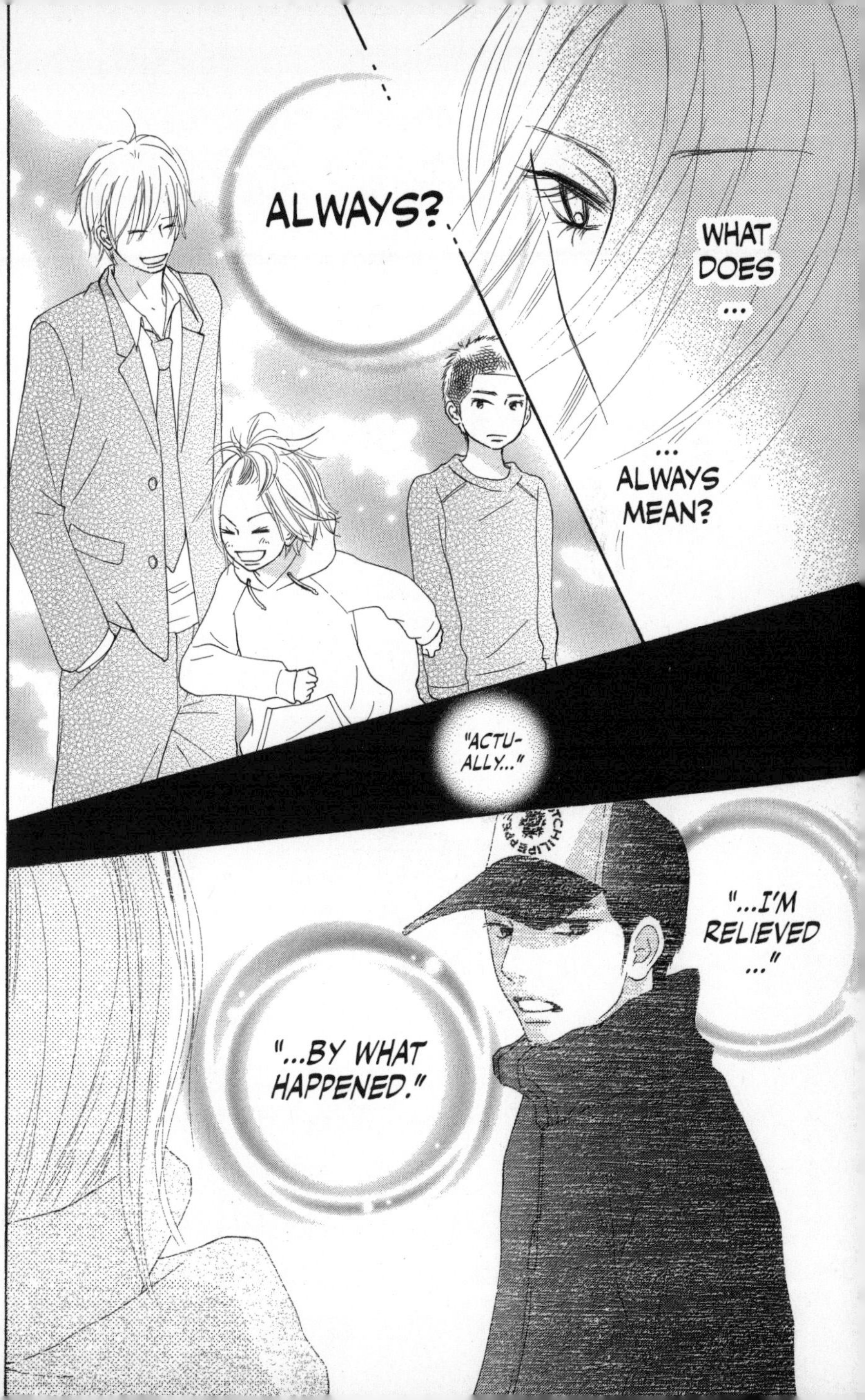
ALWAYS?
WHAT DOES ...
... ALWAYS MEAN?
"ACTU-ALLY..."
"...I'M RELIEVED ..."
"...BY WHAT HAPPENED."

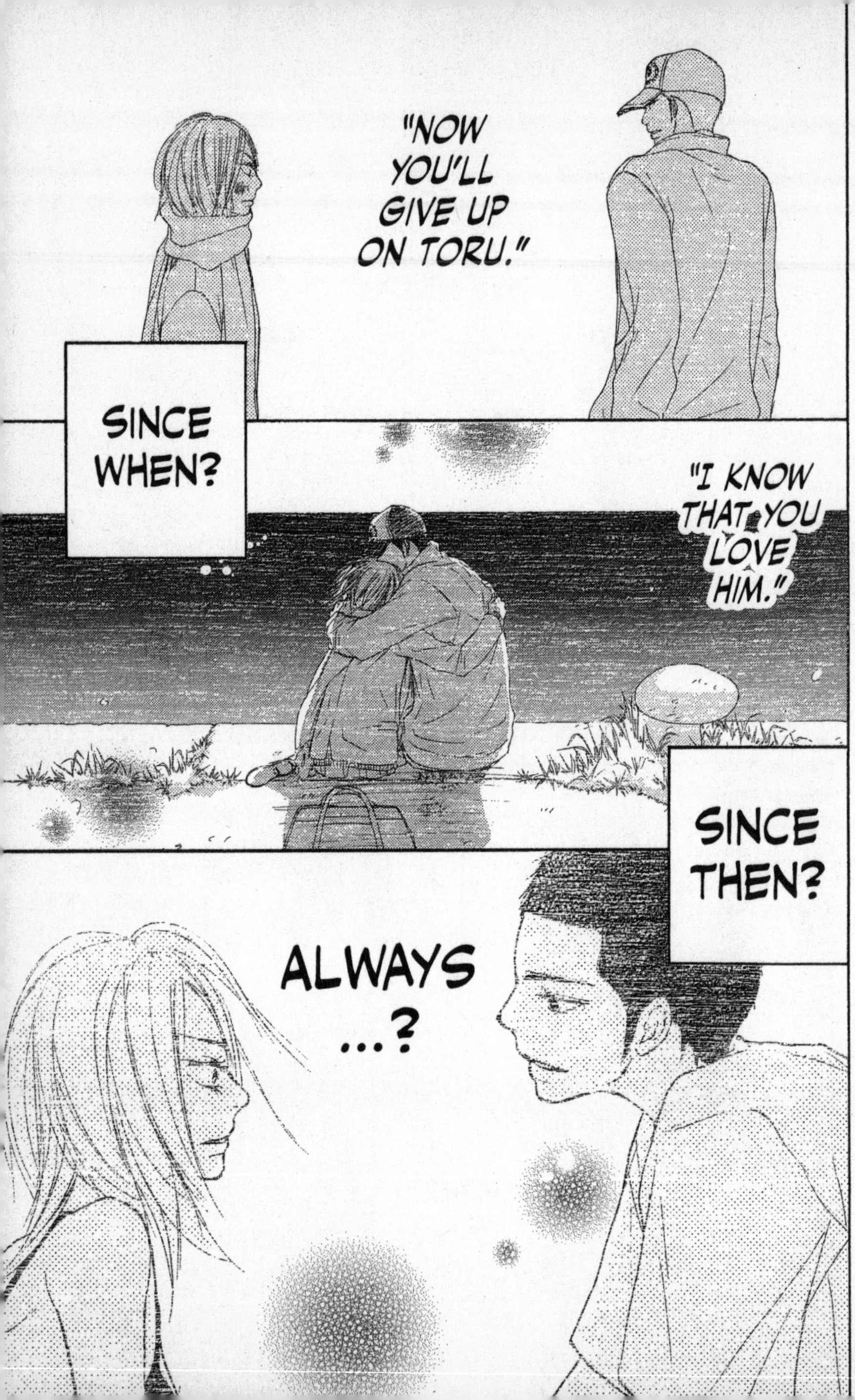
"NOW YOU'LL GIVE UP ON TORU."
SINCE WHEN?
"I KNOW THAT YOU LOVE HIM."
SINCE THEN?
ALWAYS ...?

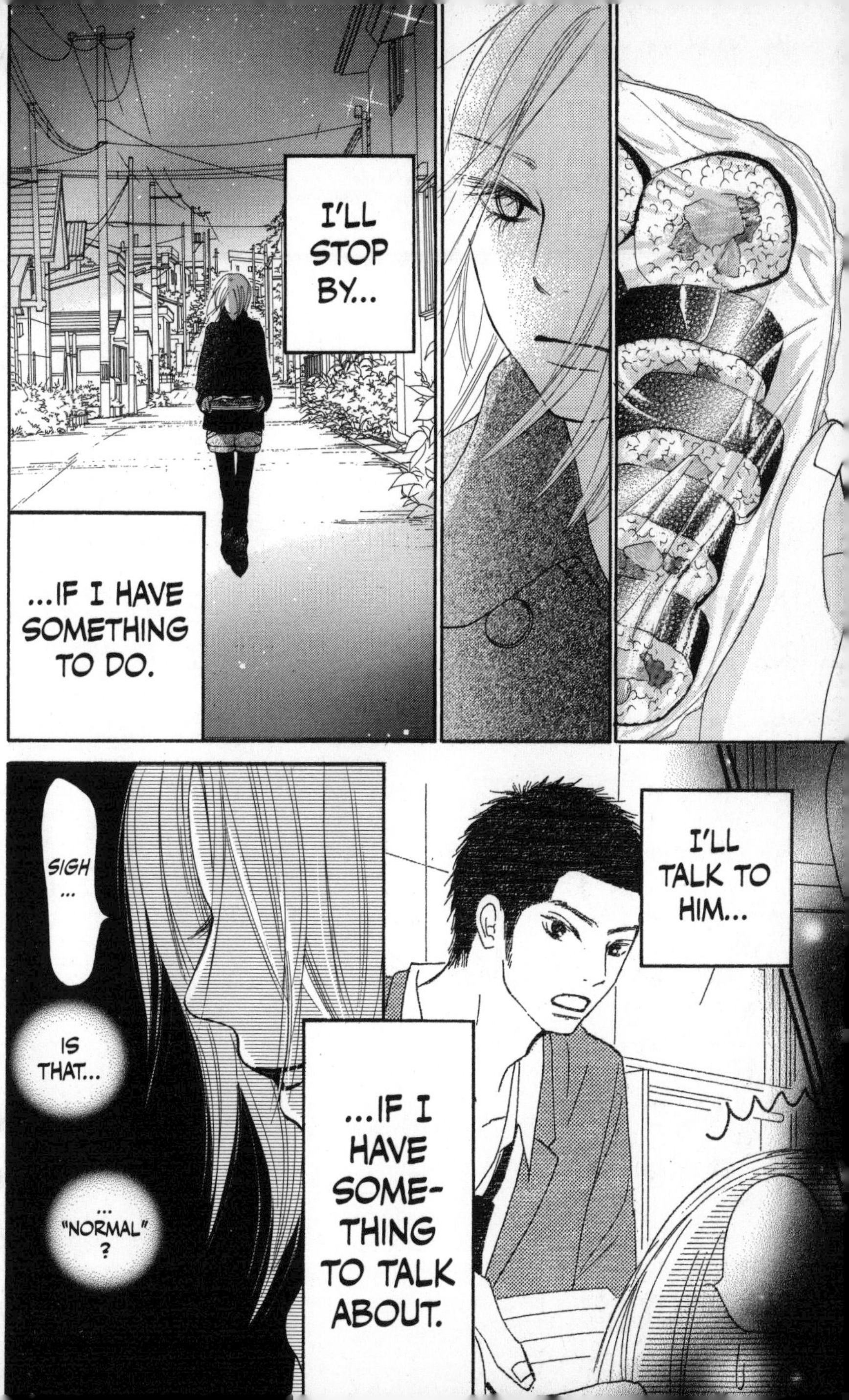
I'LL STOP BY...
...IF I HAVE SOMETHING TO DO.
I'LL TALK TO HIM...
...IF I HAVE SOME-THING TO TALK ABOUT.
SIGH ...
IS THAT...
... "NORMAL" ?

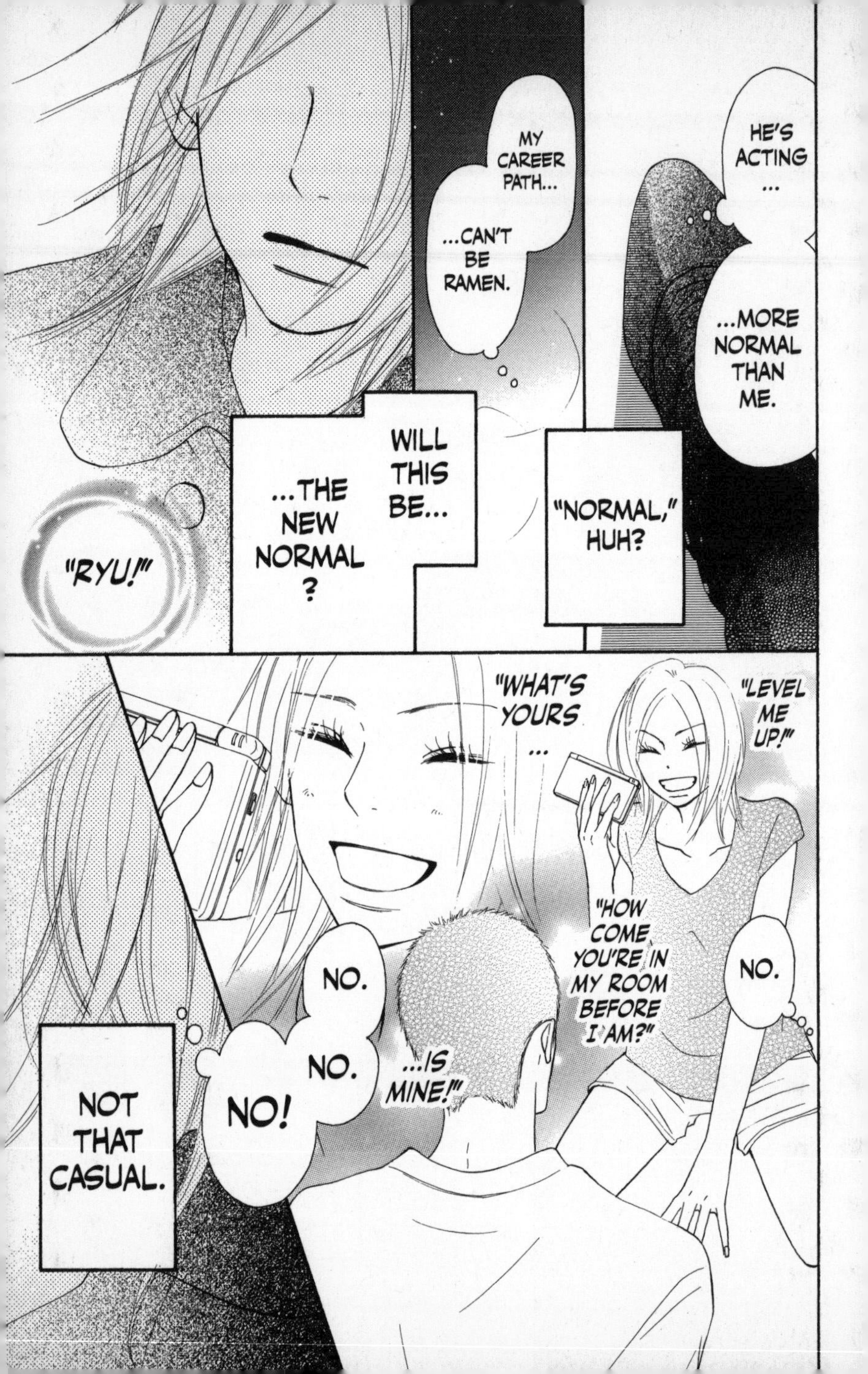
HE'S ACTING ...
...MORE NORMAL THAN ME.
"NORMAL," HUH?
MY CAREER PATH...
...CAN'T BE RAMEN.
WILL THIS BE...
...THE NEW NORMAL ?
"RYU!"
"LEVEL ME UP!"
"WHAT'S YOURS ...
"HOW COME YOU'RE IN MY ROOM BEFORE I AM?"
NO.
...IS MINE!"
NO.
NO.
NO!
NOT THAT CASUAL.

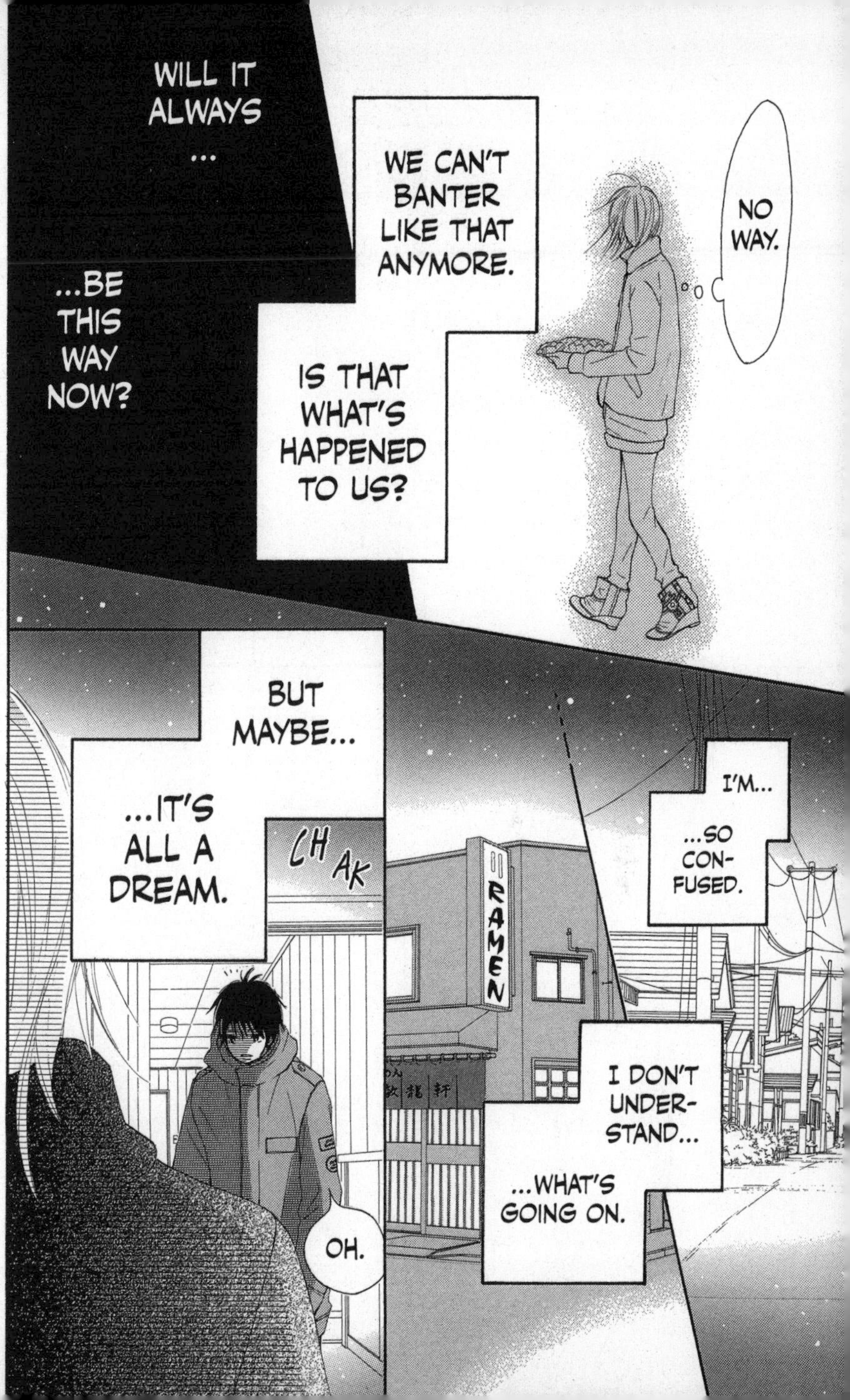
NO WAY.
WE CAN'T BANTER LIKE THAT ANYMORE.
IS THAT WHAT'S HAPPENED TO US?
WILL IT ALWAYS ...
...BE THIS WAY NOW?
I'M...
...SO CON-FUSED.
RAMEN
I DON'T UNDER-STAND...
...WHAT'S GOING ON.
BUT MAYBE...
...IT'S ALL A DREAM.
CHAK
OH.

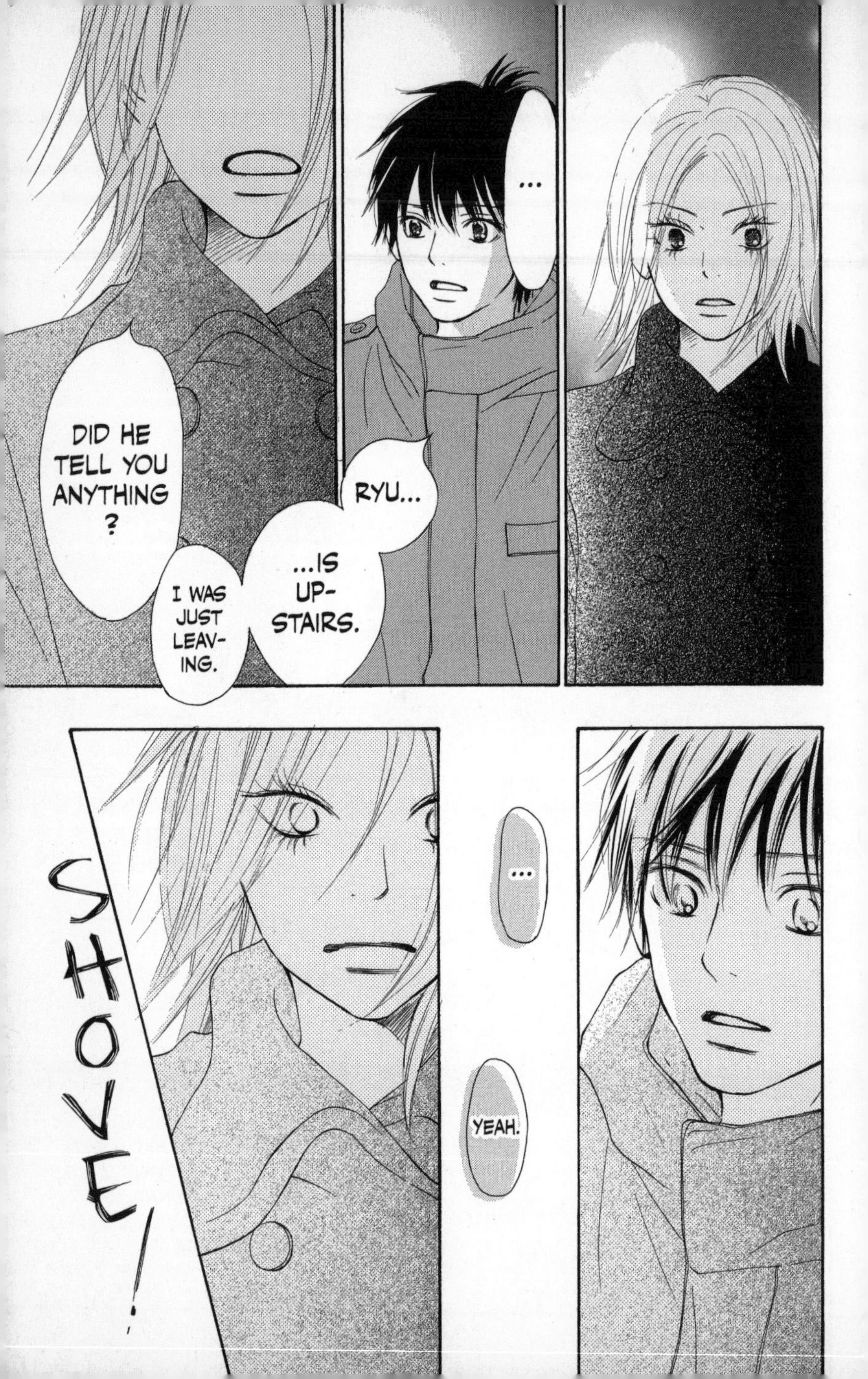
...
RYU...
...IS UP-STAIRS.
I WAS JUST LEAVING.
DID HE TELL YOU ANYTHING?
...
YEAH.
SHOVE!

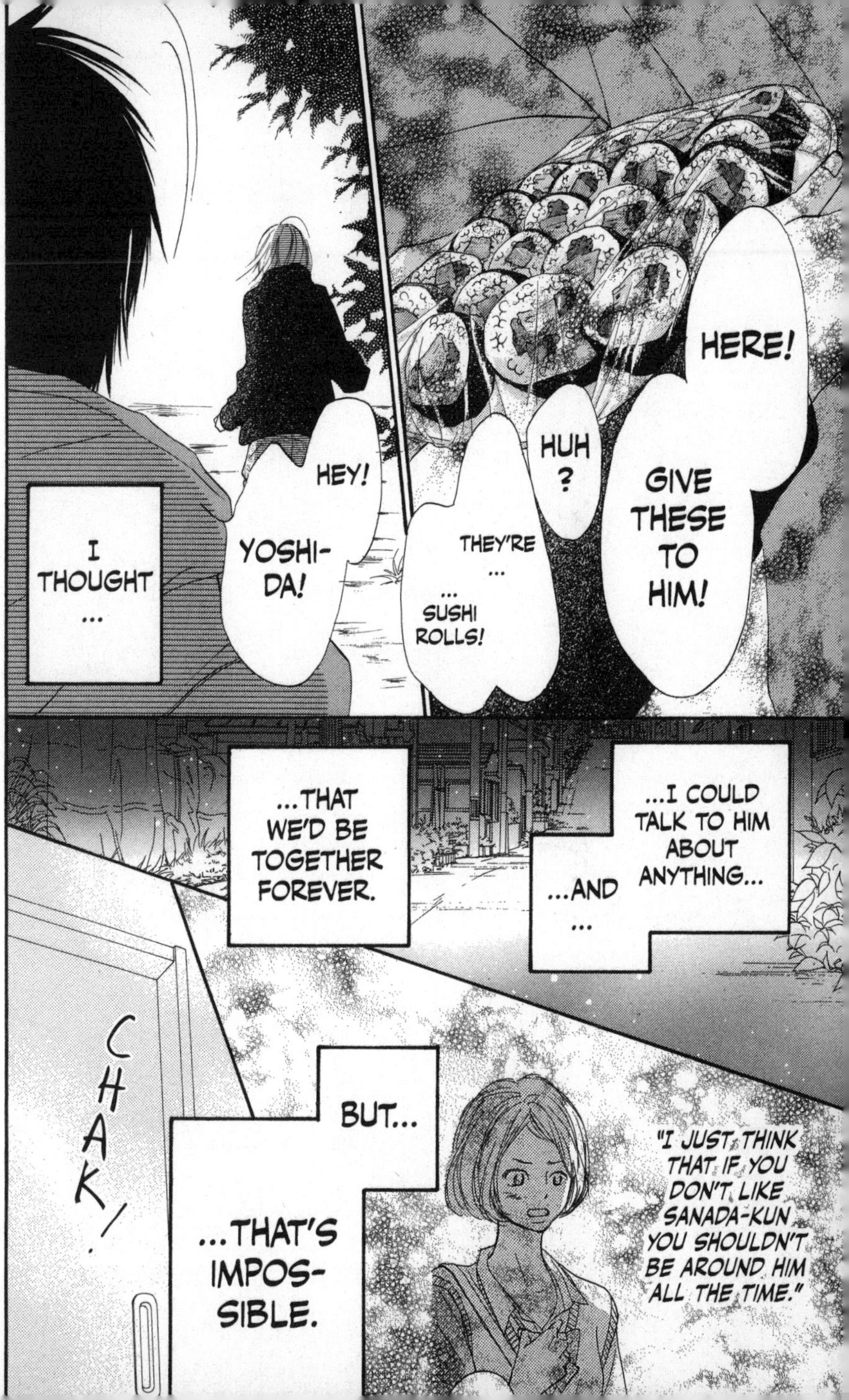
HERE!
GIVE THESE TO HIM!
HUH?
THEY'RE... ...SUSHI ROLLS!
HEY! YOSHI-DA!
I THOUGHT...
...I COULD TALK TO HIM ABOUT ANYTHING...
...AND...
...THAT WE'D BE TOGETHER FOREVER.
"I JUST THINK THAT IF YOU DON'T LIKE SANADA-KUN YOU SHOULDN'T BE AROUND HIM ALL THE TIME."
BUT...
...THAT'S IMPOS-SIBLE.
CHAK!

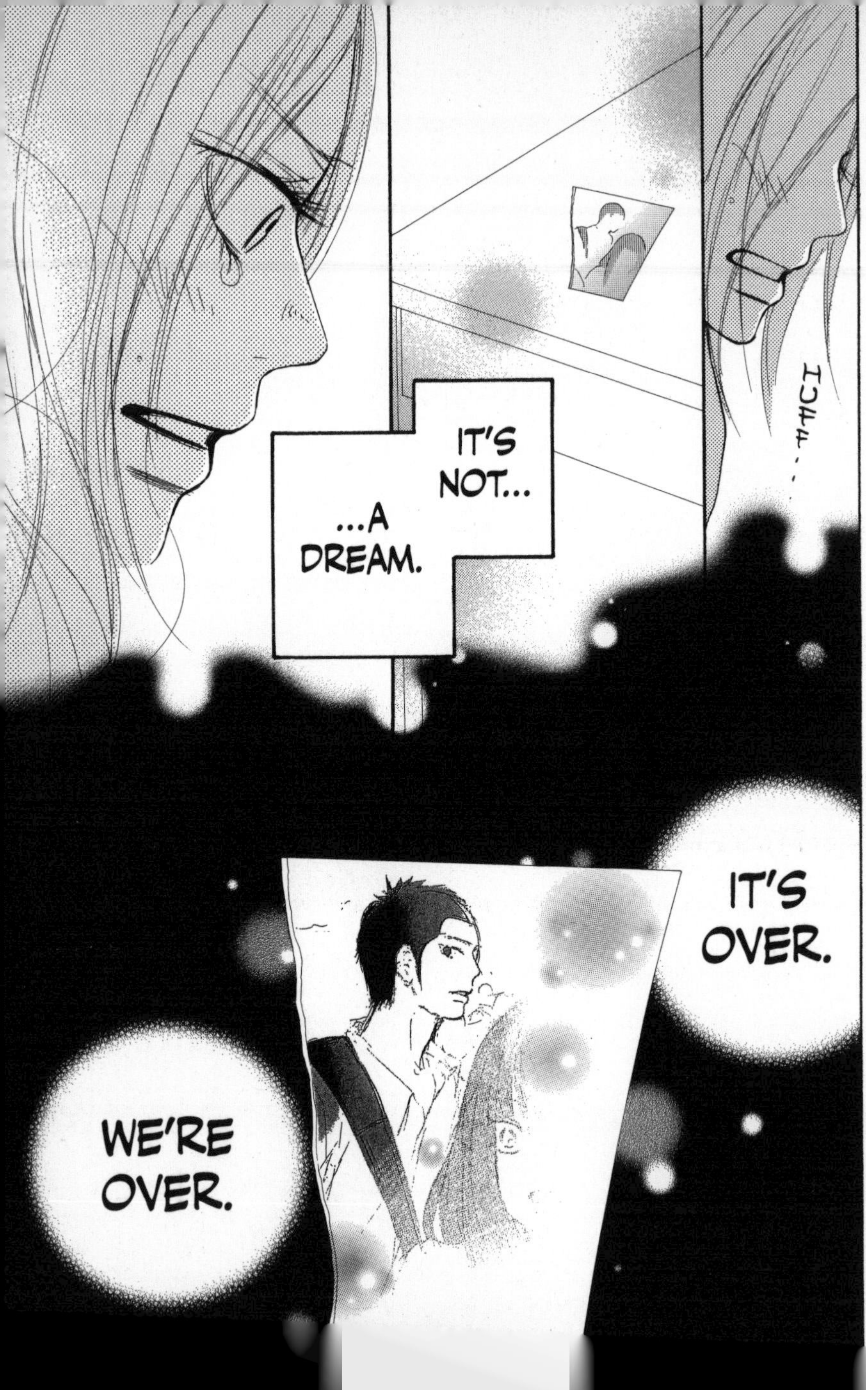
HUFF...
IT'S NOT...
...A DREAM.
IT'S OVER.
WE'RE OVER.

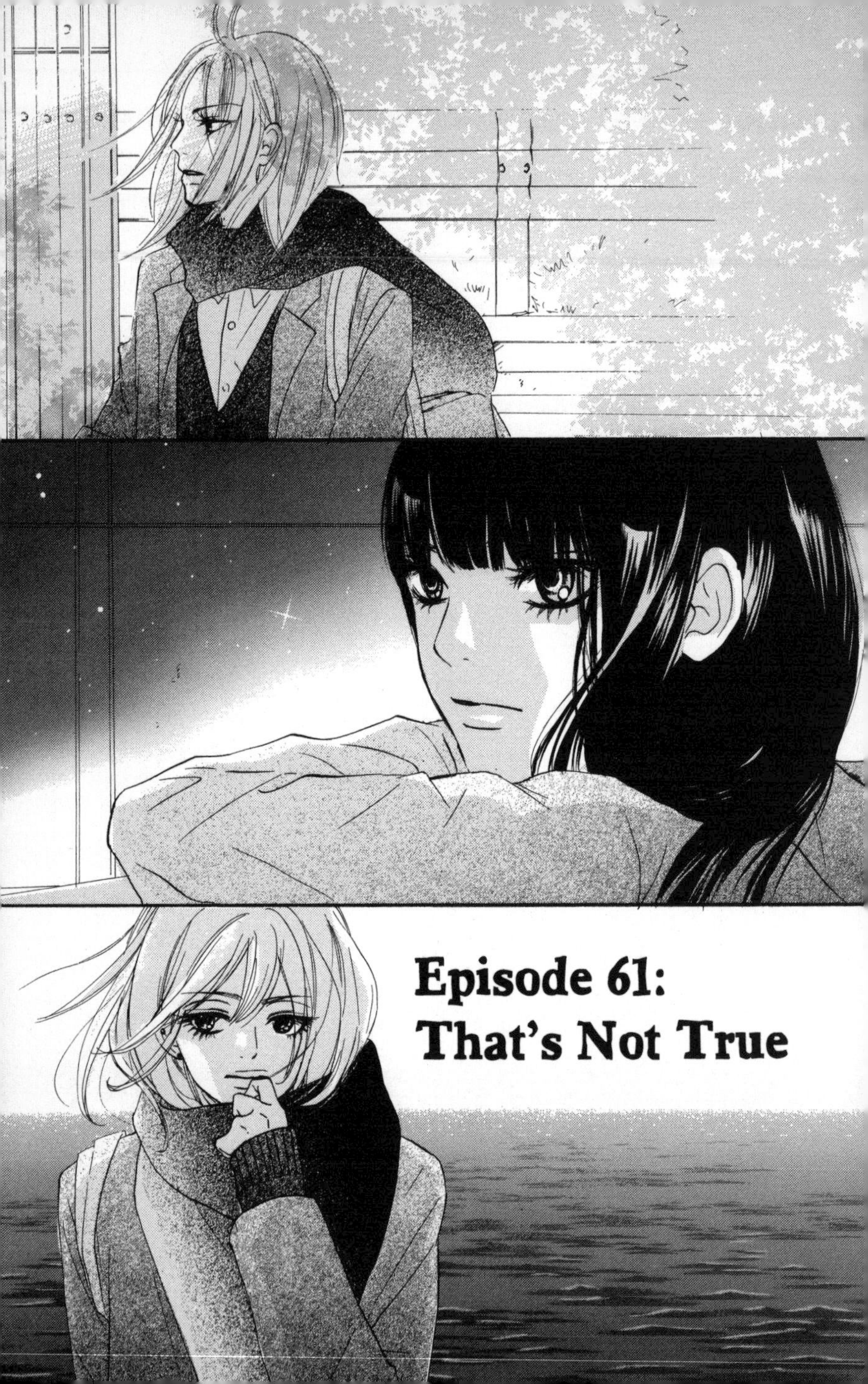
Episode 61:
That's Not True

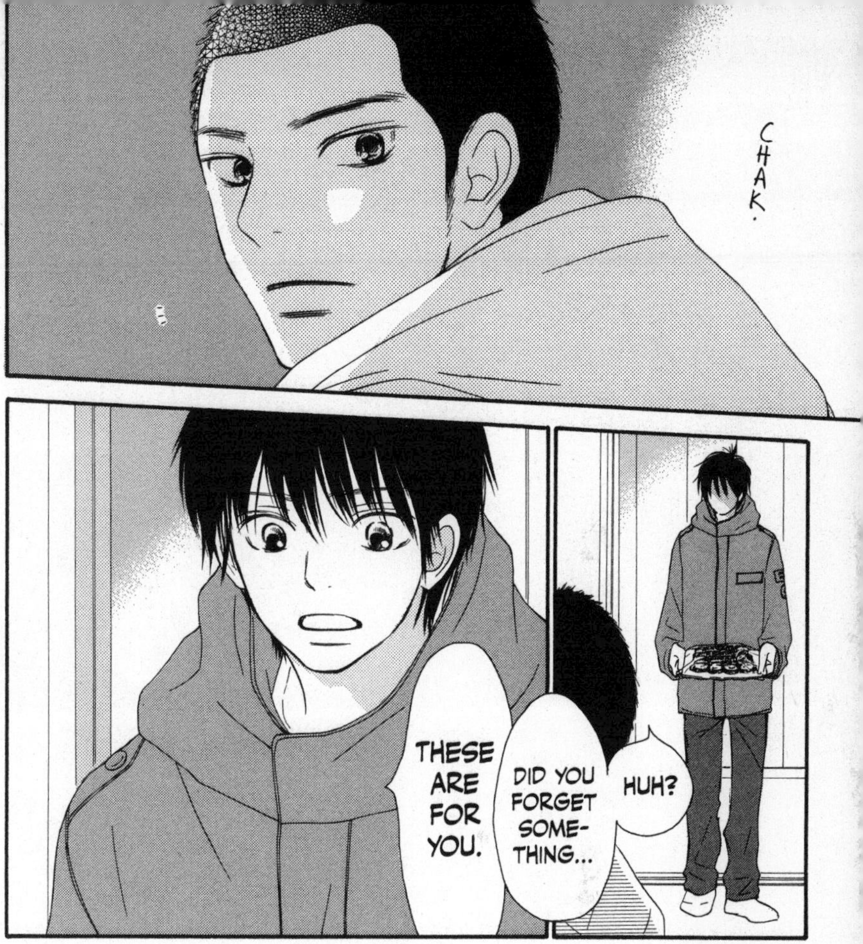
CHAK.
HUH?
DID YOU FORGET SOME-THING...
THESE ARE FOR YOU.

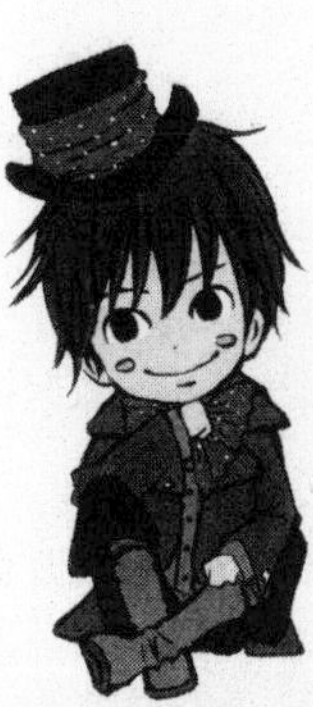

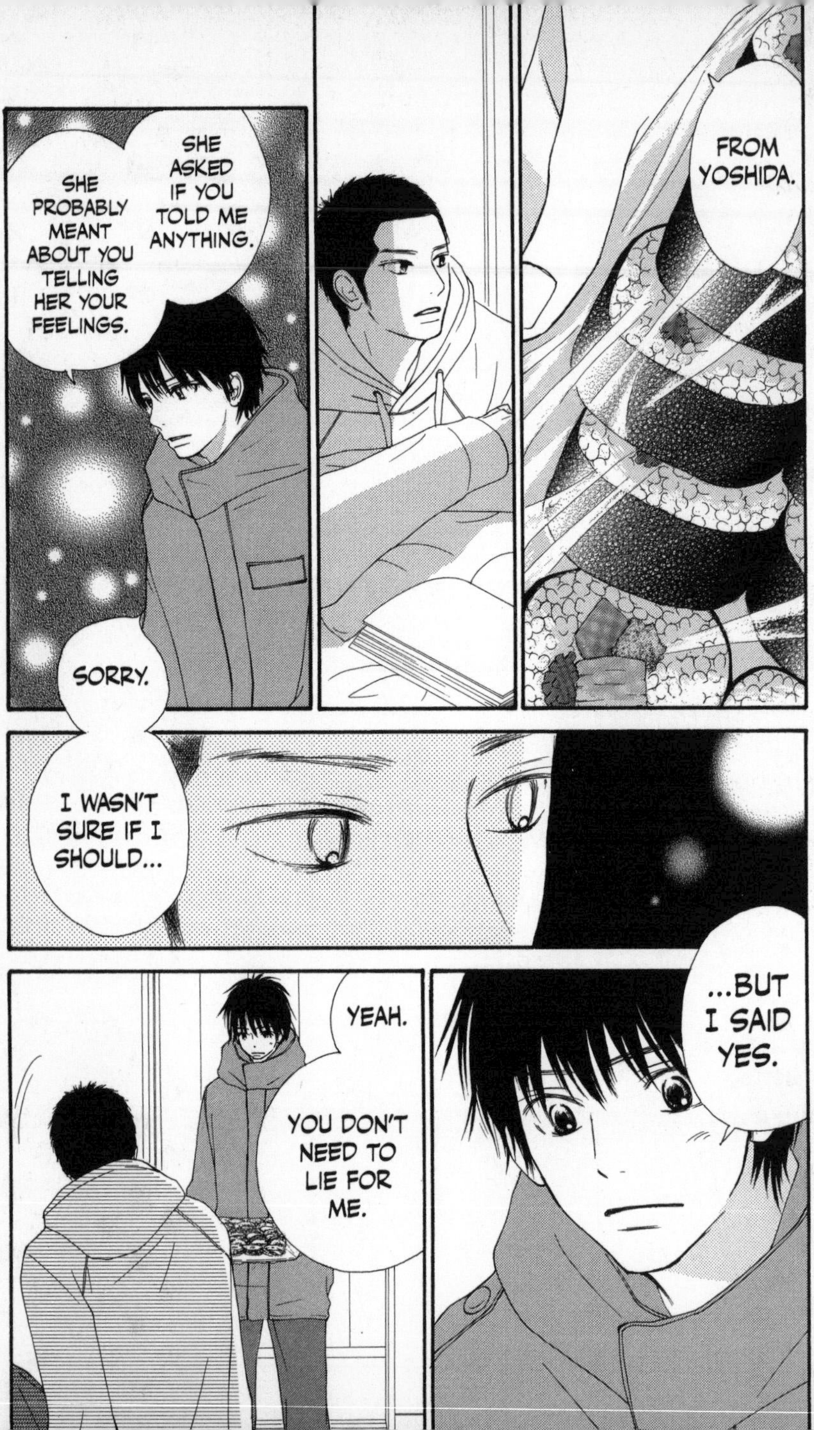
FROM YOSHIDA.
SHE ASKED IF YOU TOLD ME ANYTHING.
SHE PROBABLY MEANT ABOUT YOU TELLING HER YOUR FEELINGS.
SORRY.
I WASN'T SURE IF I SHOULD...
...BUT I SAID YES.
YEAH.
YOU DON'T NEED TO LIE FOR ME.

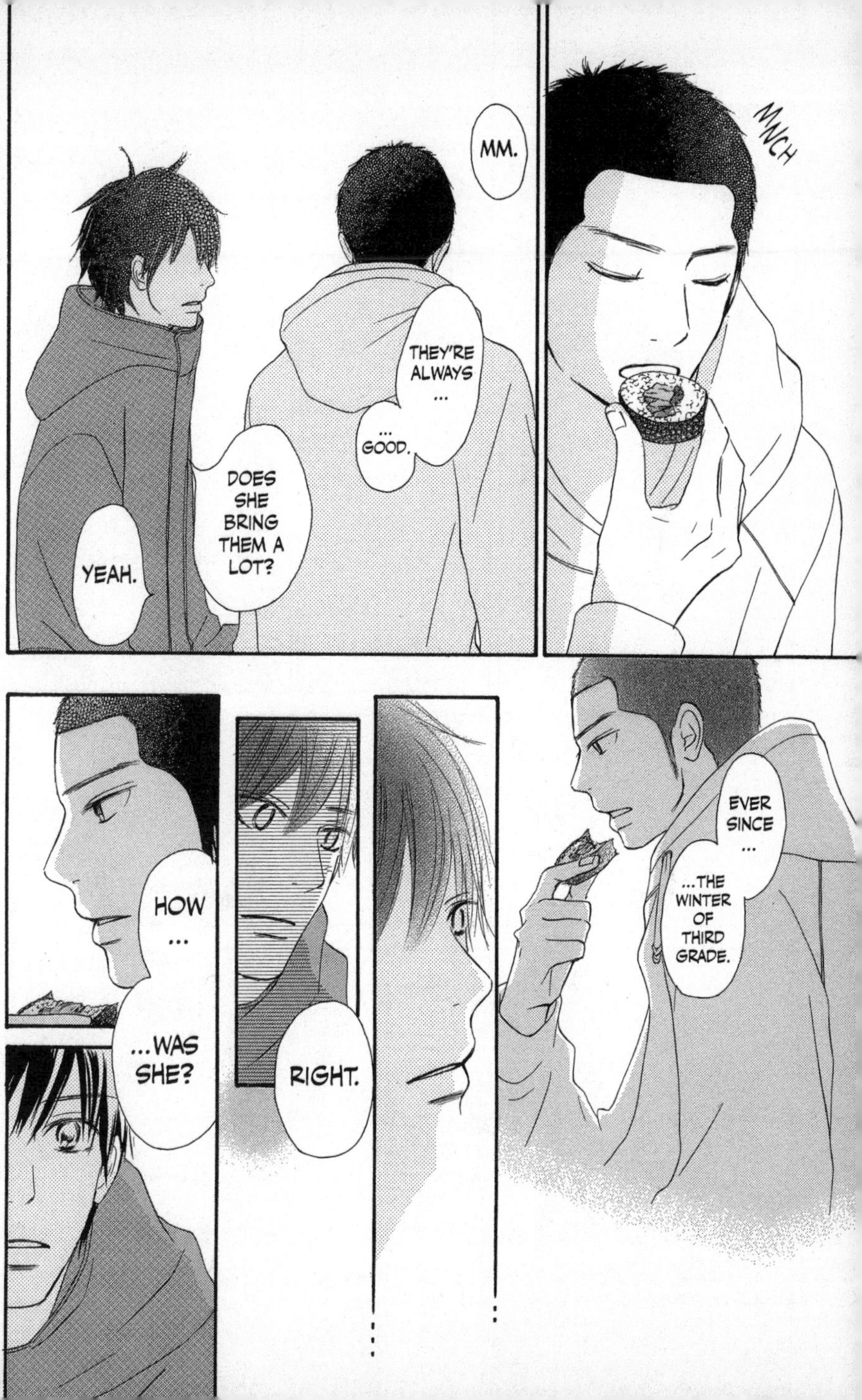
MNCH
MM.
THEY'RE ALWAYS ...
... GOOD.
DOES SHE BRING THEM A LOT?
YEAH.
EVER SINCE ...
...THE WINTER OF THIRD GRADE.
RIGHT.
HOW ...
...WAS SHE?

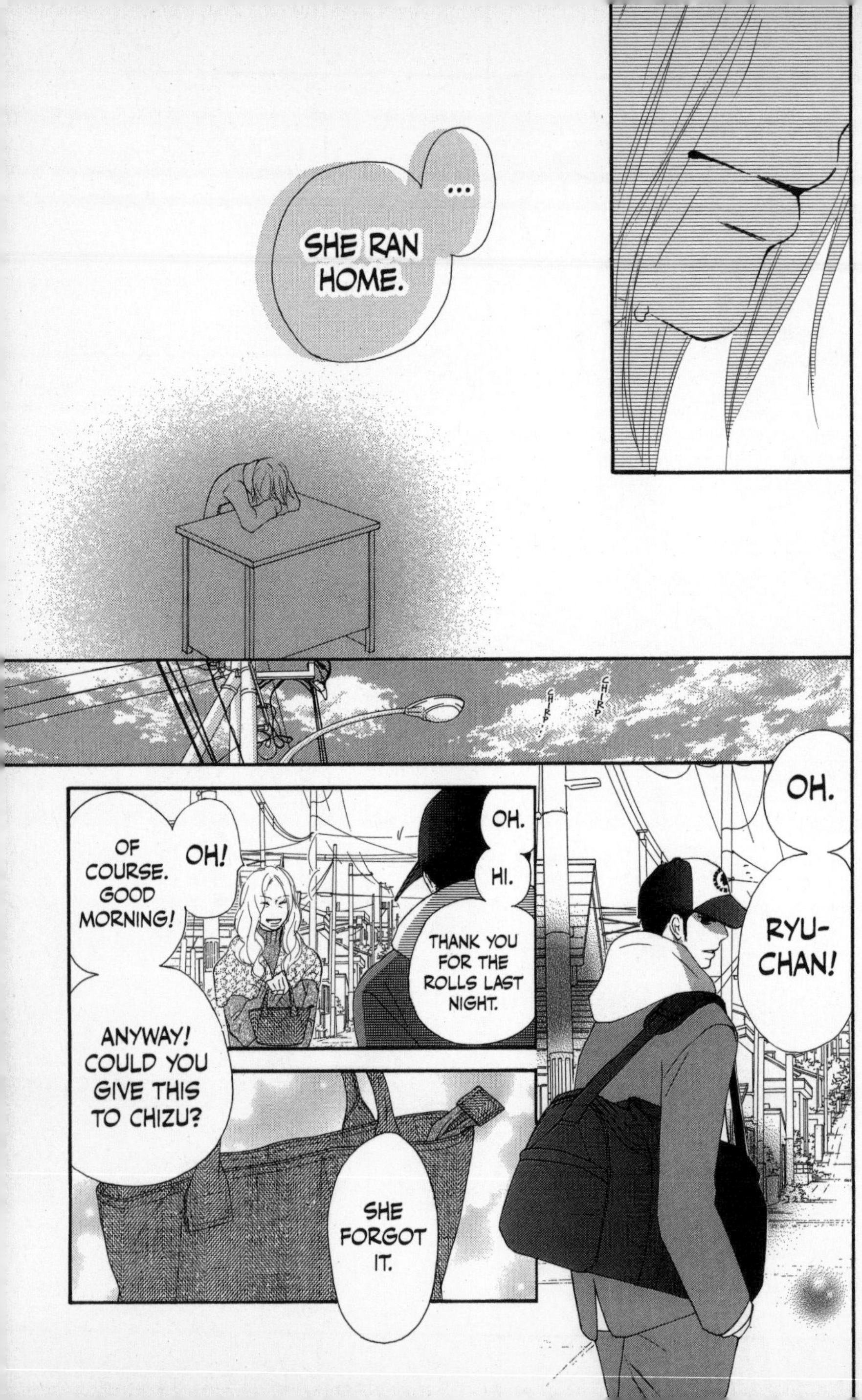
...
SHE RAN HOME.
CHIRP
CHIRP...
OH.
RYU-CHAN!
OH.
HI.
THANK YOU FOR THE ROLLS LAST NIGHT.
OH!
OF COURSE. GOOD MORNING!
ANYWAY! COULD YOU GIVE THIS TO CHIZU?
SHE FORGOT IT.

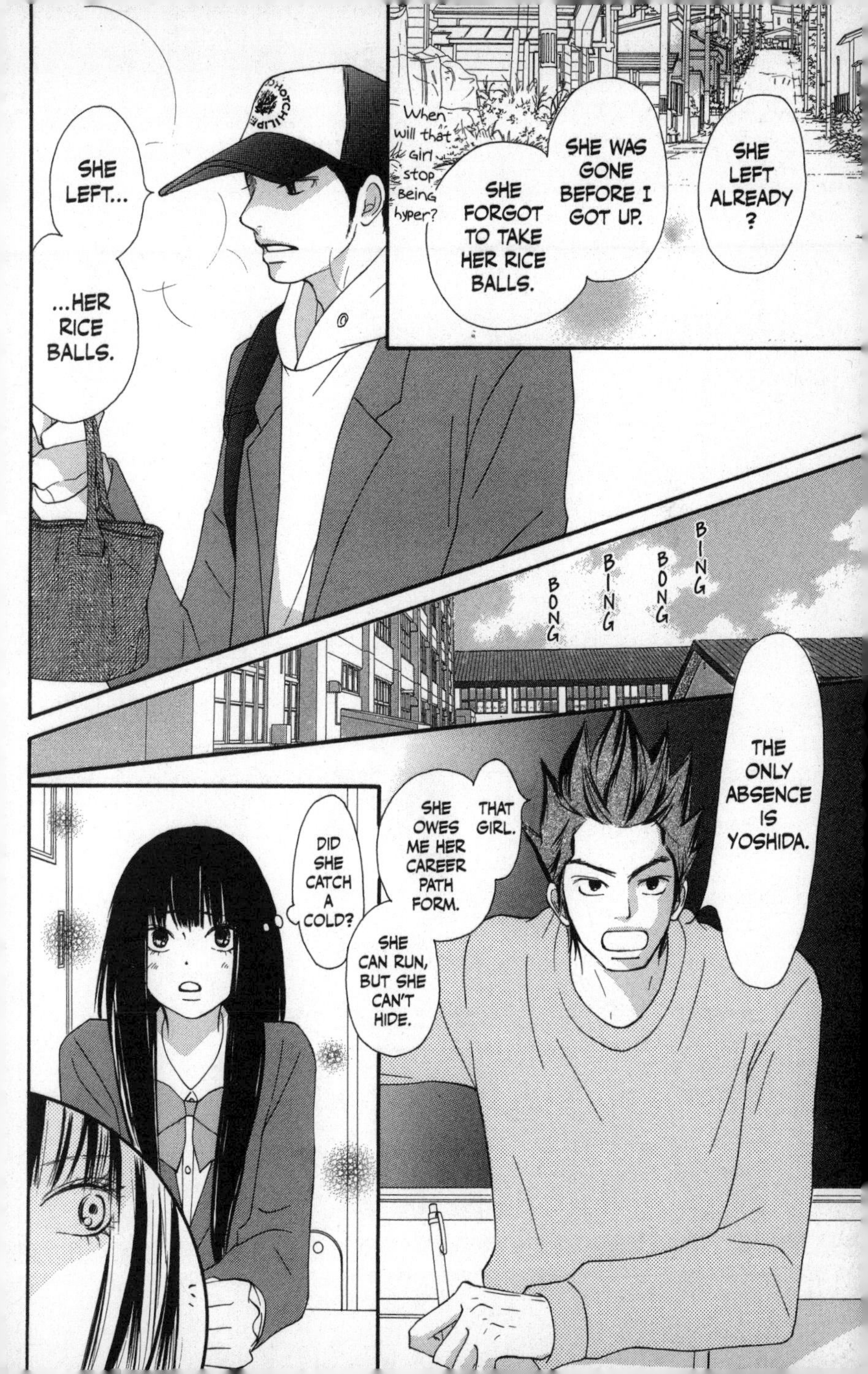
SHE LEFT ALREADY?
SHE WAS GONE BEFORE I GOT UP.
SHE FORGOT TO TAKE HER RICE BALLS.
When will that girl stop being hyper?
SHE LEFT...
...HER RICE BALLS.
BING BONG BING BONG
THE ONLY ABSENCE IS YOSHIDA.
THAT GIRL.
SHE OWES ME HER CAREER PATH FORM.
SHE CAN RUN, BUT SHE CAN'T HIDE.
DID SHE CATCH A COLD?

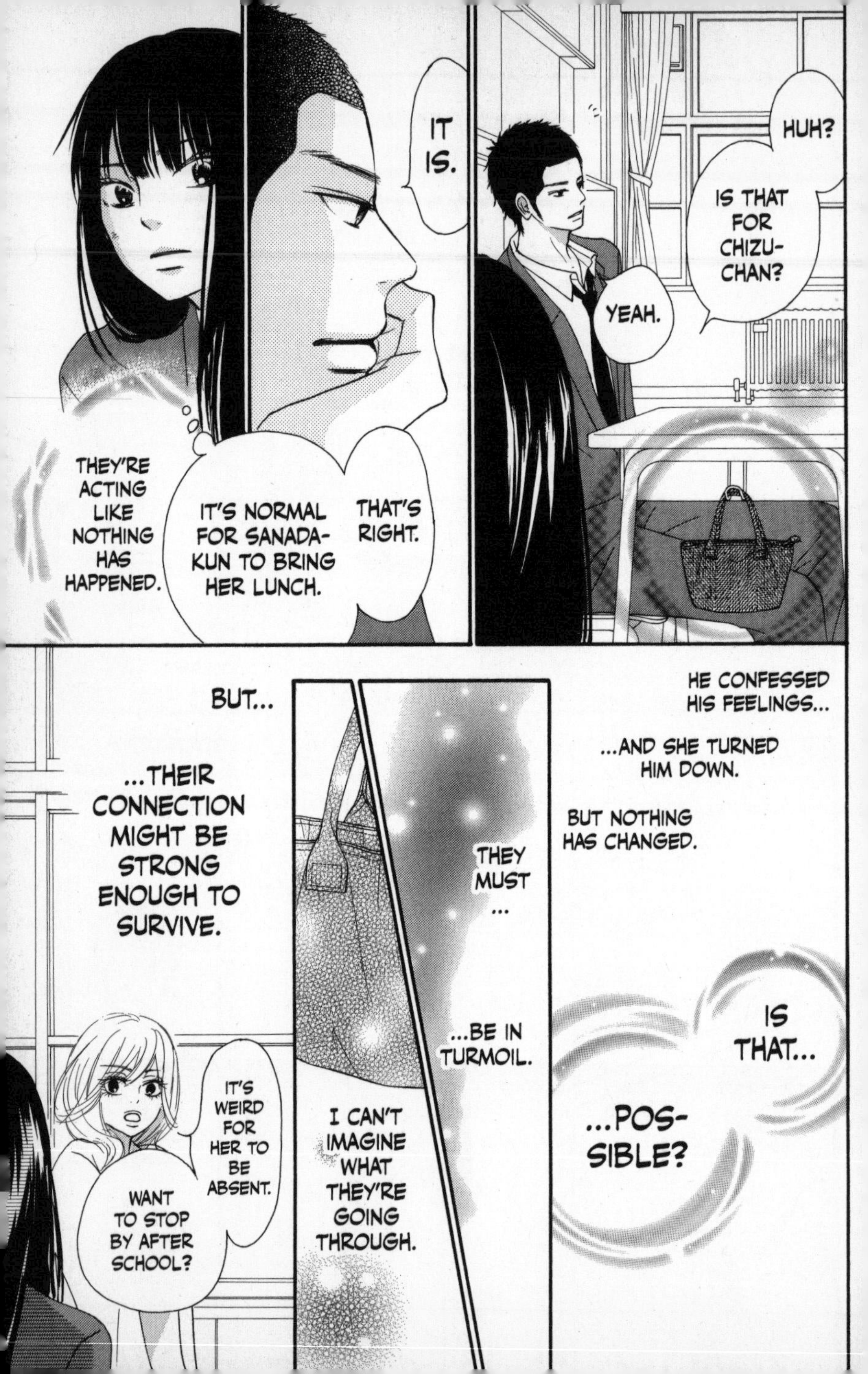
HUH?
IS THAT FOR CHIZU-CHAN?
YEAH.
IT IS.
THAT'S RIGHT.
IT'S NORMAL FOR SANADA-KUN TO BRING HER LUNCH.
THEY'RE ACTING LIKE NOTHING HAS HAPPENED.
HE CONFESSED HIS FEELINGS...
...AND SHE TURNED HIM DOWN.
BUT NOTHING HAS CHANGED.
IS THAT...
...POS-SIBLE?
THEY MUST...
...BE IN TURMOIL.
I CAN'T IMAGINE WHAT THEY'RE GOING THROUGH.
BUT...
...THEIR CONNECTION MIGHT BE STRONG ENOUGH TO SURVIVE.
IT'S WEIRD FOR HER TO BE ABSENT.
WANT TO STOP BY AFTER SCHOOL?

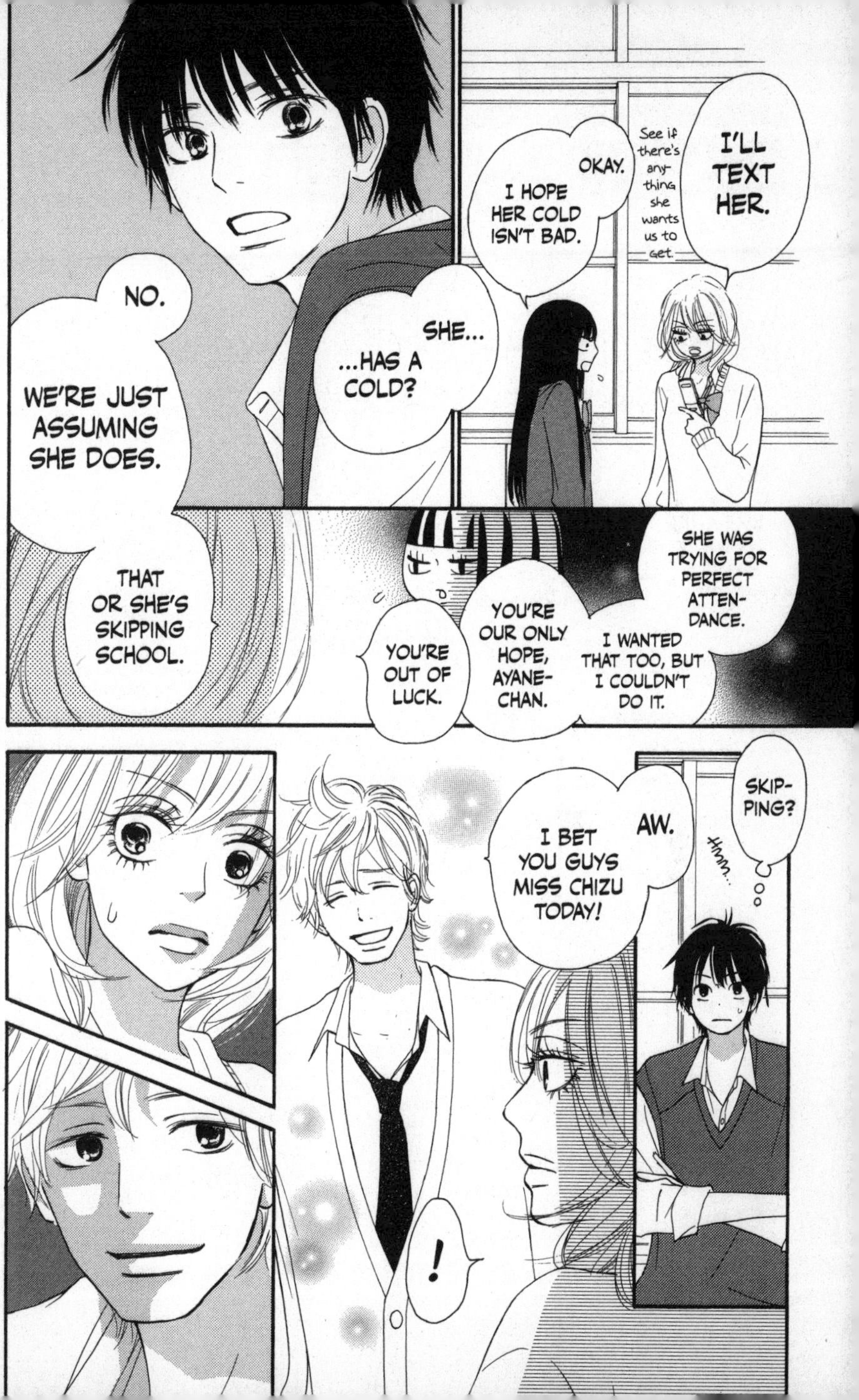
I'LL TEXT HER.
See if there's any-thing she wants us to get.
OKAY.
I HOPE HER COLD ISN'T BAD.
SHE...
...HAS A COLD?
NO.
WE'RE JUST ASSUMING SHE DOES.
SHE WAS TRYING FOR PERFECT ATTEN-DANCE.
I WANTED THAT TOO, BUT I COULDN'T DO IT.
YOU'RE OUR ONLY HOPE, AYANE-CHAN.
YOU'RE OUT OF LUCK.
THAT OR SHE'S SKIPPING SCHOOL.
SKIP-PING?
Hmm...
AW.
I BET YOU GUYS MISS CHIZU TODAY!
!

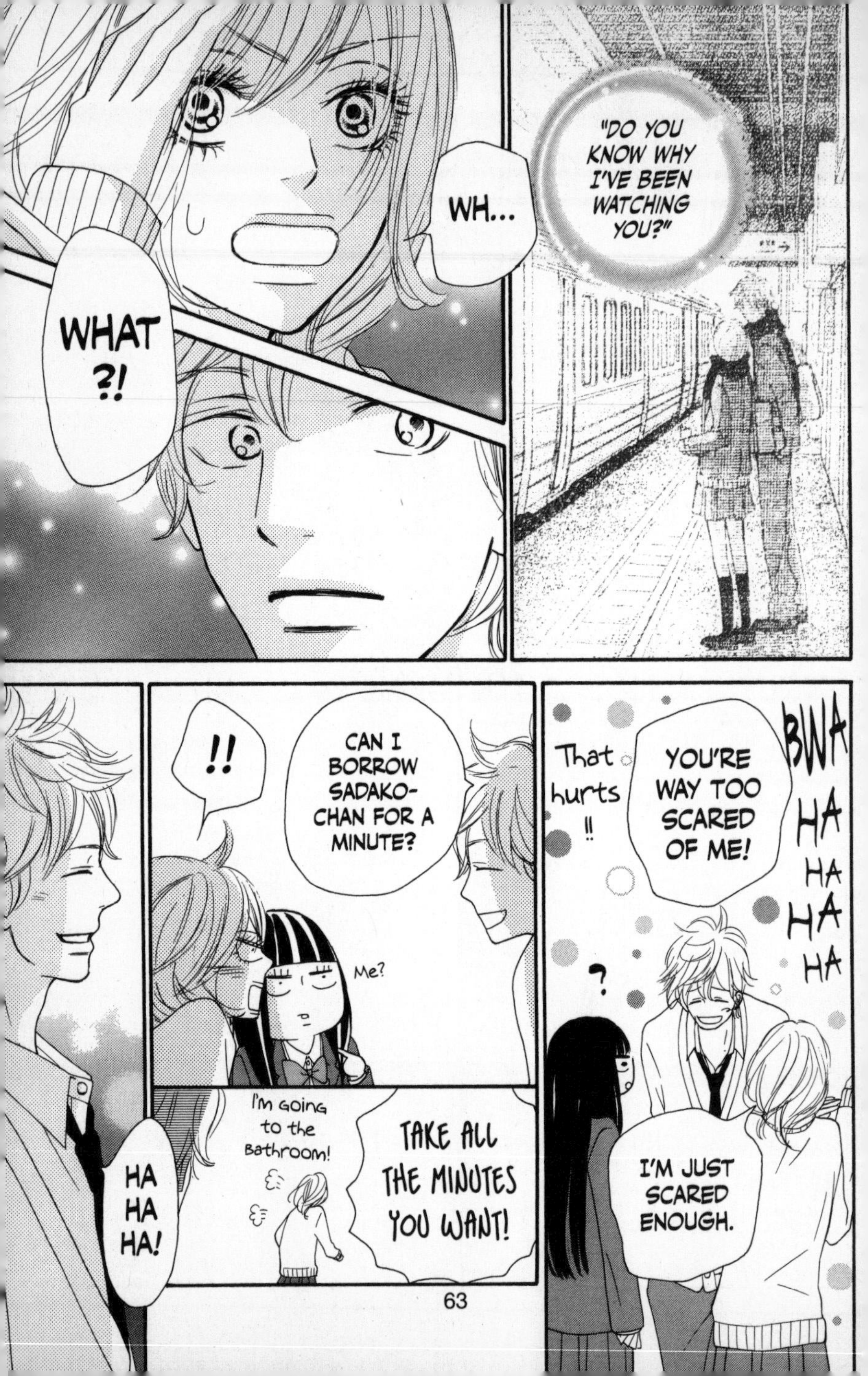
"DO YOU KNOW WHY I'VE BEEN WATCHING YOU?"
WH...
WHAT ?!
BWA HA HA HA HA HA
YOU'RE WAY TOO SCARED OF ME!
That hurts !!
?
I'M JUST SCARED ENOUGH.
CAN I BORROW SADAKO-CHAN FOR A MINUTE?
!!
Me?
TAKE ALL THE MINUTES YOU WANT!
I'm going to the Bathroom!
HA HA HA!

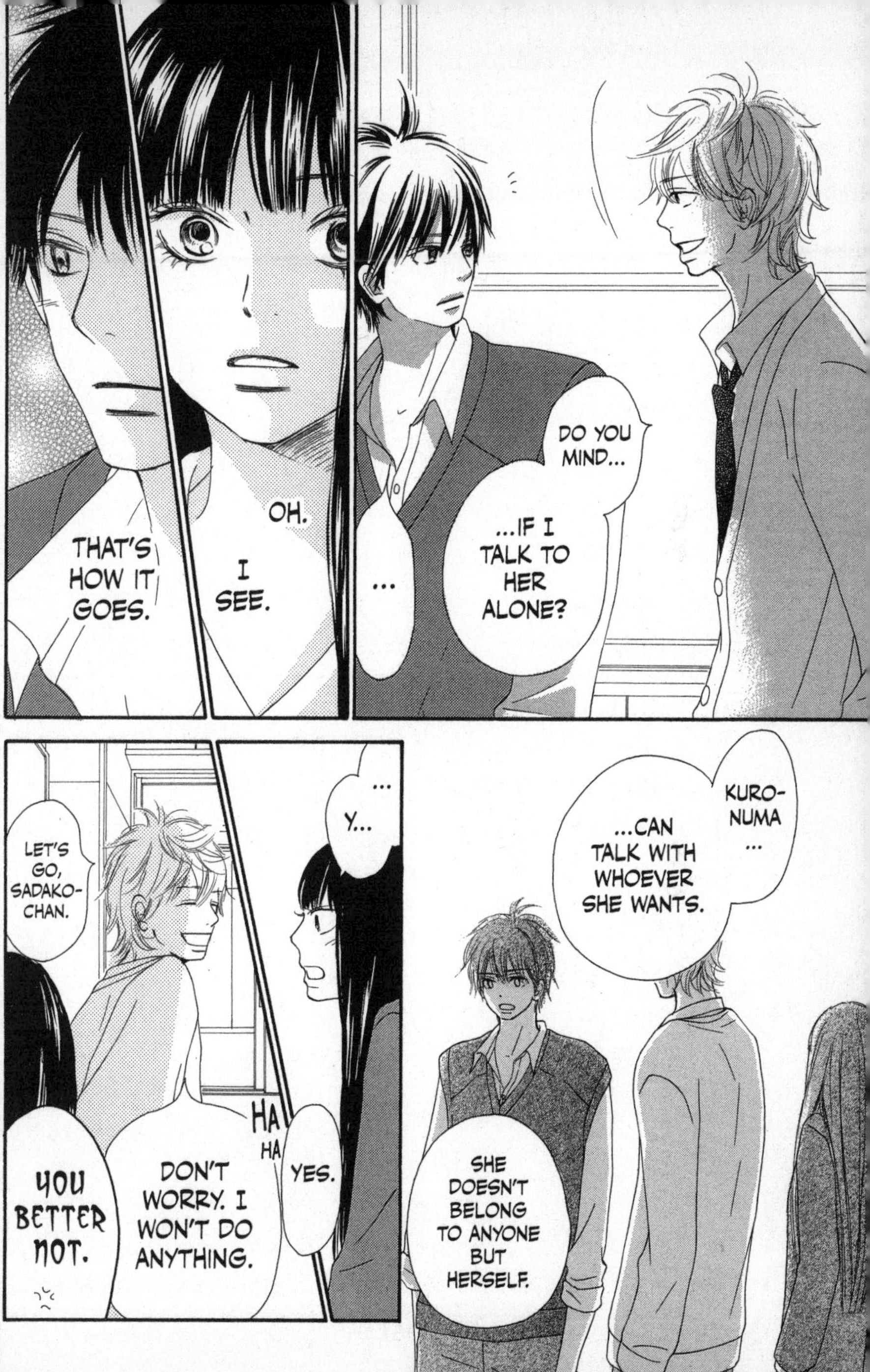
DO YOU MIND...
...IF I TALK TO HER ALONE?
...
OH.
I SEE.
THAT'S HOW IT GOES.
KURO-NUMA...
...CAN TALK WITH WHOEVER SHE WANTS.
SHE DOESN'T BELONG TO ANYONE BUT HERSELF.
... Y...
YES.
LET'S GO, SADAKO-CHAN.
HA HA
DON'T WORRY. I WON'T DO ANYTHING.
YOU BETTER NOT.

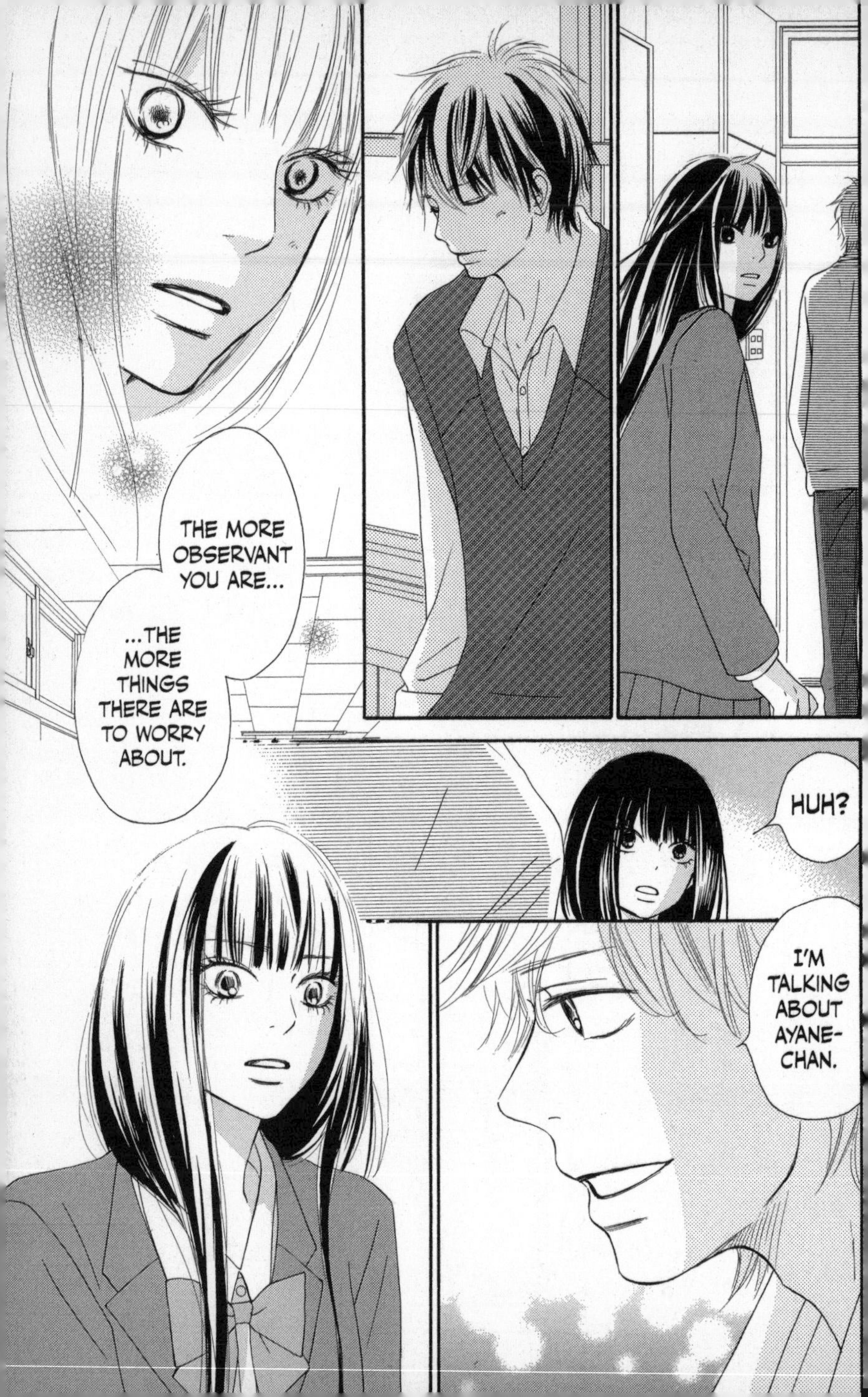
THE MORE OBSERVANT YOU ARE...
...THE MORE THINGS THERE ARE TO WORRY ABOUT.
HUH?
I'M TALKING ABOUT AYANE-CHAN.

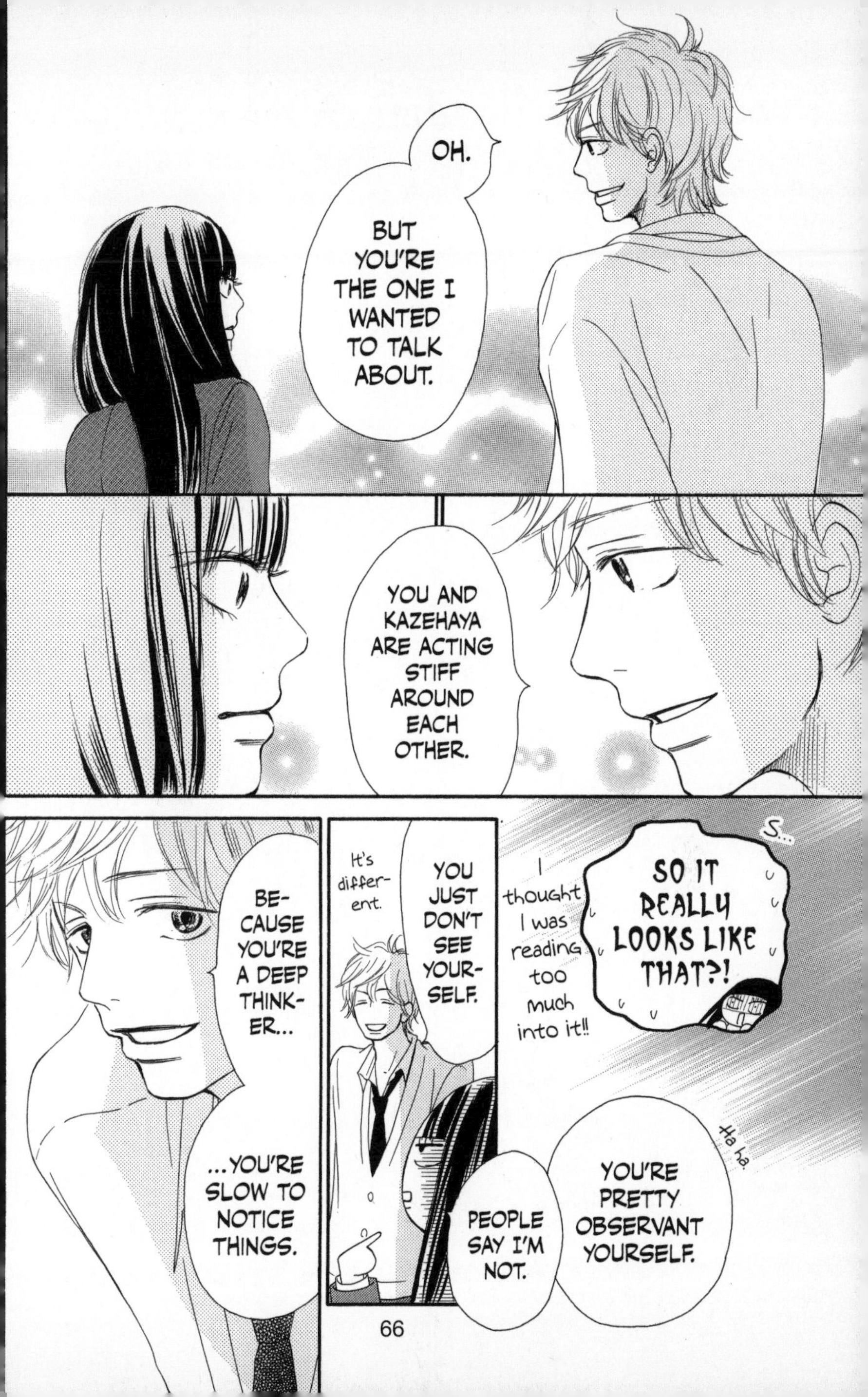
OH.
BUT YOU'RE THE ONE I WANTED TO TALK ABOUT.
YOU AND KAZEHAYA ARE ACTING STIFF AROUND EACH OTHER.
S...
SO IT REALLY LOOKS LIKE THAT?!
I thought I was reading too much into it!!
Ha ha.
YOU'RE PRETTY OBSERVANT YOURSELF.
PEOPLE SAY I'M NOT.
YOU JUST DON'T SEE YOURSELF.
It's different.
BE-CAUSE YOU'RE A DEEP THINK-ER...
...YOU'RE SLOW TO NOTICE THINGS.

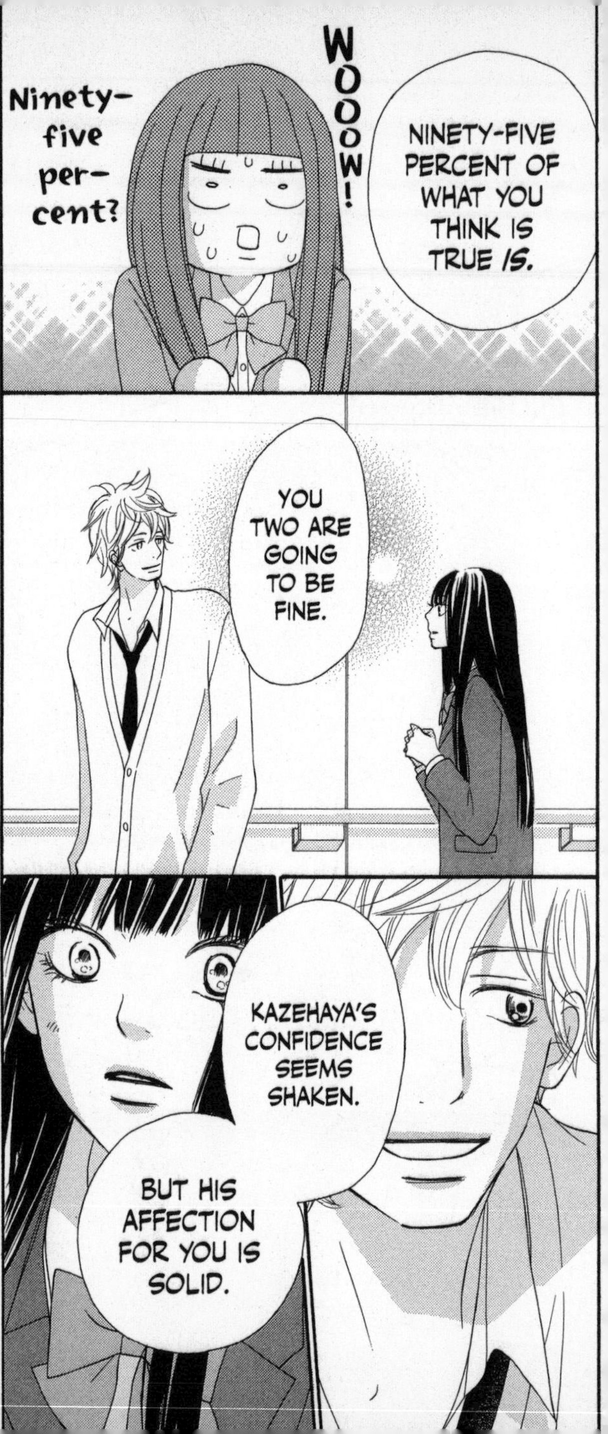
NINETY-FIVE PERCENT OF WHAT YOU THINK IS TRUE *IS.*
WOOOOW!
Ninety-five per-cent?
YOU TWO ARE GOING TO BE FINE.
KAZEHAYA'S CONFIDENCE SEEMS SHAKEN.
BUT HIS AFFECTION FOR YOU IS SOLID.

KARUPIN on JAPAN 2

This volume will be published in January! I'm writing this sidebar in the middle of November. Thinking about how much work lies ahead of me the rest of the month and in December stresses me out.

Also, I'll probably be stressed around February and April.

I'm stressed about vaccinations too! Oh no!!

I hope I'll get through the rest of 2011 without any incidents and move on to 1200--I mean, 2012. It's stressful that I made such a big mistake. Why'd I write 1200?

Big things happened in 2011. I hope I'm handling them okay. It's sobering and makes me cry to look back at the events of 2011.

That's the end of this story.

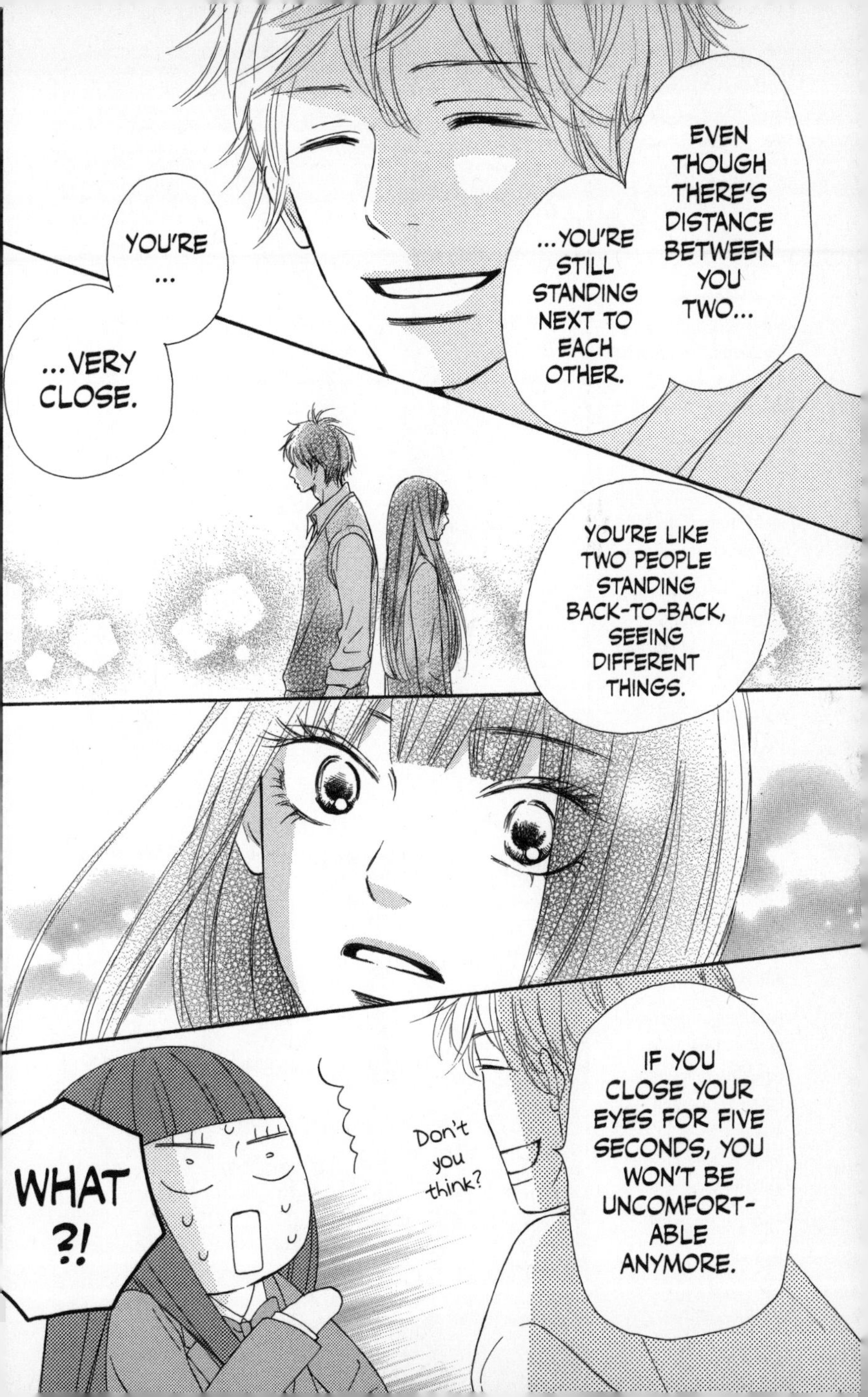
EVEN THOUGH THERE'S DISTANCE BETWEEN YOU TWO...
...YOU'RE STILL STANDING NEXT TO EACH OTHER.
YOU'RE ...
...VERY CLOSE.
YOU'RE LIKE TWO PEOPLE STANDING BACK-TO-BACK, SEEING DIFFERENT THINGS.
IF YOU CLOSE YOUR EYES FOR FIVE SECONDS, YOU WON'T BE UNCOMFORT-ABLE ANYMORE.
Don't you think?
WHAT ?!

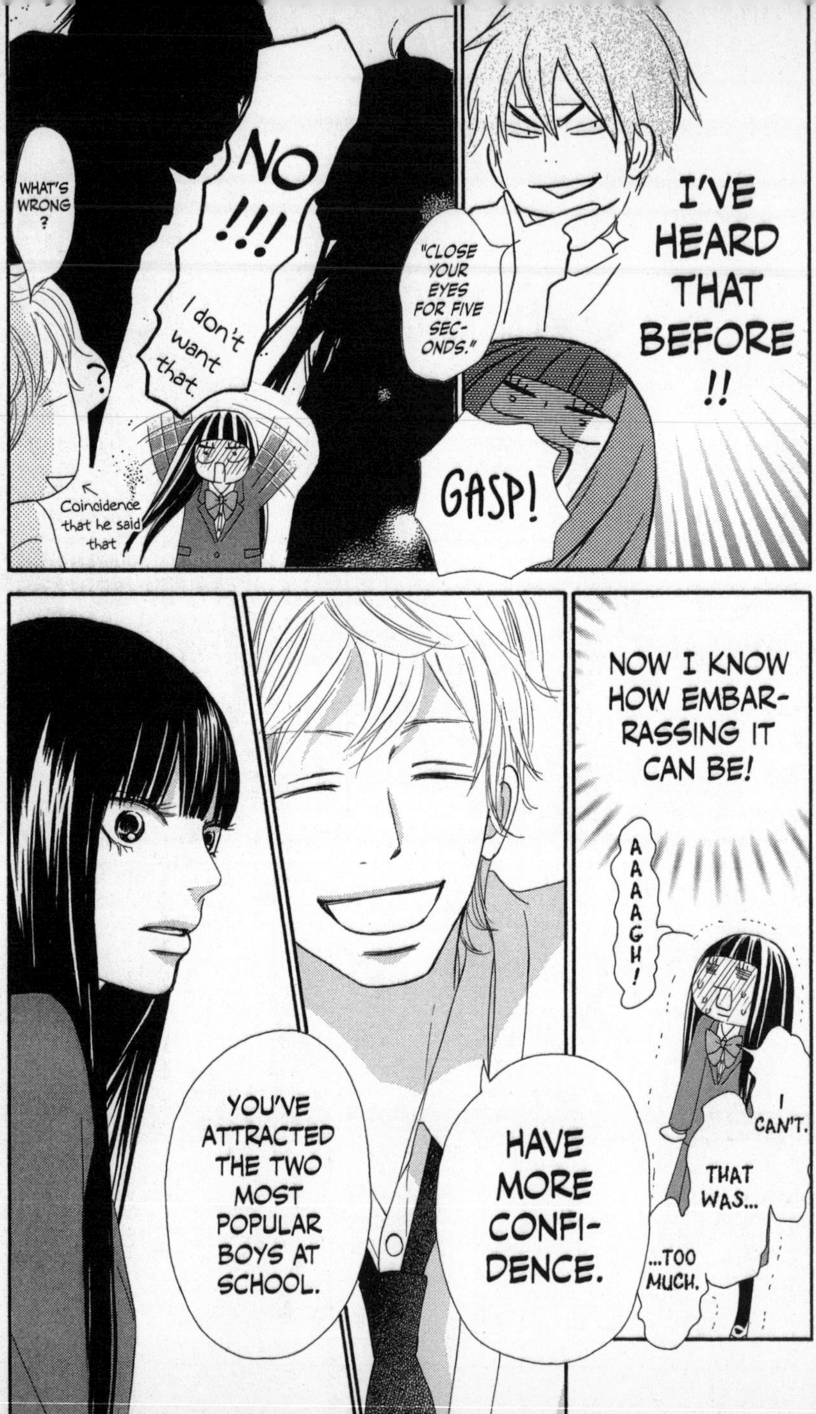
I'VE HEARD THAT BEFORE!!
"CLOSE YOUR EYES FOR FIVE SECONDS."
GASP!
NO!!!
I don't want that.
WHAT'S WRONG?
?
Coincidence that he said that
NOW I KNOW HOW EMBARRASSING IT CAN BE!
AAAAAGH!
I CAN'T.
THAT WAS...
...TOO MUCH.
HAVE MORE CONFIDENCE.
YOU'VE ATTRACTED THE TWO MOST POPULAR BOYS AT SCHOOL.

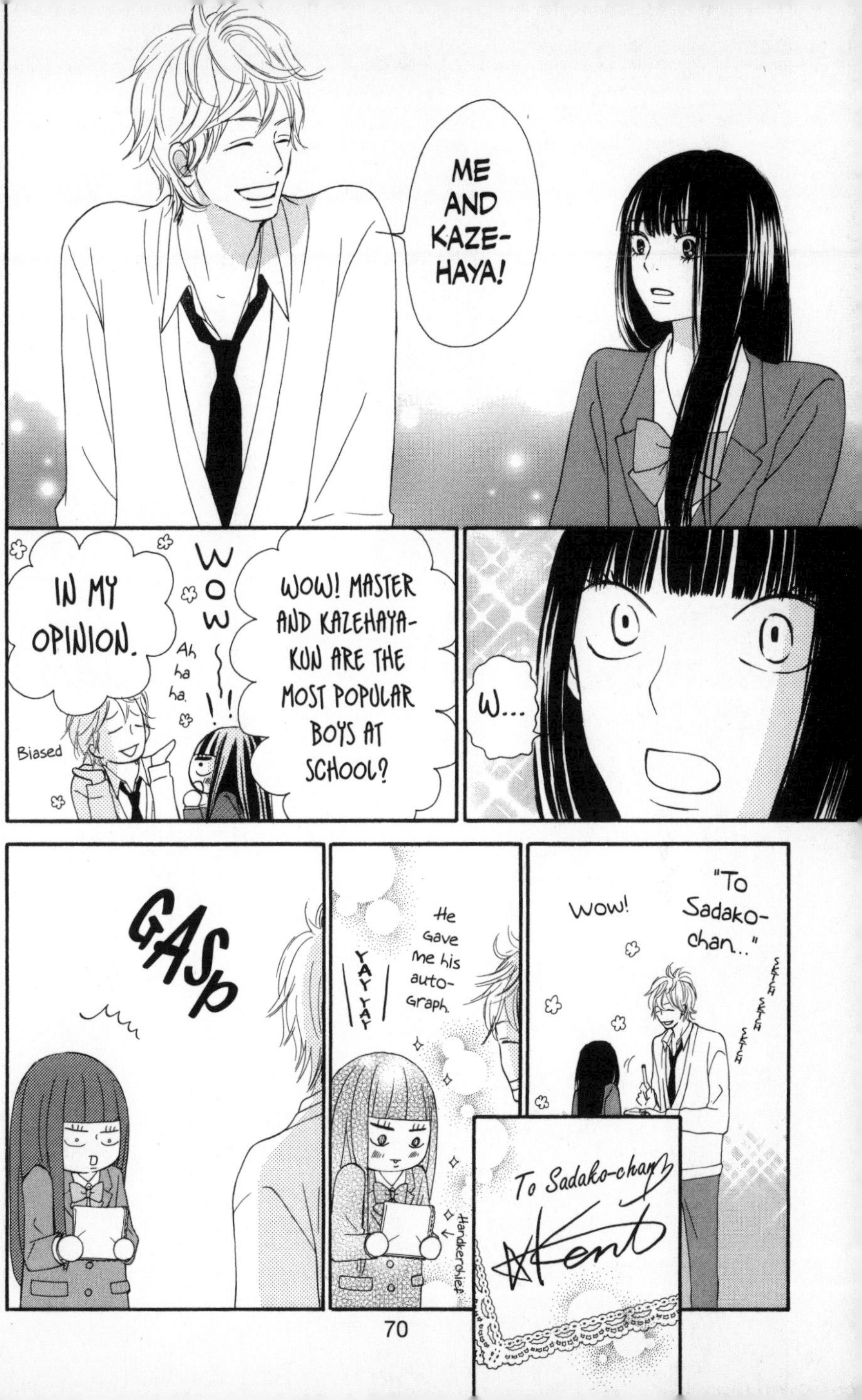
ME AND KAZE-HAYA!
W...
WOW! MASTER AND KAZEHAYA-KUN ARE THE MOST POPULAR BOYS AT SCHOOL?
WOW~!!
Ah ha ha.
IN MY OPINION.
Biased
"To Sadako-chan.."
WOW!
SKETCH SKETCH SKETCH
To Sadako-chan
Kent
He gave me his autograph.
YAY YAY
Handkerchief
GASP

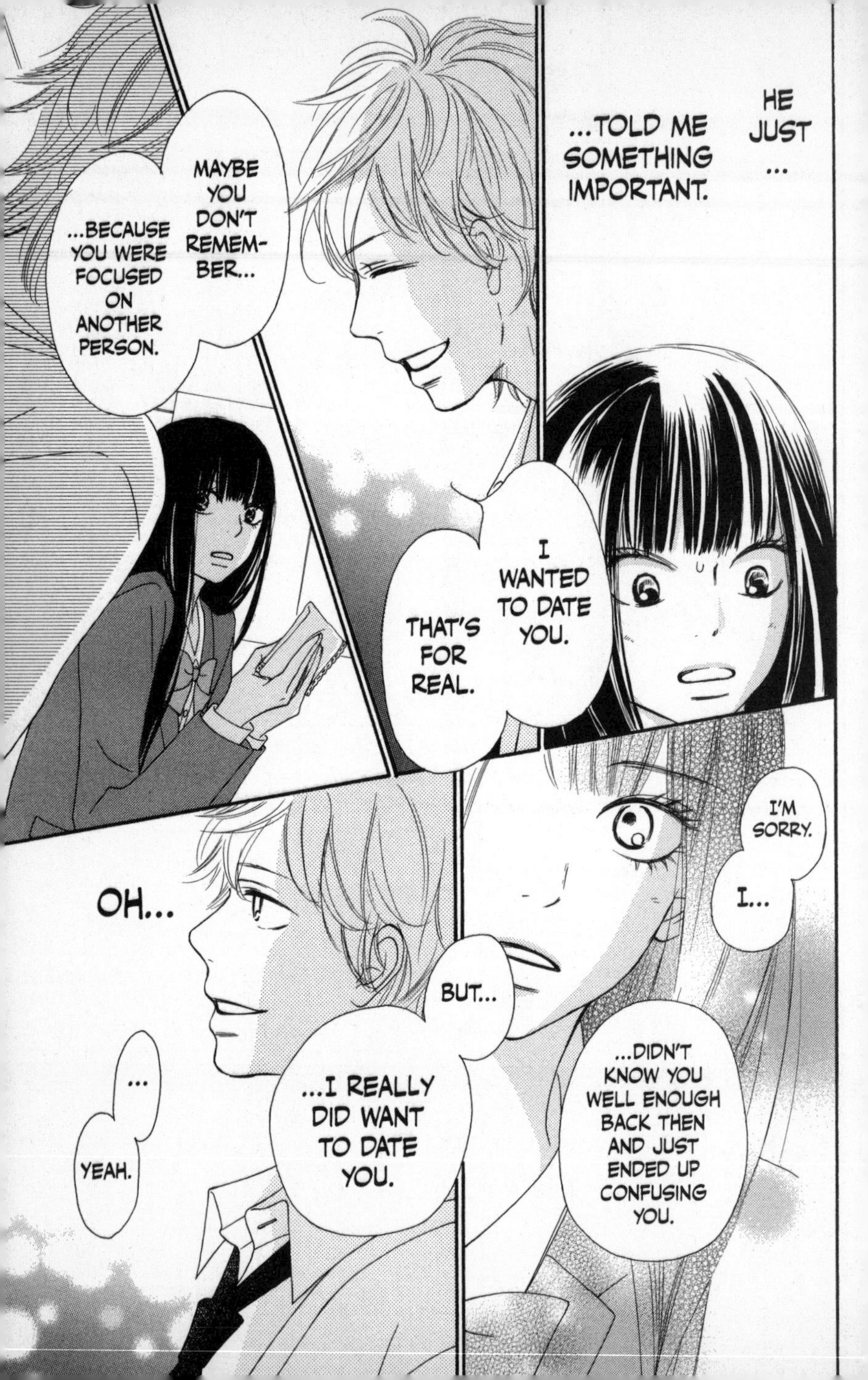

MAYBE YOU DON'T REMEMBER...
...BECAUSE YOU WERE FOCUSED ON ANOTHER PERSON.
I WANTED TO DATE YOU.
THAT'S FOR REAL.
HE JUST ...
...TOLD ME SOMETHING IMPORTANT.
I'M SORRY.
I...
...DIDN'T KNOW YOU WELL ENOUGH BACK THEN AND JUST ENDED UP CONFUSING YOU.
BUT...
...I REALLY DID WANT TO DATE YOU.
OH...
...
YEAH.

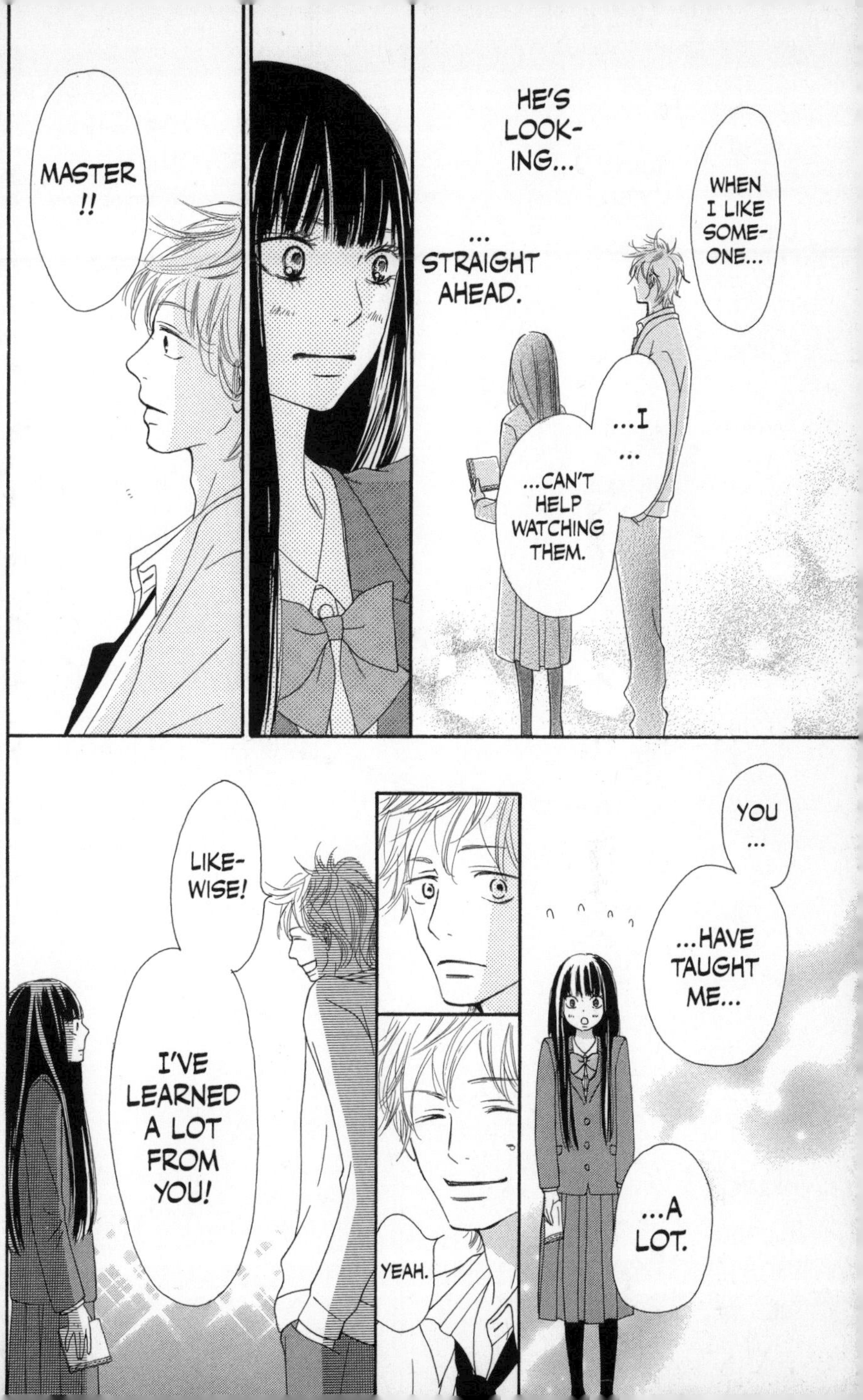
WHEN I LIKE SOME-ONE...
...I ...
...CAN'T HELP WATCHING THEM.
HE'S LOOK-ING...
... STRAIGHT AHEAD.
MASTER !!
YOU ...
...HAVE TAUGHT ME...
...A LOT.
YEAH.
LIKE-WISE!
I'VE LEARNED A LOT FROM YOU!

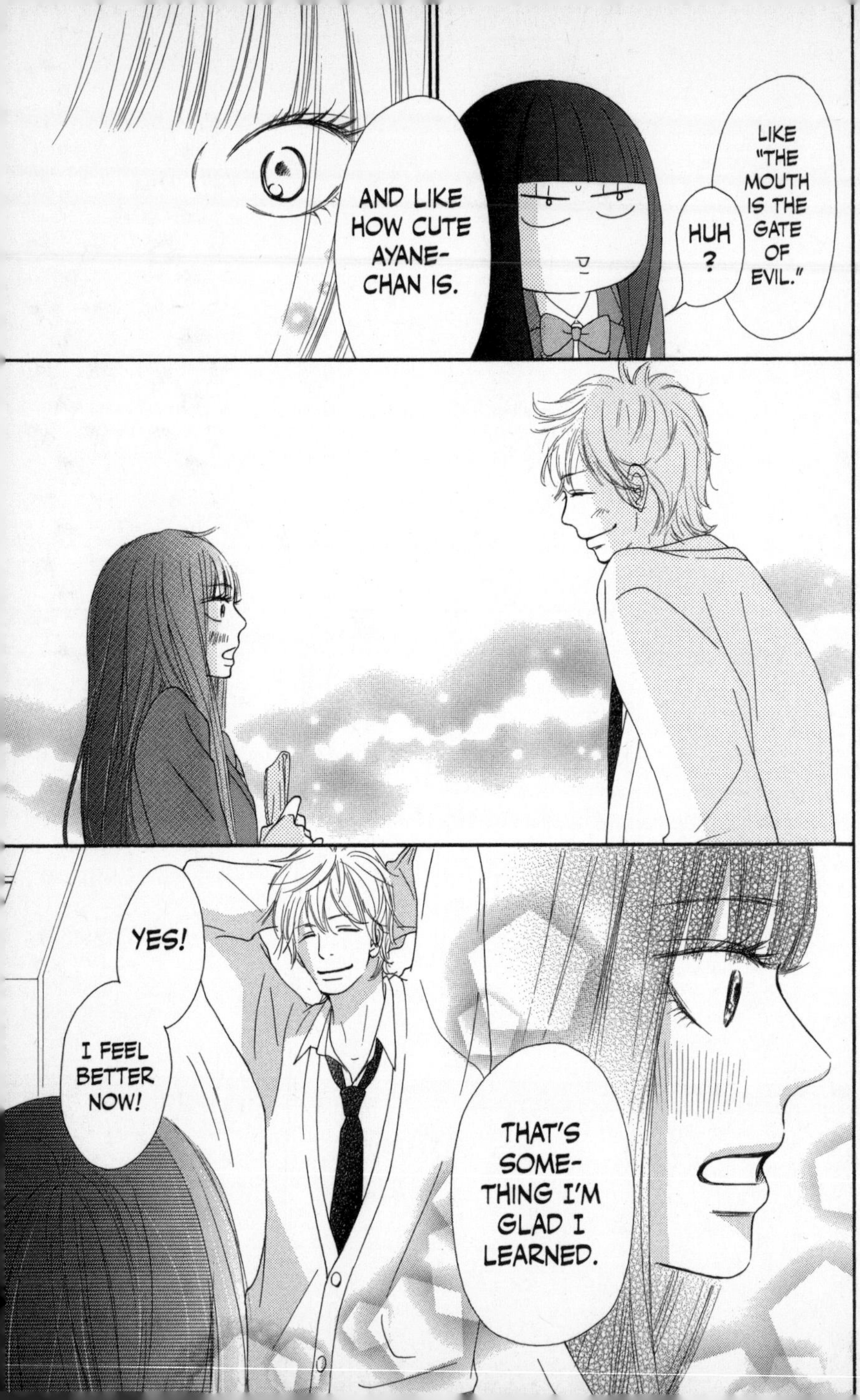
LIKE "THE MOUTH IS THE GATE OF EVIL."
HUH?
AND LIKE HOW CUTE AYANE-CHAN IS.
THAT'S SOME-THING I'M GLAD I LEARNED.
YES!
I FEEL BETTER NOW!

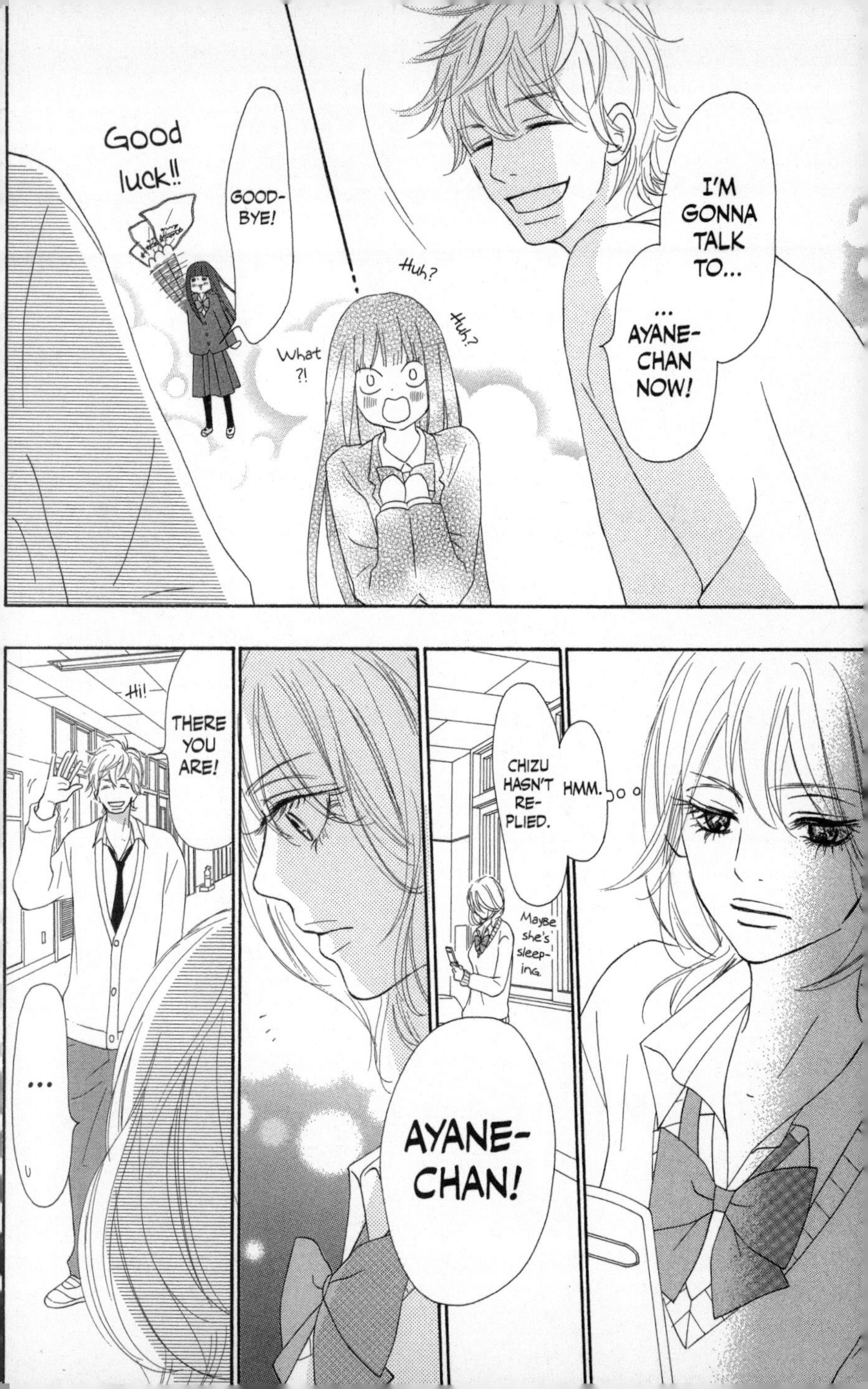
I'M GONNA TALK TO...
...AYANE-CHAN NOW!
Huh?
Huh?
What?!
GOOD-BYE!
Good luck!!
HMM.
CHIZU HASN'T RE-PLIED.
Maybe she's sleep-ing.
AYANE-CHAN!
THERE YOU ARE!
Hi!
...

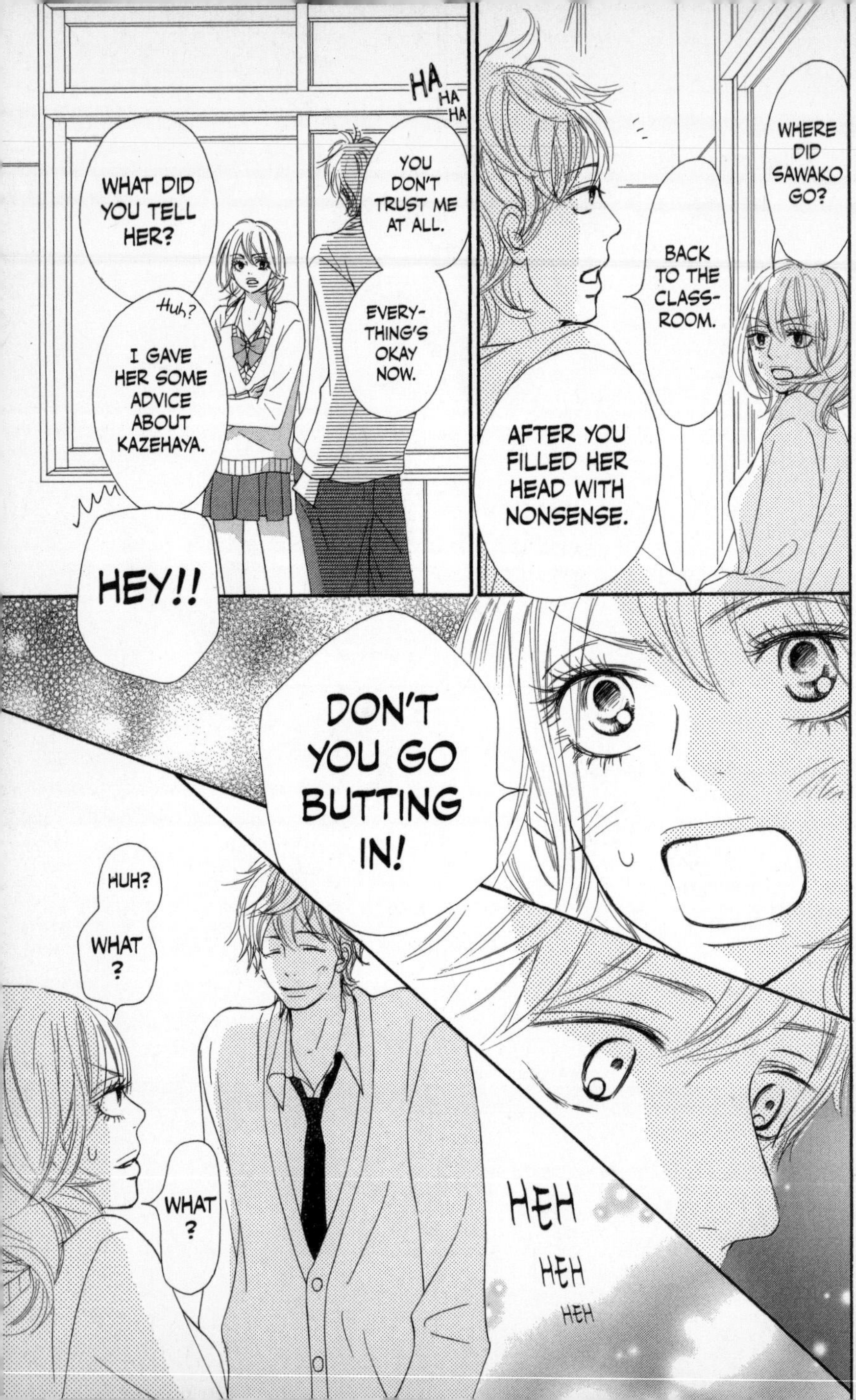
WHERE DID SAWAKO GO?
BACK TO THE CLASSROOM.
AFTER YOU FILLED HER HEAD WITH NONSENSE.
HA HA HA
YOU DON'T TRUST ME AT ALL.
EVERYTHING'S OKAY NOW.
WHAT DID YOU TELL HER?
Huh?
I GAVE HER SOME ADVICE ABOUT KAZEHAYA.
MUU
HEY!!
DON'T YOU GO BUTTING IN!
HEH HEH HEH
HUH?
WHAT?
WHAT?

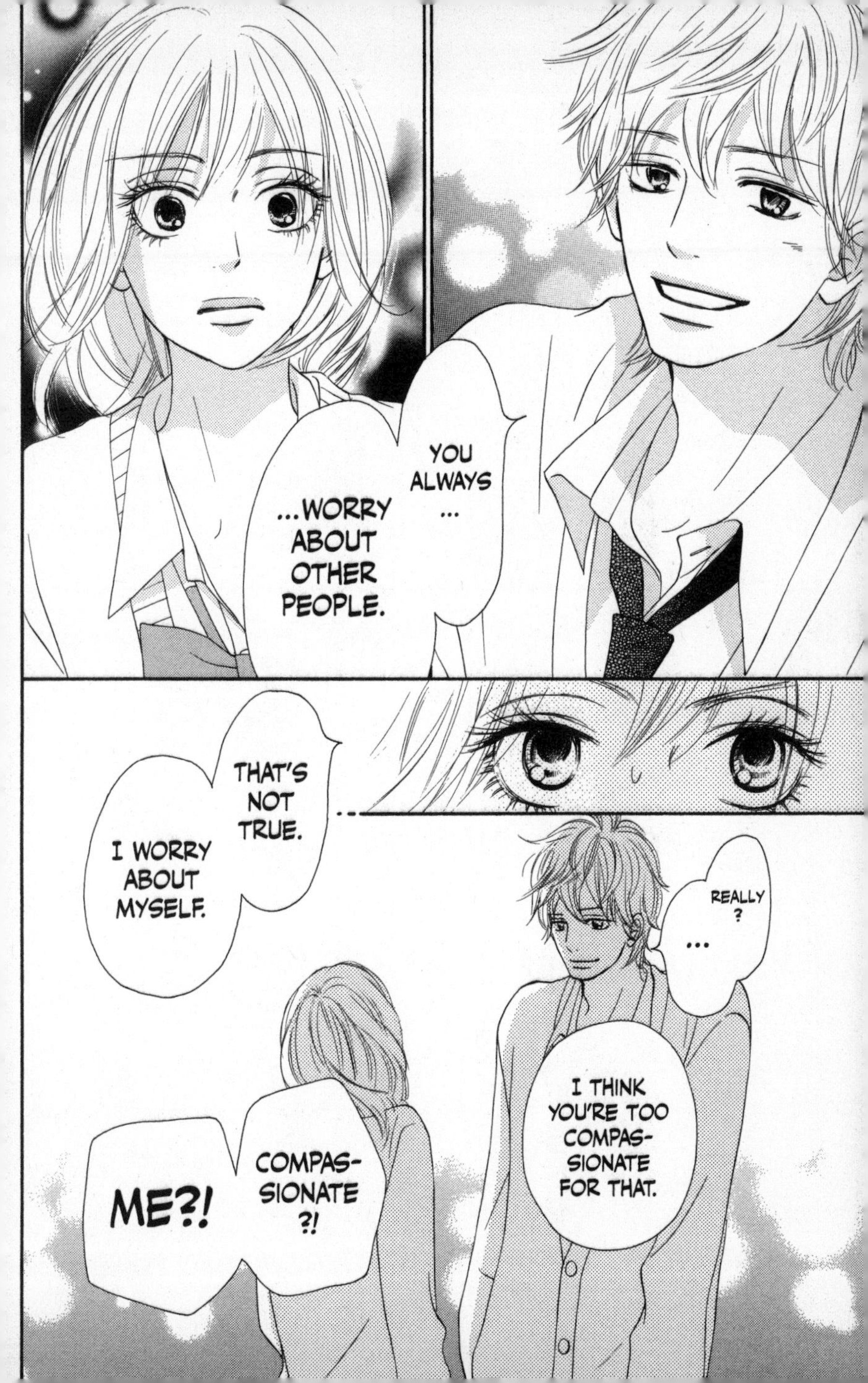
YOU ALWAYS ...
...WORRY ABOUT OTHER PEOPLE.
...
THAT'S NOT TRUE.
I WORRY ABOUT MYSELF.
REALLY ? ...
I THINK YOU'RE TOO COMPAS- SIONATE FOR THAT.
COMPAS- SIONATE ?!
ME?!

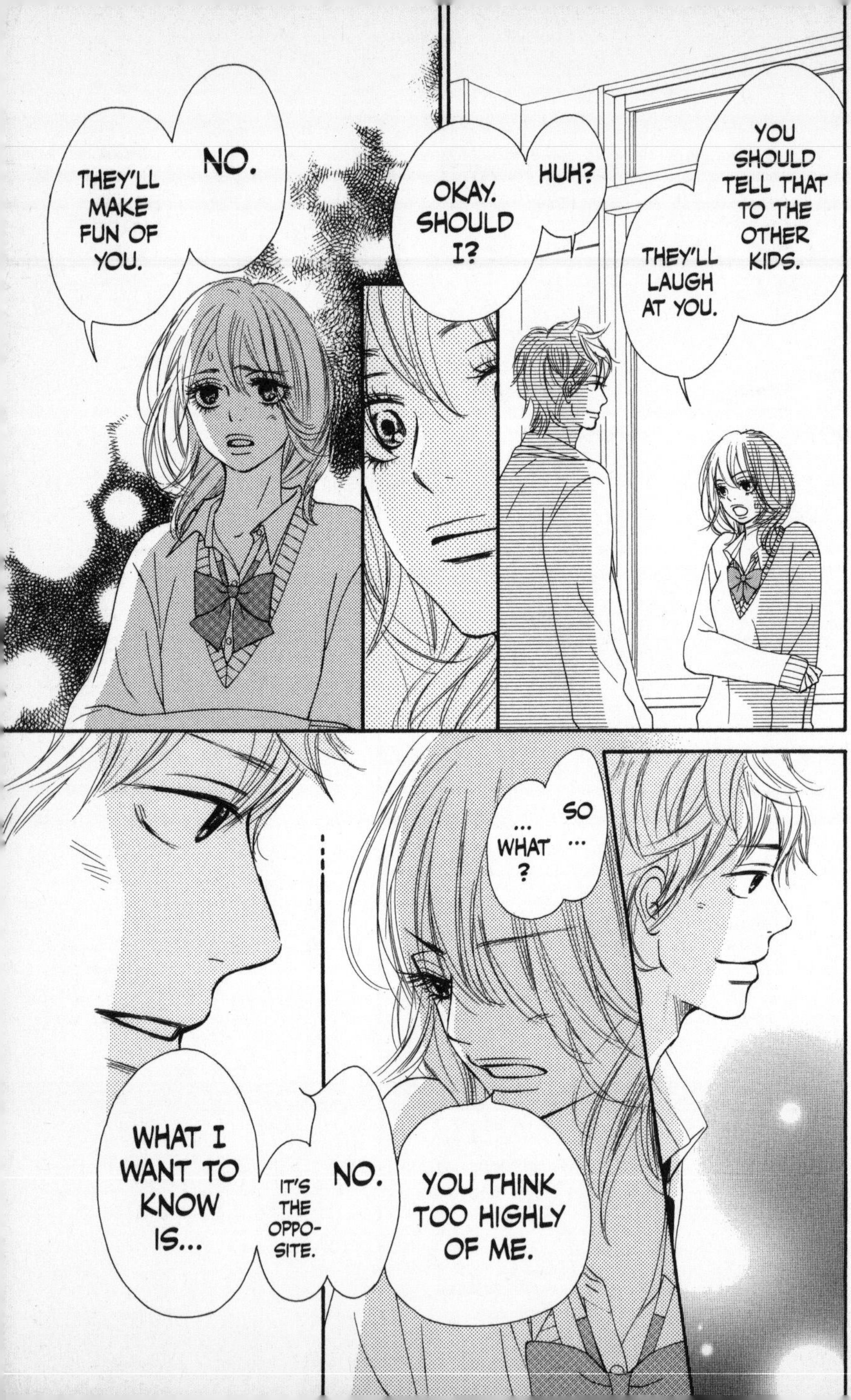

YOU SHOULD TELL THAT TO THE OTHER KIDS.
THEY'LL LAUGH AT YOU.
HUH?
OKAY. SHOULD I?
NO.
THEY'LL MAKE FUN OF YOU.
SO ...
... WHAT ?
YOU THINK TOO HIGHLY OF ME.
NO.
IT'S THE OPPO-SITE.
WHAT I WANT TO KNOW IS...

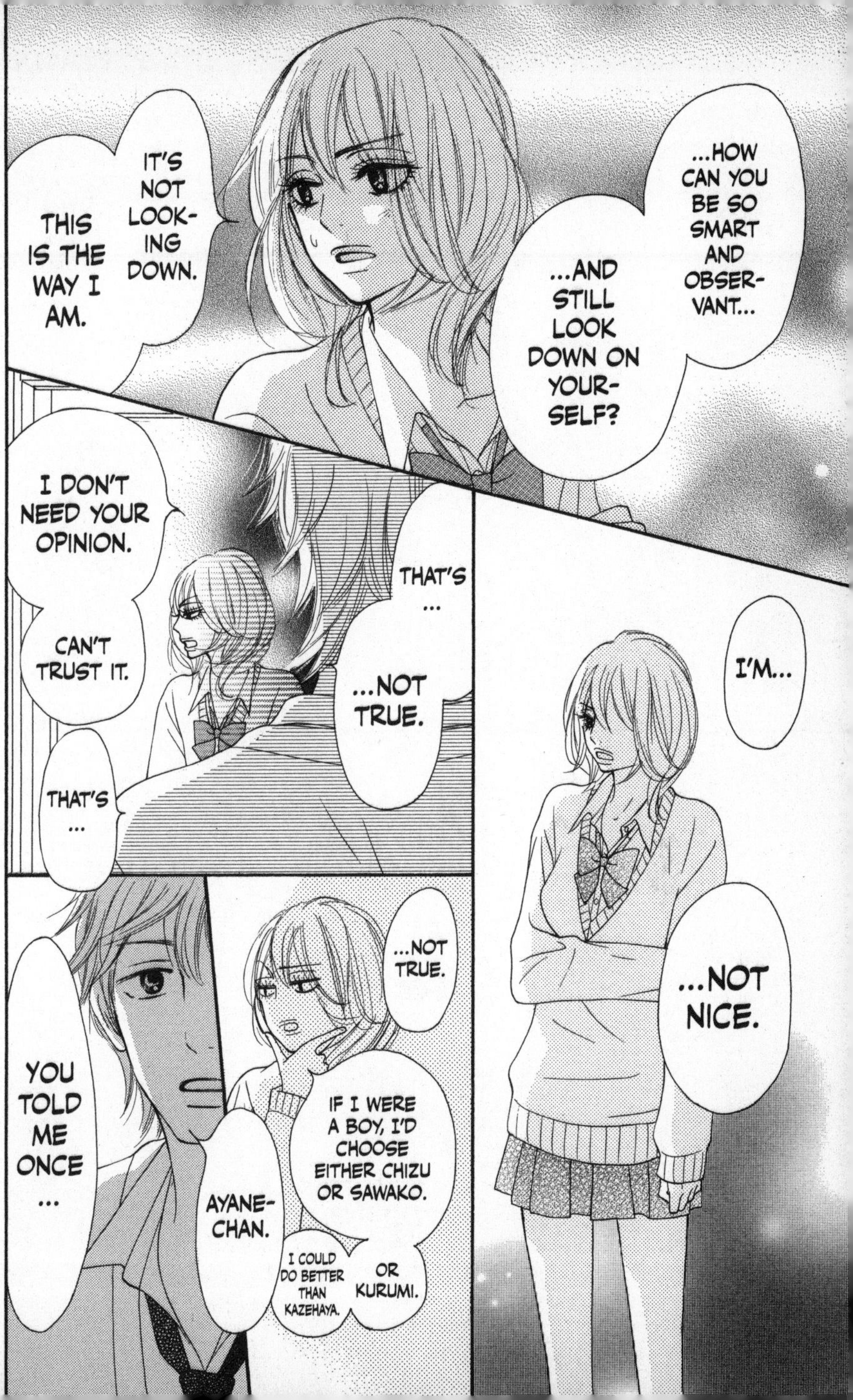
...HOW CAN YOU BE SO SMART AND OBSERVANT...
...AND STILL LOOK DOWN ON YOURSELF?
IT'S NOT LOOKING DOWN.
THIS IS THE WAY I AM.
I'M...
...NOT NICE.
THAT'S ...
...NOT TRUE.
I DON'T NEED YOUR OPINION.
CAN'T TRUST IT.
THAT'S ...
...NOT TRUE.
IF I WERE A BOY, I'D CHOOSE EITHER CHIZU OR SAWAKO.
OR KURUMI.
I COULD DO BETTER THAN KAZEHAYA.
AYANE-CHAN.
YOU TOLD ME ONCE ...

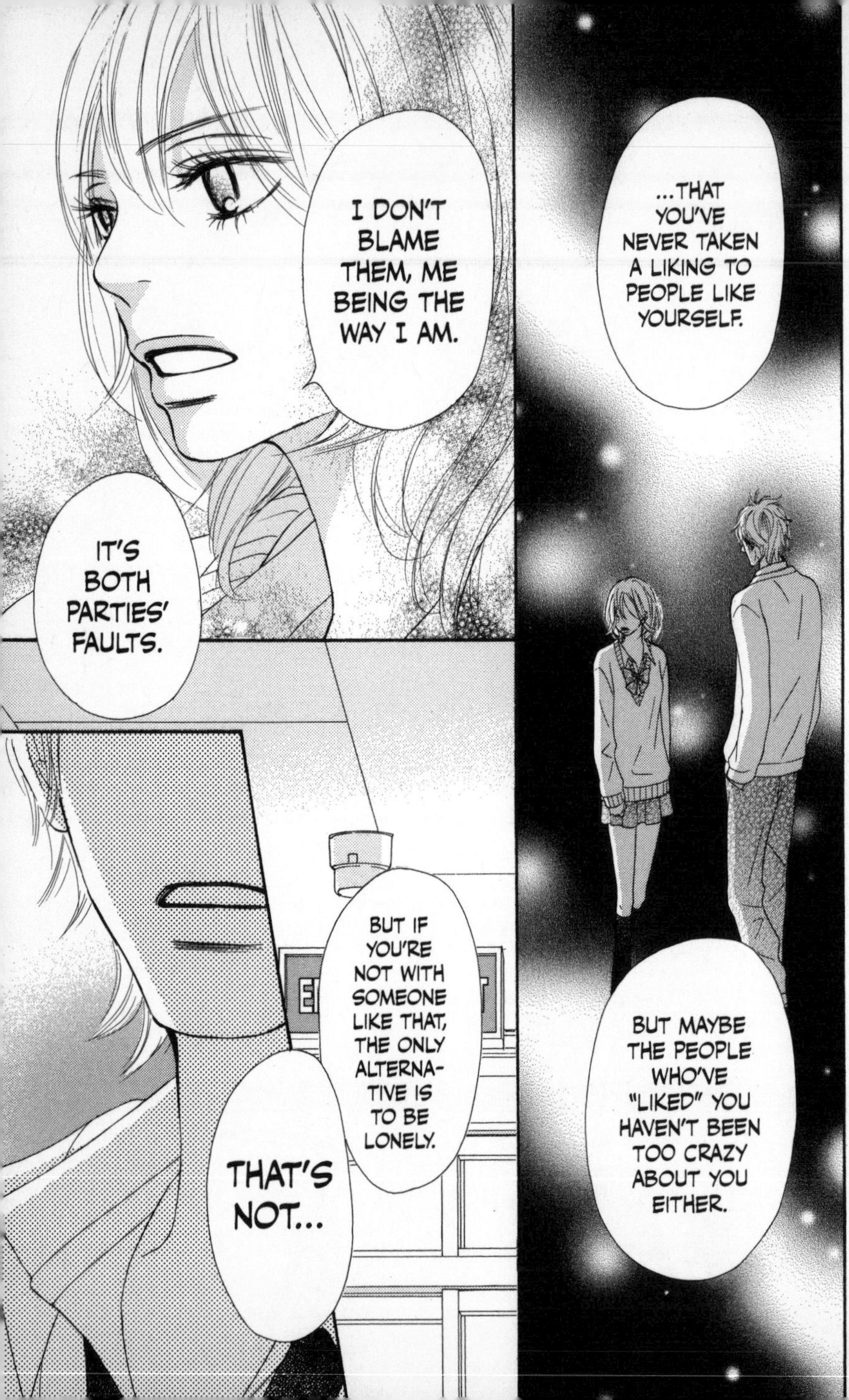
...THAT YOU'VE NEVER TAKEN A LIKING TO PEOPLE LIKE YOURSELF.
BUT MAYBE THE PEOPLE WHO'VE "LIKED" YOU HAVEN'T BEEN TOO CRAZY ABOUT YOU EITHER.
I DON'T BLAME THEM, ME BEING THE WAY I AM.
IT'S BOTH PARTIES' FAULTS.
BUT IF YOU'RE NOT WITH SOMEONE LIKE THAT, THE ONLY ALTERNATIVE IS TO BE LONELY.
THAT'S NOT...

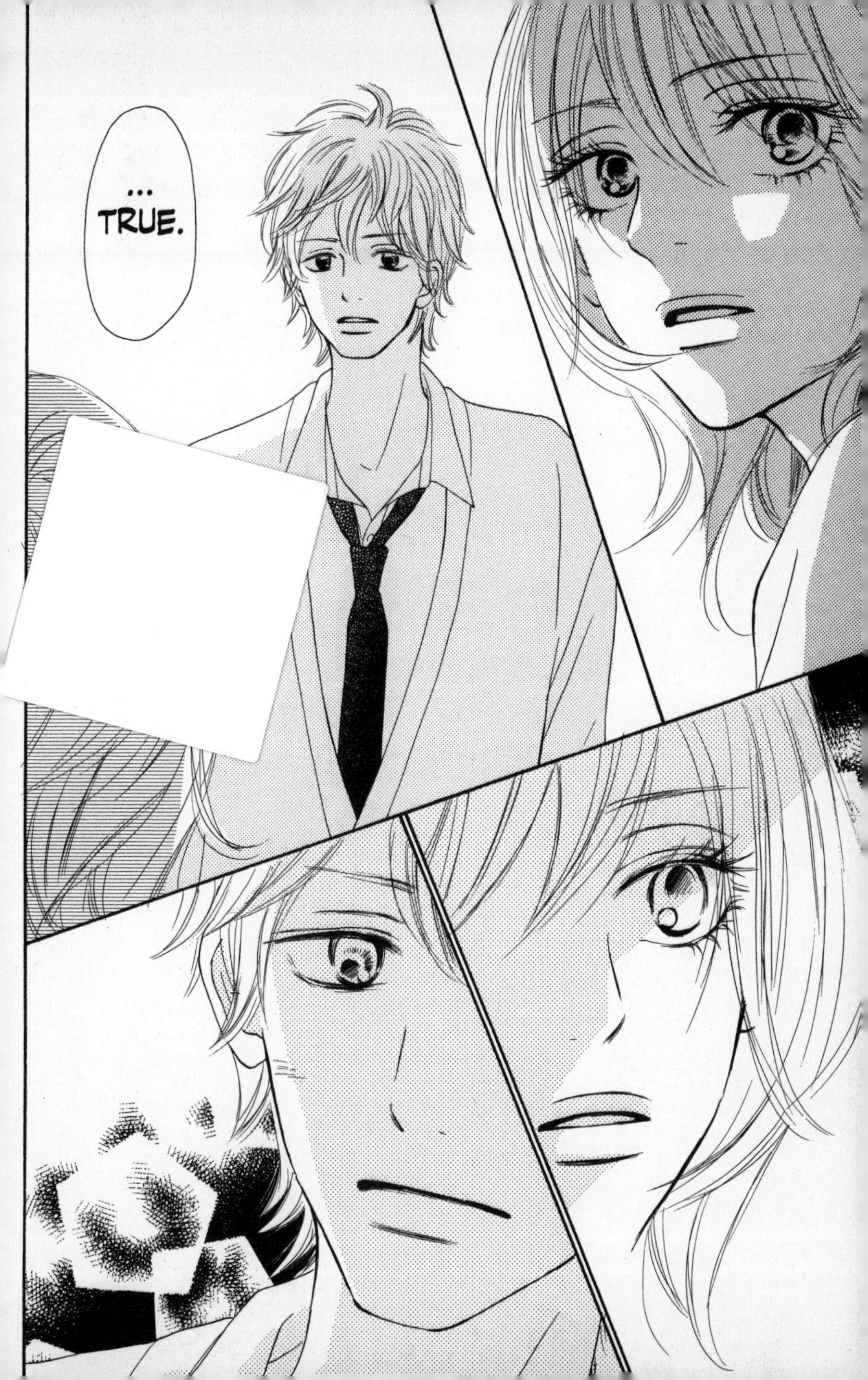
...TRUE.

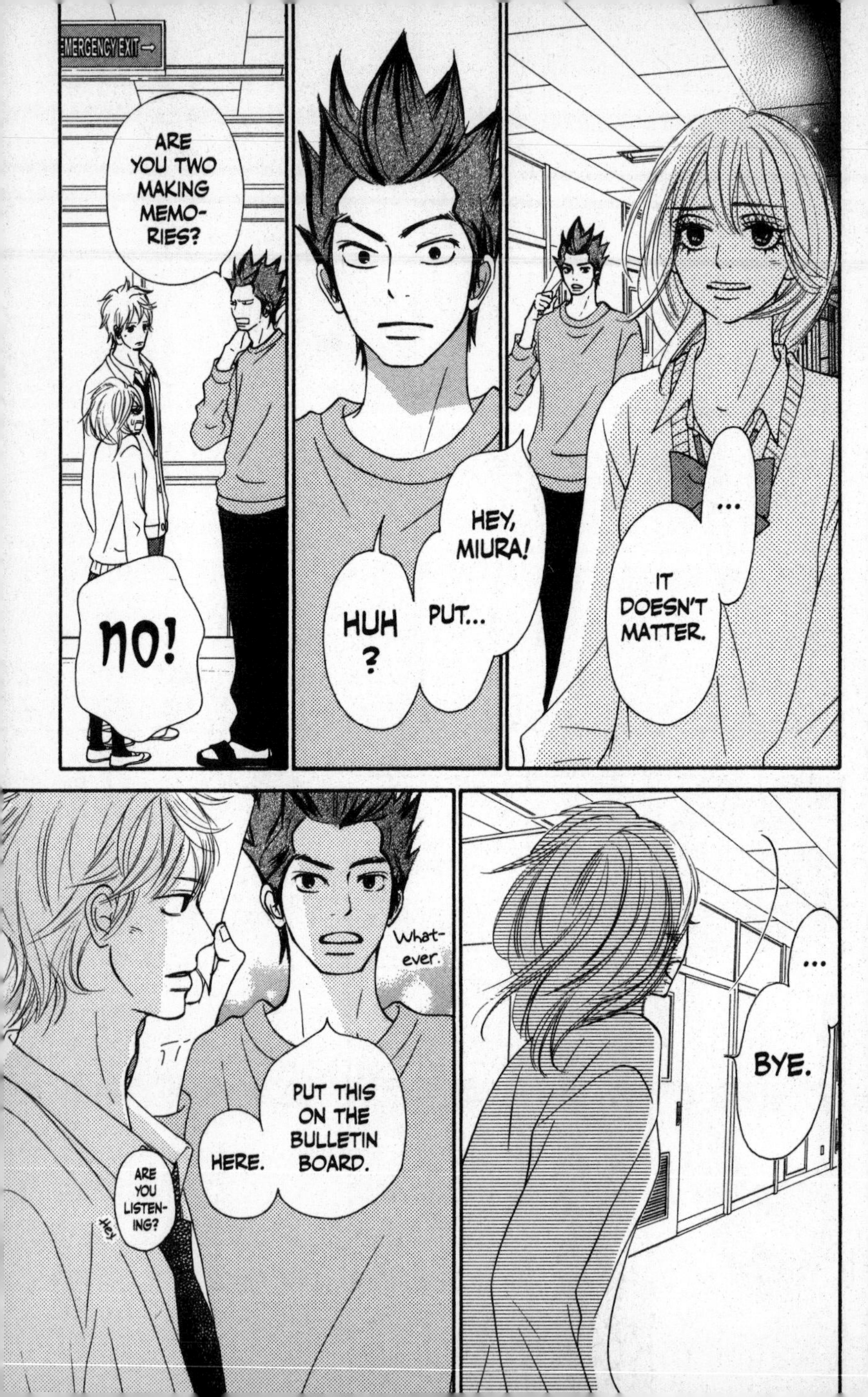
...
IT DOESN'T MATTER.
HEY, MIURA!
PUT...
HUH?
EMERGENCY EXIT
ARE YOU TWO MAKING MEMORIES?
no!
...
BYE.
What-ever.
PUT THIS ON THE BULLETIN BOARD.
HERE.
ARE YOU LISTENING?
HEY

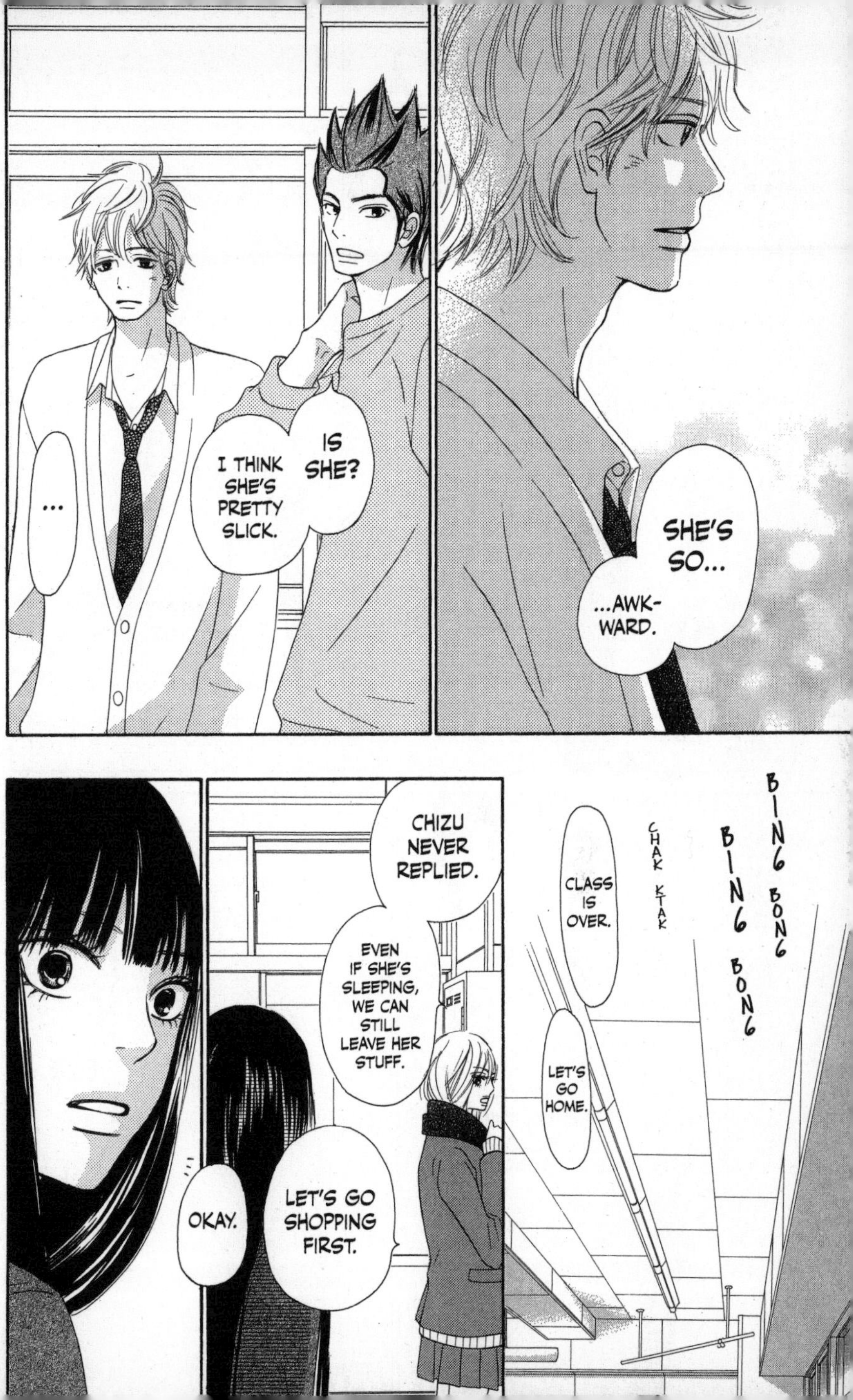
SHE'S SO...
...AWK-WARD.
IS SHE?
I THINK SHE'S PRETTY SLICK.
...
BING BONG
BING BONG
CHAK KTAK
CLASS IS OVER.
LET'S GO HOME.
CHIZU NEVER REPLIED.
EVEN IF SHE'S SLEEPING, WE CAN STILL LEAVE HER STUFF.
LET'S GO SHOPPING FIRST.
OKAY.

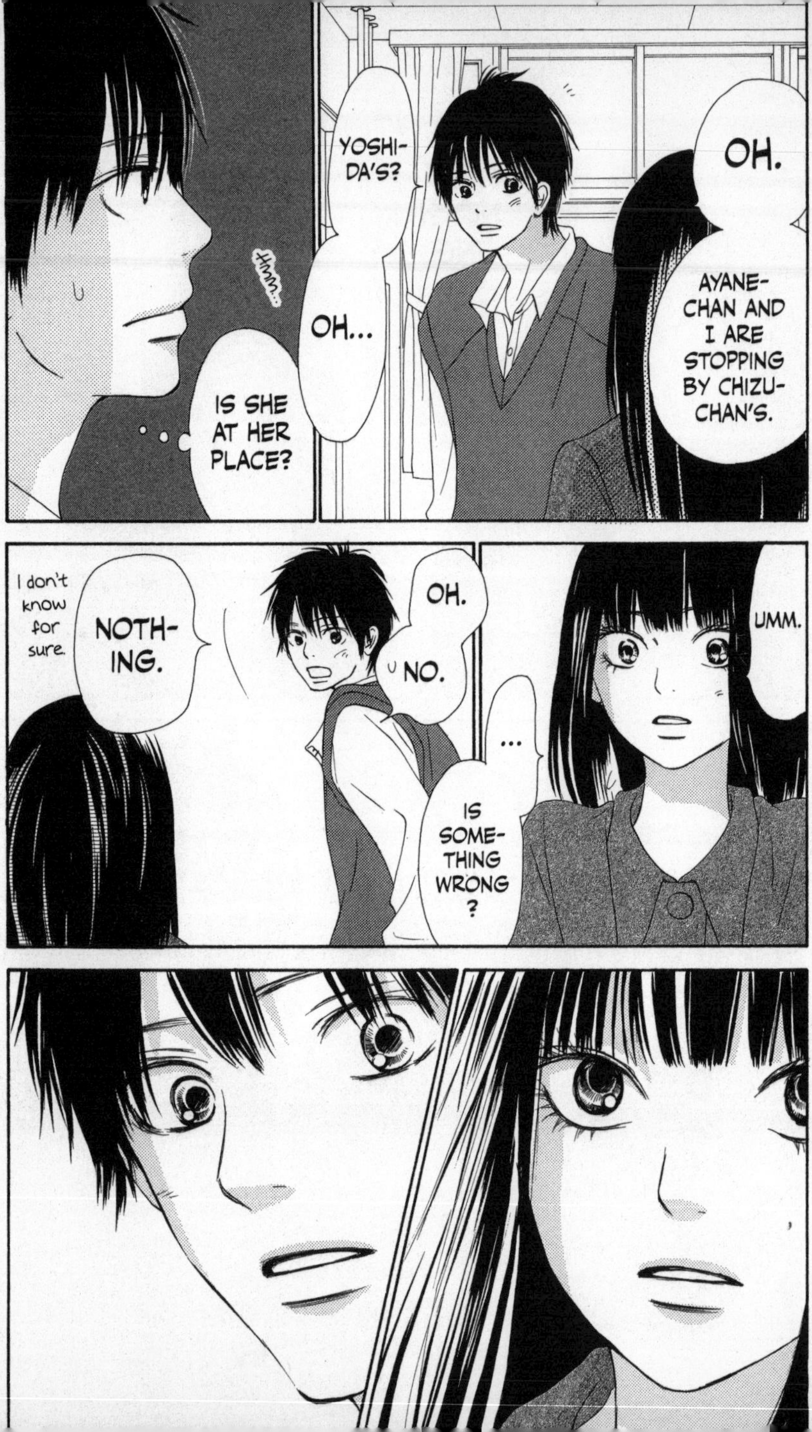
OH.
AYANE-CHAN AND I ARE STOPPING BY CHIZU-CHAN'S.
YOSHIDA'S?
OH...
Hmm...
IS SHE AT HER PLACE?
UMM.
...
IS SOMETHING WRONG?
OH.
NO.
NOTHING.
I don't know for sure.

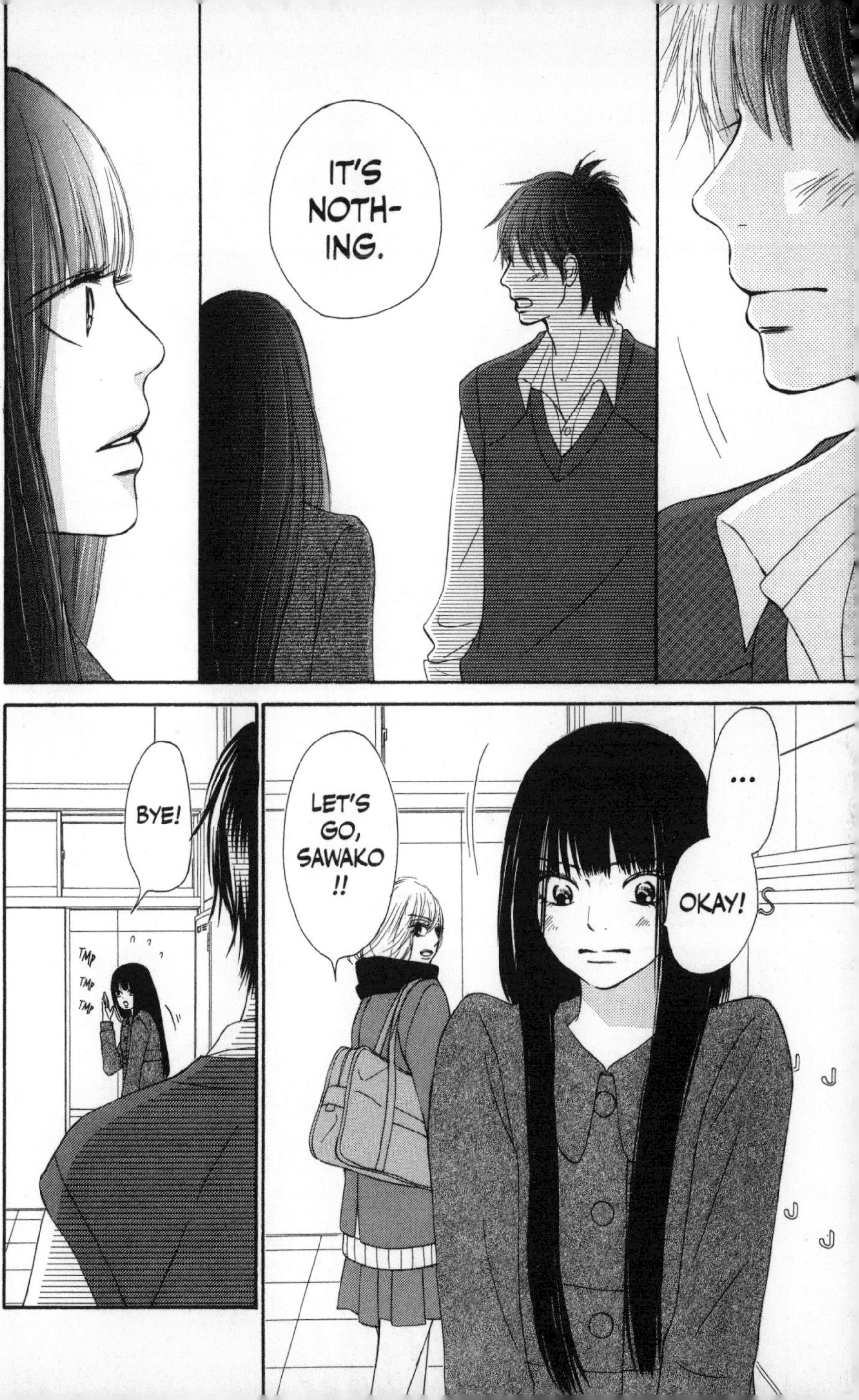
IT'S NOTH-ING.
...
OKAY!
LET'S GO, SAWAKO !!
BYE!
TMP
TMP
TMP

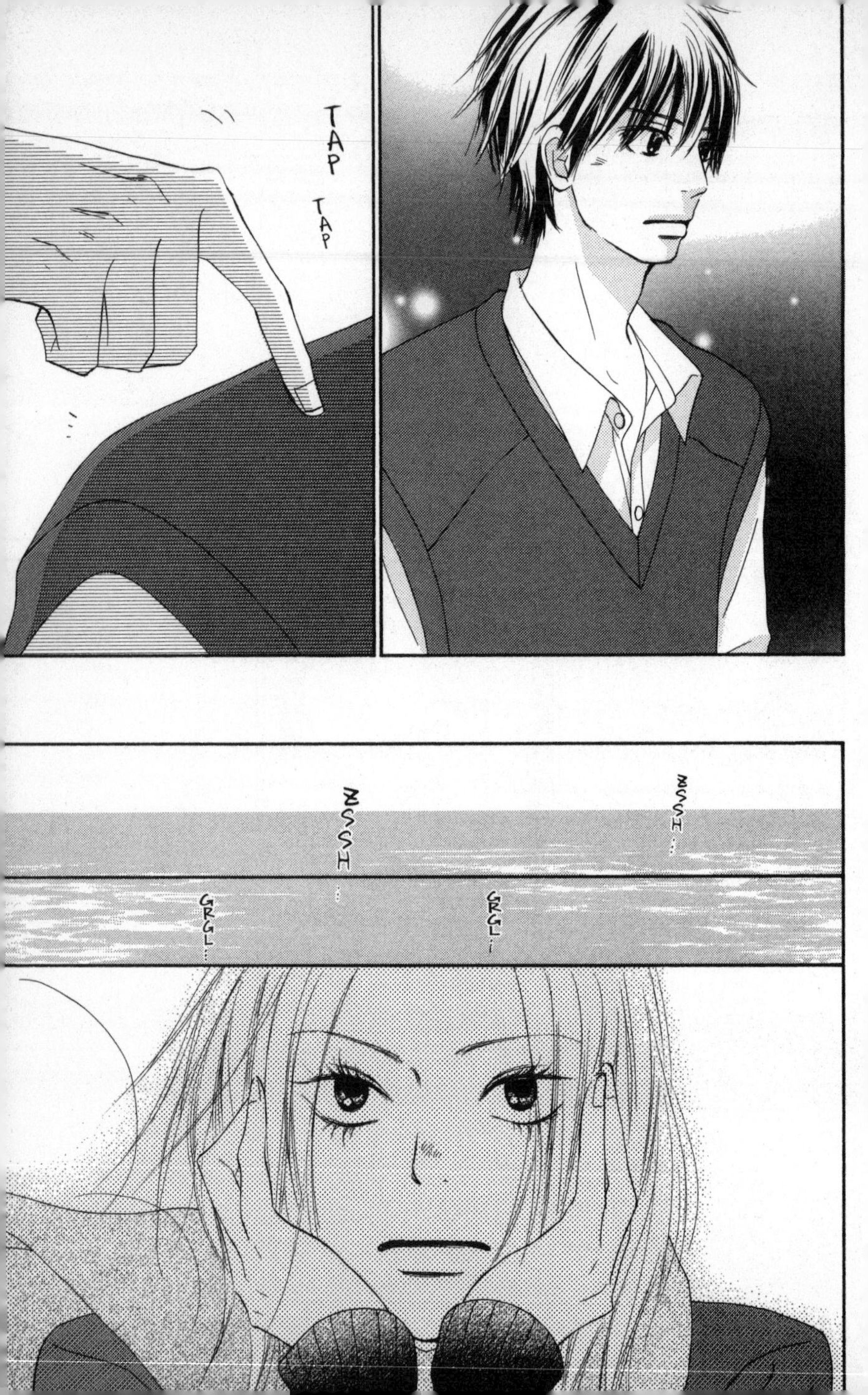
TAP
TAP
ZSSH...
ZSSH...
GRGL
GRGL...

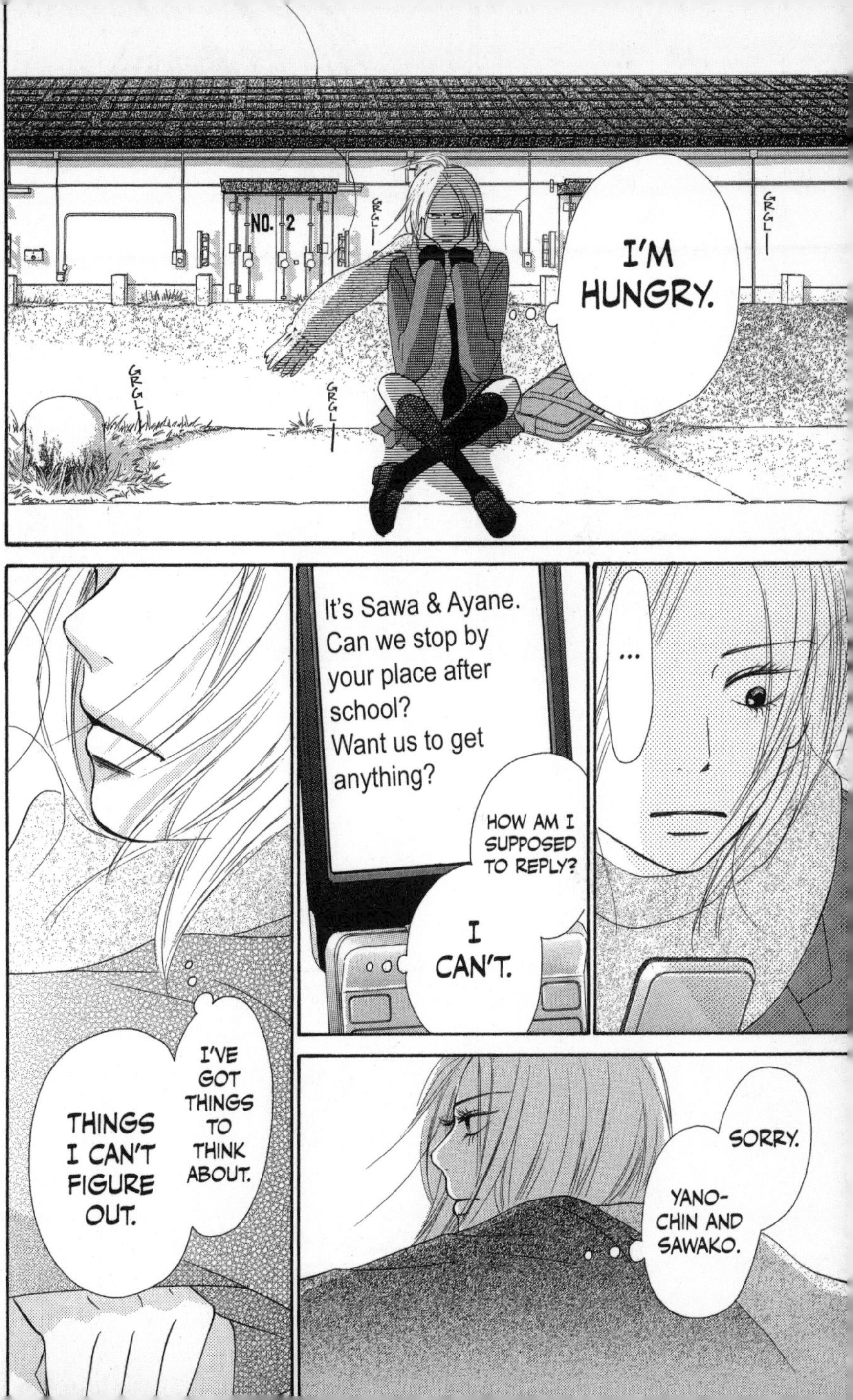
GRGL
I'M HUNGRY.
GRGL
GRGL
GRGL
...
It's Sawa & Ayane. Can we stop by your place after school? Want us to get anything?
HOW AM I SUPPOSED TO REPLY?
I CAN'T.
SORRY.
YANO-CHIN AND SAWAKO.
I'VE GOT THINGS TO THINK ABOUT.
THINGS I CAN'T FIGURE OUT.

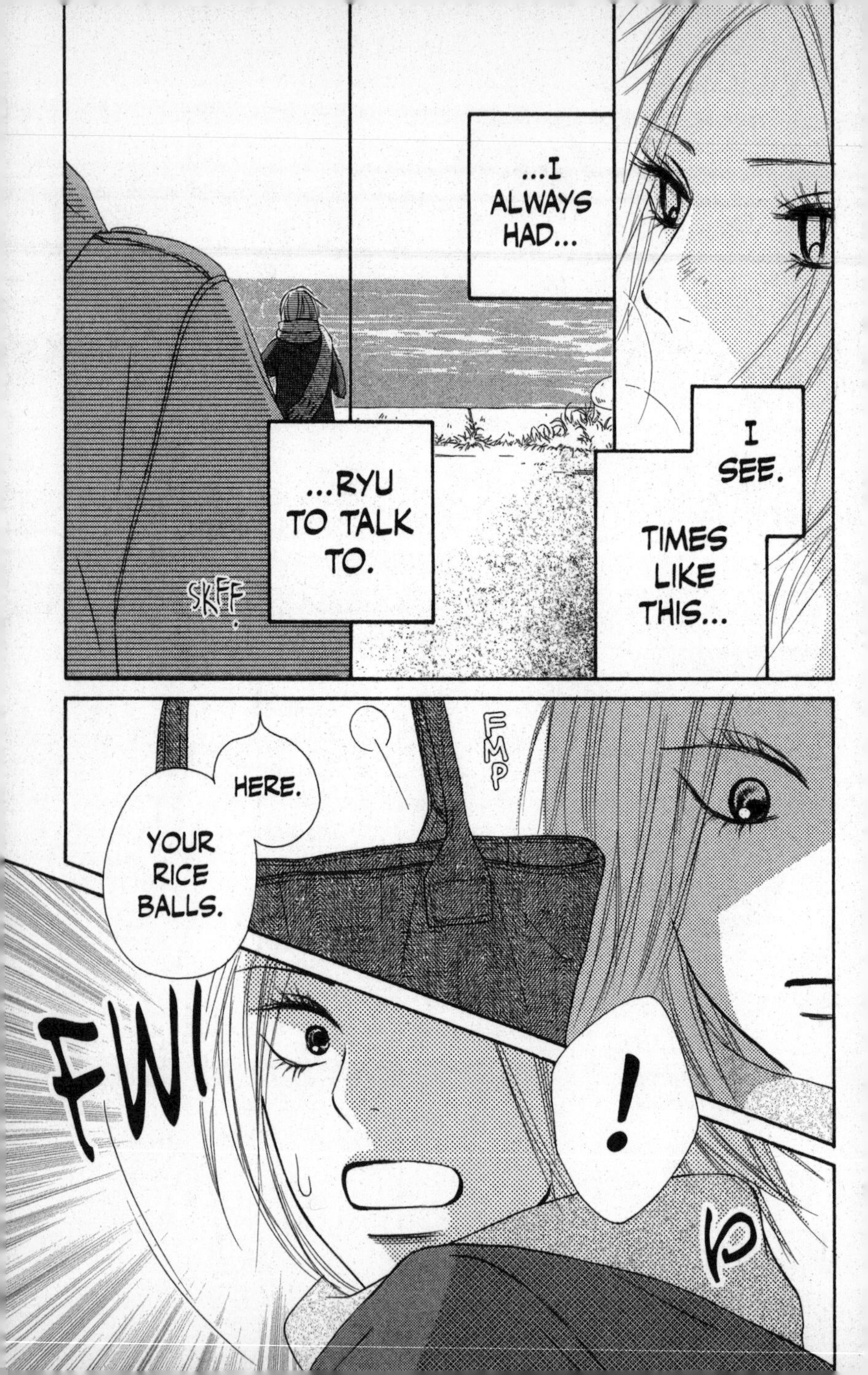
I SEE.
TIMES LIKE THIS...
...I ALWAYS HAD...
...RYU TO TALK TO.
SKFF
FMP
HERE.
YOUR RICE BALLS.
!
FWI

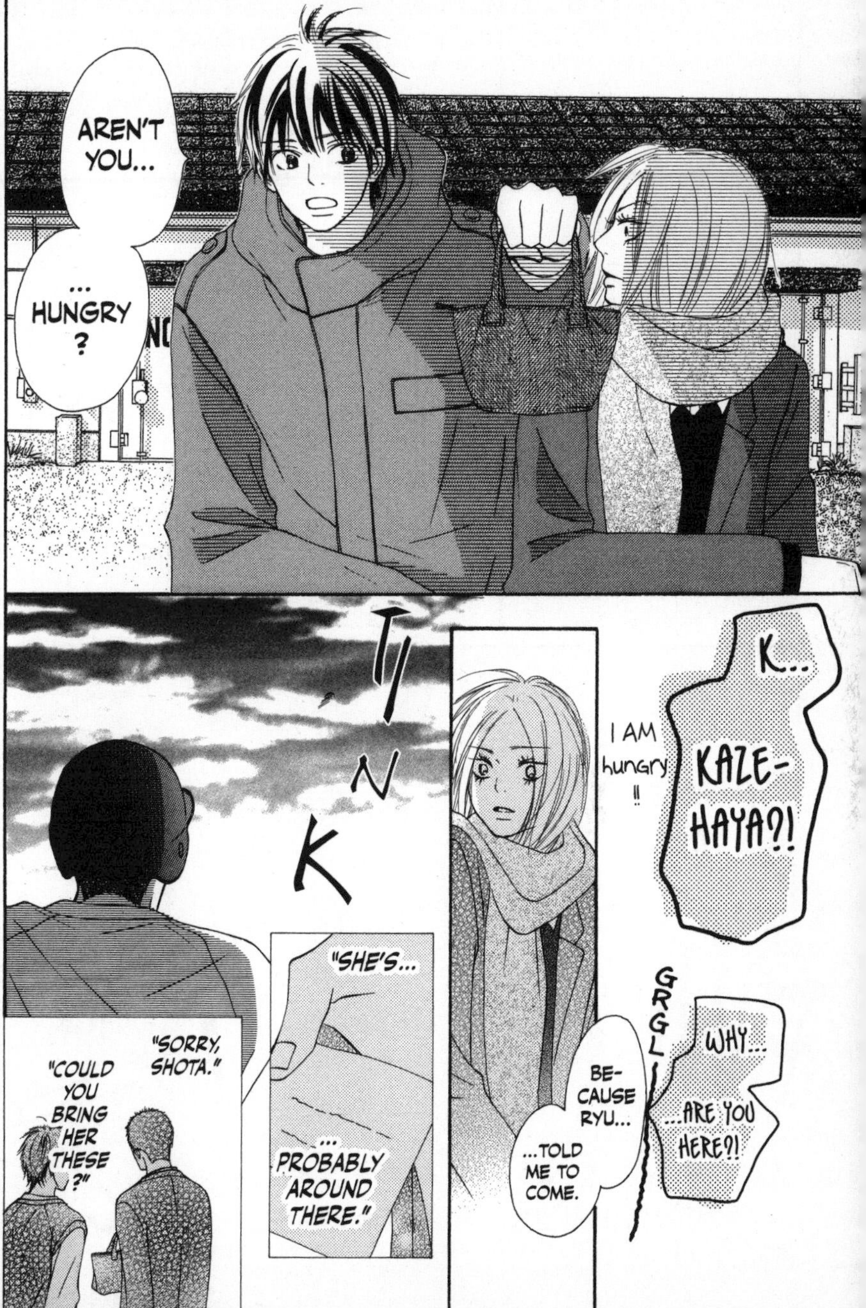
AREN'T YOU...
... HUNGRY ?
K... KAZE-HAYA?!
I AM hungry !!
GRGL
WHY... ...ARE YOU HERE?!
BE-CAUSE RYU...
...TOLD ME TO COME.
TINK
"SHE'S...
... PROBABLY AROUND THERE."
"SORRY, SHOTA."
"COULD YOU BRING HER THESE?"

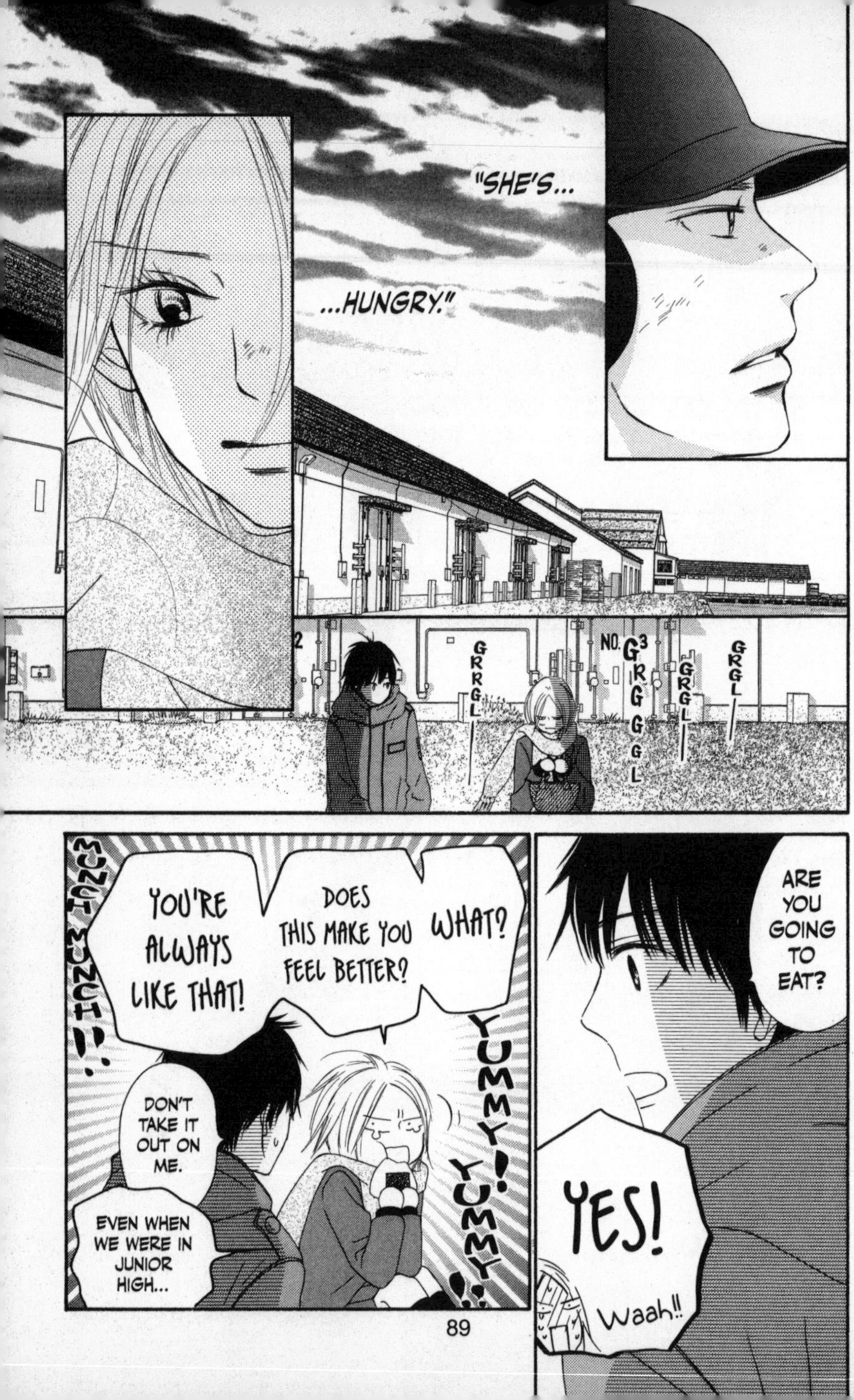
"SHE'S...
...HUNGRY."
GRRGL
NO. 3
GRGGGL
GRGL
GRGL
ARE YOU GOING TO EAT?
YES!
Waah!!
WHAT?
DOES THIS MAKE YOU FEEL BETTER?
YOU'RE ALWAYS LIKE THAT!
MUNCH MUNCH!!
YUMMY! YUMMY!!
DON'T TAKE IT OUT ON ME.
EVEN WHEN WE WERE IN JUNIOR HIGH...

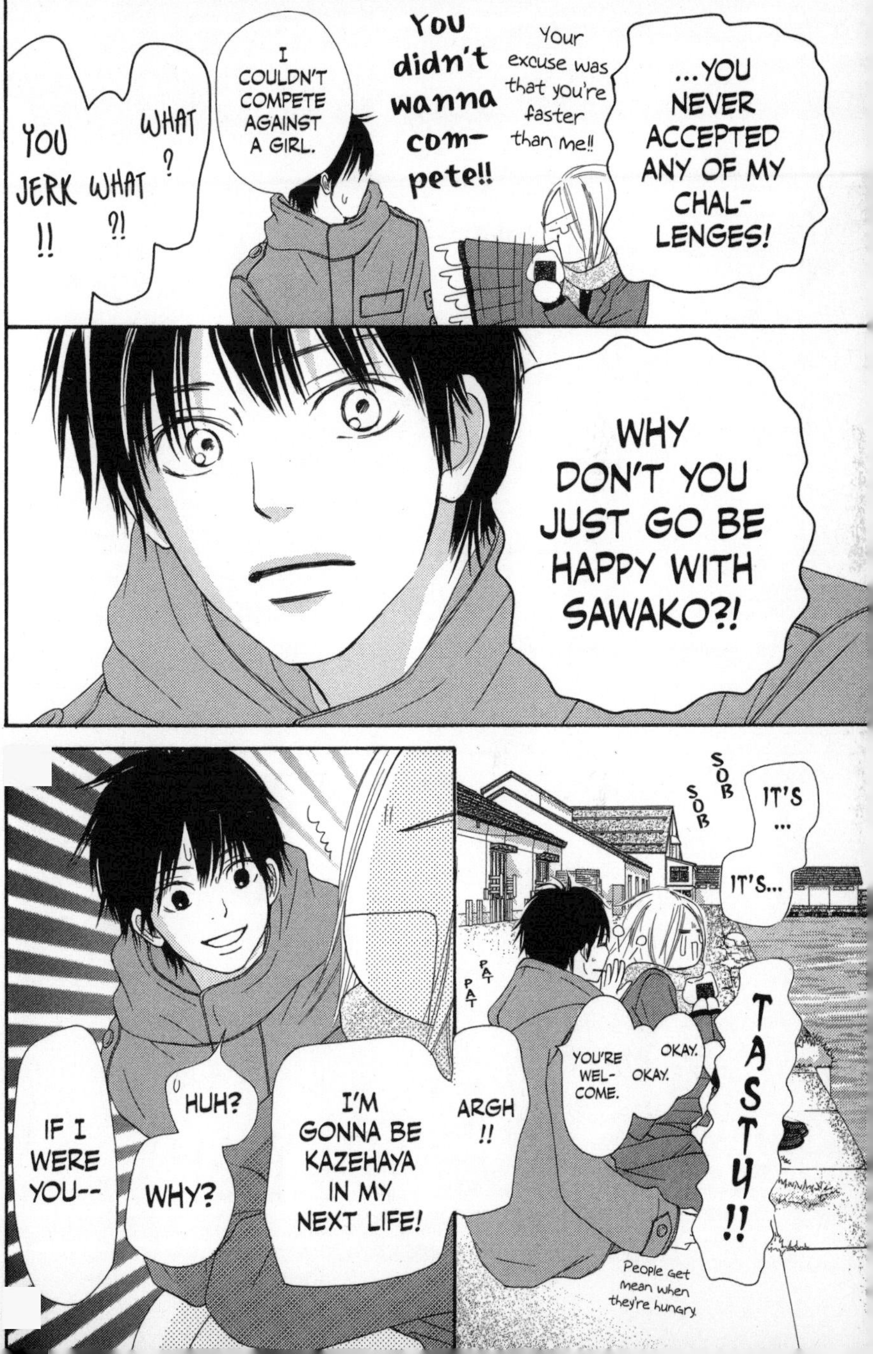
...YOU NEVER ACCEPTED ANY OF MY CHALLENGES!
Your excuse was that you're faster than me!!
You didn't wanna compete!!
I COULDN'T COMPETE AGAINST A GIRL.
WHAT? WHAT?!
YOU JERK!!
WHY DON'T YOU JUST GO BE HAPPY WITH SAWAKO?!
SOB SOB
IT'S... IT'S...
TASTY!!
OKAY. OKAY.
YOU'RE WELCOME.
PAT PAT
People get mean when they're hungry.
ARGH!!
I'M GONNA BE KAZEHAYA IN MY NEXT LIFE!
HUH? WHY?
IF I WERE YOU--

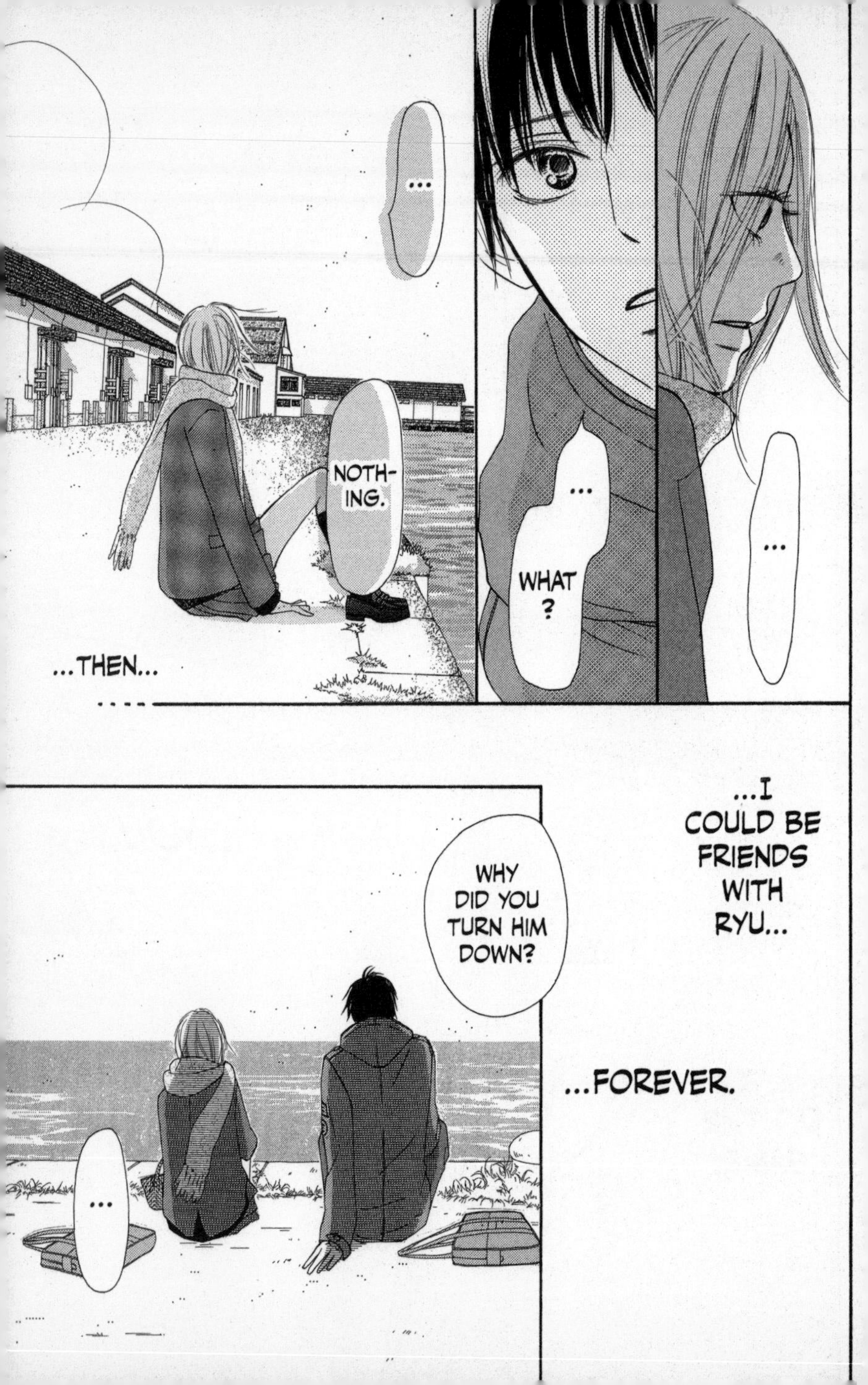
...
...
WHAT?
...
NOTH-ING.
...THEN...
...I COULD BE FRIENDS WITH RYU...
...FOREVER.
WHY DID YOU TURN HIM DOWN?
...

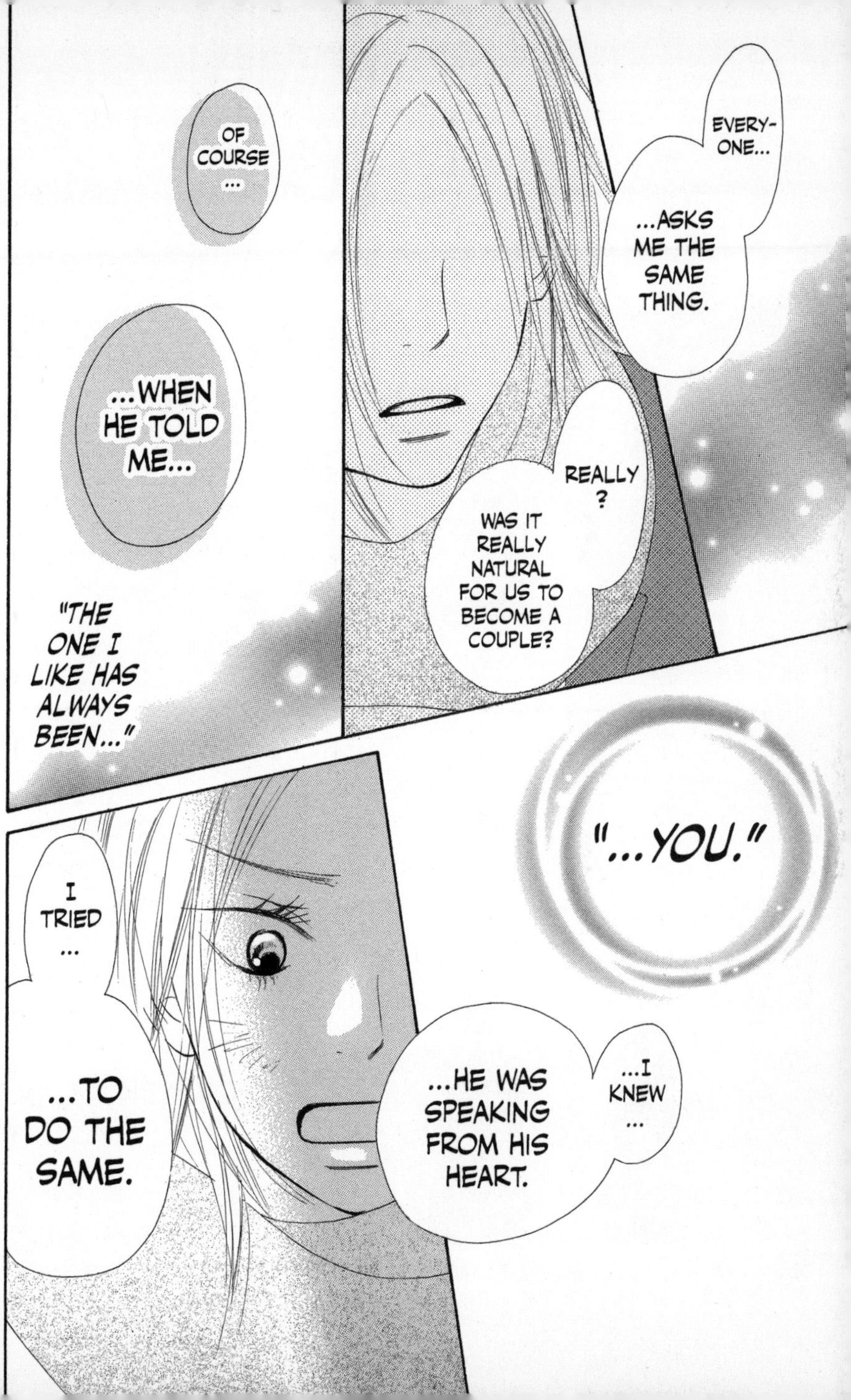
EVERY-ONE...
...ASKS ME THE SAME THING.
REALLY?
WAS IT REALLY NATURAL FOR US TO BECOME A COUPLE?
OF COURSE...
...WHEN HE TOLD ME...
"THE ONE I LIKE HAS ALWAYS BEEN..."
"...YOU."
...I KNEW...
...HE WAS SPEAKING FROM HIS HEART.
I TRIED...
...TO DO THE SAME.

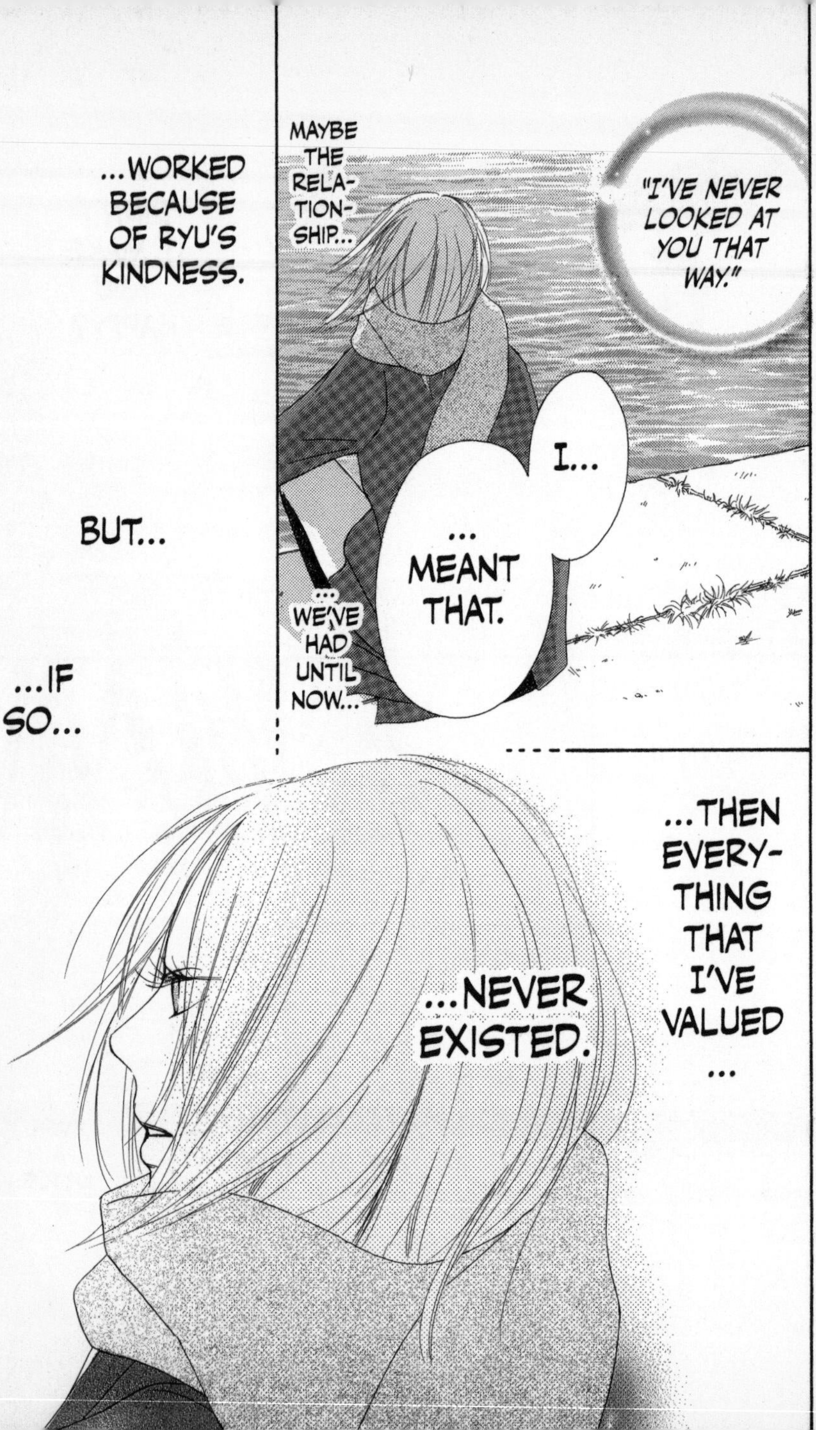
"I'VE NEVER LOOKED AT YOU THAT WAY."
I...
...MEANT THAT.
MAYBE THE RELATIONSHIP...
...WE'VE HAD UNTIL NOW...
...WORKED BECAUSE OF RYU'S KINDNESS.
BUT...
...IF SO...
...THEN EVERYTHING THAT I'VE VALUED...
...NEVER EXISTED.

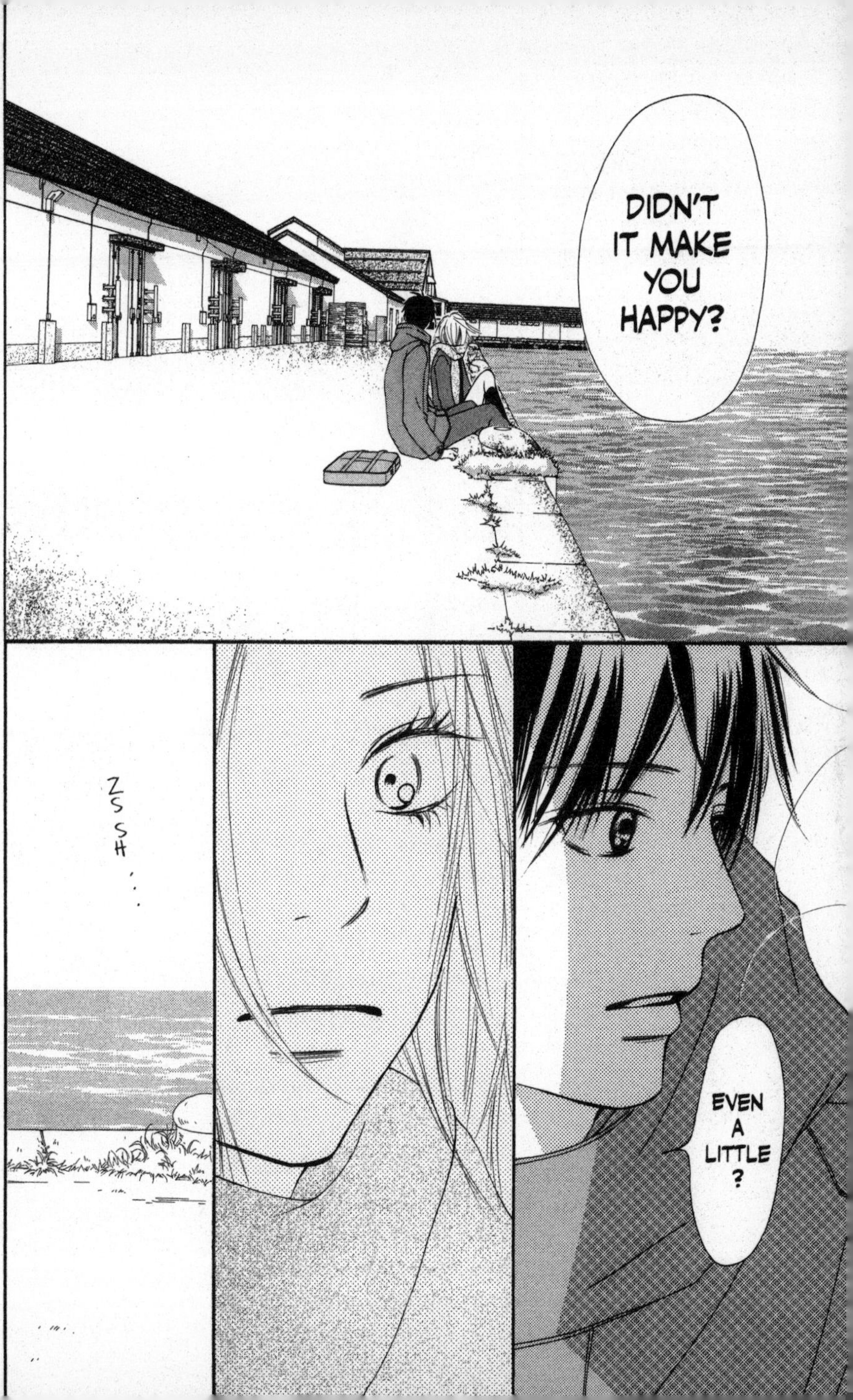
DIDN'T IT MAKE YOU HAPPY?
ZSSH...
EVEN A LITTLE?

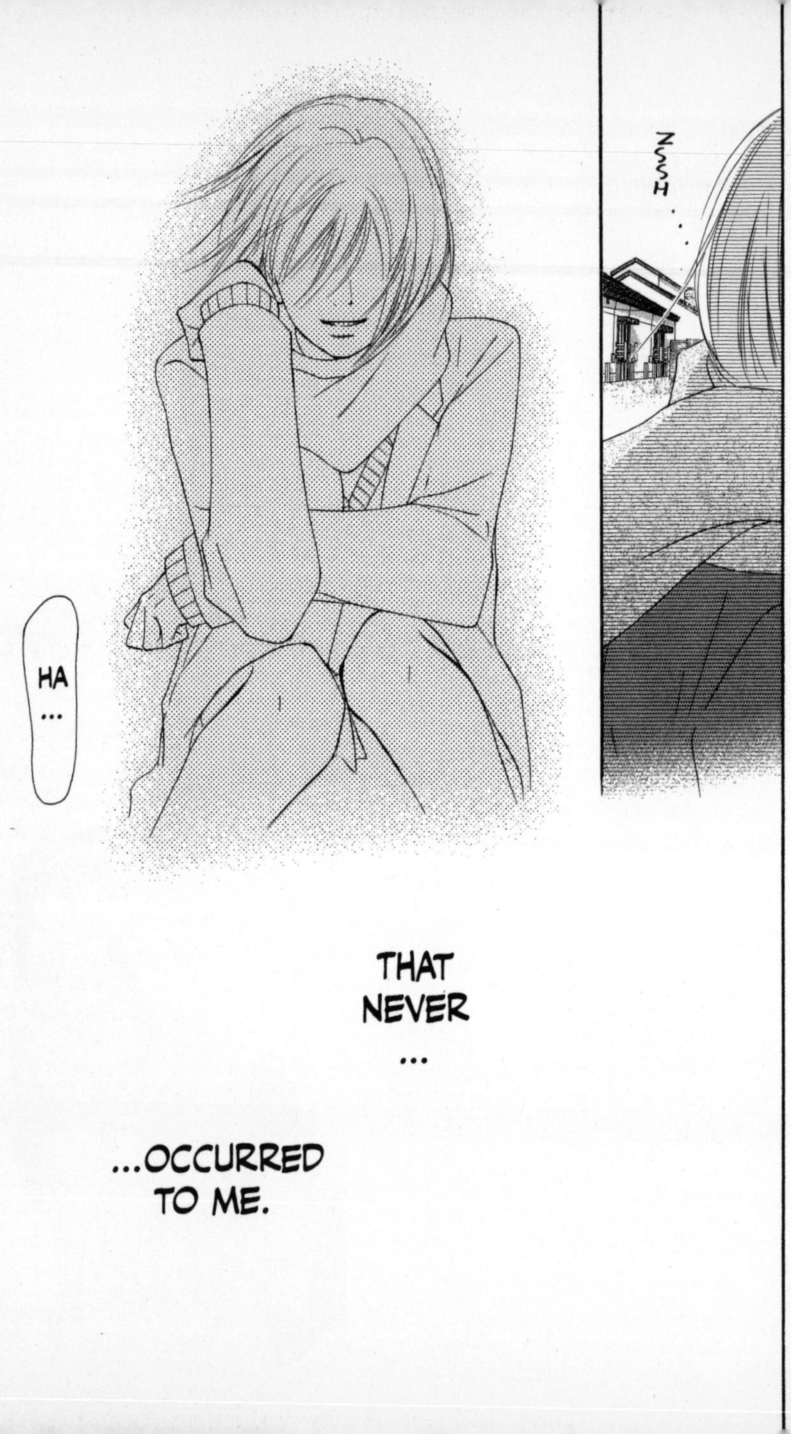
ZSSH . . .
HA ...
THAT NEVER ...
...OCCURRED TO ME.

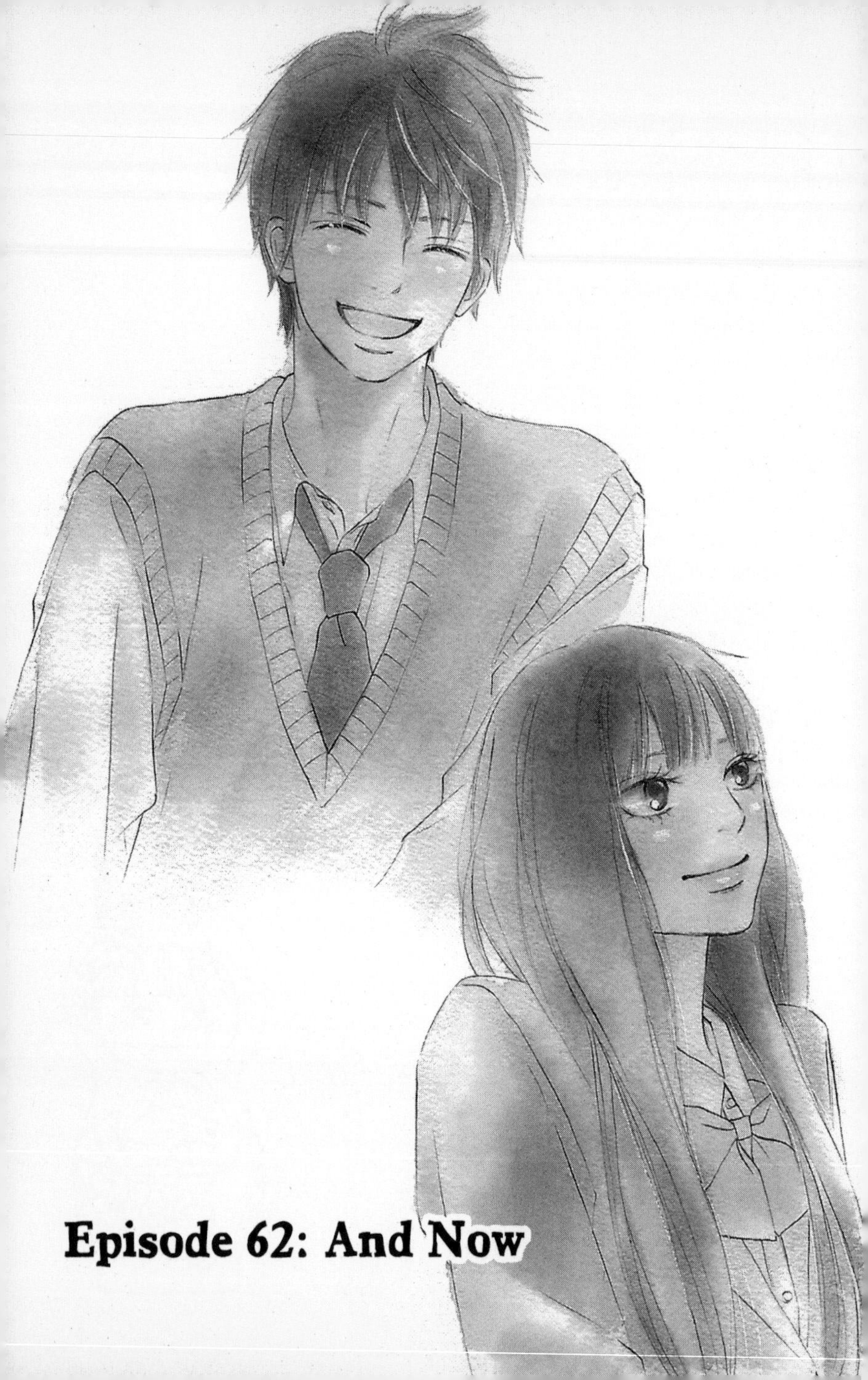
Episode 62: And Now

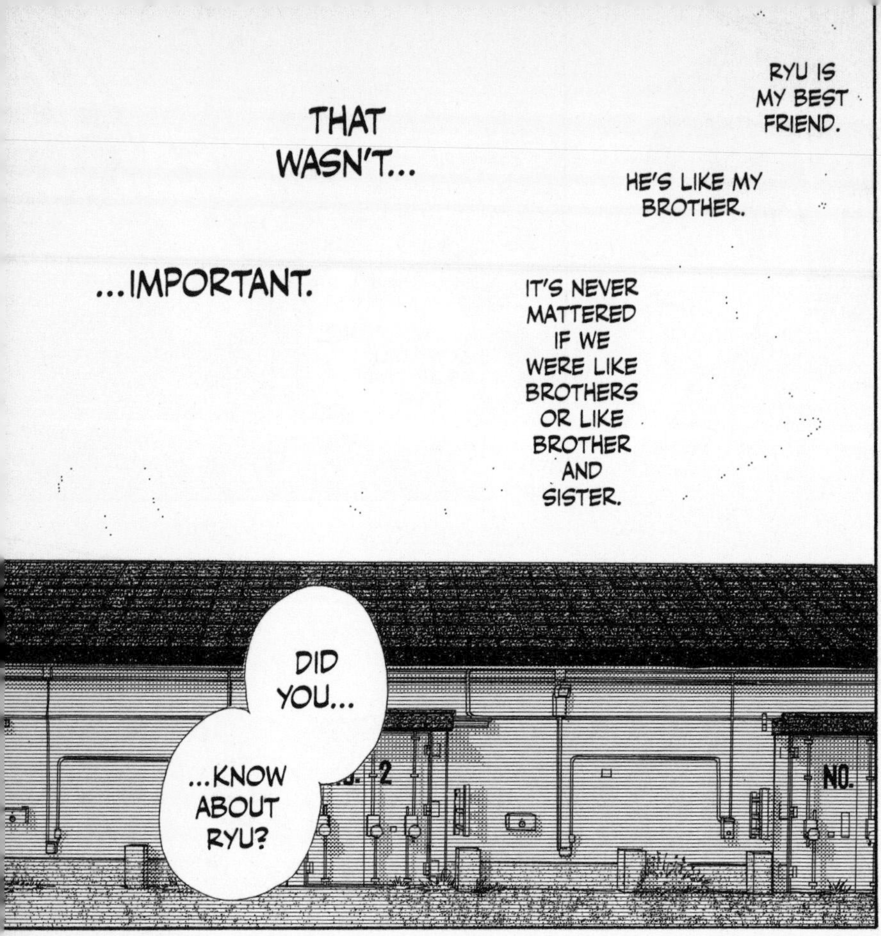
RYU IS MY BEST FRIEND.
HE'S LIKE MY BROTHER.
IT'S NEVER MATTERED IF WE WERE LIKE BROTHERS OR LIKE BROTHER AND SISTER.
THAT WASN'T...
...IMPORTANT.
DID YOU...
...KNOW ABOUT RYU?

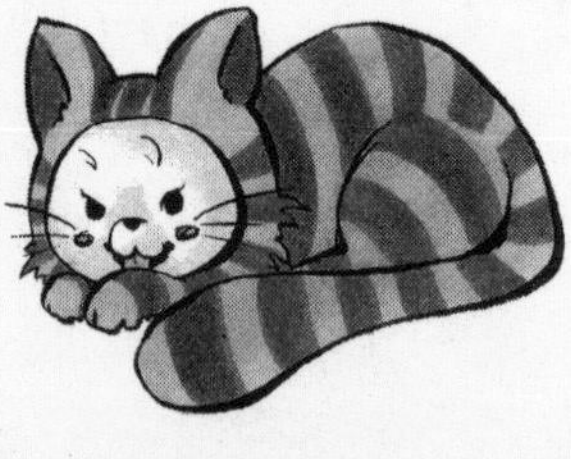

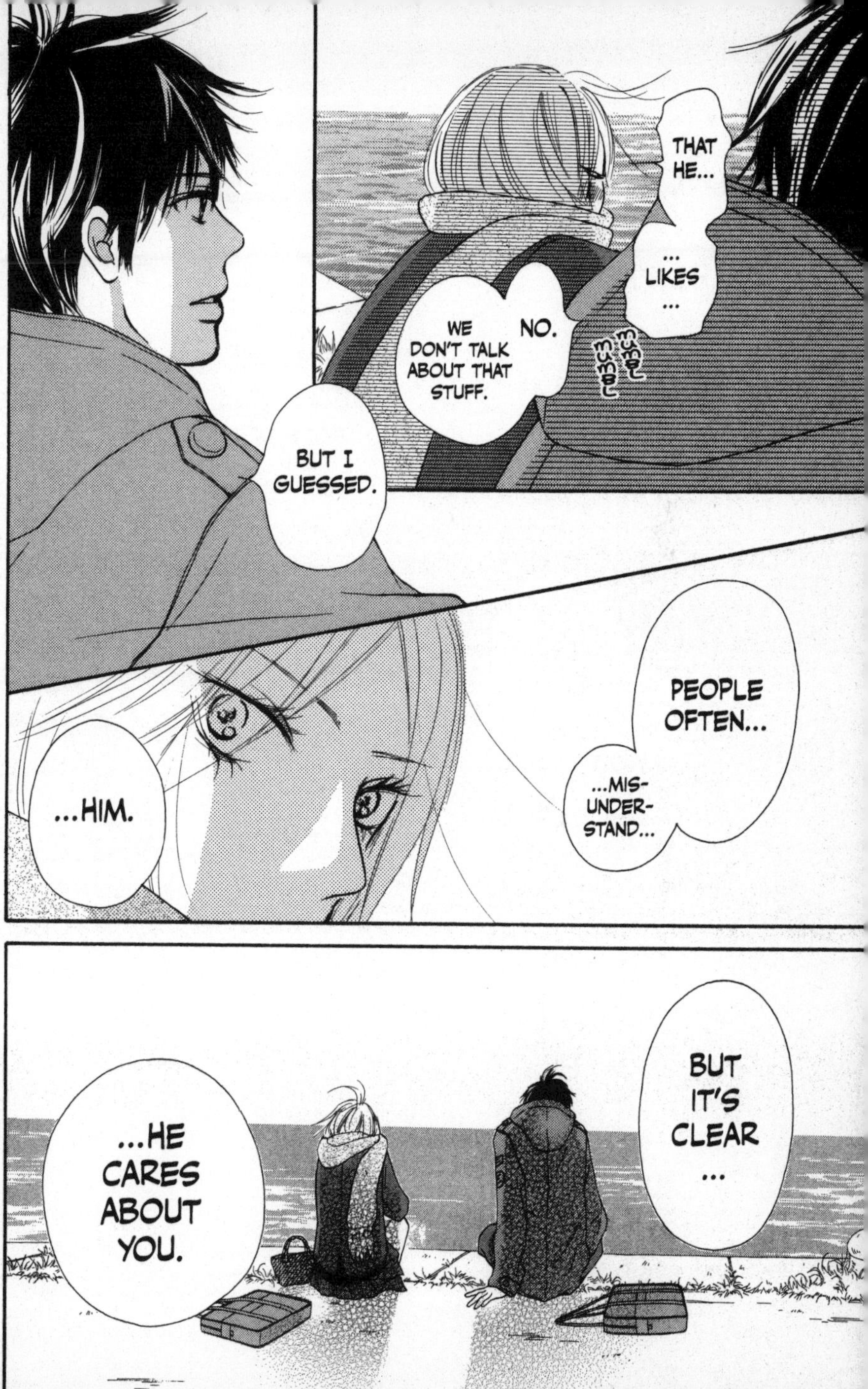
THAT HE...
...LIKES...
MUMBLE MUMBLE
NO.
WE DON'T TALK ABOUT THAT STUFF.
BUT I GUESSED.
PEOPLE OFTEN...
...MIS-UNDERSTAND...
...HIM.
BUT IT'S CLEAR...
...HE CARES ABOUT YOU.

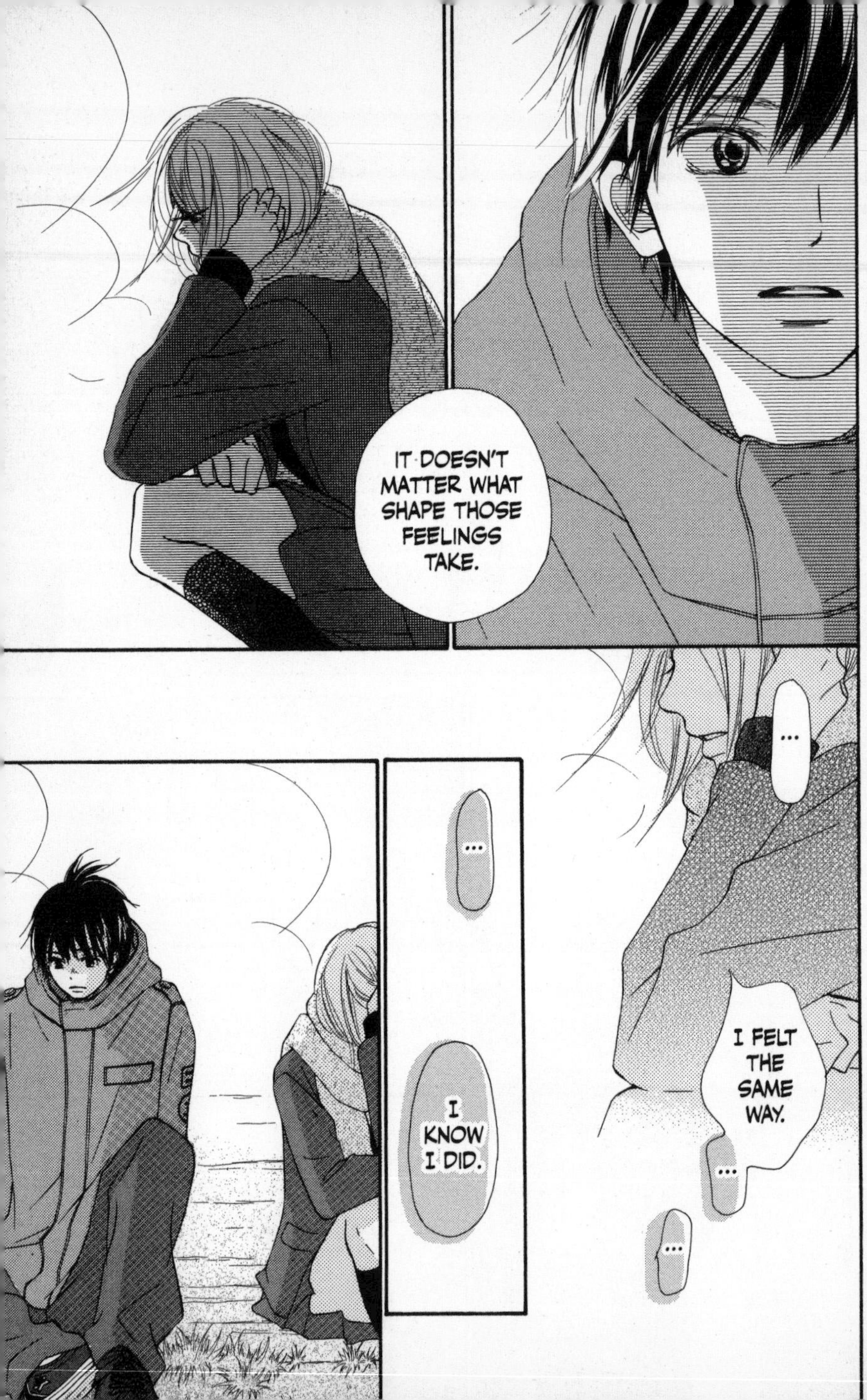
IT DOESN'T MATTER WHAT SHAPE THOSE FEELINGS TAKE.
...
I FELT THE SAME WAY.
...
...
...
I KNOW I DID.

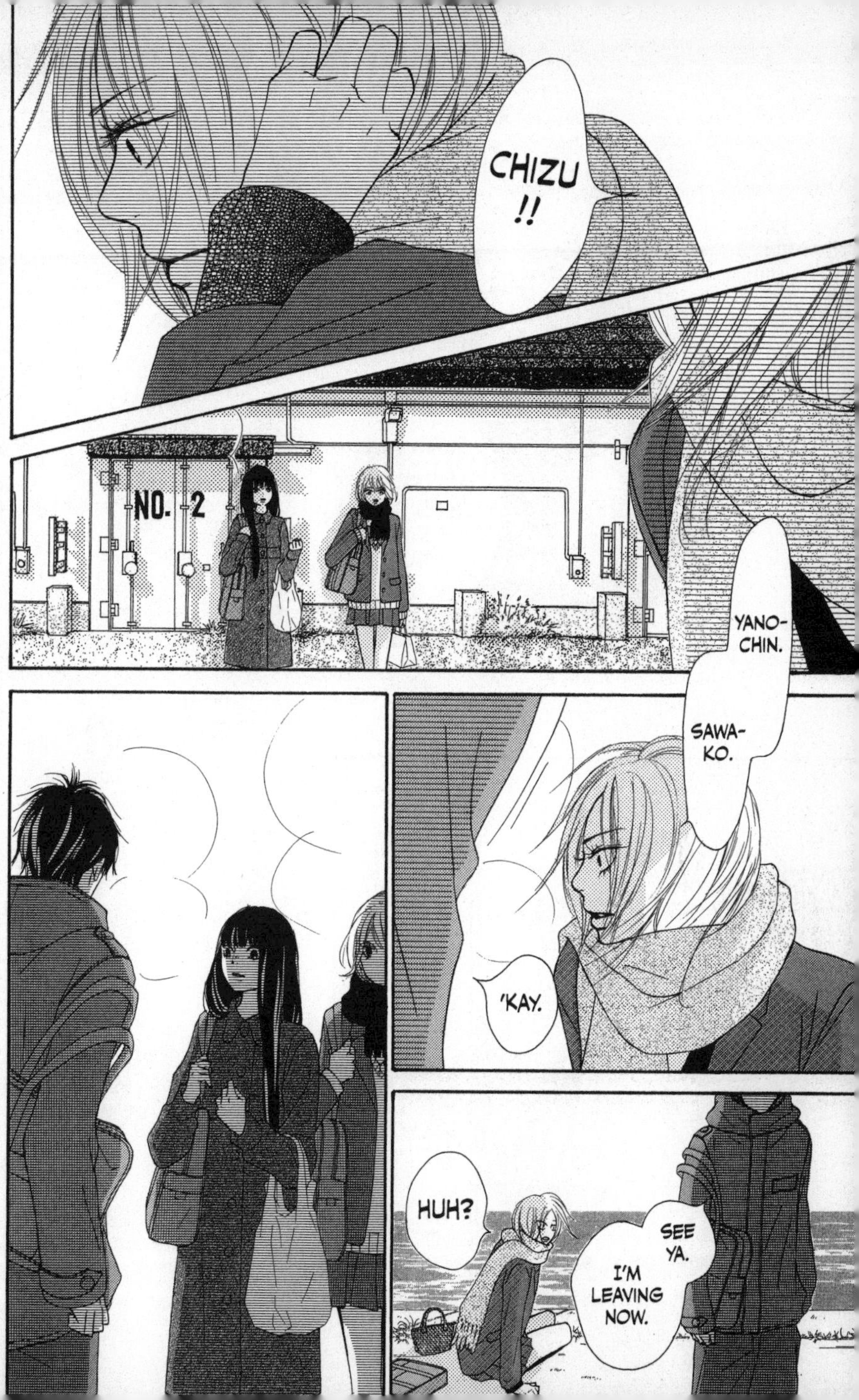
CHIZU !!
YANO-CHIN.
SAWA-KO.
'KAY.
SEE YA.
I'M LEAVING NOW.
HUH?

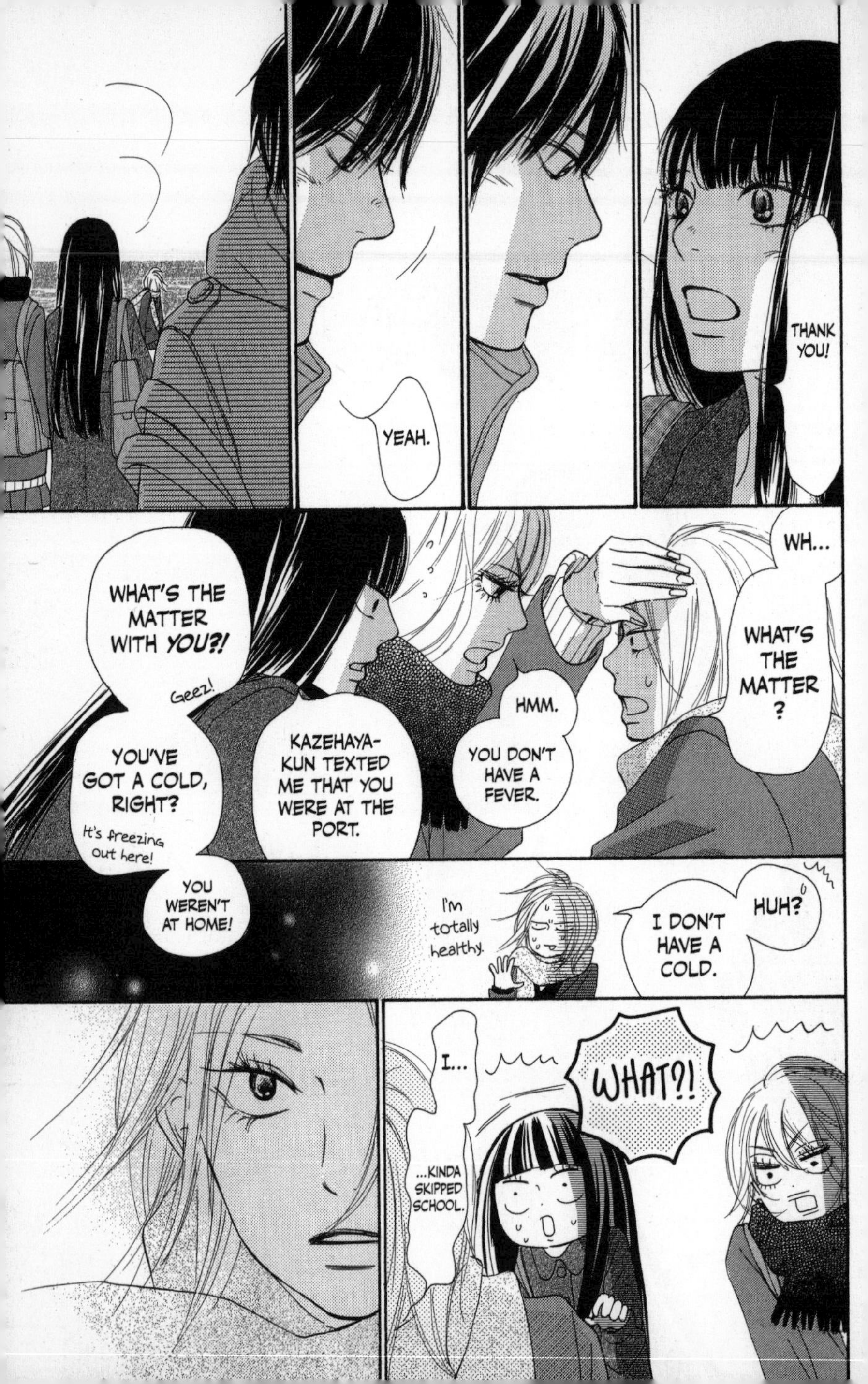
THANK YOU!
YEAH.
WH...
WHAT'S THE MATTER?
HMM.
YOU DON'T HAVE A FEVER.
WHAT'S THE MATTER WITH *YOU?!*
Geez!
KAZEHAYA-KUN TEXTED ME THAT YOU WERE AT THE PORT.
YOU'VE GOT A COLD, RIGHT?
It's freezing out here!
YOU WEREN'T AT HOME!
HUH?
I DON'T HAVE A COLD.
I'm totally healthy.
WHAT?!
I...
...KINDA SKIPPED SCHOOL.

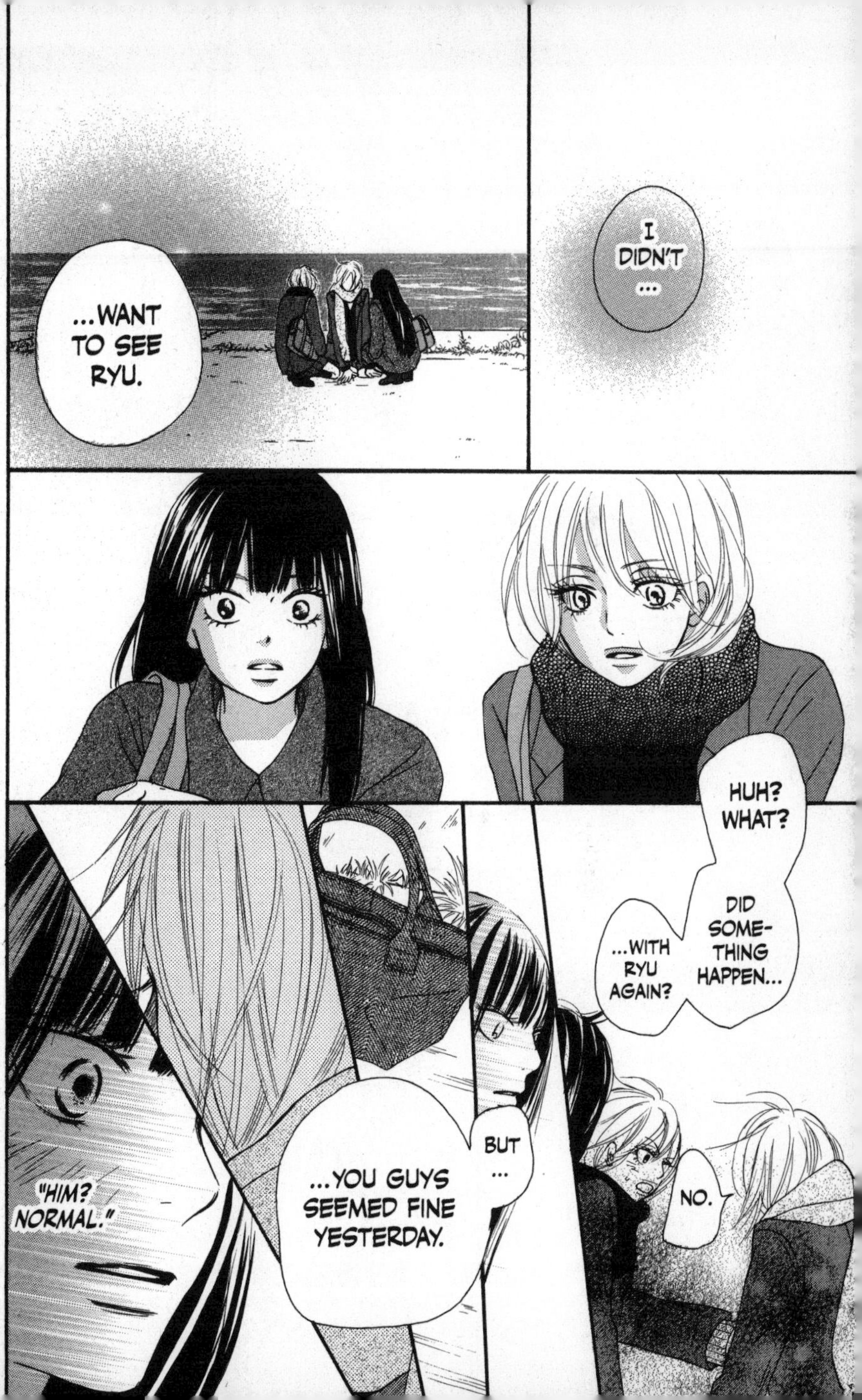
I DIDN'T ...
...WANT TO SEE RYU.
HUH? WHAT?
DID SOME-THING HAPPEN...
...WITH RYU AGAIN?
NO.
BUT ...
...YOU GUYS SEEMED FINE YESTERDAY.
"HIM? NORMAL."

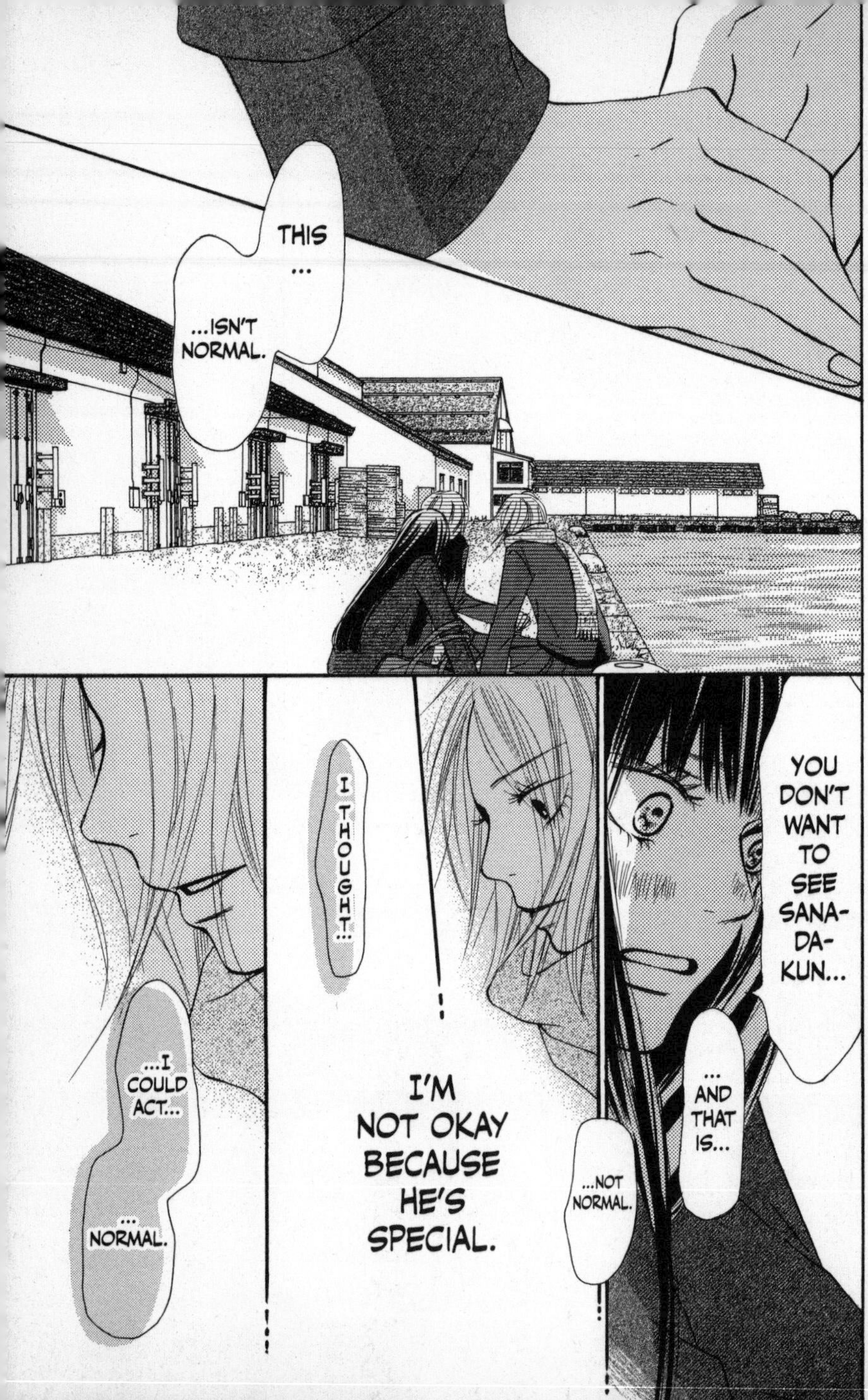
THIS ...
...ISN'T NORMAL.
YOU DON'T WANT TO SEE SANA-DA-KUN...
... AND THAT IS...
...NOT NORMAL.
I THOUGHT...
I'M NOT OKAY BECAUSE HE'S SPECIAL.
...I COULD ACT...
... NORMAL.

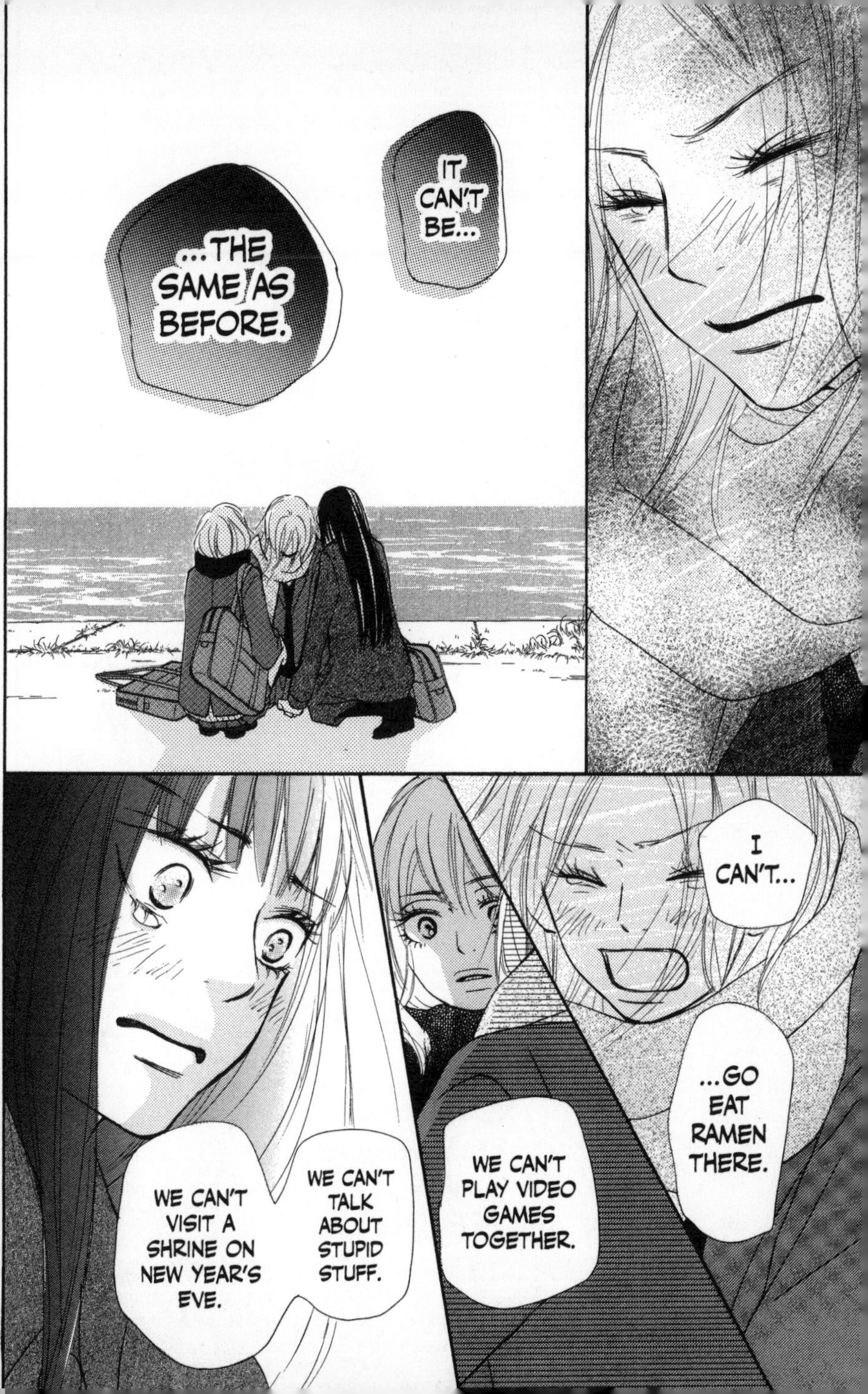
IT CAN'T BE...
...THE SAME AS BEFORE.
I CAN'T...
...GO EAT RAMEN THERE.
WE CAN'T PLAY VIDEO GAMES TOGETHER.
WE CAN'T TALK ABOUT STUPID STUFF.
WE CAN'T VISIT A SHRINE ON NEW YEAR'S EVE.

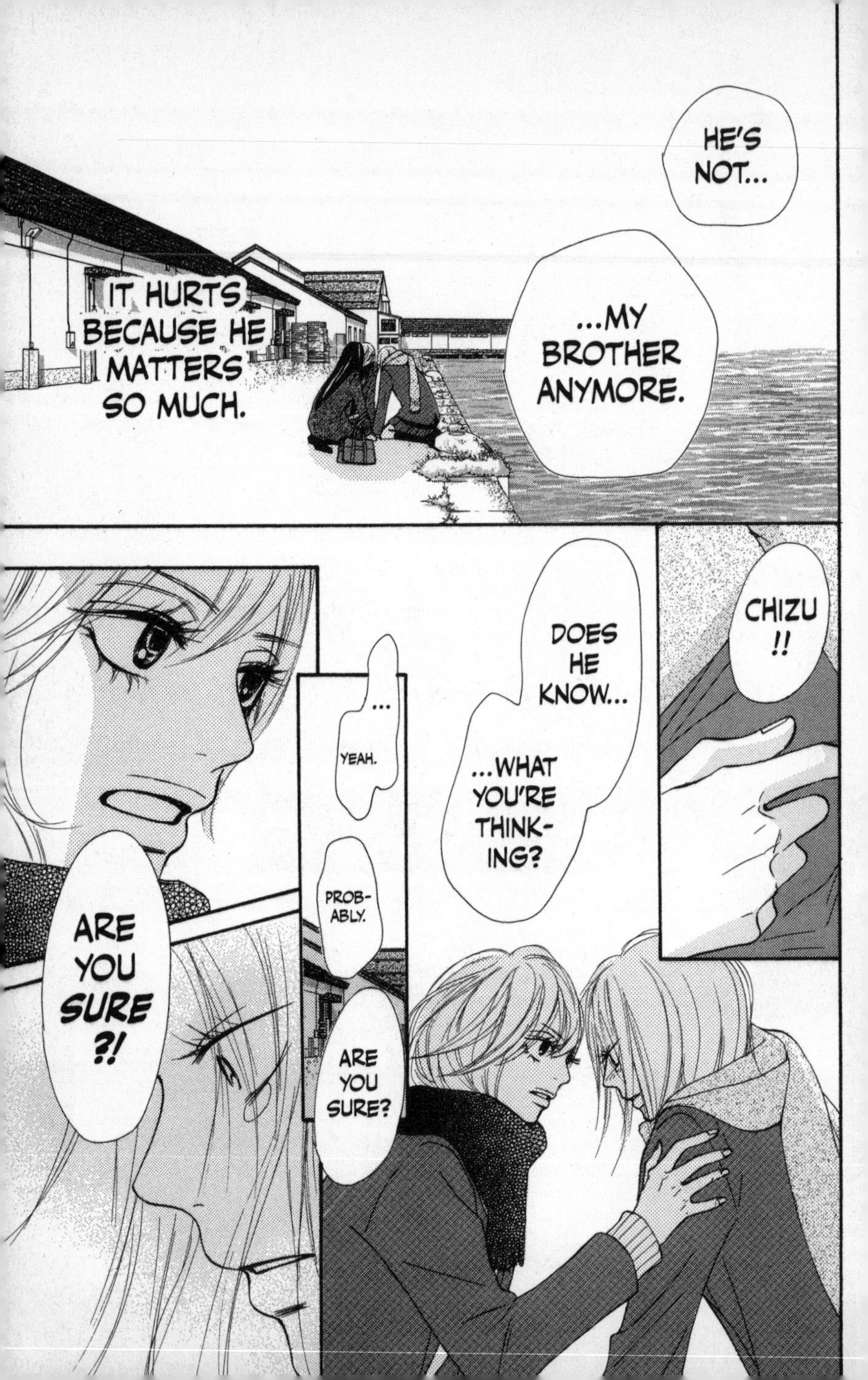
HE'S NOT...
...MY BROTHER ANYMORE.
IT HURTS BECAUSE HE MATTERS SO MUCH.
CHIZU !!
DOES HE KNOW...
...WHAT YOU'RE THINK-ING?
...
YEAH.
PROB-ABLY.
ARE YOU SURE?
ARE YOU SURE ?!

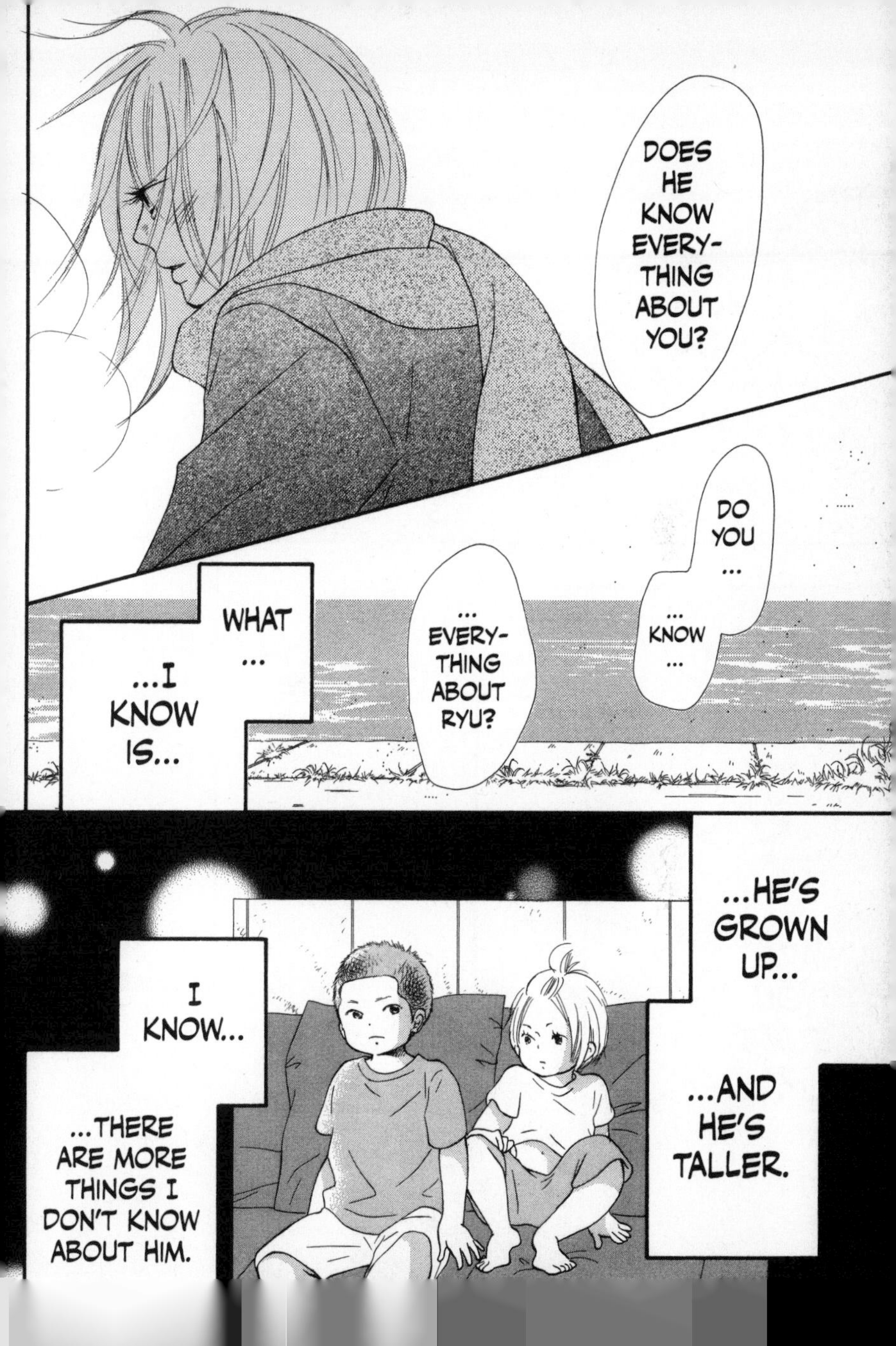
DOES HE KNOW EVERY-THING ABOUT YOU?
DO YOU ... ... KNOW ...
... EVERY-THING ABOUT RYU?
WHAT ...
...I KNOW IS...
...HE'S GROWN UP...
...AND HE'S TALLER.
I KNOW...
...THERE ARE MORE THINGS I DON'T KNOW ABOUT HIM.

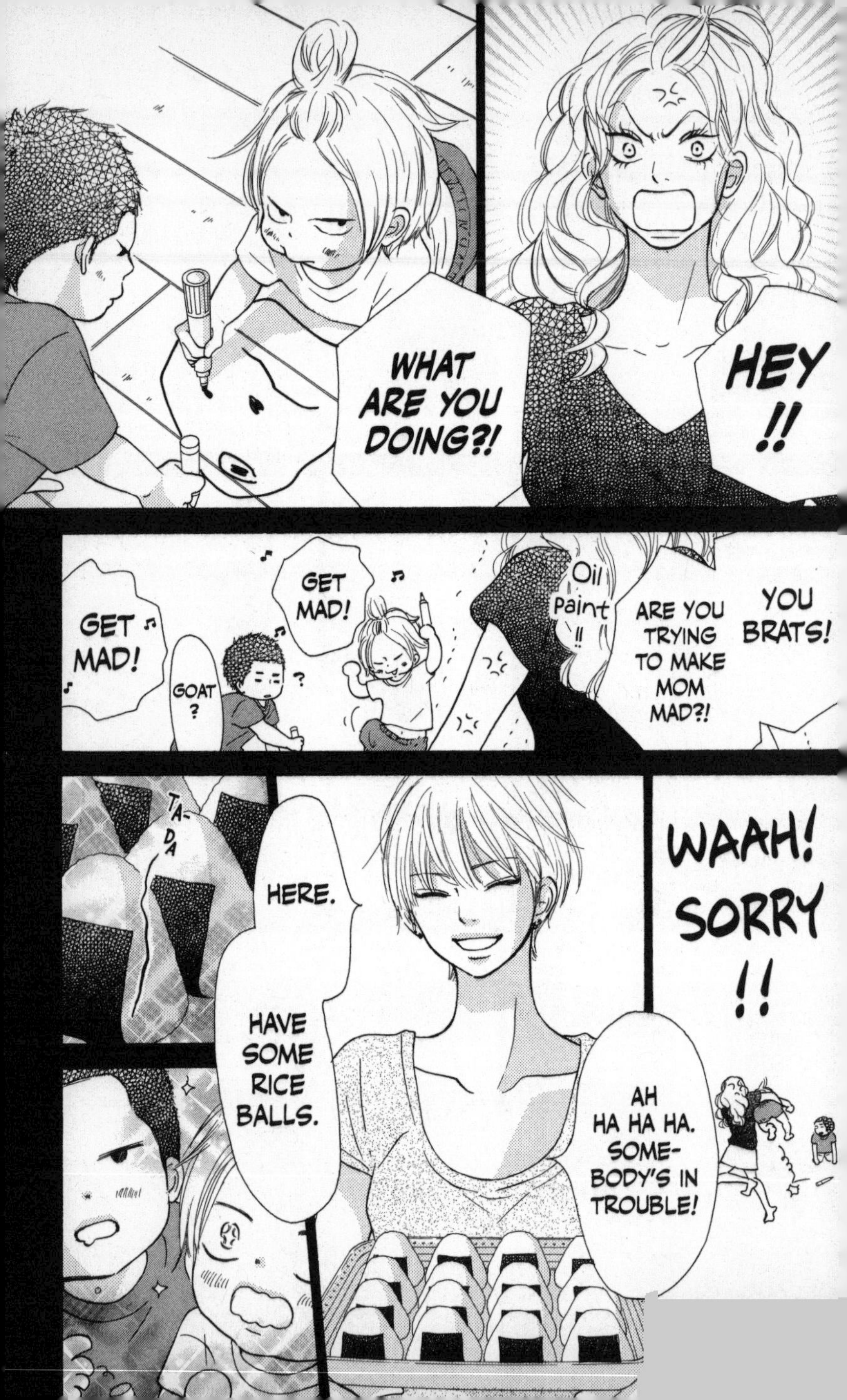
HEY !!
WHAT ARE YOU DOING?!
YOU BRATS!
ARE YOU TRYING TO MAKE MOM MAD?!
Oil paint !!
GET MAD!
GET MAD!
GOAT ?
WAAH! SORRY !!
AH HA HA HA. SOME-BODY'S IN TROUBLE!
HERE.
HAVE SOME RICE BALLS.
TA-DA

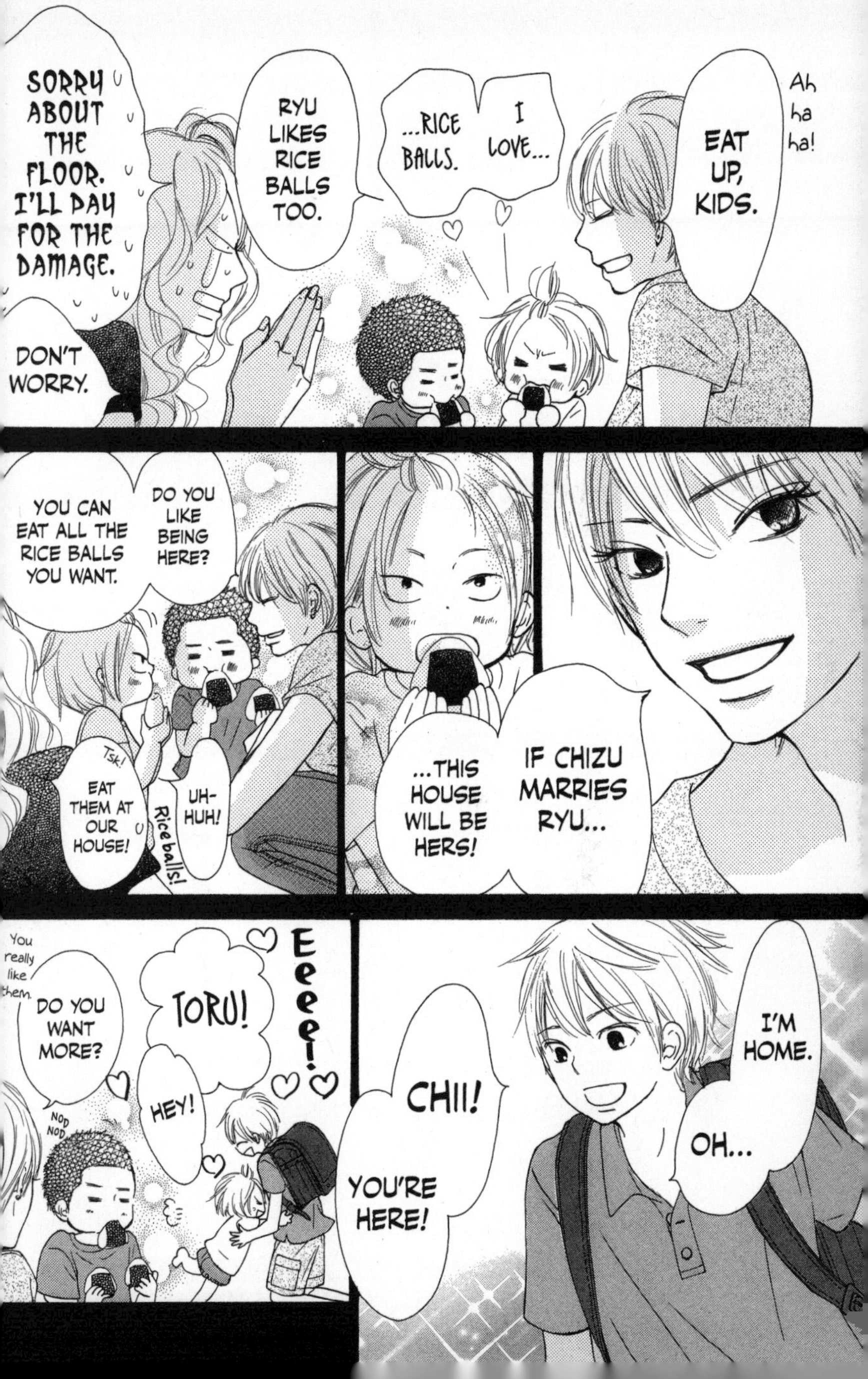
Ah ha ha!
EAT UP, KIDS.
I LOVE...
...RICE BALLS.
RYU LIKES RICE BALLS TOO.
SORRY ABOUT THE FLOOR. I'LL PAY FOR THE DAMAGE.
DON'T WORRY.
IF CHIZU MARRIES RYU...
...THIS HOUSE WILL BE HERS!
DO YOU LIKE BEING HERE?
YOU CAN EAT ALL THE RICE BALLS YOU WANT.
UH-HUH!
Rice balls!
Tsk!
EAT THEM AT OUR HOUSE!
I'M HOME.
OH...
CHII!
YOU'RE HERE!
Eeee!
TORU!
HEY!
DO YOU WANT MORE?
You really like them.
NOD NOD

In this volume, Sawako and Kazehaya spend a lot of time on the sidelines. Look forward to seeing more of them in the next volume!

Speaking of Sawako, a Sawako Kuronuma figure came out in 2011. It came with an adorable Maru-chan!

When I see different representations of Sawako, it takes me back to when I was still writing one-shots of *Kimi ni Todoke*. SIGH... She's in color, and moves, and she looks sort of like a real person and sorta like a doll.

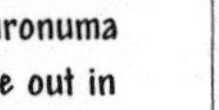

WOW!!!!

Her hair doesn't grow.

Sawako the Figure, Magazine Special Prize Sawako and my friend's handmade felt Sawako are all in a corner of my studio with my favorite things.

They're cute. I'm happy for you, Sawako. I'm happy for you, Karuho. SIGH...

CLICK

KITAHORO ELEMENTARY SCHOOL

HAPPY ENTRANCE CEREMONY

READY?

ONE, TWO...

THREE!!

SOB... THEY'RE ALL GROWN UP.

DON'T BREAK ANYTHING AT SCHOOL!

OKAY!

I'M GLAD YOU'RE IN THE SAME CLASS!

YEAH.

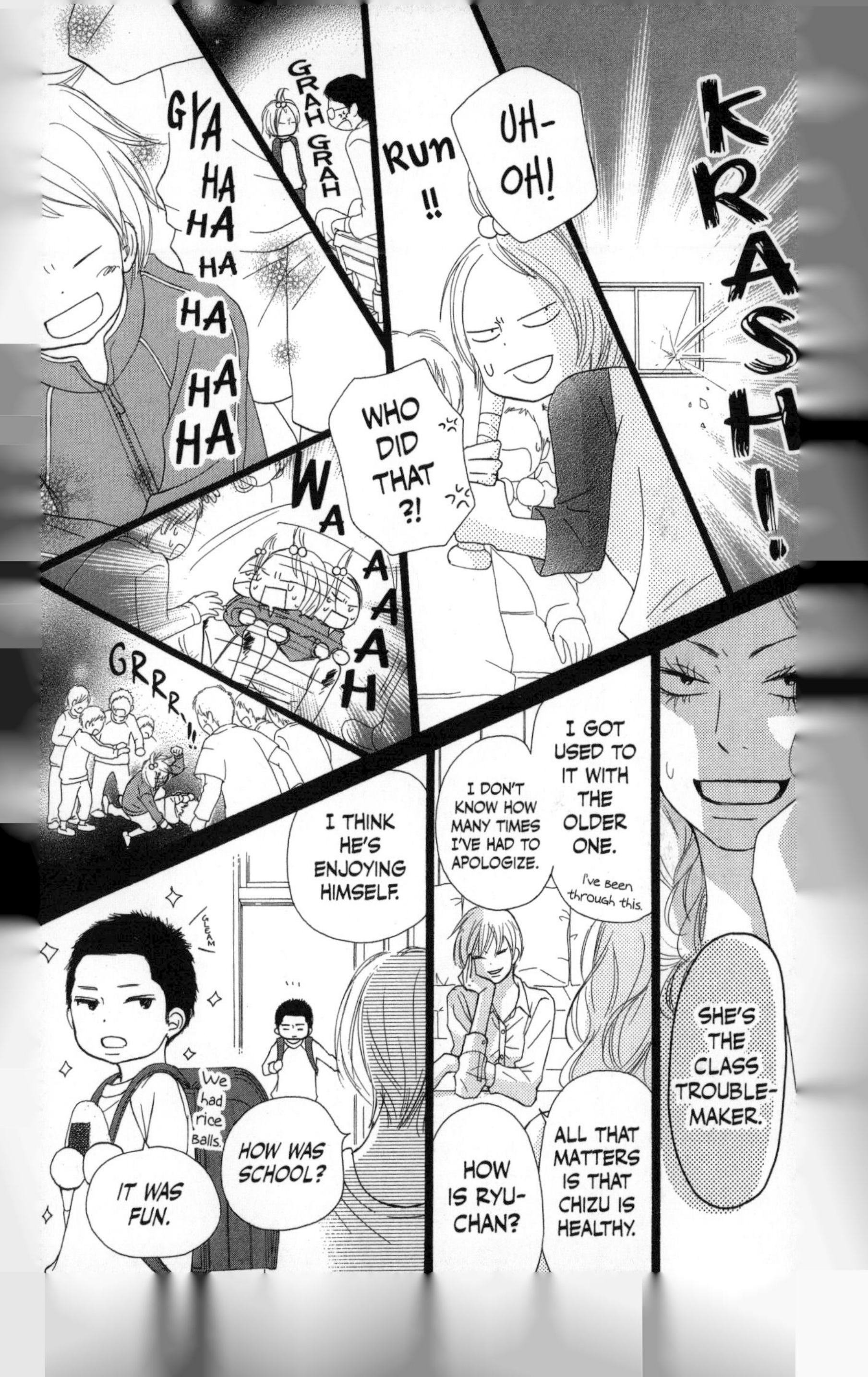
KRASH!!
UH-OH!
RUN!!
WHO DID THAT?!
GRAH GRAH GRAH
GYA HA HA HA HA HA HA HA
WAAAAAH
GRRR...!!
SHE'S THE CLASS TROUBLE-MAKER.
I GOT USED TO IT WITH THE OLDER ONE.
I've been through this.
I DON'T KNOW HOW MANY TIMES I'VE HAD TO APOLOGIZE.
ALL THAT MATTERS IS THAT CHIZU IS HEALTHY.
HOW IS RYU-CHAN?
I THINK HE'S ENJOYING HIMSELF.
GLEAM
HOW WAS SCHOOL?
We had rice balls.
IT WAS FUN.

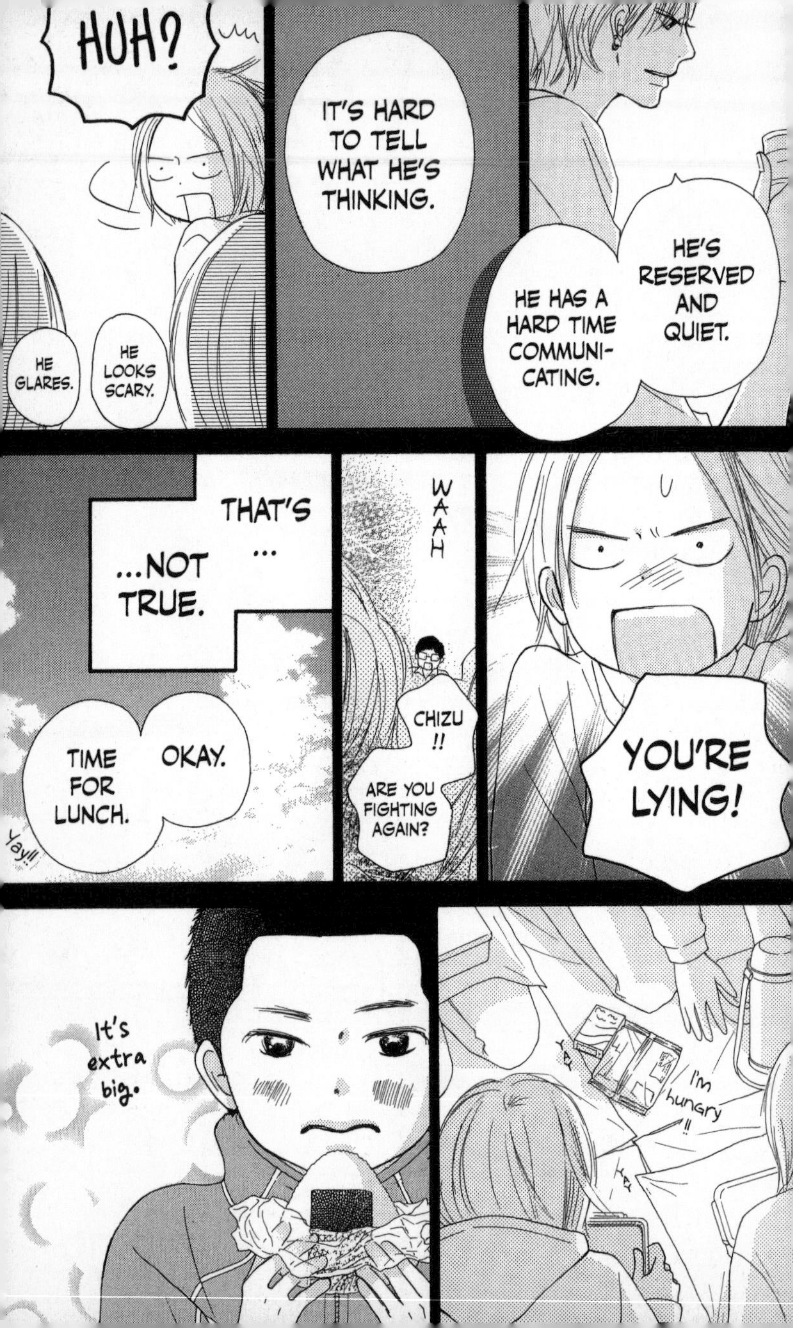
HE'S RESERVED AND QUIET.
HE HAS A HARD TIME COMMUNI-CATING.
IT'S HARD TO TELL WHAT HE'S THINKING.
HUH?
HE LOOKS SCARY.
HE GLARES.
YOU'RE LYING!
WAAH
CHIZU!!
ARE YOU FIGHTING AGAIN?
THAT'S...
...NOT TRUE.
OKAY.
TIME FOR LUNCH.
Yay!!
I'm hungry!!
It's extra big.

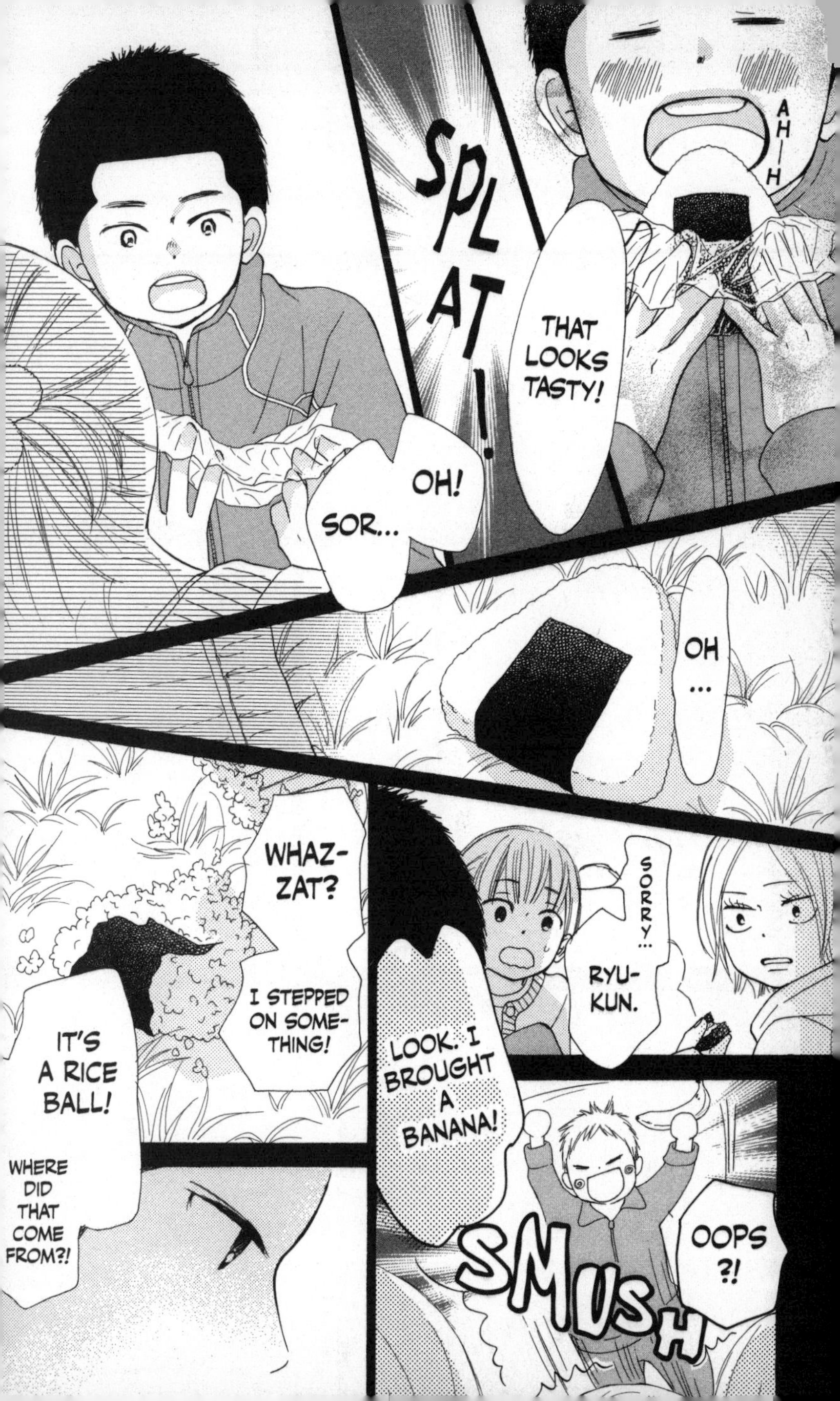
AH-H
THAT LOOKS TASTY!
SPLAT!
OH!
SOR...
OH...
SORRY...
RYU-KUN.
WHAZ-ZAT?
I STEPPED ON SOME-THING!
IT'S A RICE BALL!
LOOK. I BROUGHT A BANANA!
OOPS?!
SMUSH
WHERE DID THAT COME FROM?!

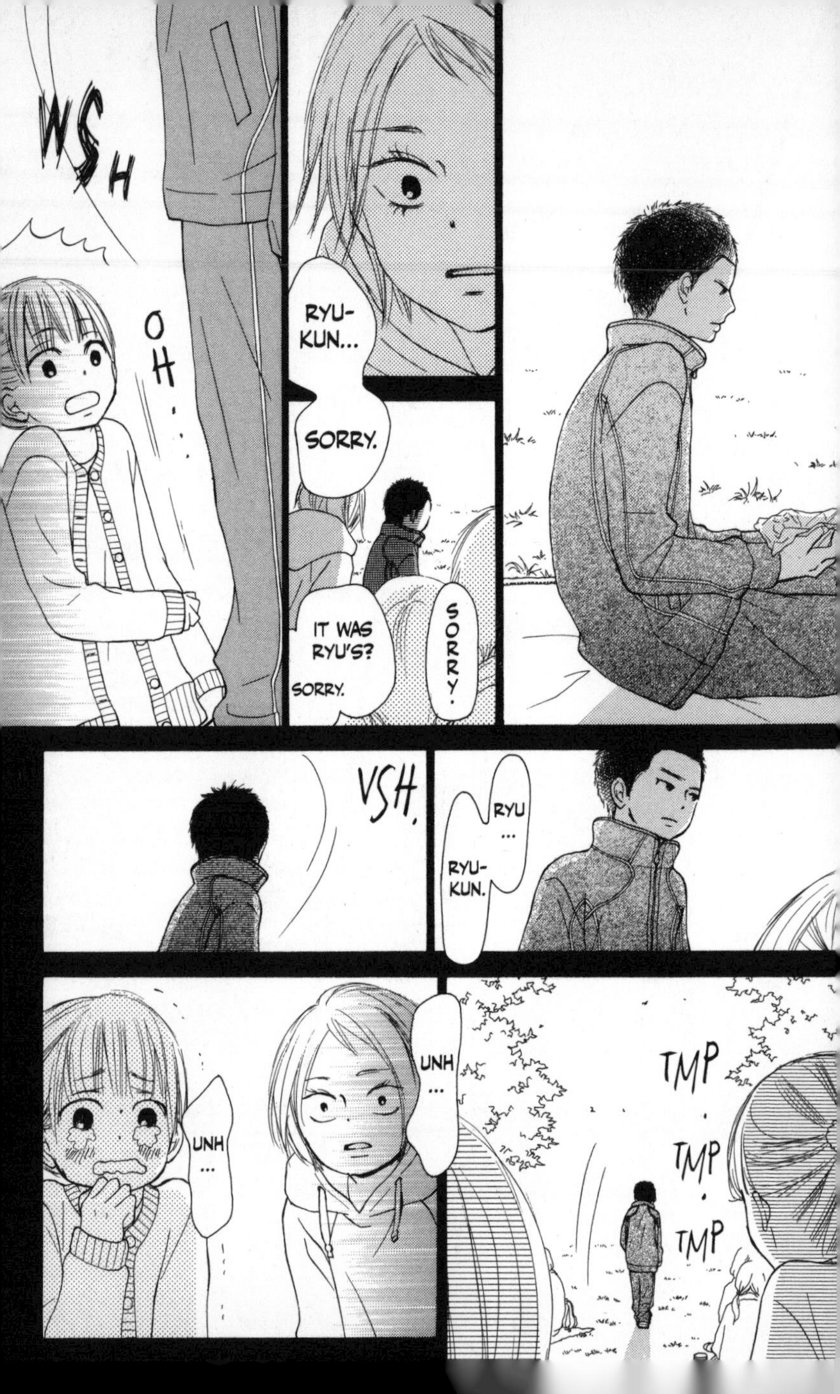
RYU-KUN...
SORRY.
SORRY.
IT WAS RYU'S?
SORRY.
WSH
OH...
RYU... RYU-KUN.
VSH.
TMP TMP TMP
UNH...
UNH...

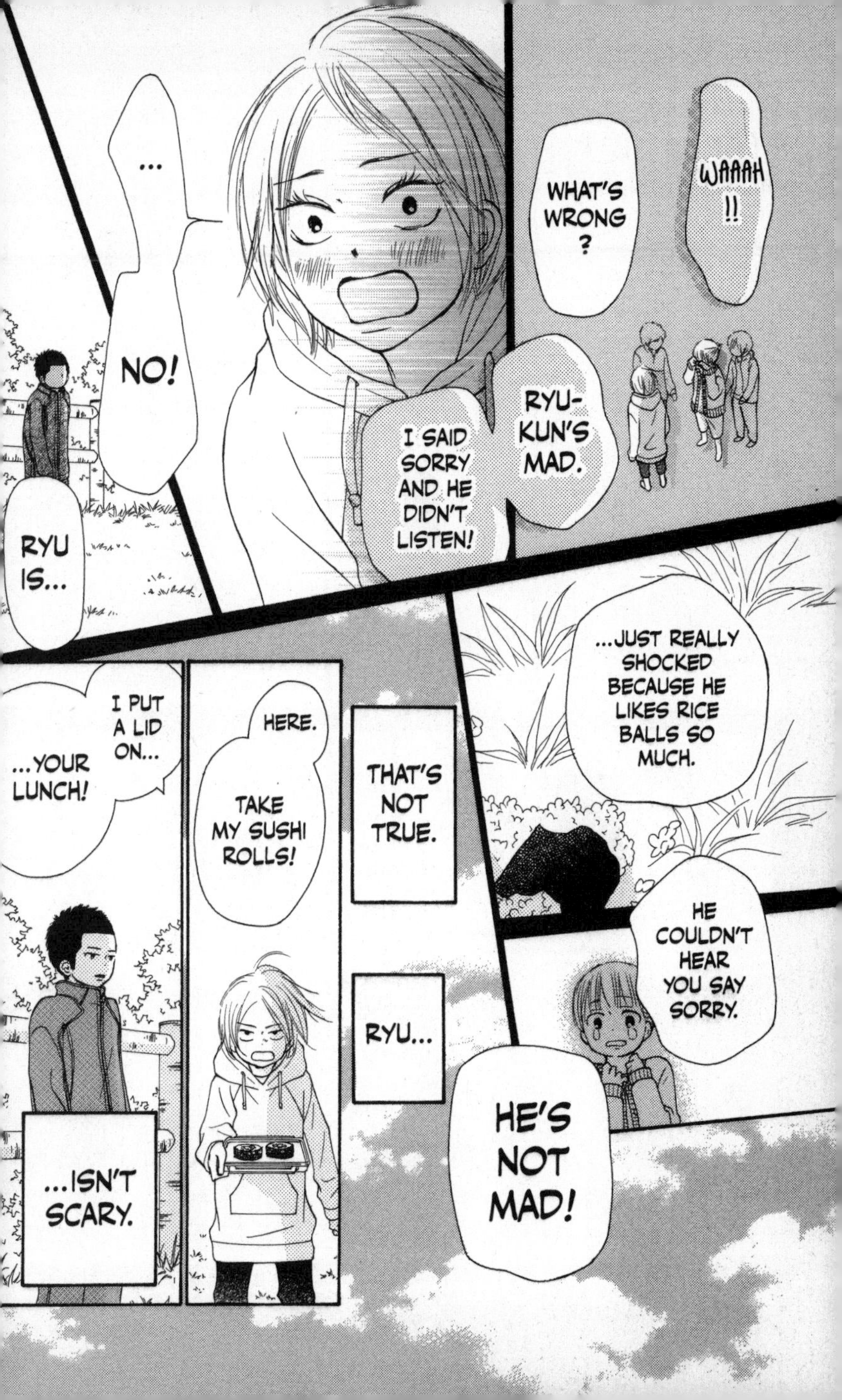
WAAAH !!
WHAT'S WRONG ?
RYU-KUN'S MAD.
I SAID SORRY AND HE DIDN'T LISTEN!
...
NO!
RYU IS...
...JUST REALLY SHOCKED BECAUSE HE LIKES RICE BALLS SO MUCH.
HE COULDN'T HEAR YOU SAY SORRY.
HE'S NOT MAD!
THAT'S NOT TRUE.
RYU...
HERE.
TAKE MY SUSHI ROLLS!
I PUT A LID ON...
...YOUR LUNCH!
...ISN'T SCARY.

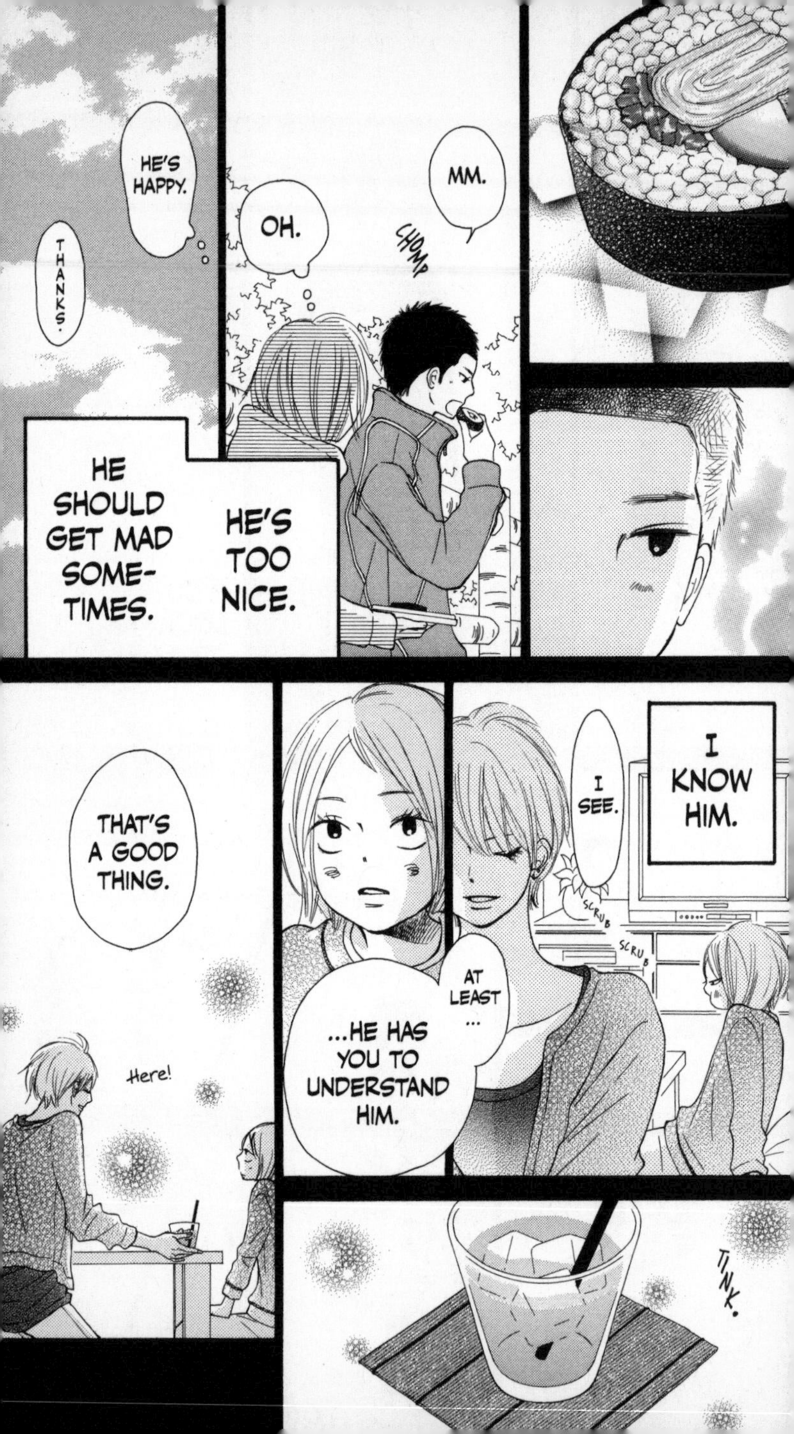
MM.
CHOMP
OH.
HE'S HAPPY.
THANKS.
HE'S TOO NICE.
HE SHOULD GET MAD SOME-TIMES.
I KNOW HIM.
I SEE.
SCRUB
SCRUB
AT LEAST...
...HE HAS YOU TO UNDERSTAND HIM.
TINK.
THAT'S A GOOD THING.
Here!

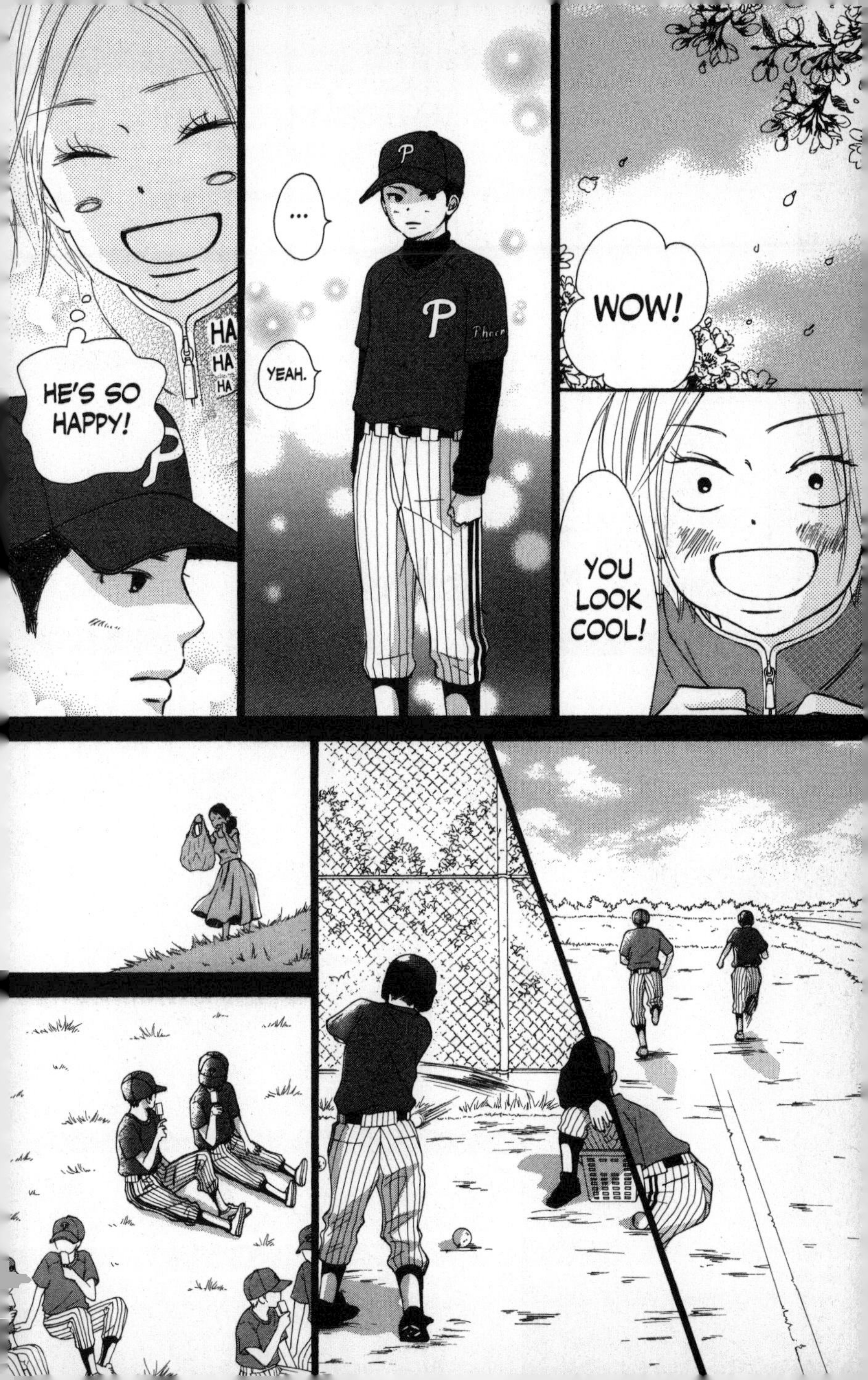
WOW!
YOU LOOK COOL!
...
YEAH.
HA HA HA
HE'S SO HAPPY!

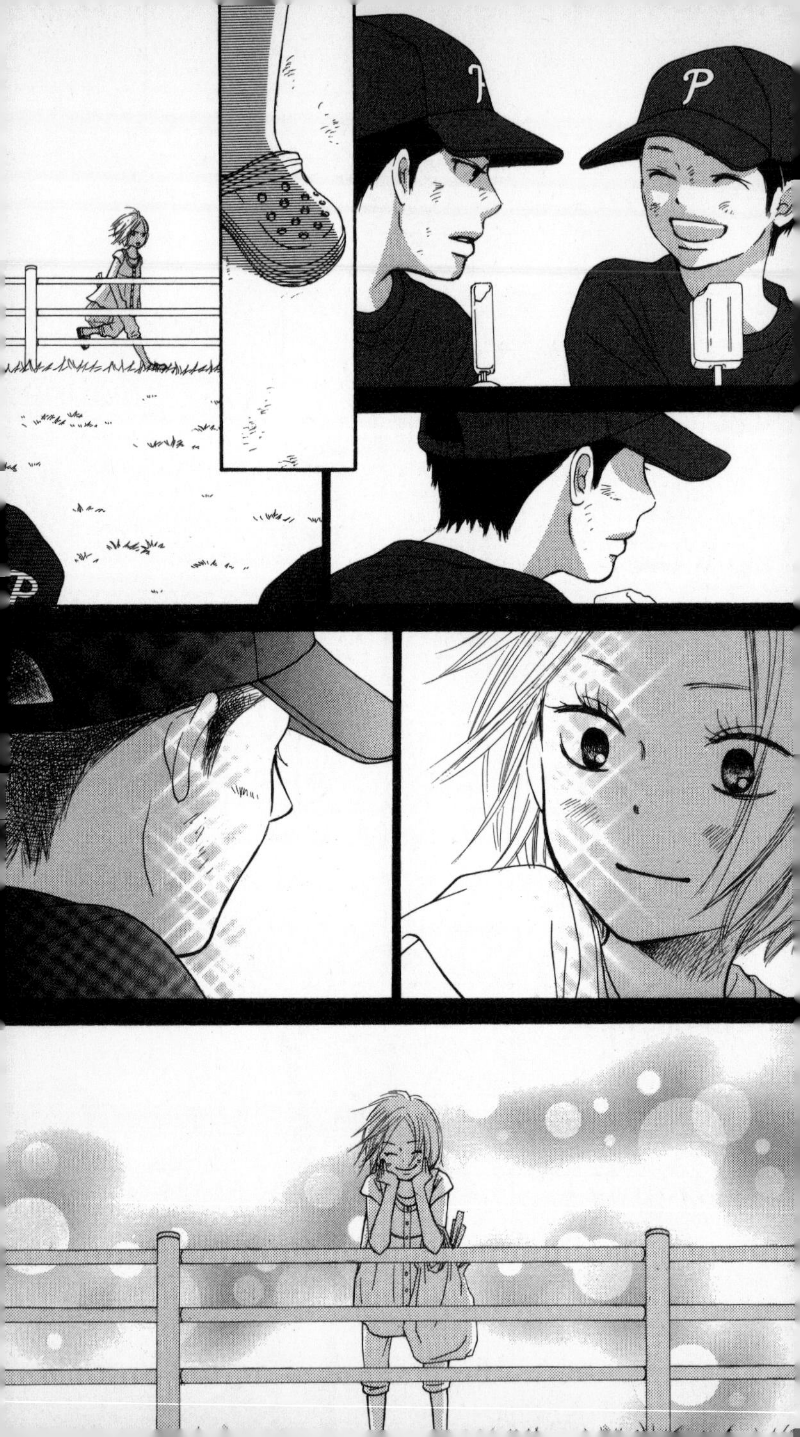

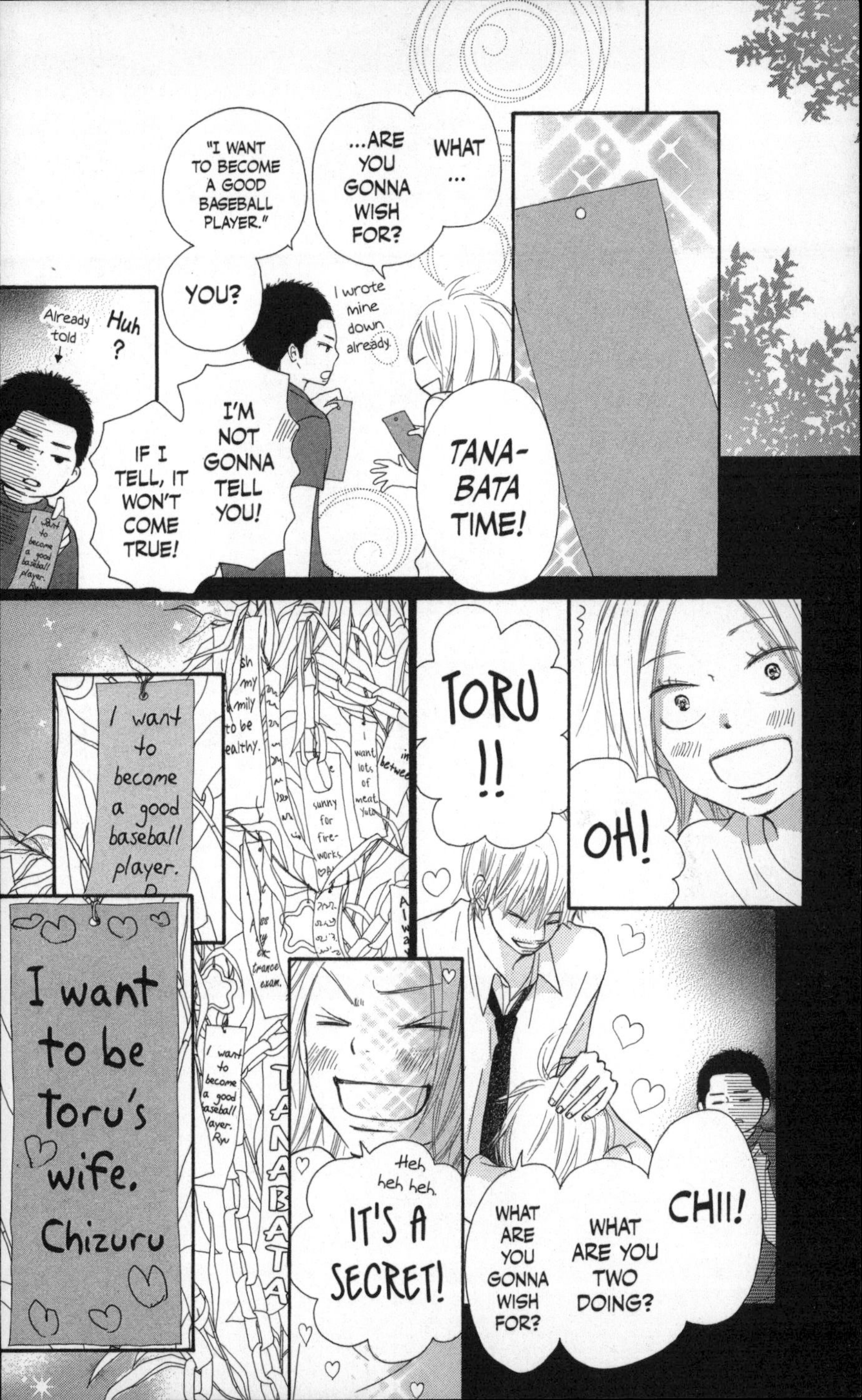

TANABATA TIME!
WHAT ...
...ARE YOU GONNA WISH FOR?
I wrote mine down already.
"I WANT TO BECOME A GOOD BASEBALL PLAYER."
YOU?
Huh?
Already told
I'M NOT GONNA TELL YOU!
IF I TELL, IT WON'T COME TRUE!
OH!
TORU!!
CHII!
WHAT ARE YOU TWO DOING?
WHAT ARE YOU GONNA WISH FOR?
Heh heh heh.
IT'S A SECRET!
TANABATA
I want lots of meat. Yuta
sunny for fire-works.
I want to become a good baseball player. Ryu
I want to become a good baseball player.
I want to be toru's wife. Chizuru

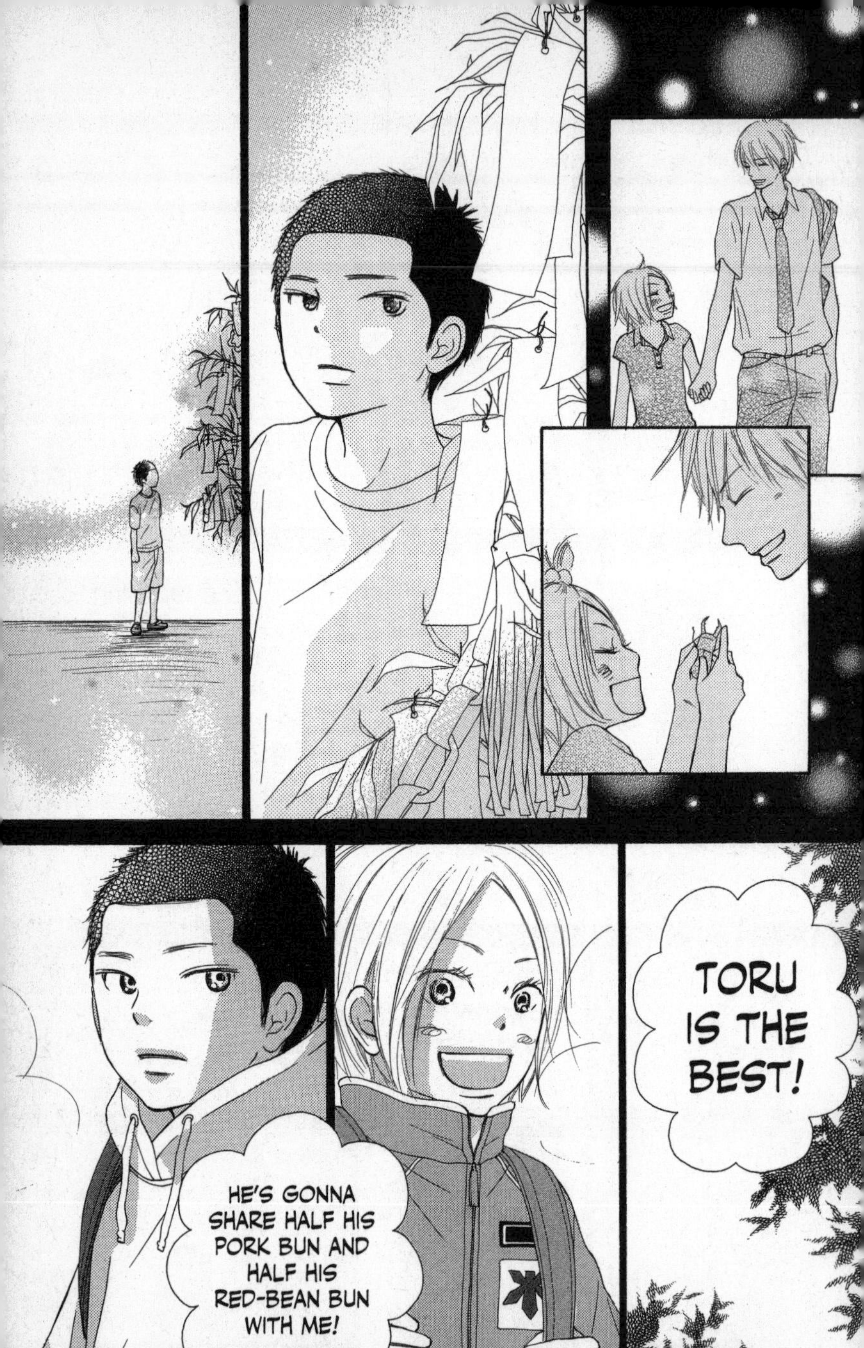
TORU IS THE BEST!
HE'S GONNA SHARE HALF HIS PORK BUN AND HALF HIS RED-BEAN BUN WITH ME!

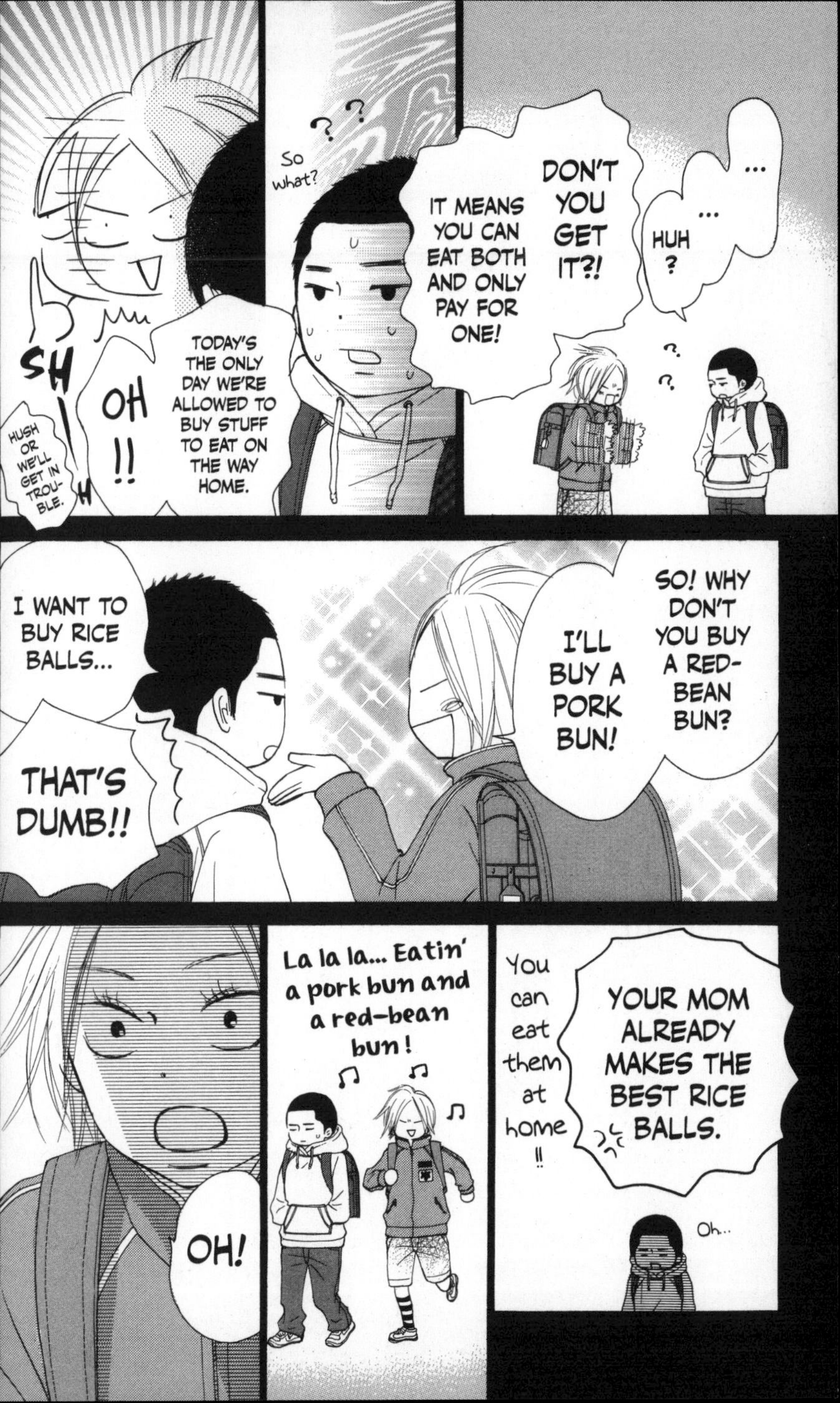
...
... HUH ?
DON'T YOU GET IT?!
IT MEANS YOU CAN EAT BOTH AND ONLY PAY FOR ONE!
So what?
TODAY'S THE ONLY DAY WE'RE ALLOWED TO BUY STUFF TO EAT ON THE WAY HOME.
OH !!
SHH
HUSH OR WE'LL GET IN TROUBLE.
SO! WHY DON'T YOU BUY A RED-BEAN BUN?
I'LL BUY A PORK BUN!
I WANT TO BUY RICE BALLS...
THAT'S DUMB!!
YOUR MOM ALREADY MAKES THE BEST RICE BALLS.
You can eat them at home !!
Oh...
La la la... Eatin' a pork bun and a red-bean bun!
OH!

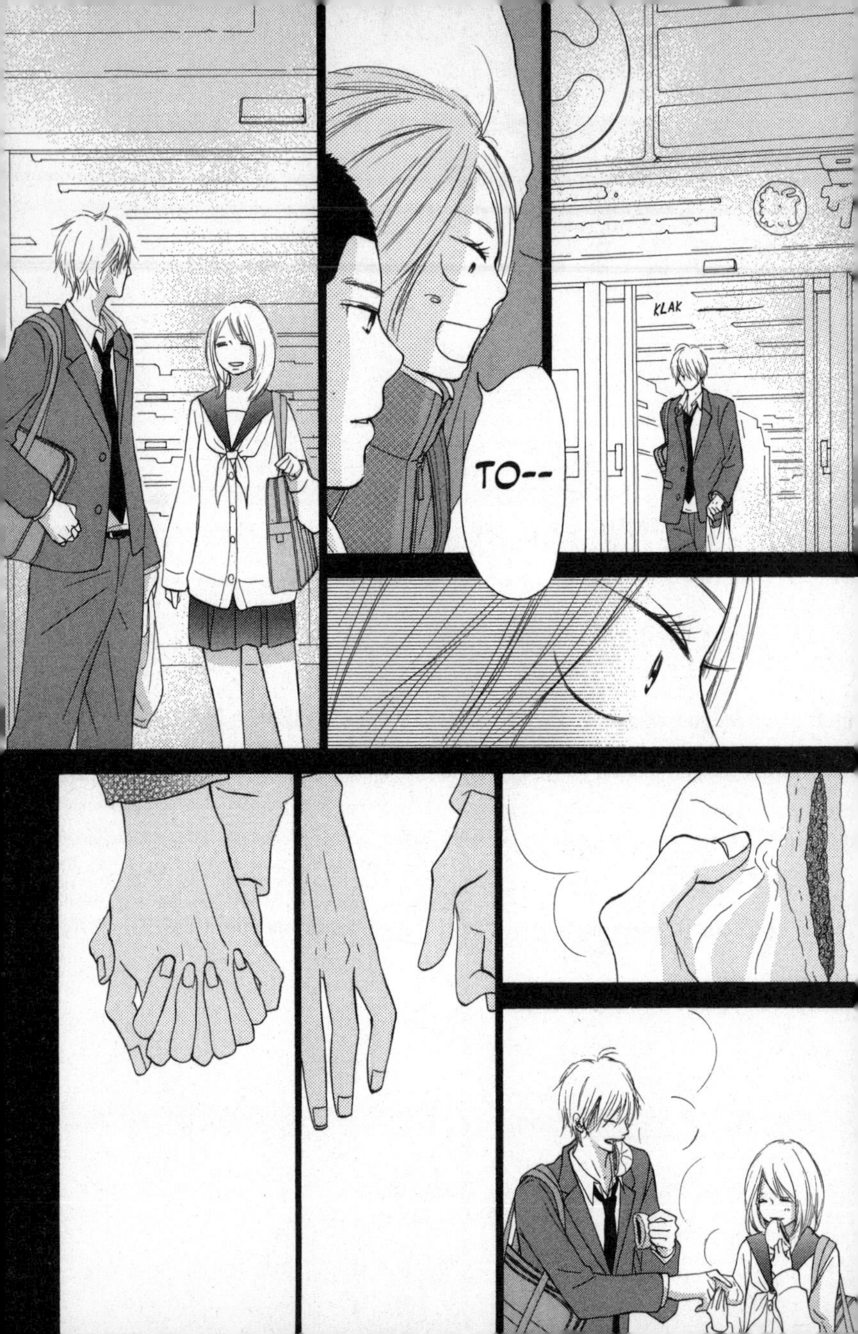
KLAK
TO--

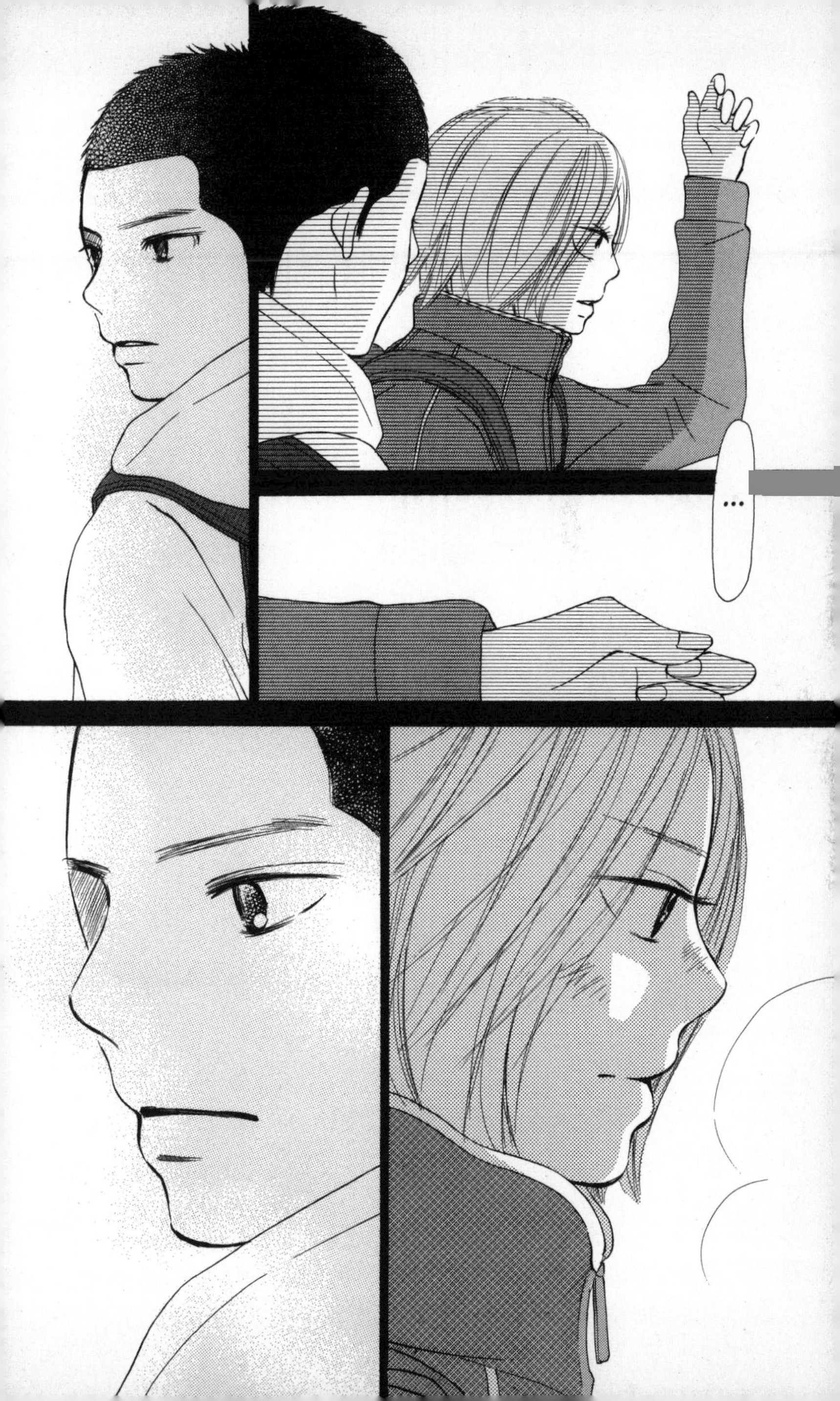
...

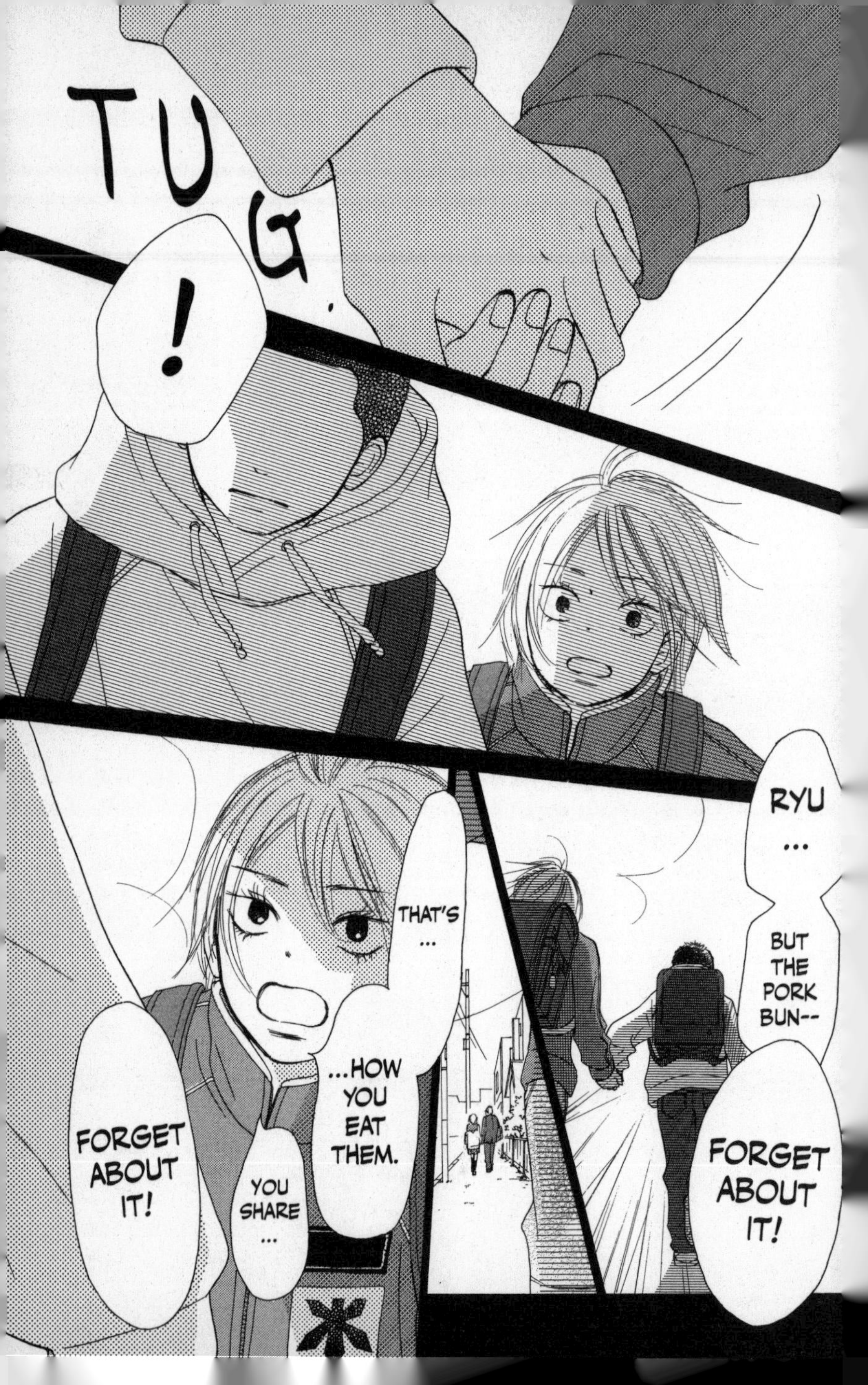
TUG
!
RYU ...
BUT THE PORK BUN--
FORGET ABOUT IT!
THAT'S ...
YOU SHARE ...
...HOW YOU EAT THEM.
FORGET ABOUT IT!

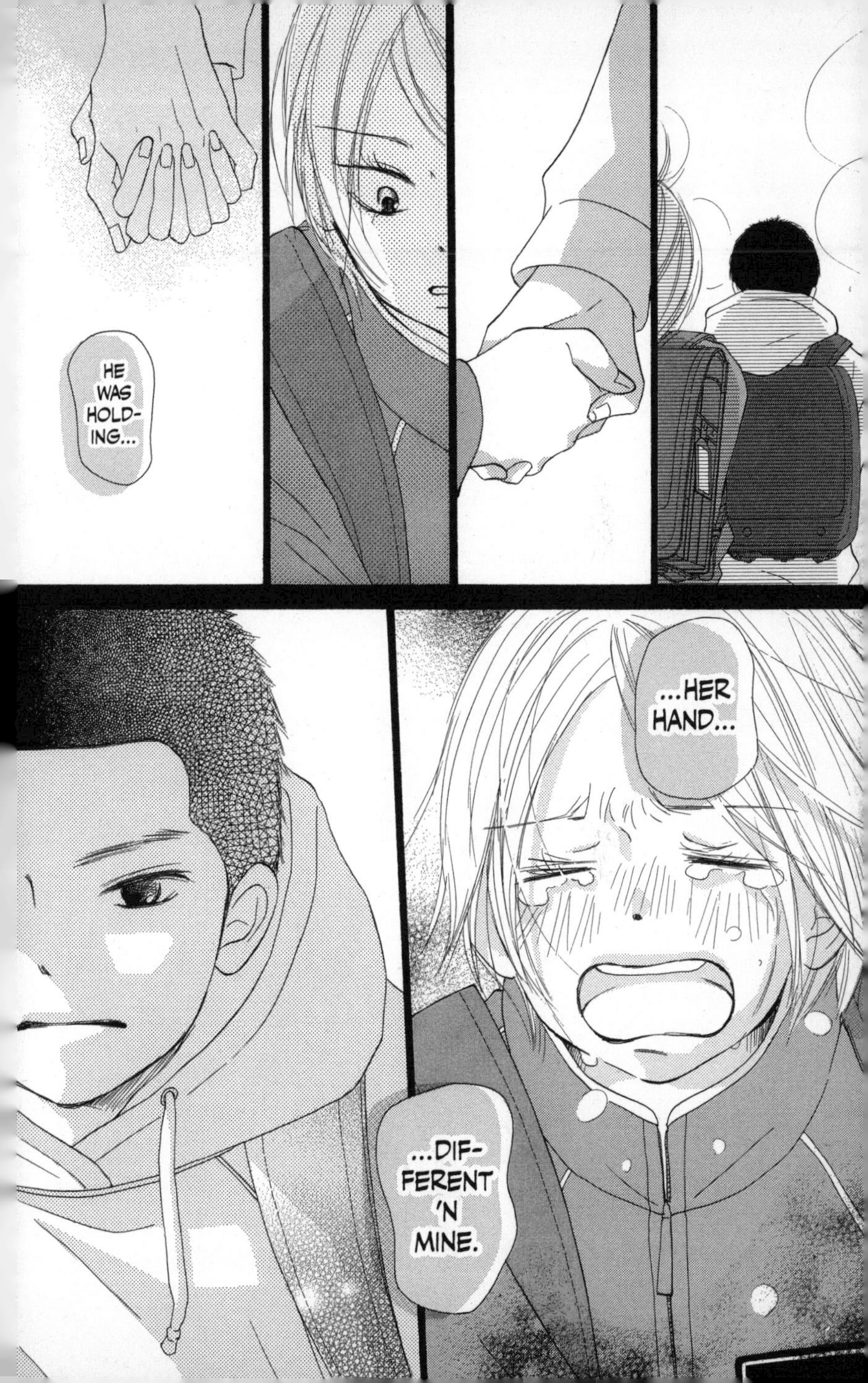
HE WAS HOLD-ING...
...HER HAND...
...DIF-FERENT 'N MINE.

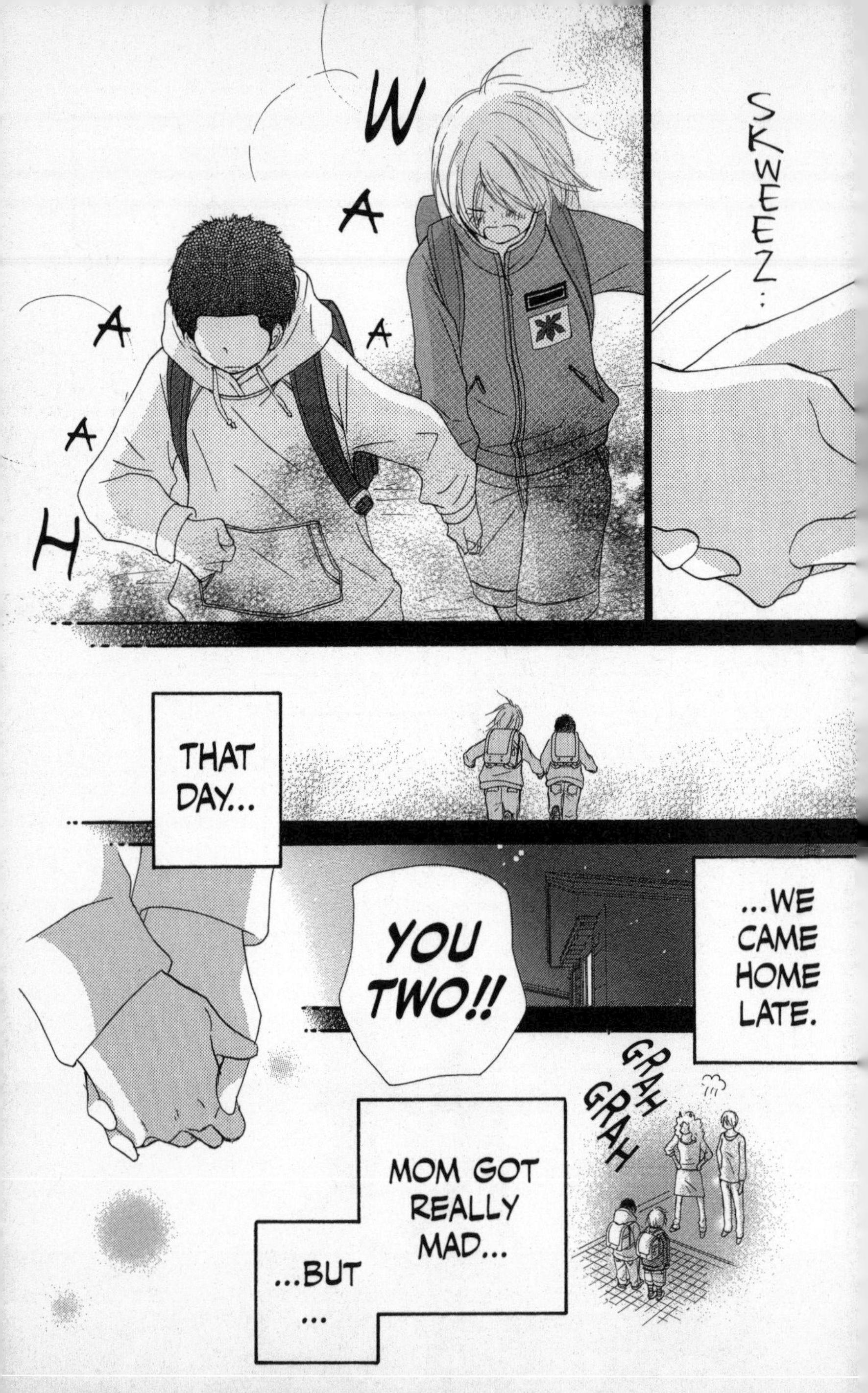
SKWEEZ...
WAAAAH
THAT DAY...
...WE CAME HOME LATE.
YOU TWO!!
GRAH GRAH
MOM GOT REALLY MAD...
...BUT ...

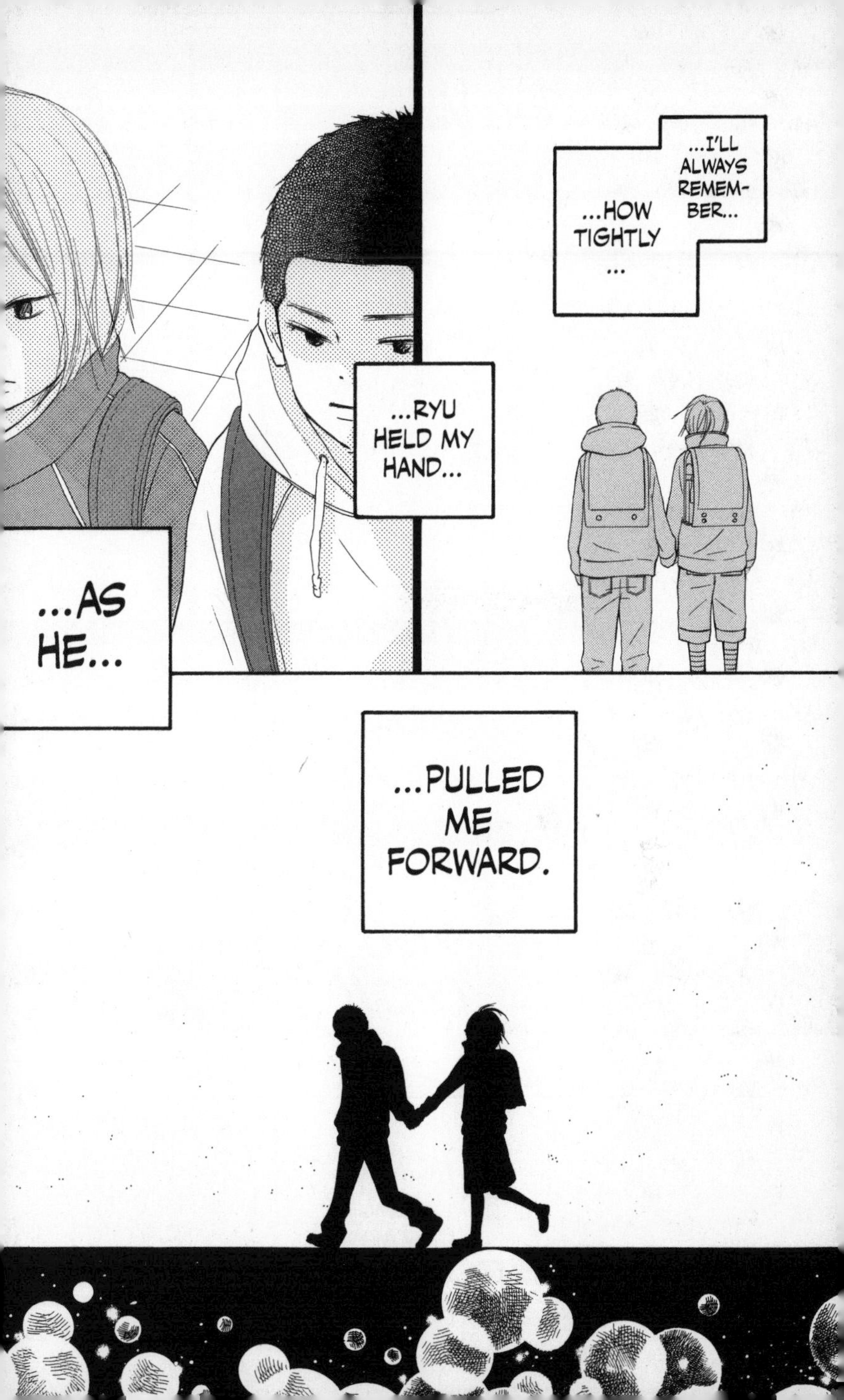
...I'LL ALWAYS REMEMBER...
...HOW TIGHTLY ...
...RYU HELD MY HAND...
...AS HE...
...PULLED ME FORWARD.

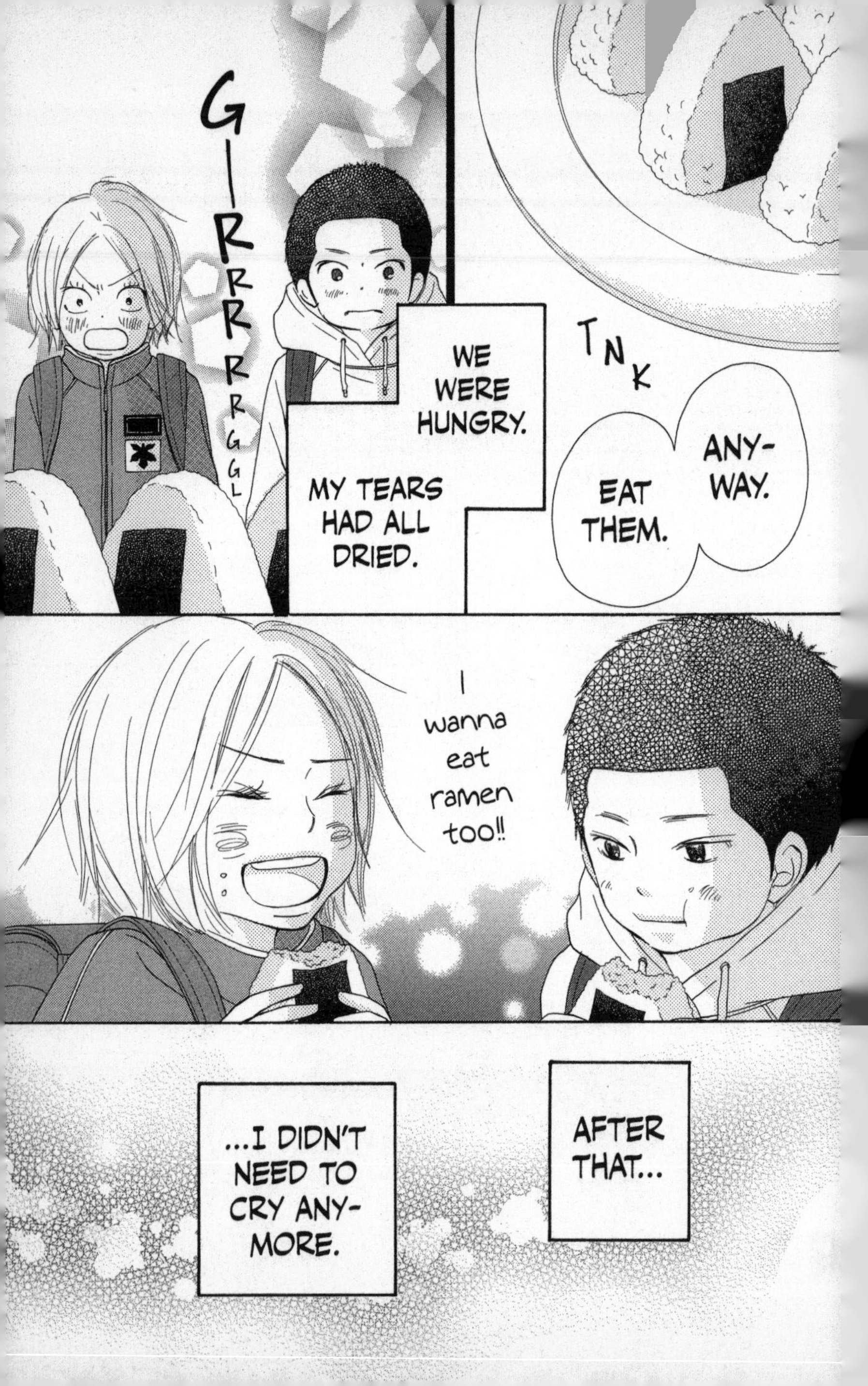
TNK
ANY-WAY. EAT THEM.
WE WERE HUNGRY.
MY TEARS HAD ALL DRIED.
GIRRRRRGGL
I wanna eat ramen too!!
AFTER THAT...
...I DIDN'T NEED TO CRY ANY-MORE.

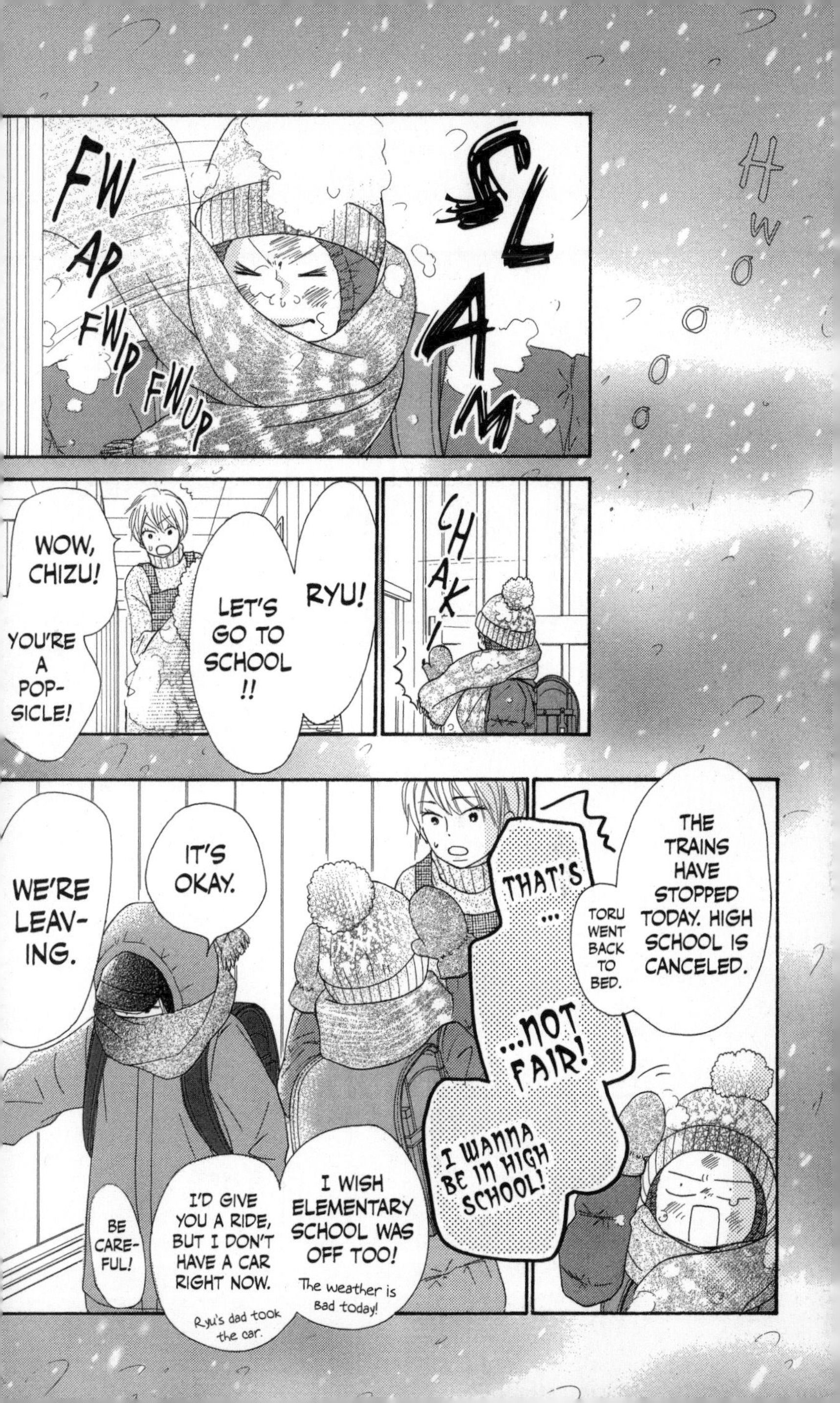
HWOOOOOO
SLAM
FWAP FWIP FWUP
CHAKI
RYU!
LET'S GO TO SCHOOL!!
WOW, CHIZU!
YOU'RE A POPSICLE!
THE TRAINS HAVE STOPPED TODAY. HIGH SCHOOL IS CANCELED.
TORU WENT BACK TO BED.
THAT'S...
...not FAIR!
I WANNA BE IN HIGH SCHOOL!
IT'S OKAY.
WE'RE LEAVING.
I WISH ELEMENTARY SCHOOL WAS OFF TOO!
The weather is Bad today!
I'D GIVE YOU A RIDE, BUT I DON'T HAVE A CAR RIGHT NOW.
Ryu's dad took the car.
BE CAREFUL!

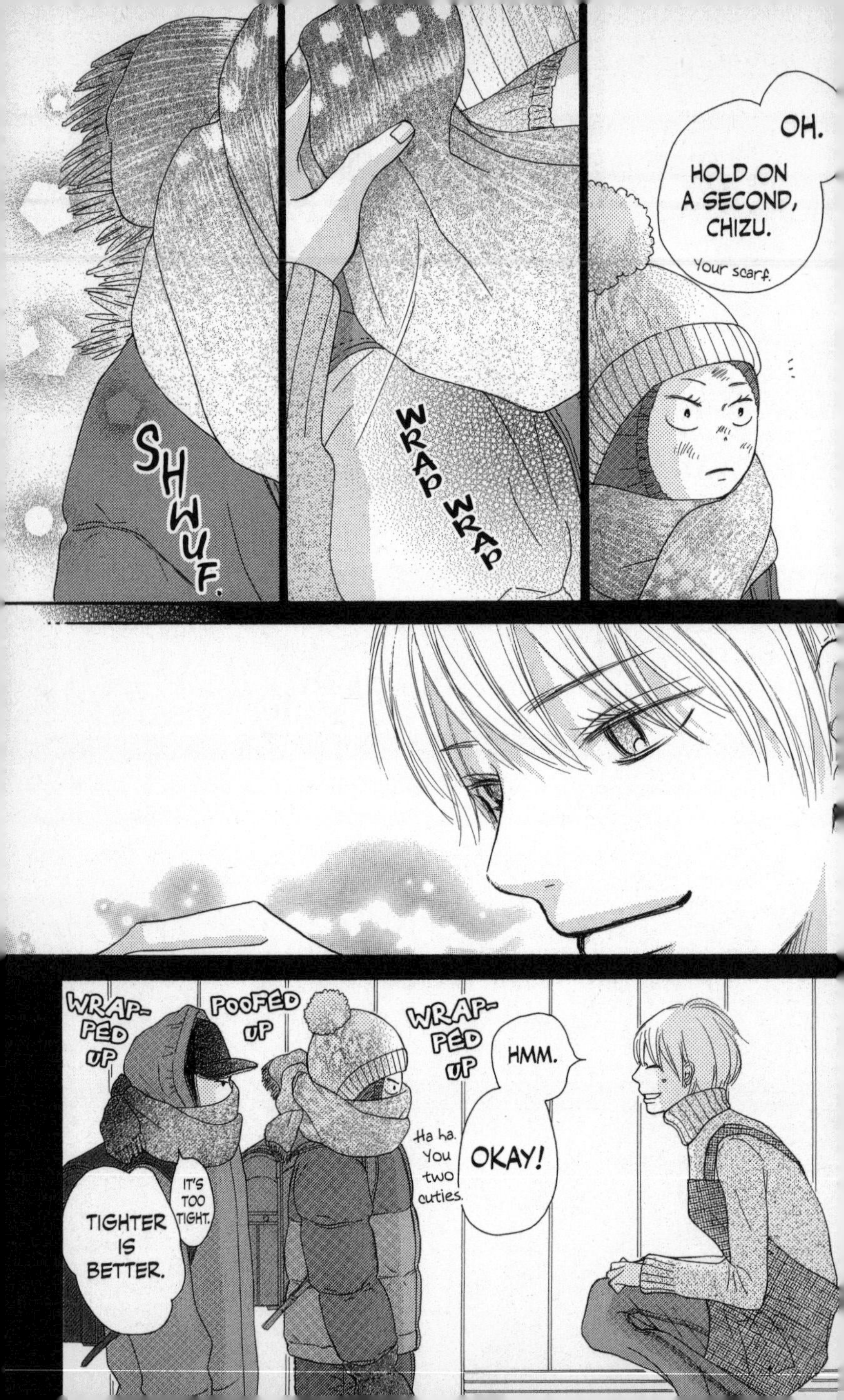
OH.
HOLD ON A SECOND, CHIZU.
Your scarf.
WRAP WRAP
SHWUF.
HMM.
OKAY!
Ha ha. You two cuties.
WRAP-PED UP
POOFED UP
WRAP-PED UP
IT'S TOO TIGHT.
TIGHTER IS BETTER.

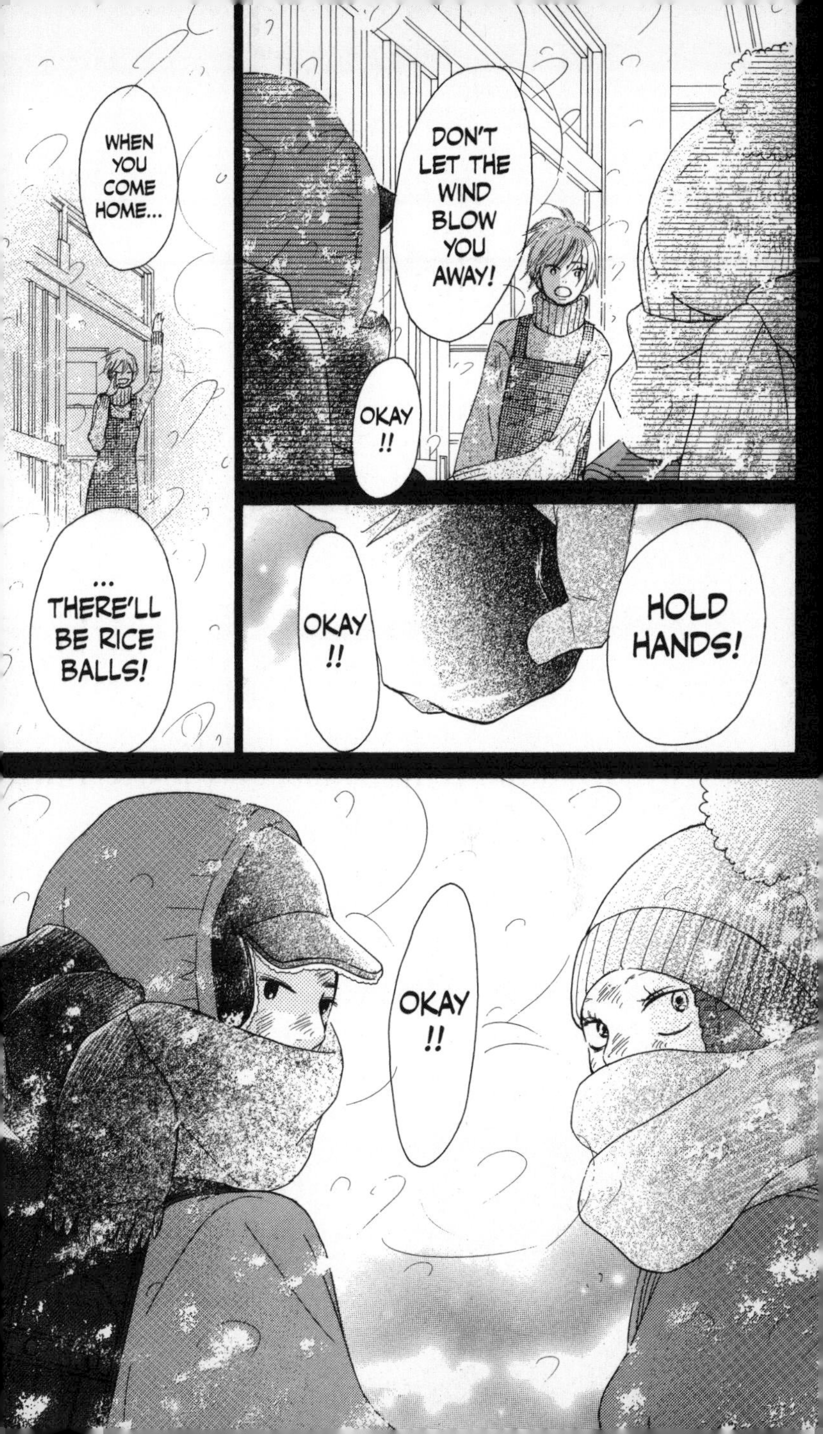
DON'T LET THE WIND BLOW YOU AWAY!
OKAY!!
HOLD HANDS!
OKAY!!
WHEN YOU COME HOME...
...THERE'LL BE RICE BALLS!
OKAY!!

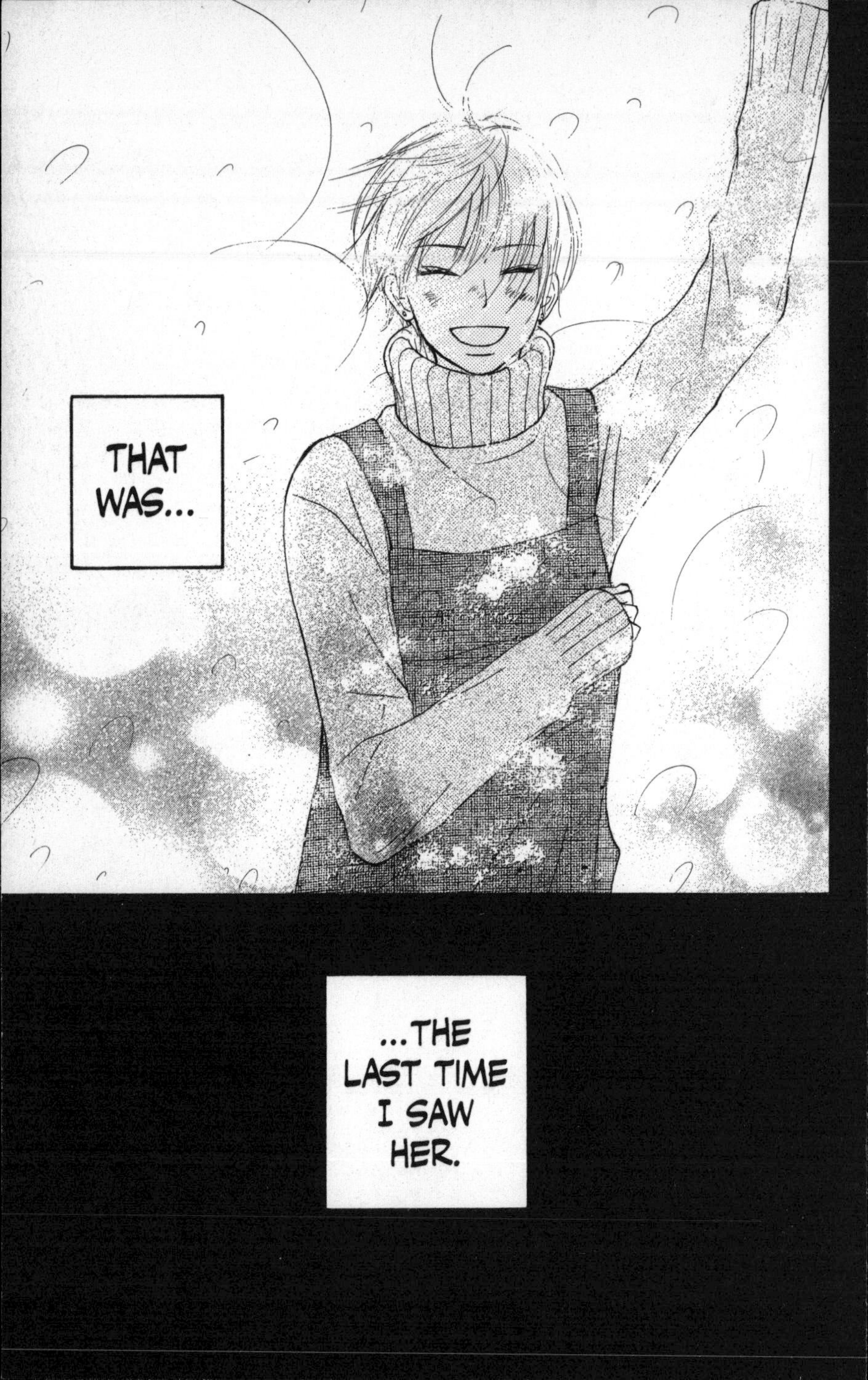
THAT WAS...
...THE LAST TIME I SAW HER.

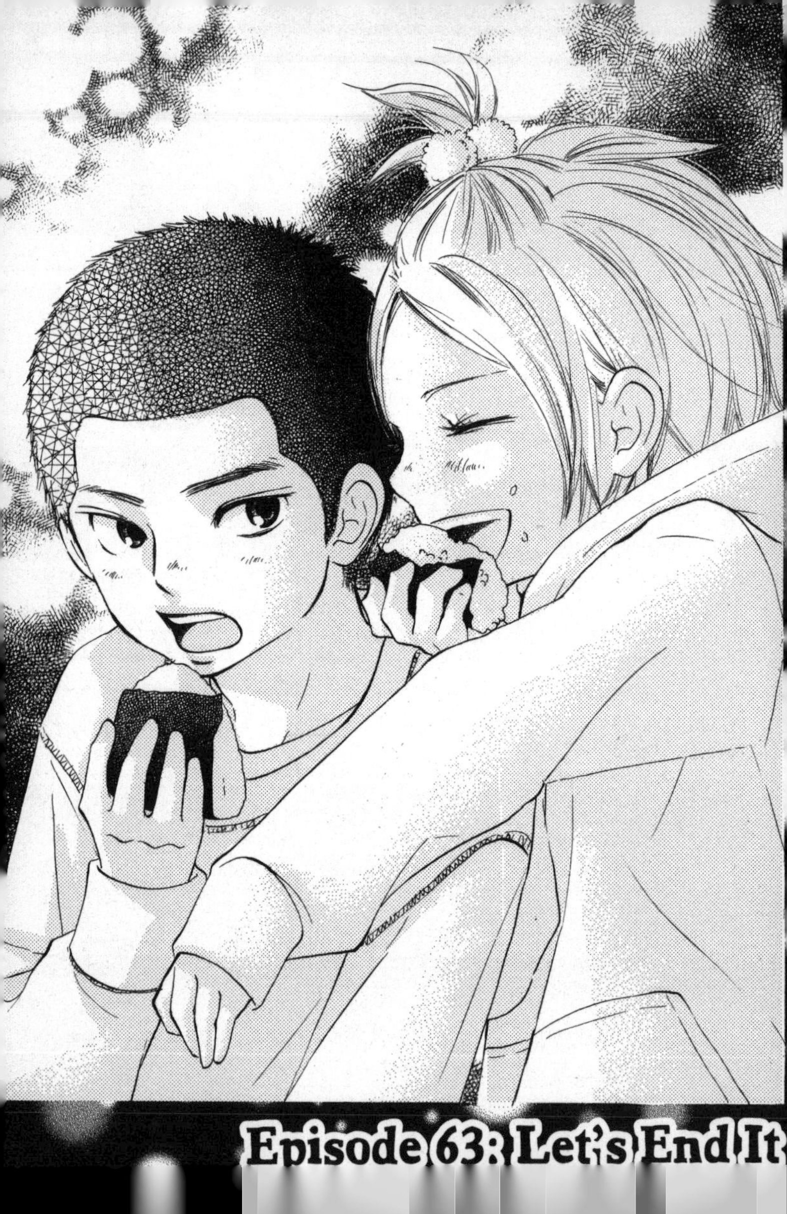

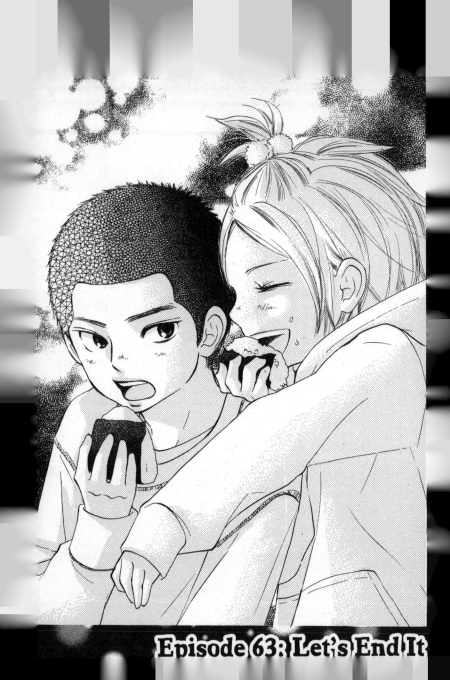

Episode 63: Let's End It

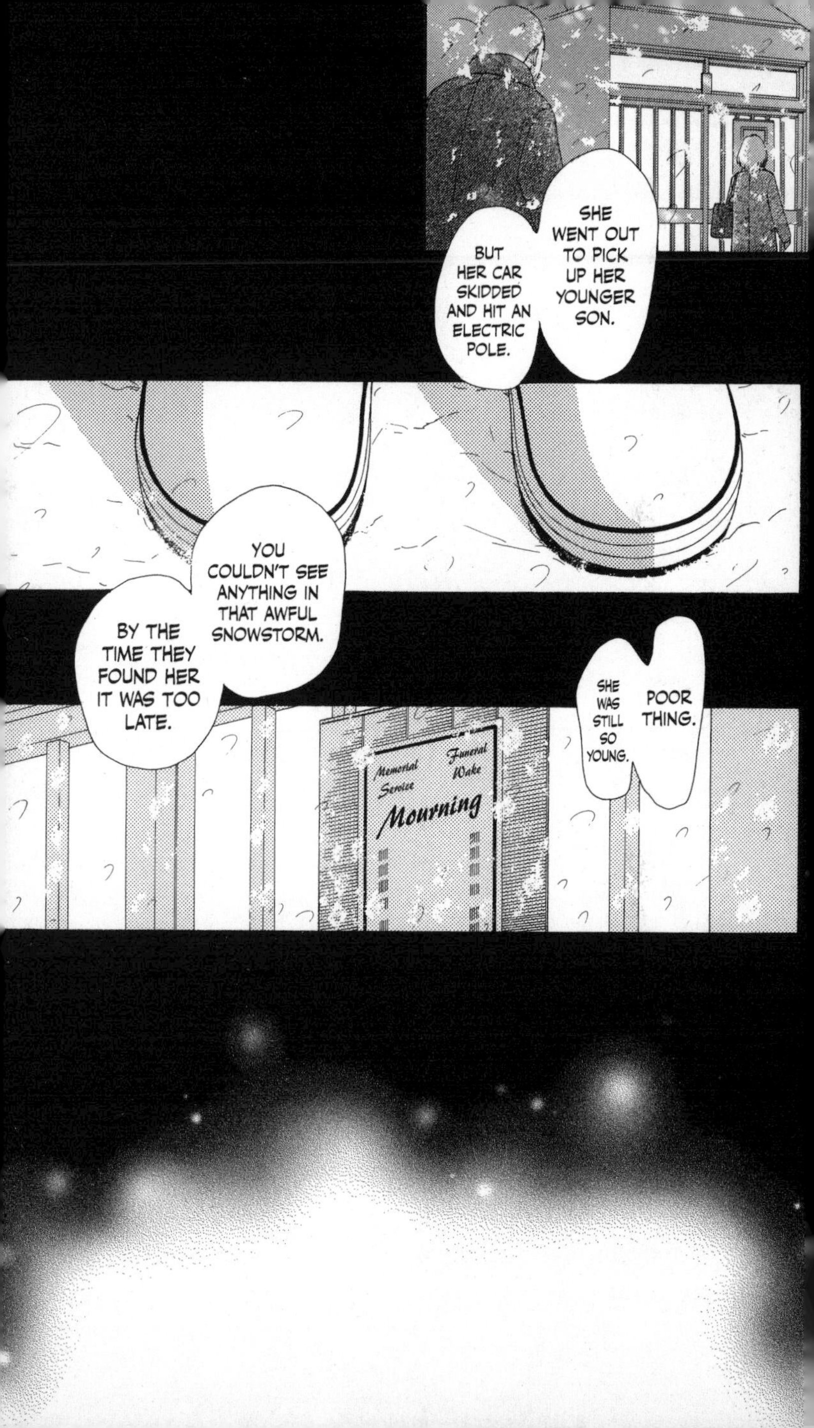
SHE WENT OUT TO PICK UP HER YOUNGER SON.
BUT HER CAR SKIDDED AND HIT AN ELECTRIC POLE.
YOU COULDN'T SEE ANYTHING IN THAT AWFUL SNOWSTORM.
BY THE TIME THEY FOUND HER IT WAS TOO LATE.
POOR THING.
SHE WAS STILL SO YOUNG.
Funeral Wake
Memorial Service
Mourning

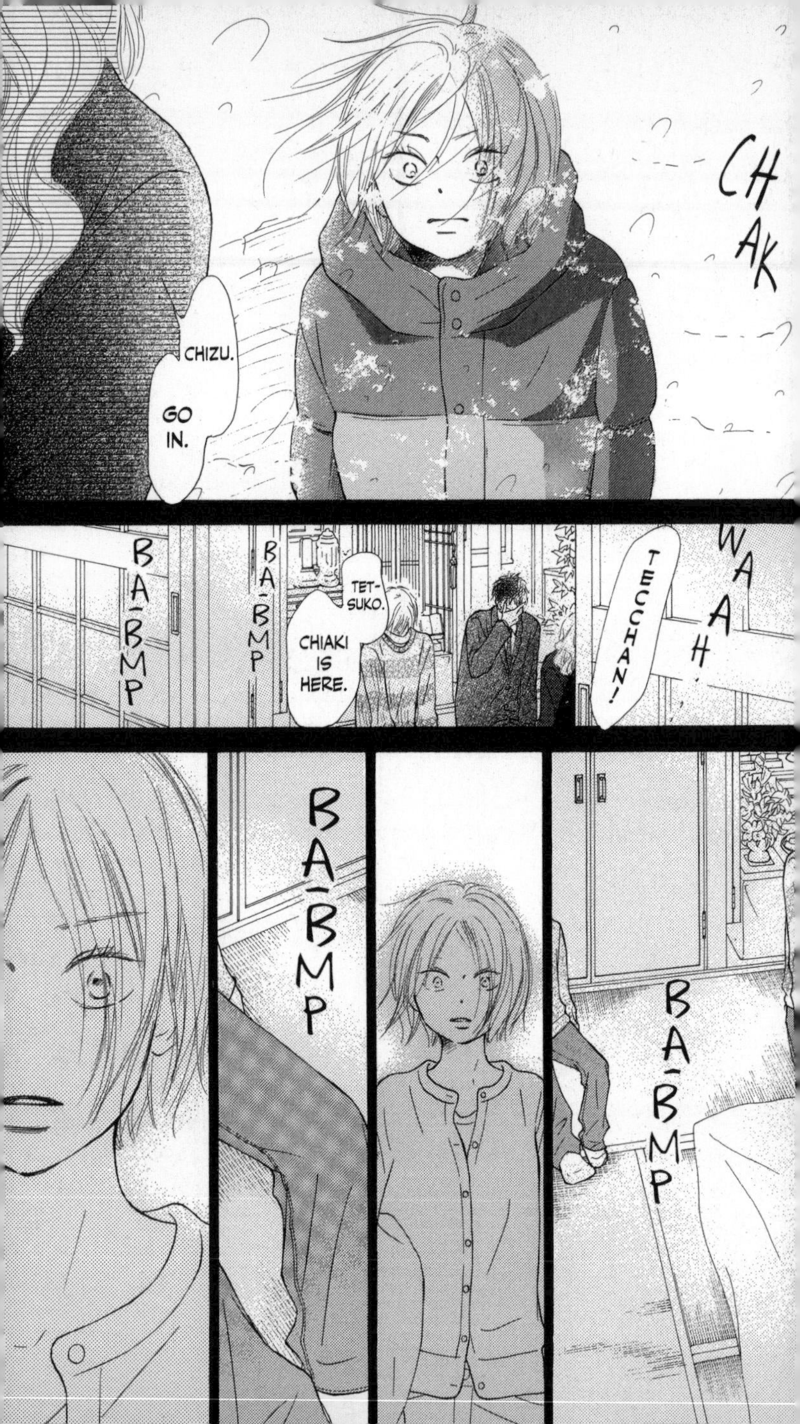
CHAK
CHIZU.
GO IN.
WAAH!
TECCHAN!
TET-SUKO.
CHIAKI IS HERE.
BA-BMP
BA-BMP
BA-BMP
BA-BMP

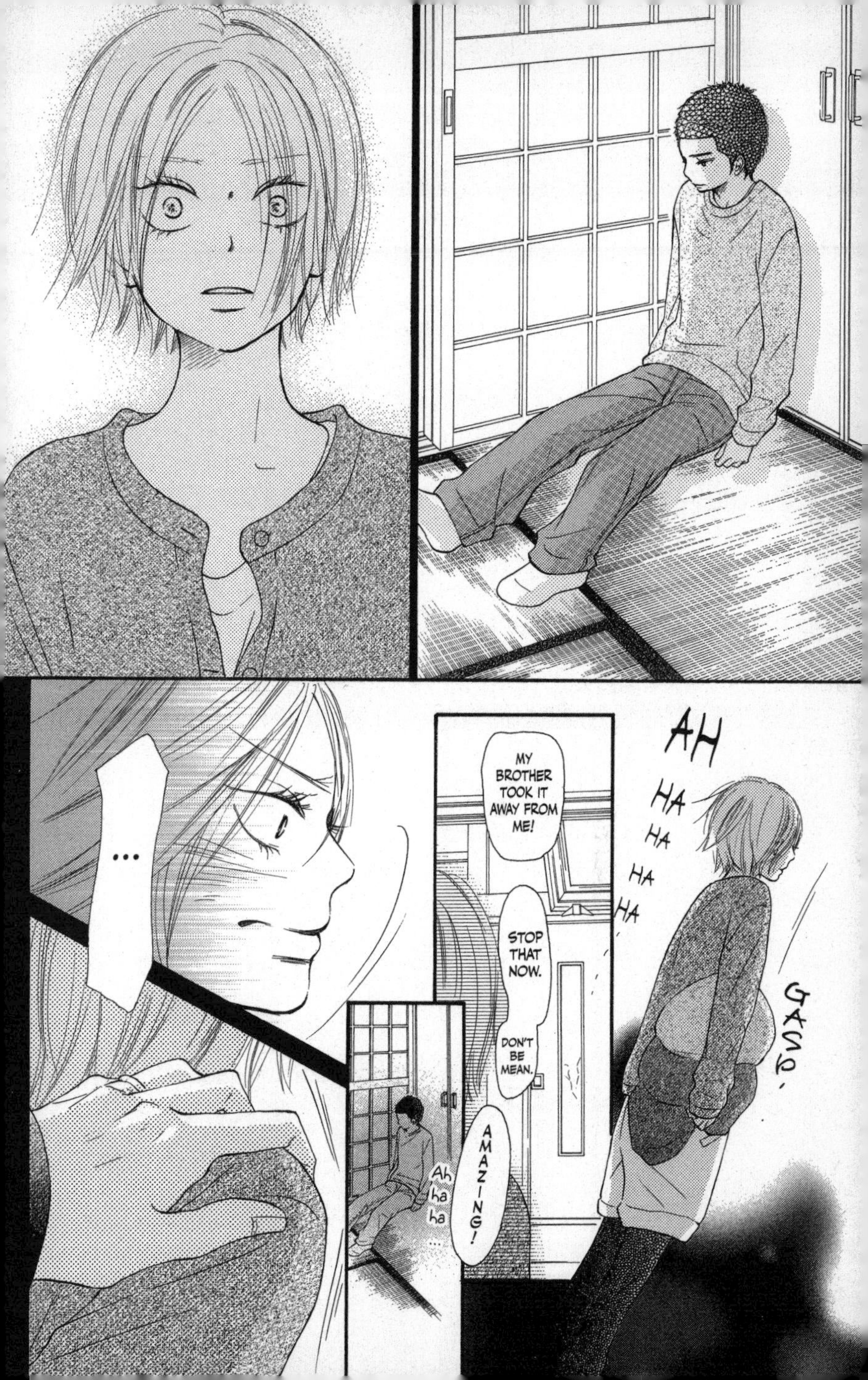
AH
HA
HA
HA
HA
GASP
MY BROTHER TOOK IT AWAY FROM ME!
STOP THAT NOW.
DON'T BE MEAN.
AMAZING!
Ah ha ha ...
...

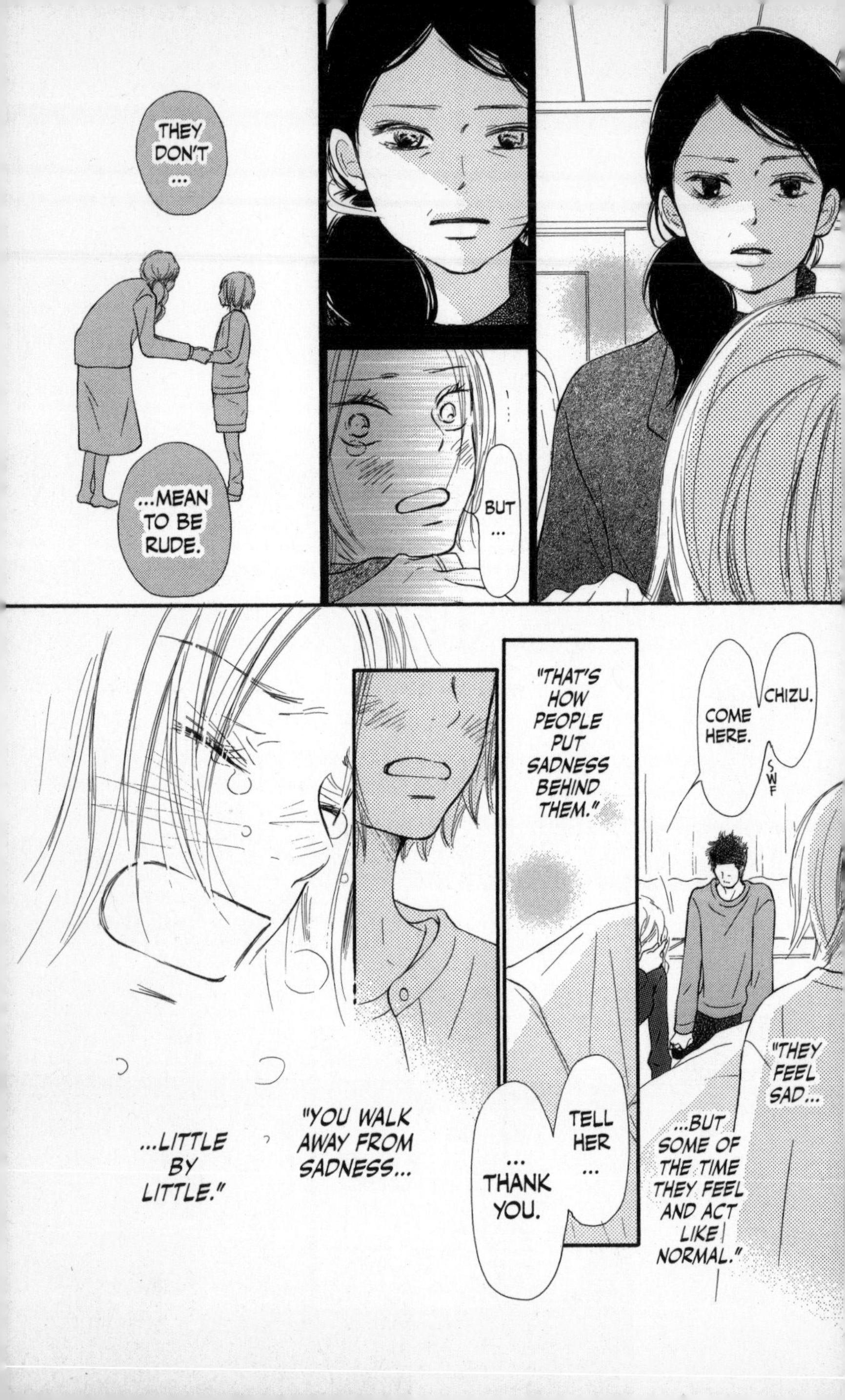
BUT ...
THEY DON'T ...
...MEAN TO BE RUDE.
CHIZU.
COME HERE.
SWF
"THEY FEEL SAD...
...BUT SOME OF THE TIME THEY FEEL AND ACT LIKE NORMAL."
"THAT'S HOW PEOPLE PUT SADNESS BEHIND THEM."
TELL HER ...
... THANK YOU.
"YOU WALK AWAY FROM SADNESS...
...LITTLE BY LITTLE."

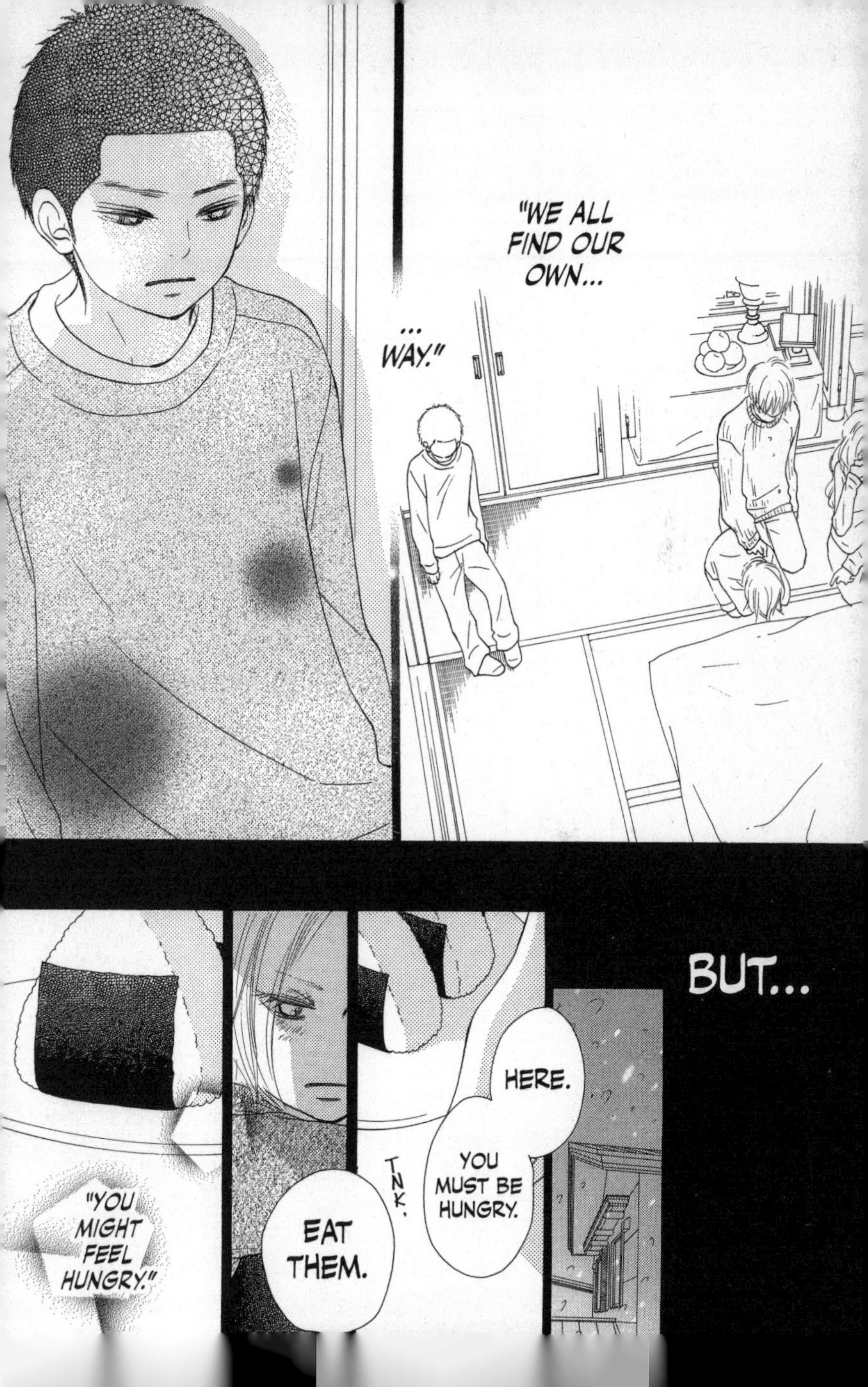
"WE ALL FIND OUR OWN...
... WAY."
BUT...
HERE.
YOU MUST BE HUNGRY.
TNK.
EAT THEM.
"YOU MIGHT FEEL HUNGRY."

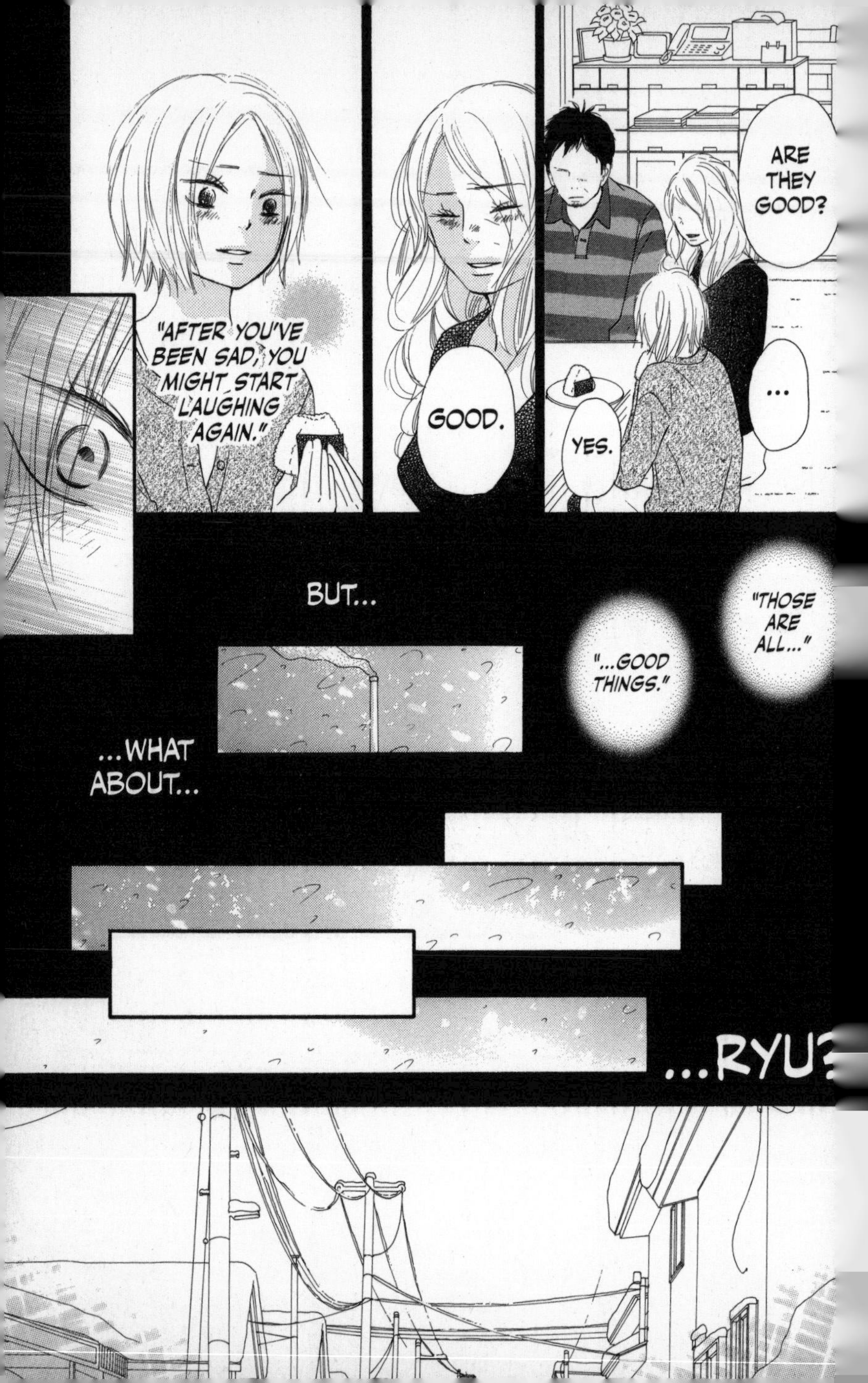
ARE THEY GOOD?
...
YES.
GOOD.
"AFTER YOU'VE BEEN SAD, YOU MIGHT START LAUGHING AGAIN."
"THOSE ARE ALL..."
"...GOOD THINGS."
BUT...
...WHAT ABOUT...
...RYU?

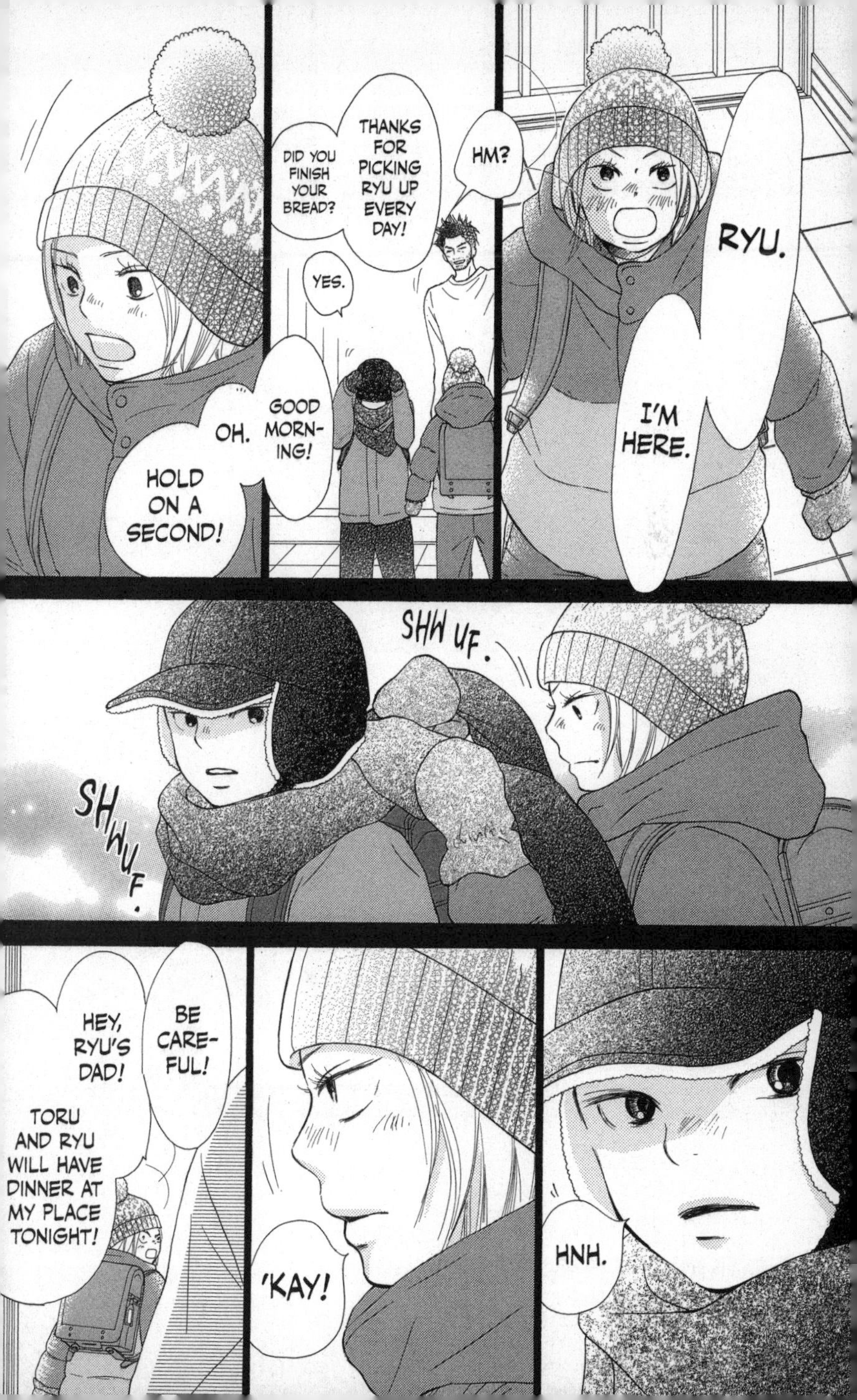
RYU.
I'M HERE.
HM?
THANKS FOR PICKING RYU UP EVERY DAY!
DID YOU FINISH YOUR BREAD?
YES.
GOOD MORNING!
OH.
HOLD ON A SECOND!
SHW UF.
SHWUF.
HNH.
'KAY!
BE CAREFUL!
HEY, RYU'S DAD!
TORU AND RYU WILL HAVE DINNER AT MY PLACE TONIGHT!

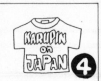

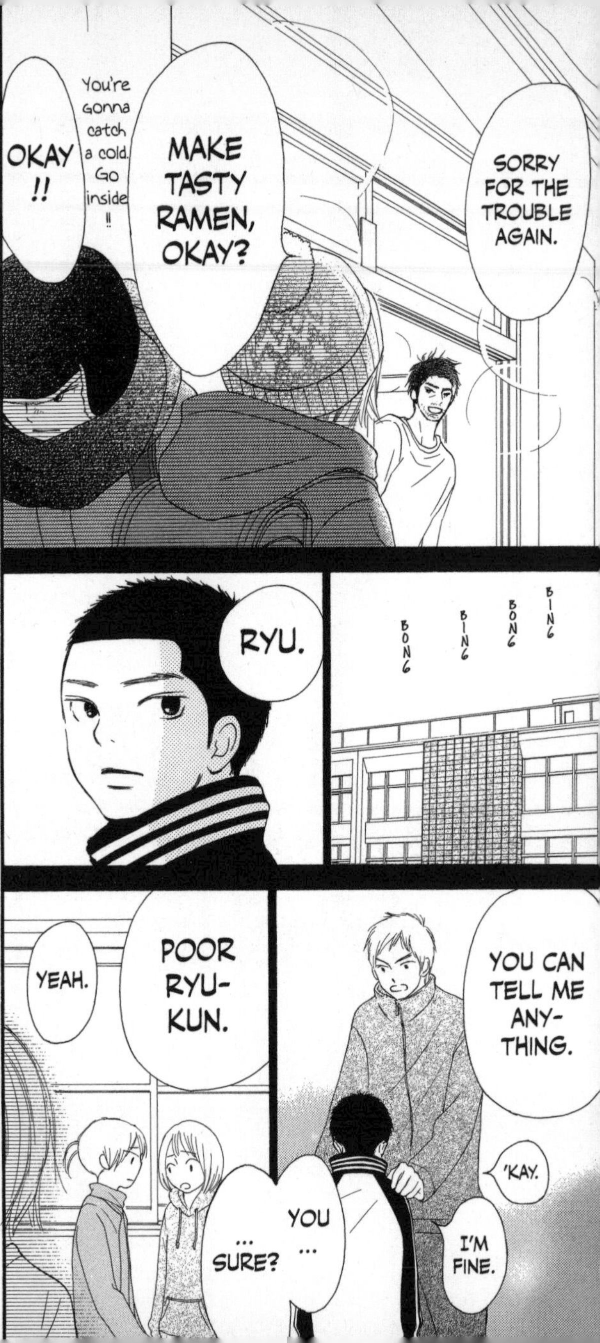
SORRY FOR THE TROUBLE AGAIN.
MAKE TASTY RAMEN, OKAY?
You're gonna catch a cold. Go inside!!
OKAY!!
BING BONG BING BONG
RYU.
YOU CAN TELL ME ANYTHING.
'KAY.
I'M FINE.
POOR RYU-KUN.
YEAH.
YOU ...
... SURE?

KARUPIN on JAPAN 4

Recently, I've been playing DVDs while I work. They're on in the background, so I hear them more than see them. I process some parts but not others, so I watch the same DVD a few times. I haven't watched many TV shows, but there are plenty of fun ones out there!! I really enjoyed *Wagahai wa Shufu de Aru* (I Am a Housewife).

Also, I never finished the anime of *Anne of Green Gables*. (Although it was always on air, I always seemed to tune in for the same episodes.)

Especially the one about strawberry juice.

When I sat down and watched it, it was really good! It was hard to believe that the characters in both *Wagahai* and *Anne* don't actually exist. They're alive inside of me. What great stuff.

Watching Anne grow up was a bittersweet feeling... Oh, is this the end of the sidebars already?! How'd that happen?! Please look forward to the next volume!

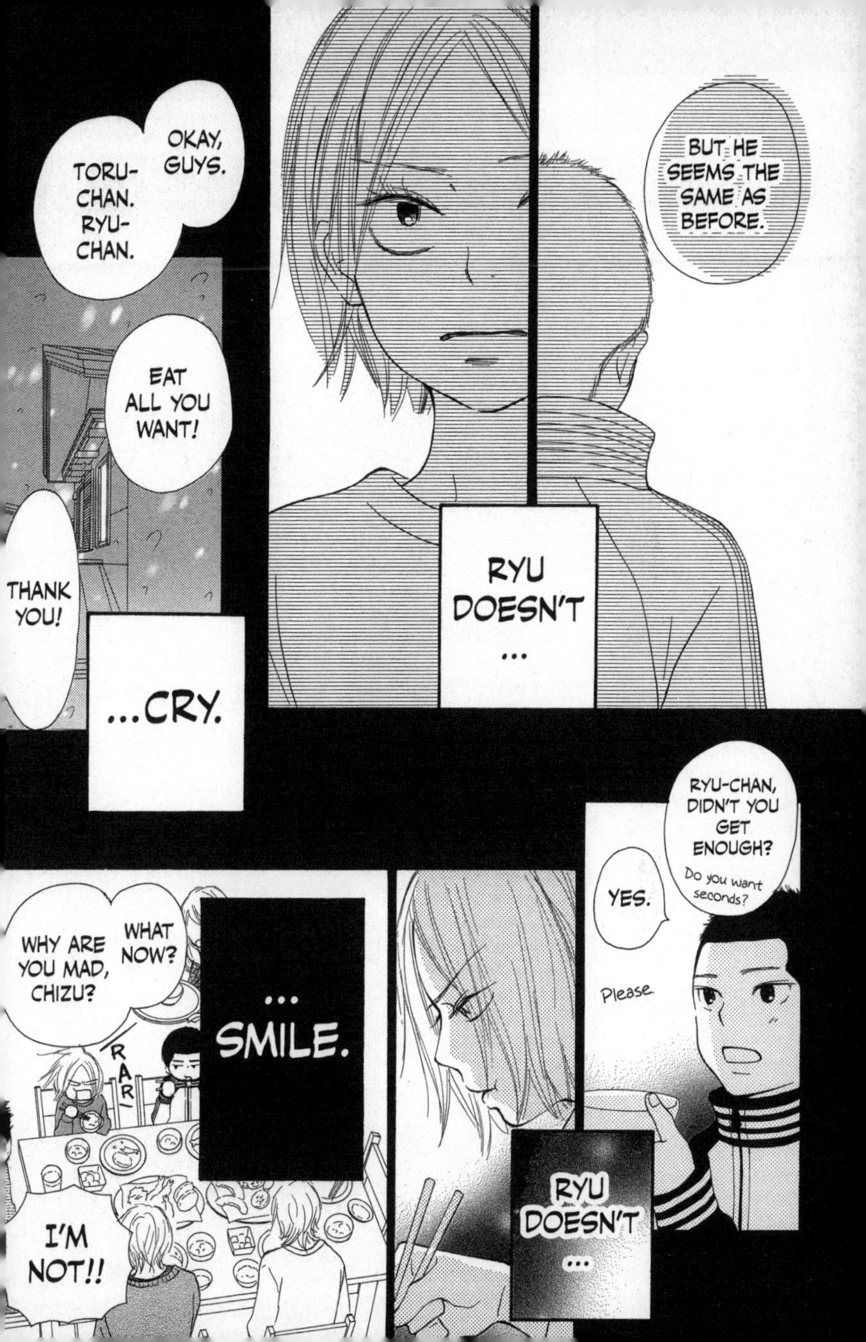
BUT HE SEEMS THE SAME AS BEFORE.
RYU DOESN'T ...
OKAY, GUYS.
TORU-CHAN. RYU-CHAN.
EAT ALL YOU WANT!
THANK YOU!
...CRY.
RYU-CHAN, DIDN'T YOU GET ENOUGH?
Do you want seconds?
YES.
Please.
RYU DOESN'T ...
... SMILE.
WHAT NOW?
WHY ARE YOU MAD, CHIZU?
RAR
I'M NOT!!

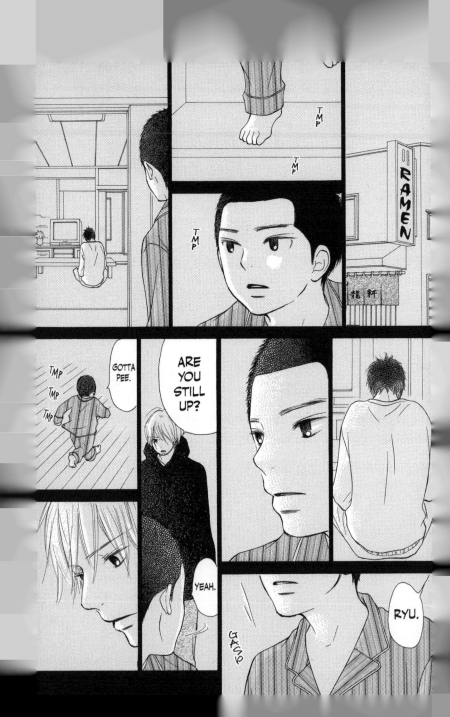

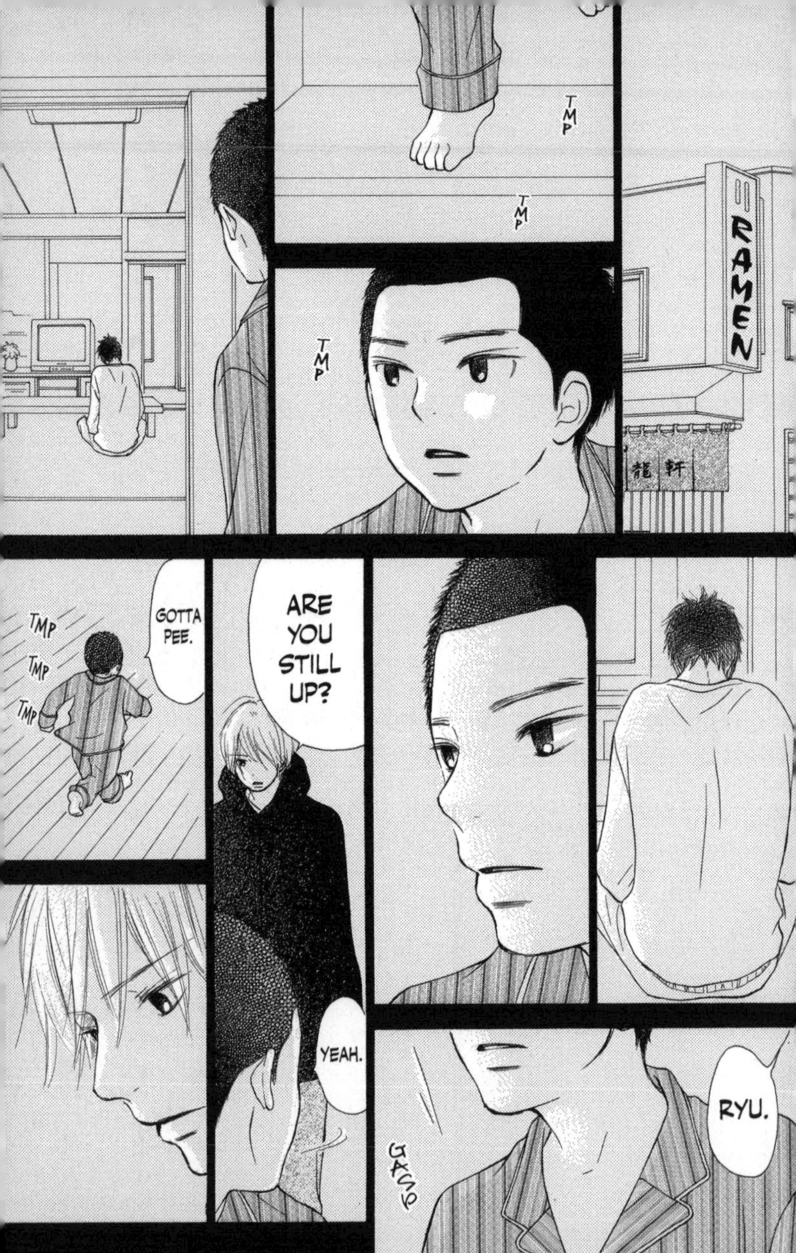
RAMEN
龍 軒
TMP
TMP
TMP
RYU.
GASP
ARE YOU STILL UP?
YEAH.
GOTTA PEE.
TMP
TMP
TMP

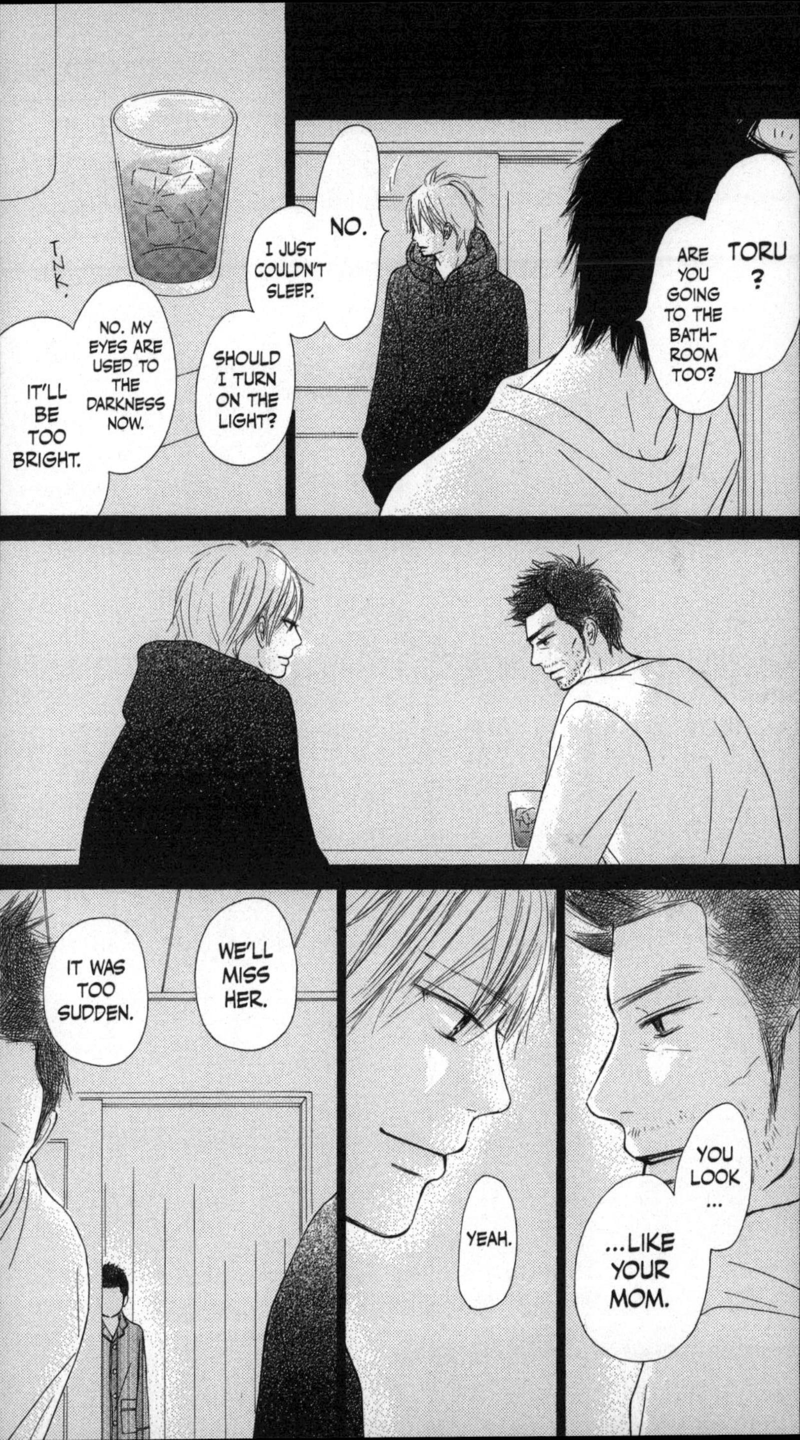
TORU?
ARE YOU GOING TO THE BATHROOM TOO?
NO.
I JUST COULDN'T SLEEP.
SHOULD I TURN ON THE LIGHT?
NO. MY EYES ARE USED TO THE DARKNESS NOW.
IT'LL BE TOO BRIGHT.
TNK.
YOU LOOK...
...LIKE YOUR MOM.
YEAH.
WE'LL MISS HER.
IT WAS TOO SUDDEN.

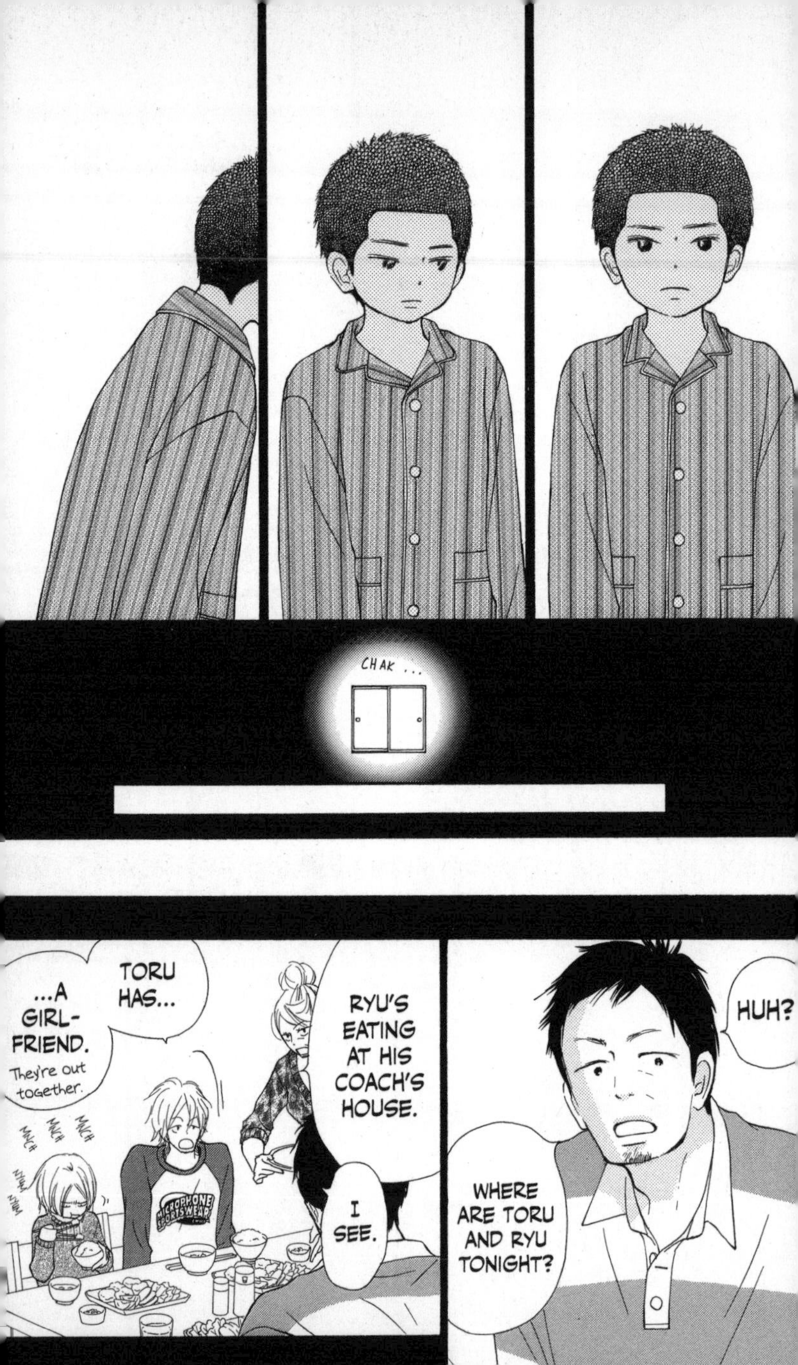
CHAK ...
HUH?
WHERE ARE TORU AND RYU TONIGHT?
RYU'S EATING AT HIS COACH'S HOUSE.
I SEE.
TORU HAS...
...A GIRL-FRIEND.
They're out together.
MNCH MNCH MNCH
MICROPHONE SPORTSWEAR

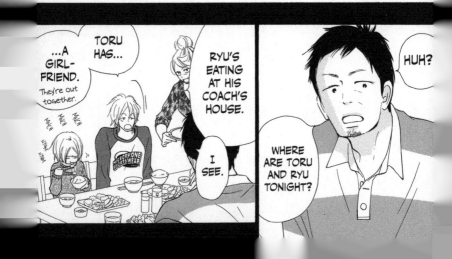

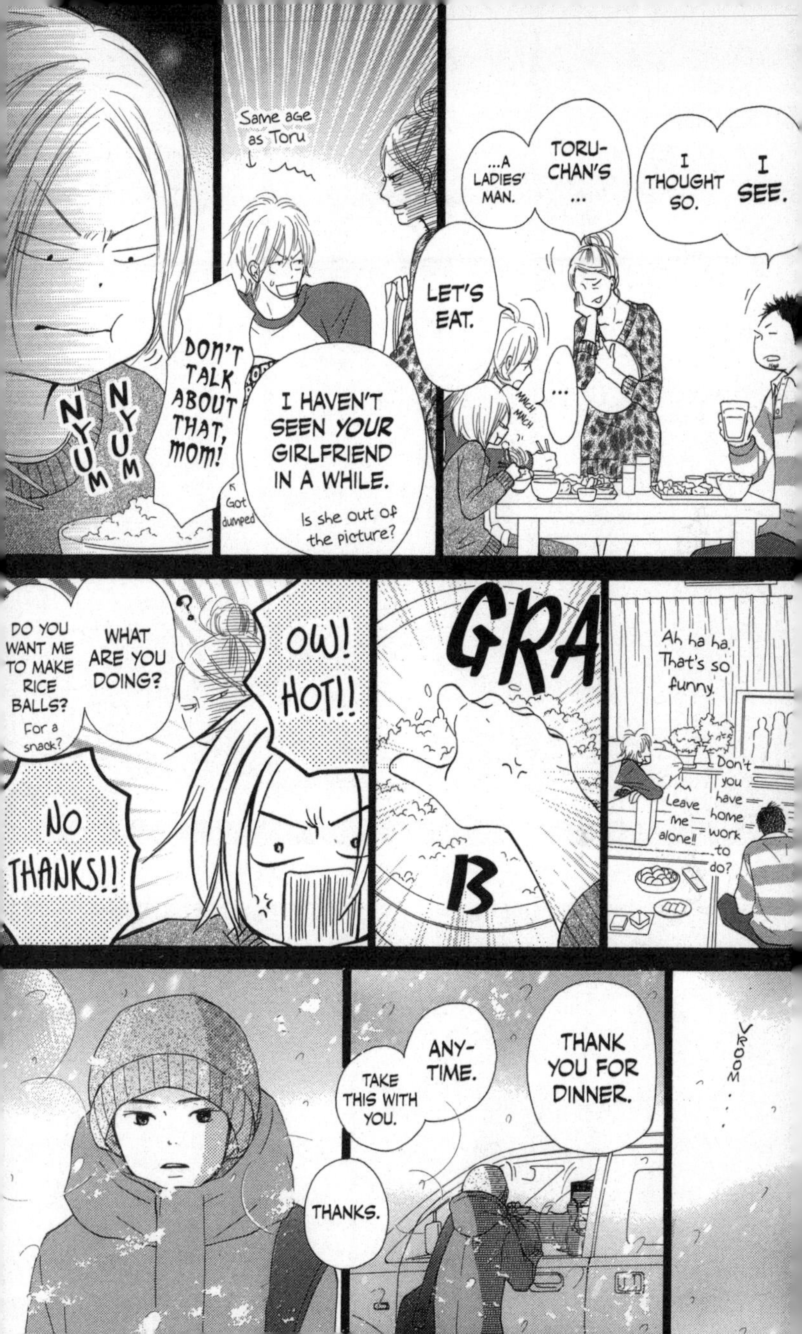
I SEE.
I THOUGHT SO.
TORU-CHAN'S...
...A LADIES' MAN.
LET'S EAT.
MNCH MNCH
...
Same age as Toru
I HAVEN'T SEEN *YOUR* GIRLFRIEND IN A WHILE.
Is she out of the picture?
DON'T TALK ABOUT THAT, MOM!
Got dumped
NYUM NYUM
Ah ha ha. That's so funny.
Don't you have homework to do?
Leave me alone!!
GRAB
OW! HOT!!
WHAT ARE YOU DOING?
DO YOU WANT ME TO MAKE RICE BALLS?
For a snack?
NO THANKS!!
VROOM...
THANK YOU FOR DINNER.
ANY-TIME.
TAKE THIS WITH YOU.
THANKS.

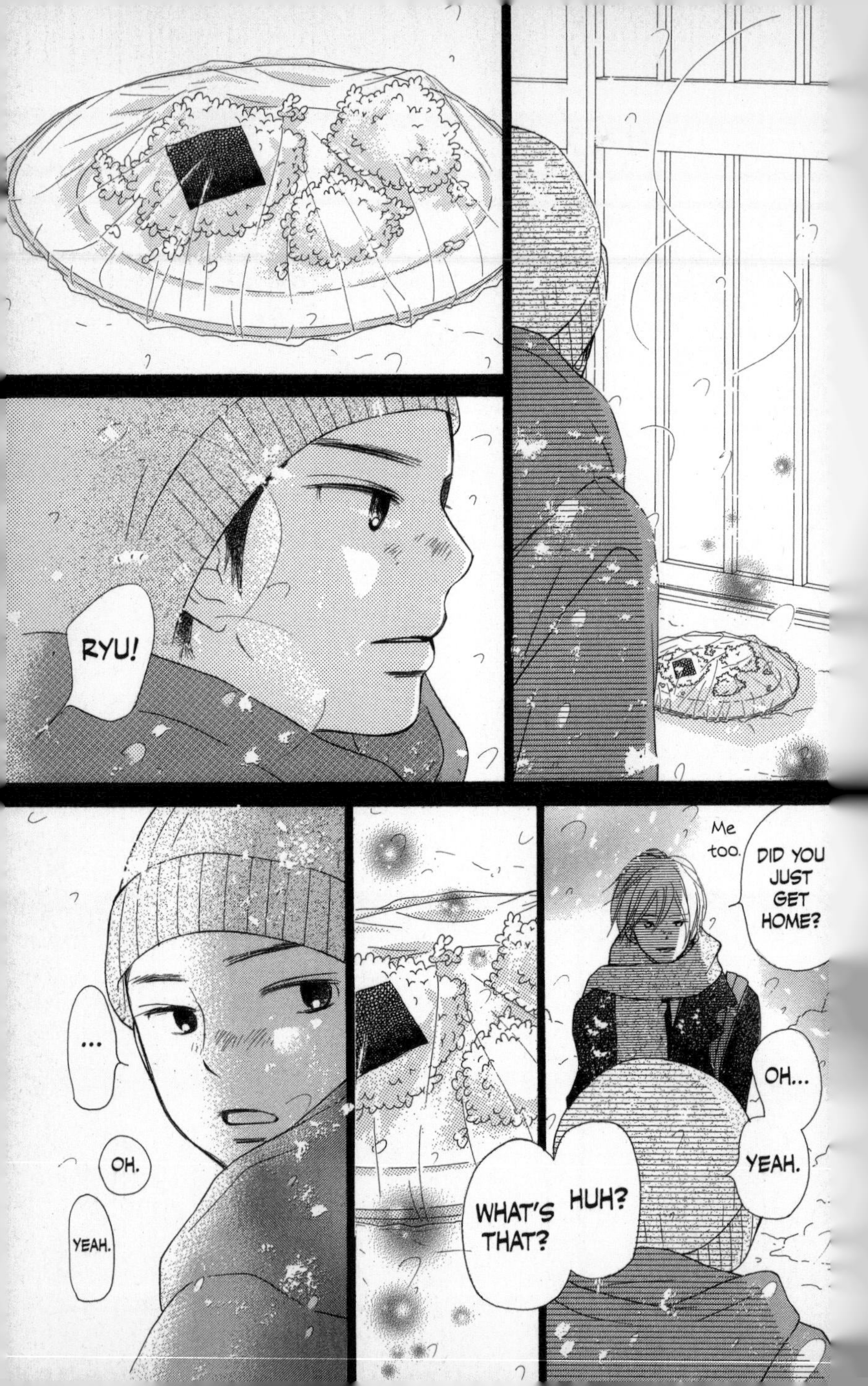
RYU!
DID YOU JUST GET HOME?
Me too.
OH...
YEAH.
HUH?
WHAT'S THAT?
...
OH.
YEAH.

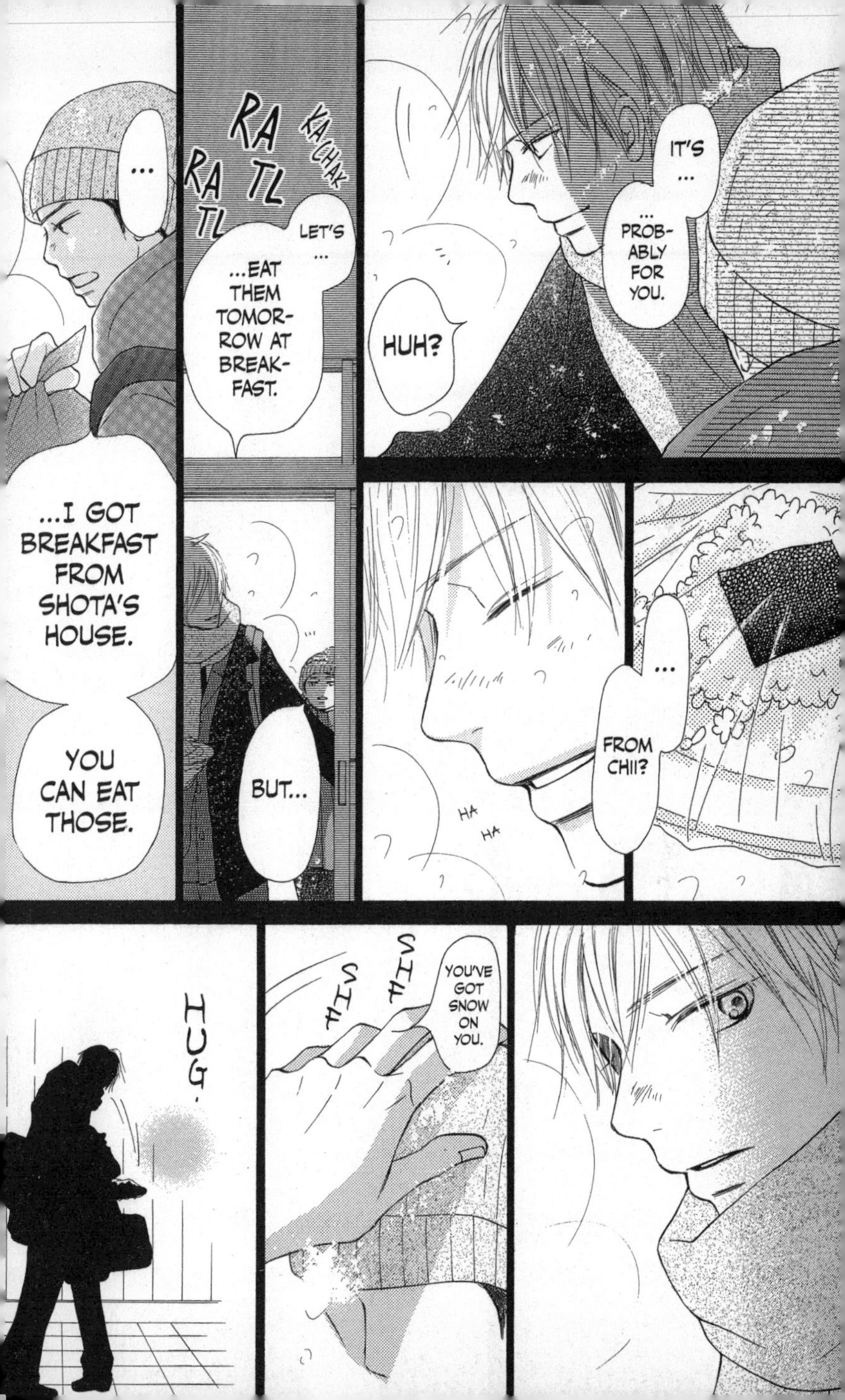
IT'S ...
... PROBABLY FOR YOU.
HUH?
KACHAK
RA TL RA TL
LET'S ...
...EAT THEM TOMORROW AT BREAKFAST.
...
FROM CHII?
HA HA
BUT...
...
...I GOT BREAKFAST FROM SHOTA'S HOUSE.
YOU CAN EAT THOSE.
SHF SHF
YOU'VE GOT SNOW ON YOU.
HUG.

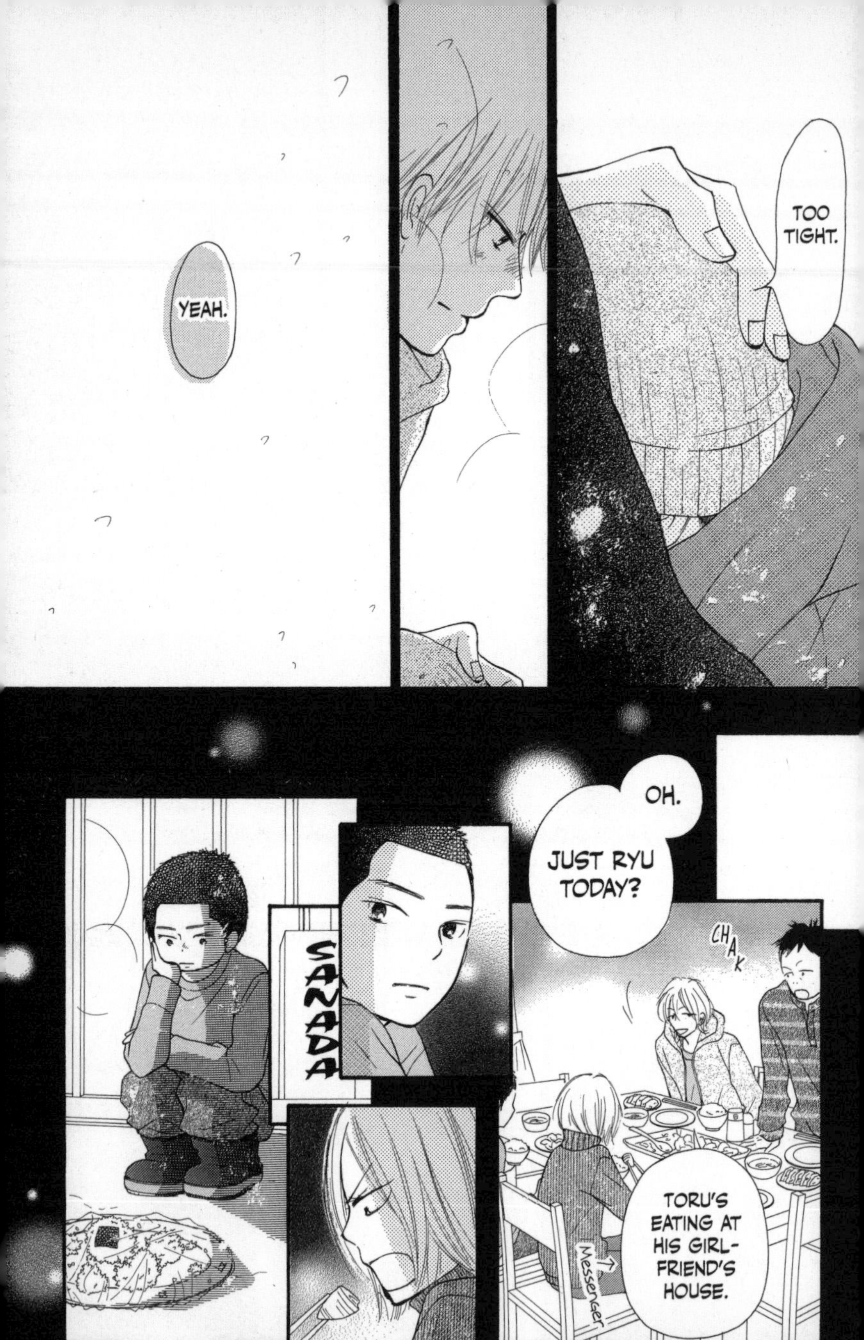
TOO TIGHT.
YEAH.
OH.
JUST RYU TODAY?
CHAK
TORU'S EATING AT HIS GIRL-FRIEND'S HOUSE.
Messenger
SANADA

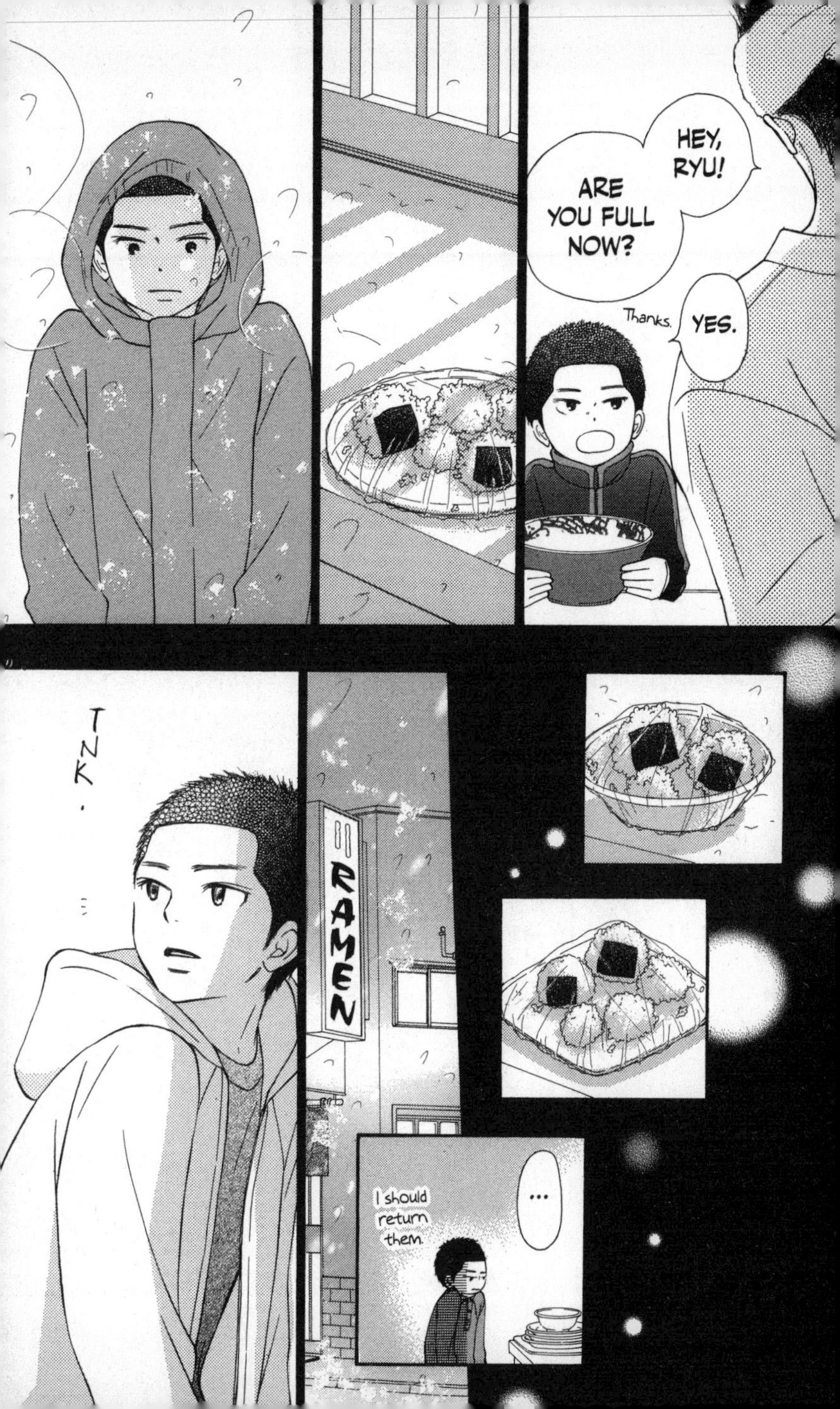
HEY, RYU!
ARE YOU FULL NOW?
YES.
Thanks.
...
I should return them.
RAMEN
TNK.

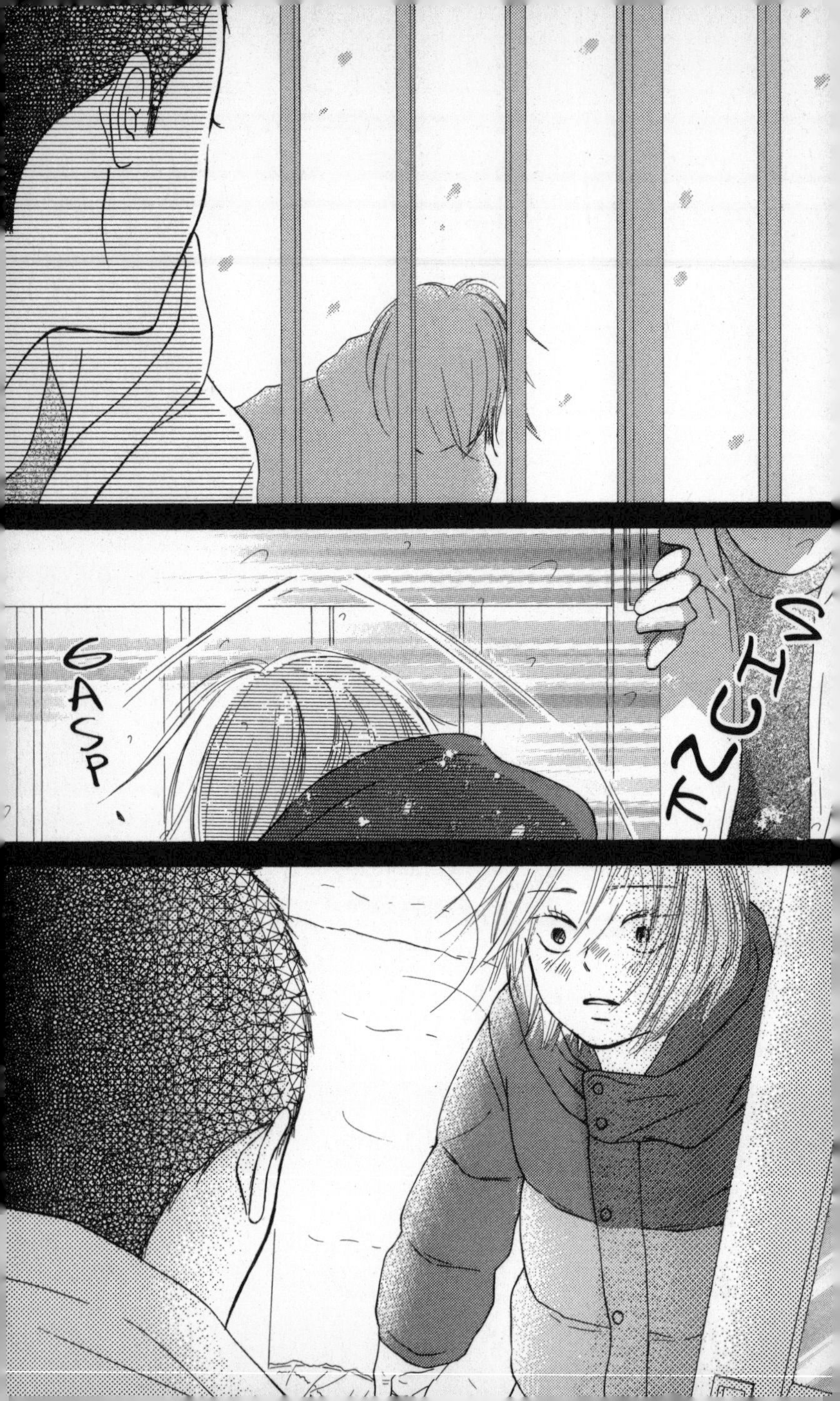
SHUNK
GASP

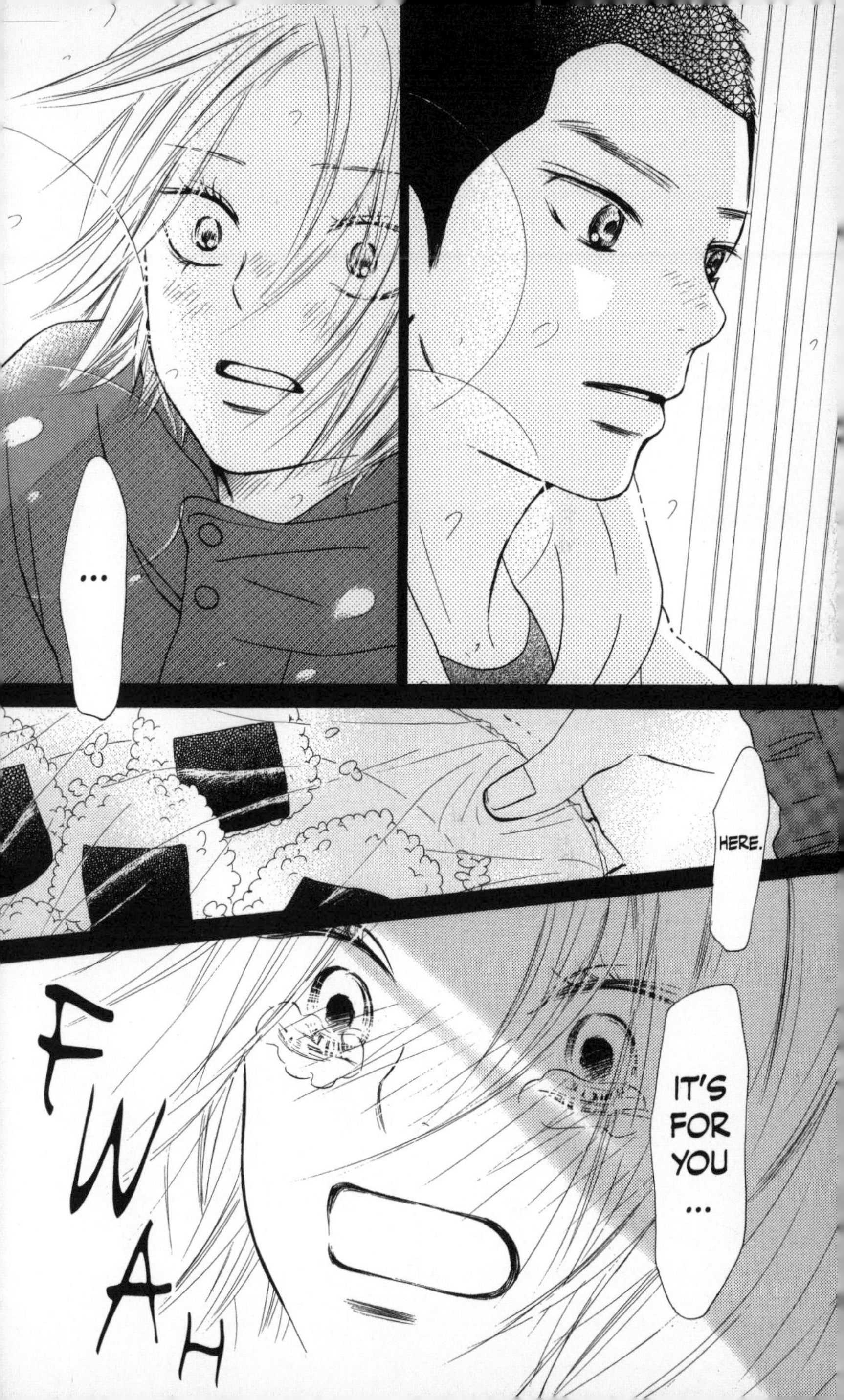
...
HERE.
IT'S FOR YOU ...
FWAH

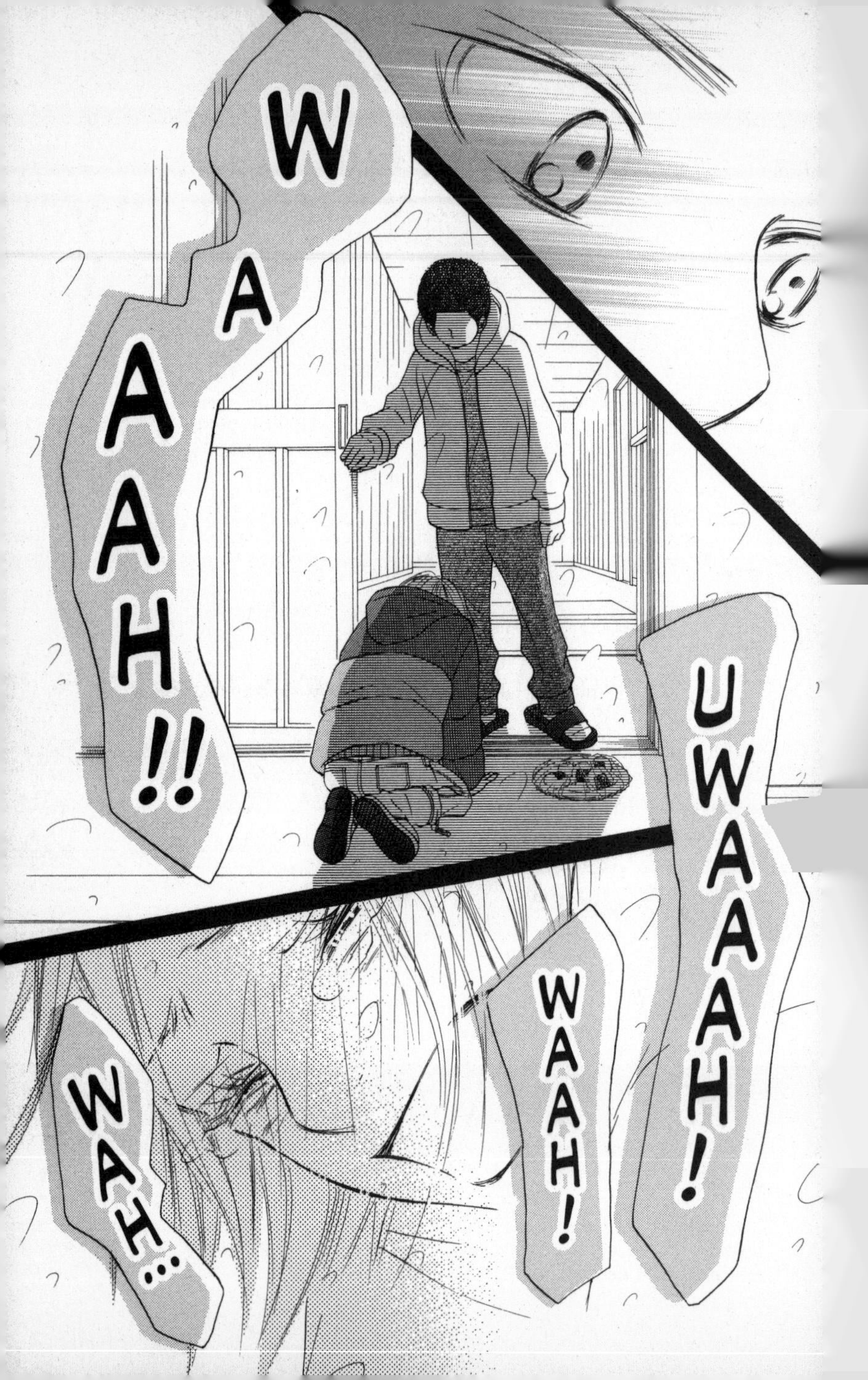
WAAAH!!
UWAAAH!
WAAH!
WAH..

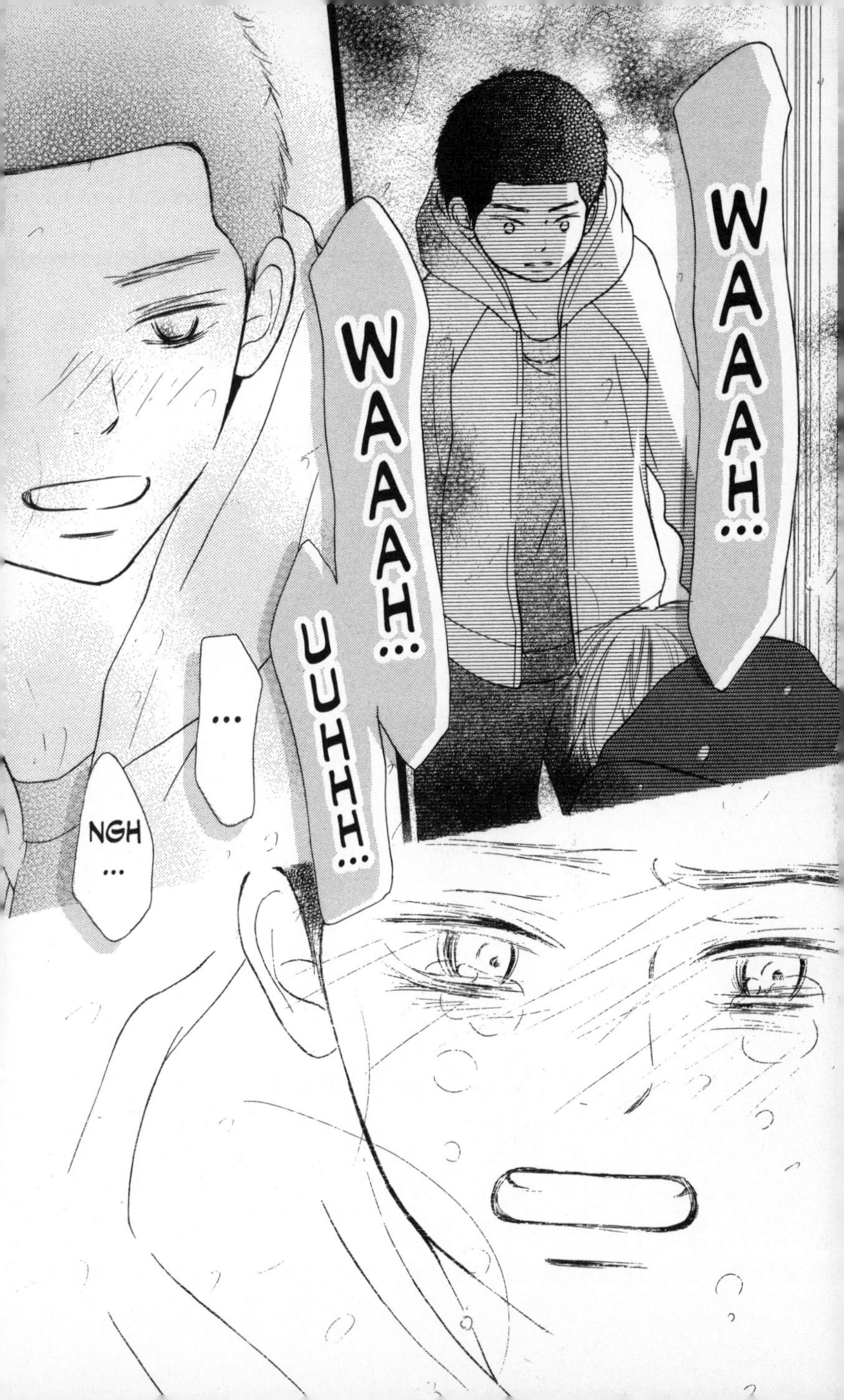
WAAAAH...
WAAAAH...
UUHHH...
...
NGH...

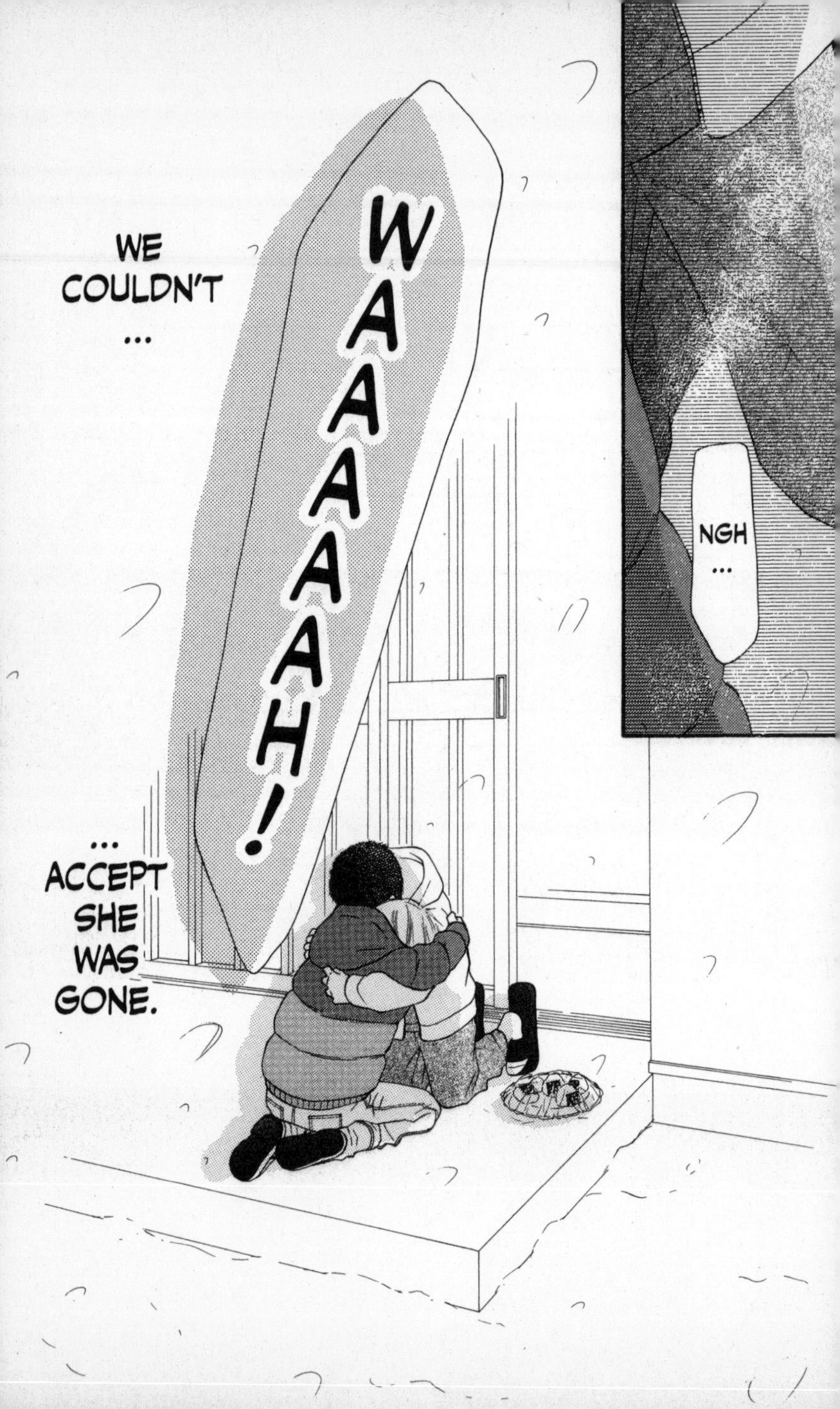
NGH ...
WE COULDN'T ...
WAAAAAH!
... ACCEPT SHE WAS GONE.

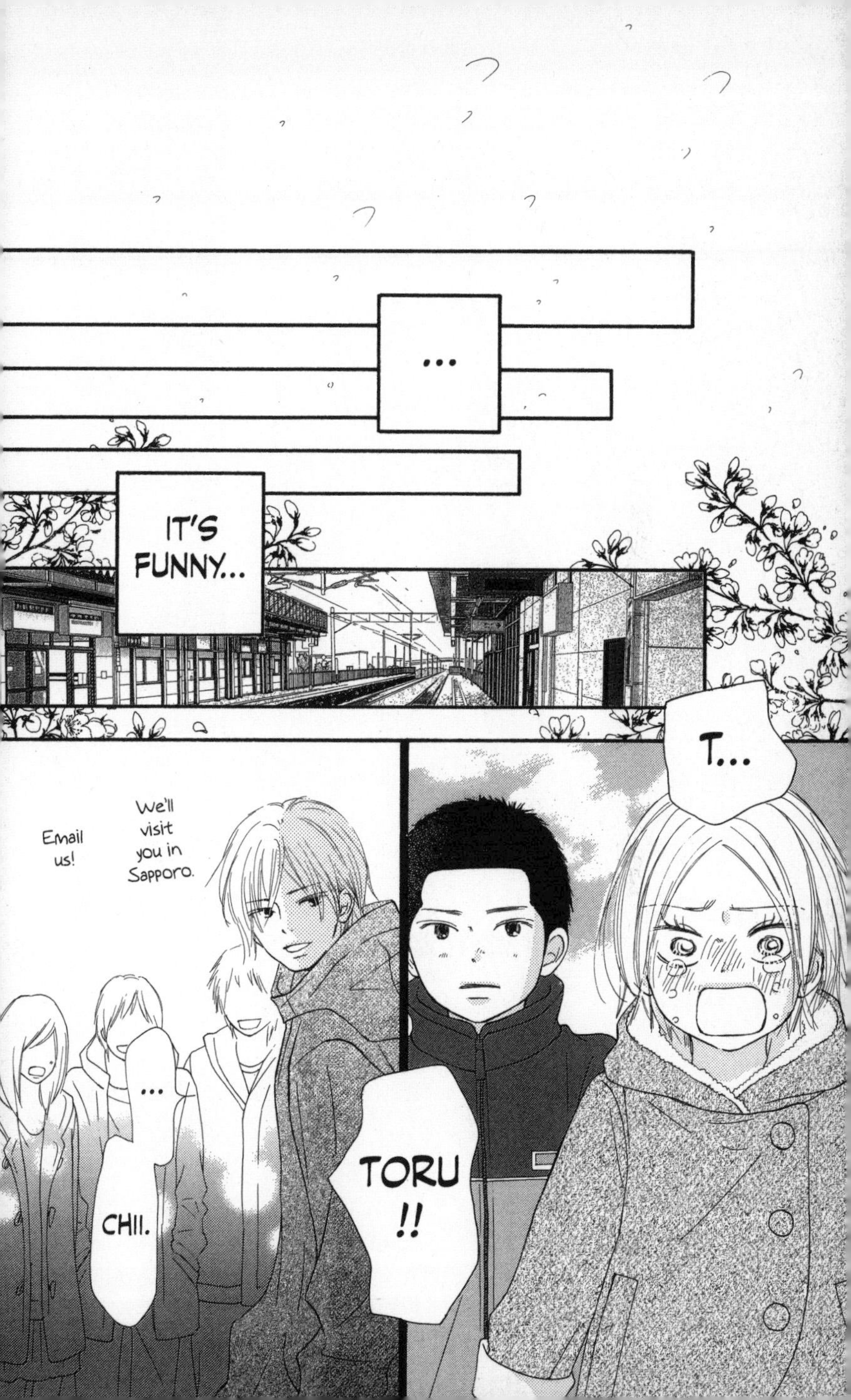
...
IT'S FUNNY...
T...
TORU !!
We'll visit you in Sapporo.
Email us!
...
CHII.

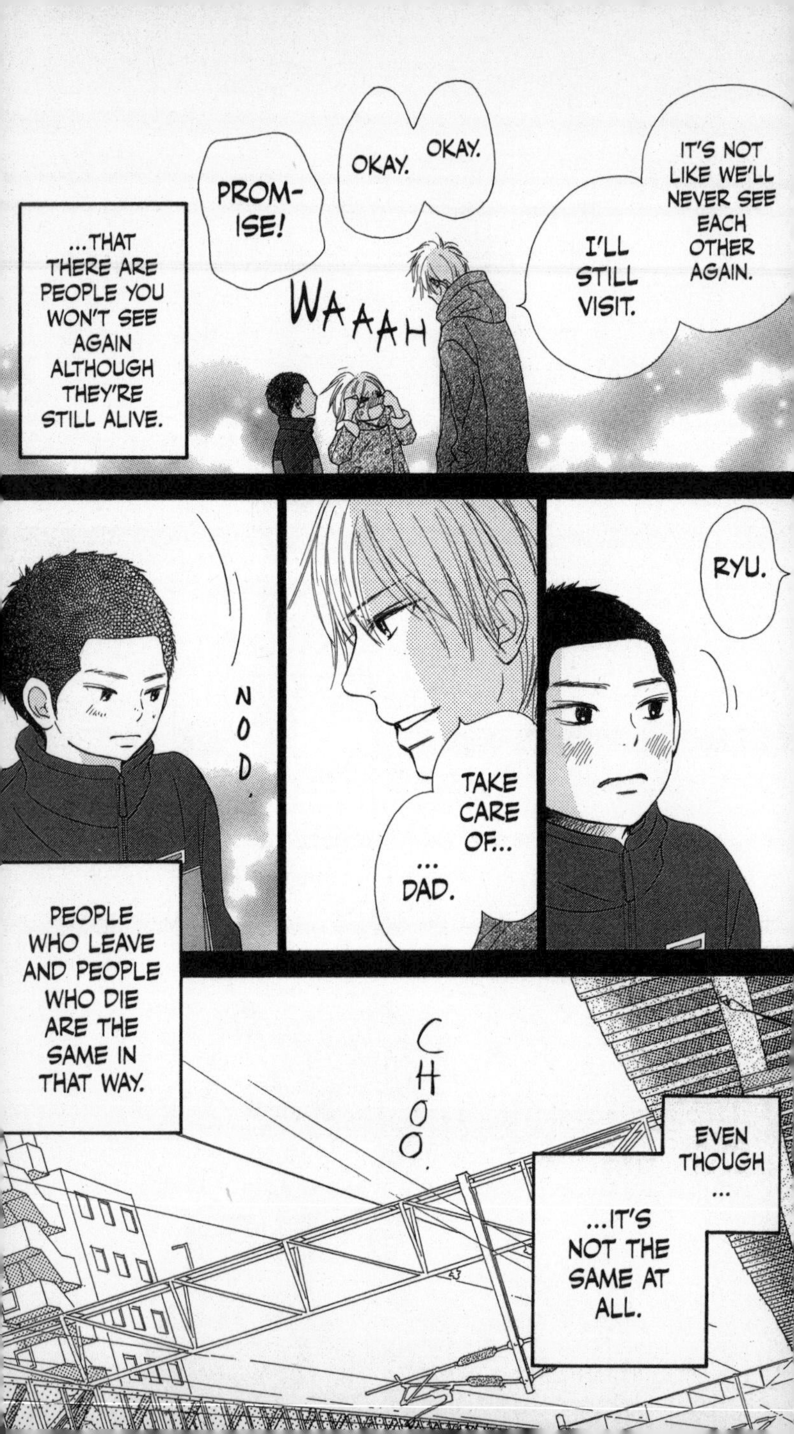
IT'S NOT LIKE WE'LL NEVER SEE EACH OTHER AGAIN.
I'LL STILL VISIT.
OKAY.
OKAY.
PROMISE!
WAAAH
...THAT THERE ARE PEOPLE YOU WON'T SEE AGAIN ALTHOUGH THEY'RE STILL ALIVE.
RYU.
TAKE CARE OF...
...DAD.
NOD.
PEOPLE WHO LEAVE AND PEOPLE WHO DIE ARE THE SAME IN THAT WAY.
EVEN THOUGH...
...IT'S NOT THE SAME AT ALL.
CHOO.

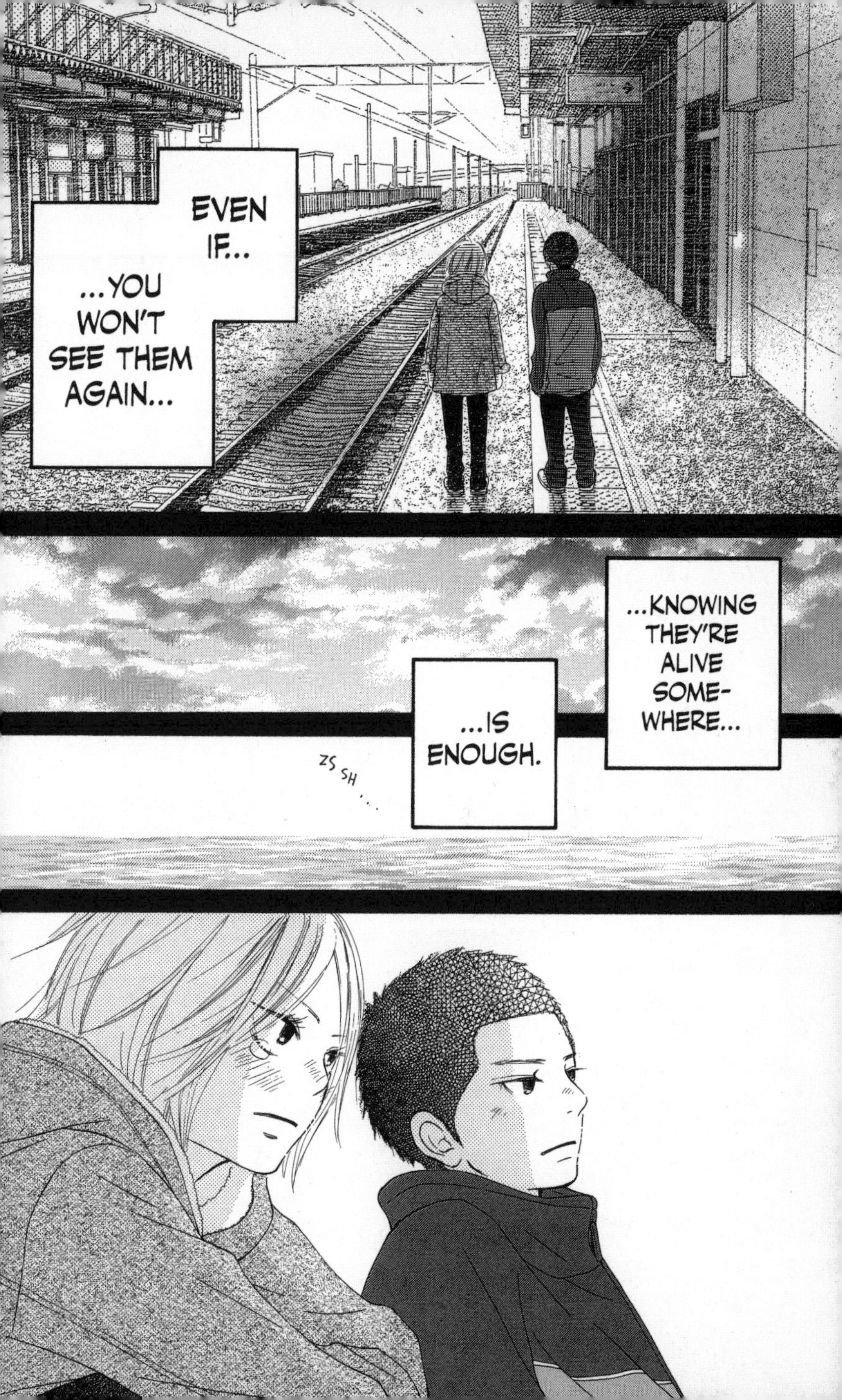
EVEN IF...
...YOU WON'T SEE THEM AGAIN...
...KNOWING THEY'RE ALIVE SOME-WHERE...
...IS ENOUGH.
SH SZ...

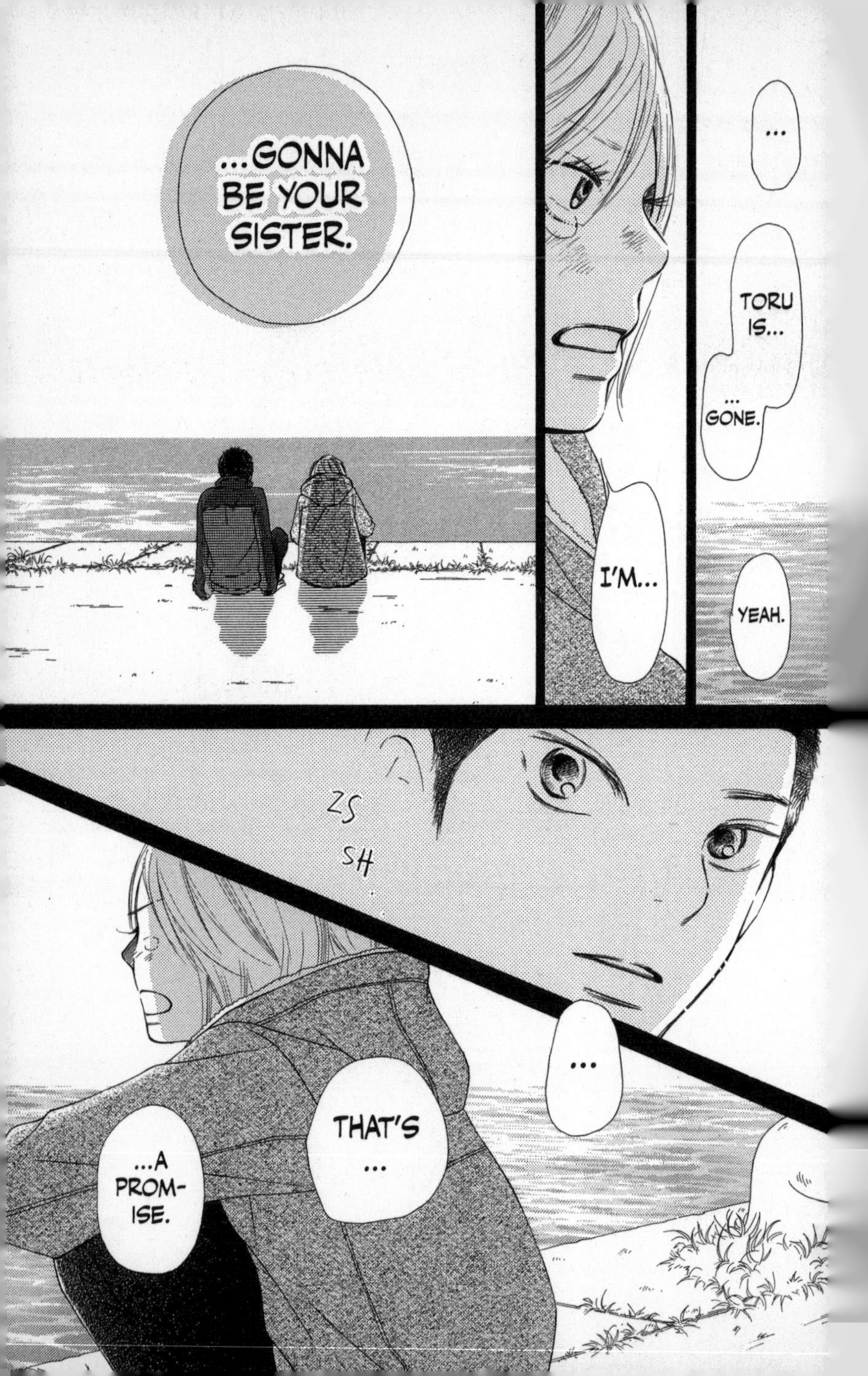
...
TORU IS...
...GONE.
YEAH.
I'M...
...GONNA BE YOUR SISTER.
ZSSH
...
THAT'S...
...A PROM-ISE.

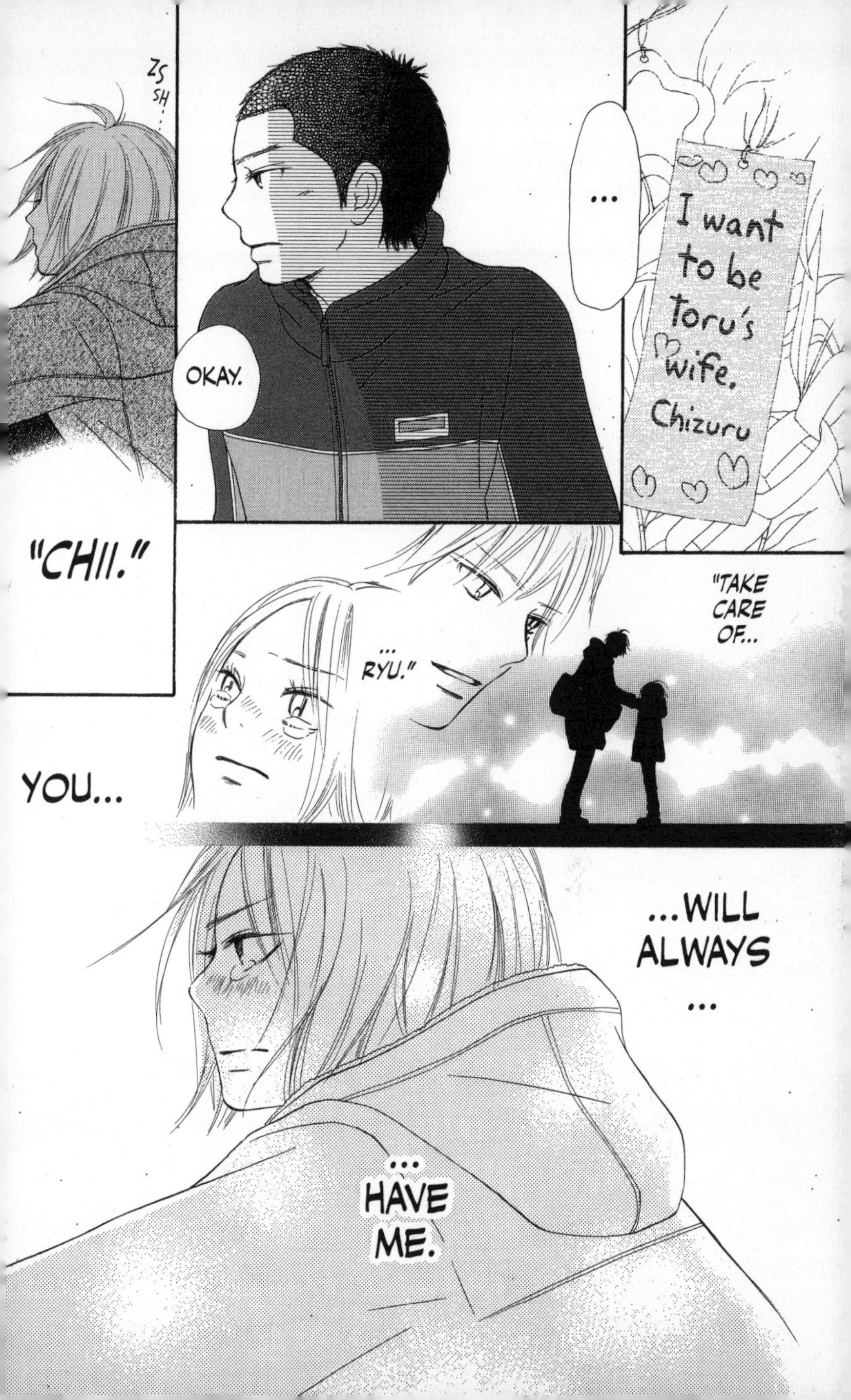
I want to be toru's wife. Chizuru
...
OKAY.
ZSSH...
"TAKE CARE OF...
... RYU."
"CHII."
YOU...
...WILL ALWAYS ...
... HAVE ME.

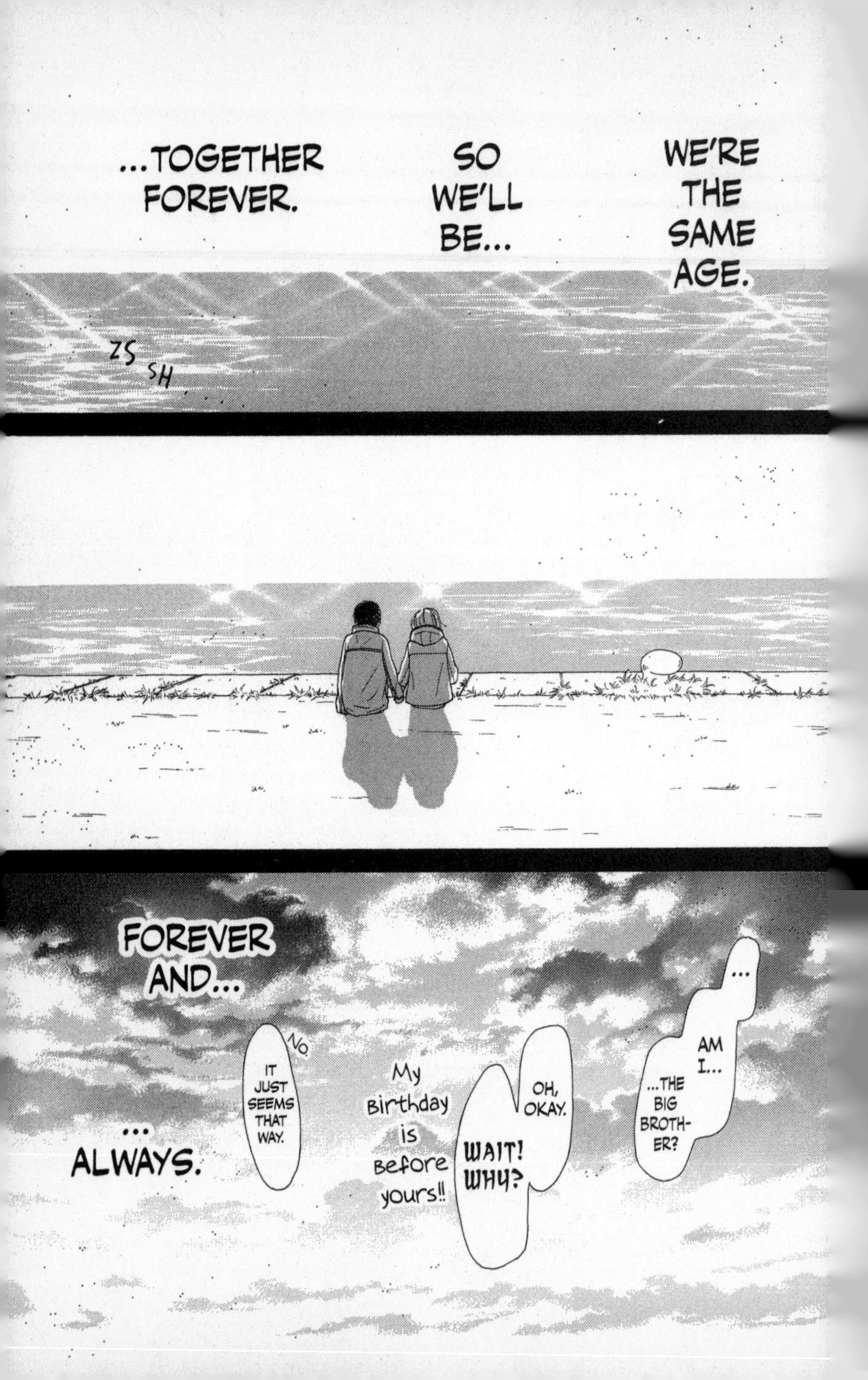
WE'RE THE SAME AGE.
SO WE'LL BE...
...TOGETHER FOREVER.
...
AM I... ...THE BIG BROTHER?
OH, OKAY.
WAIT! WHY?
My Birthday is before yours!!
NO.
IT JUST SEEMS THAT WAY.
FOREVER AND...
...ALWAYS.

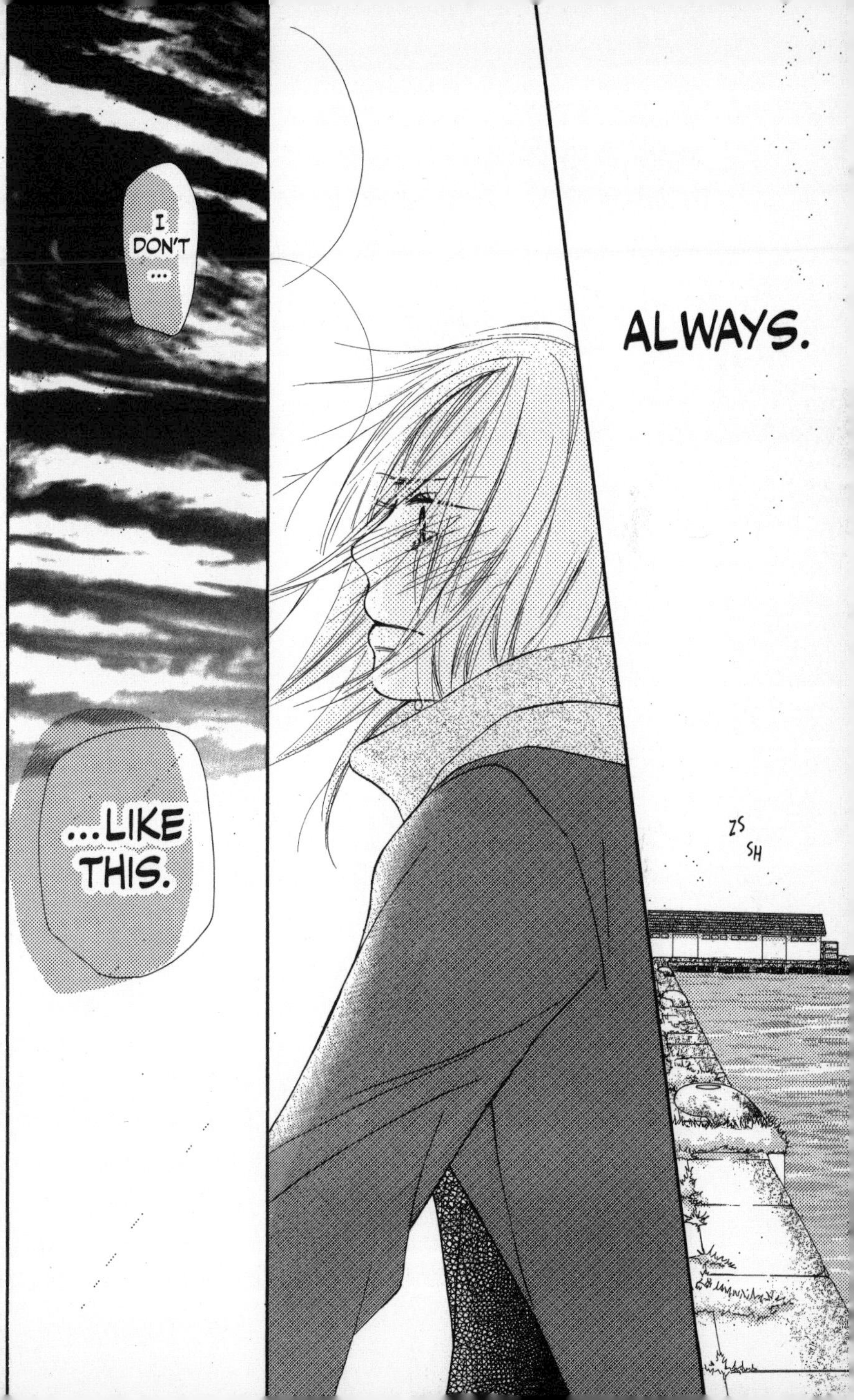
ALWAYS.
ZS SH
I DON'T ...
...LIKE THIS.

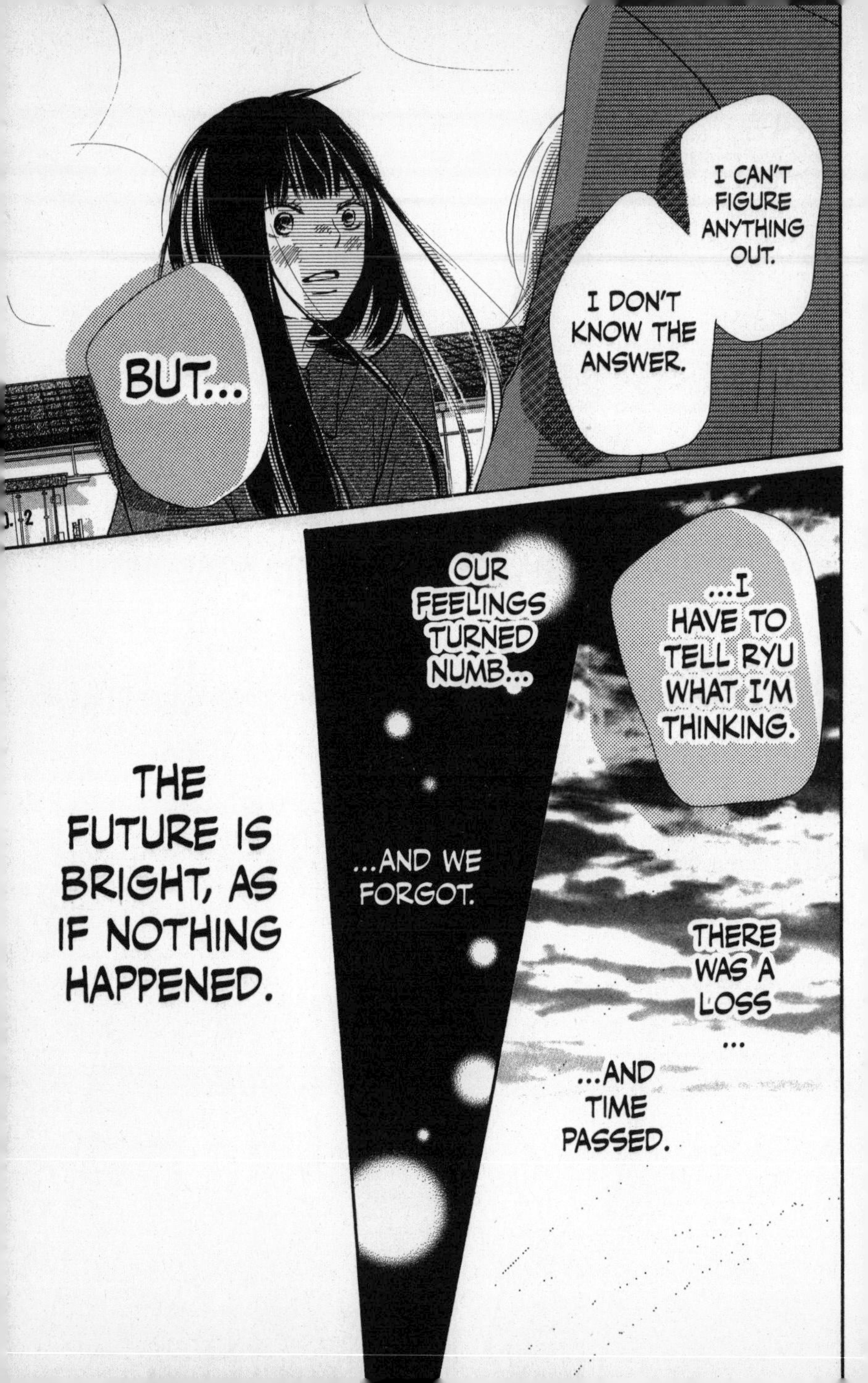
I CAN'T FIGURE ANYTHING OUT.
I DON'T KNOW THE ANSWER.
BUT...
...I HAVE TO TELL RYU WHAT I'M THINKING.
THERE WAS A LOSS ...
...AND TIME PASSED.
OUR FEELINGS TURNED NUMB...
...AND WE FORGOT.
THE FUTURE IS BRIGHT, AS IF NOTHING HAPPENED.

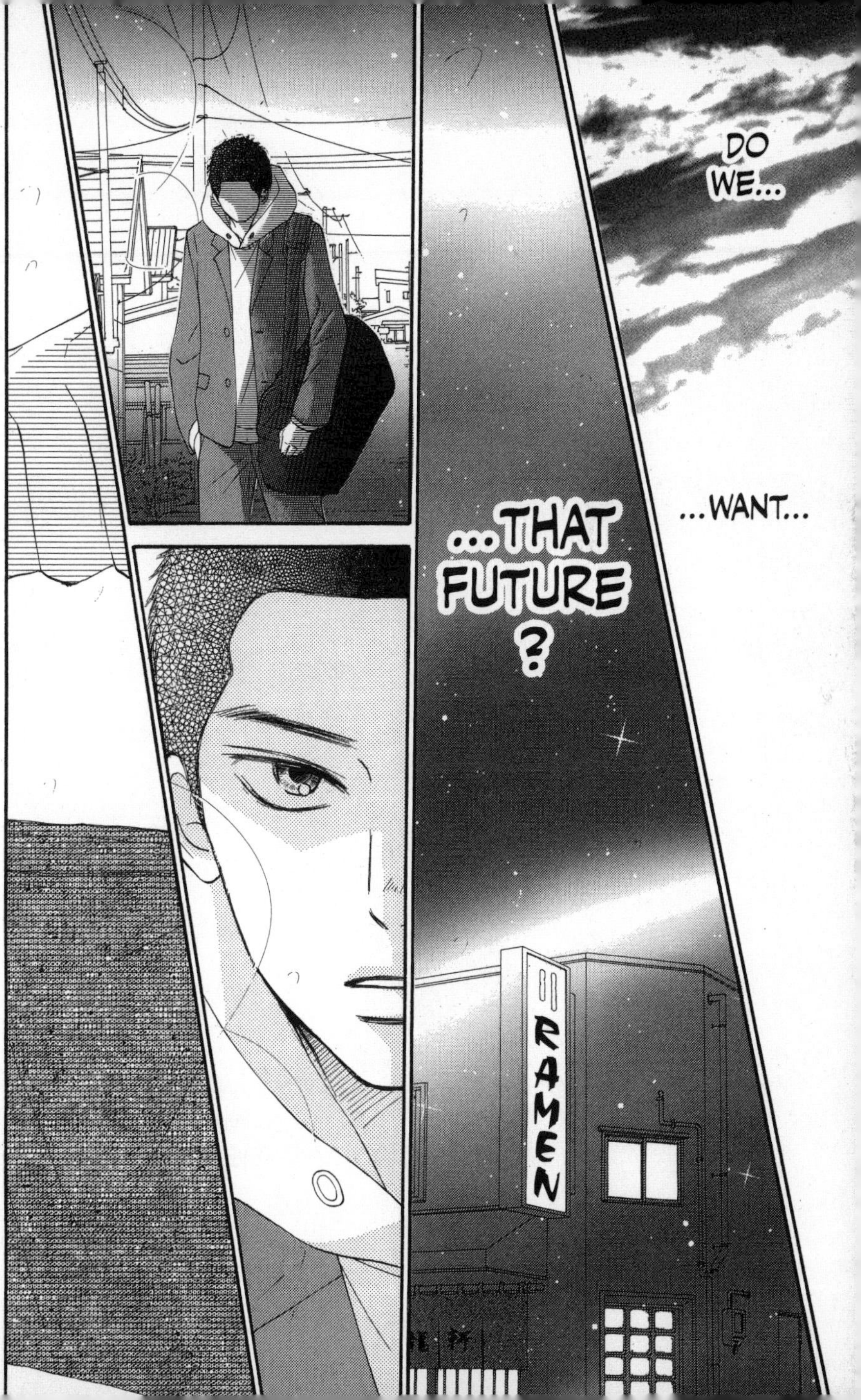
DO WE...
...WANT...
...THAT FUTURE?
RAMEN

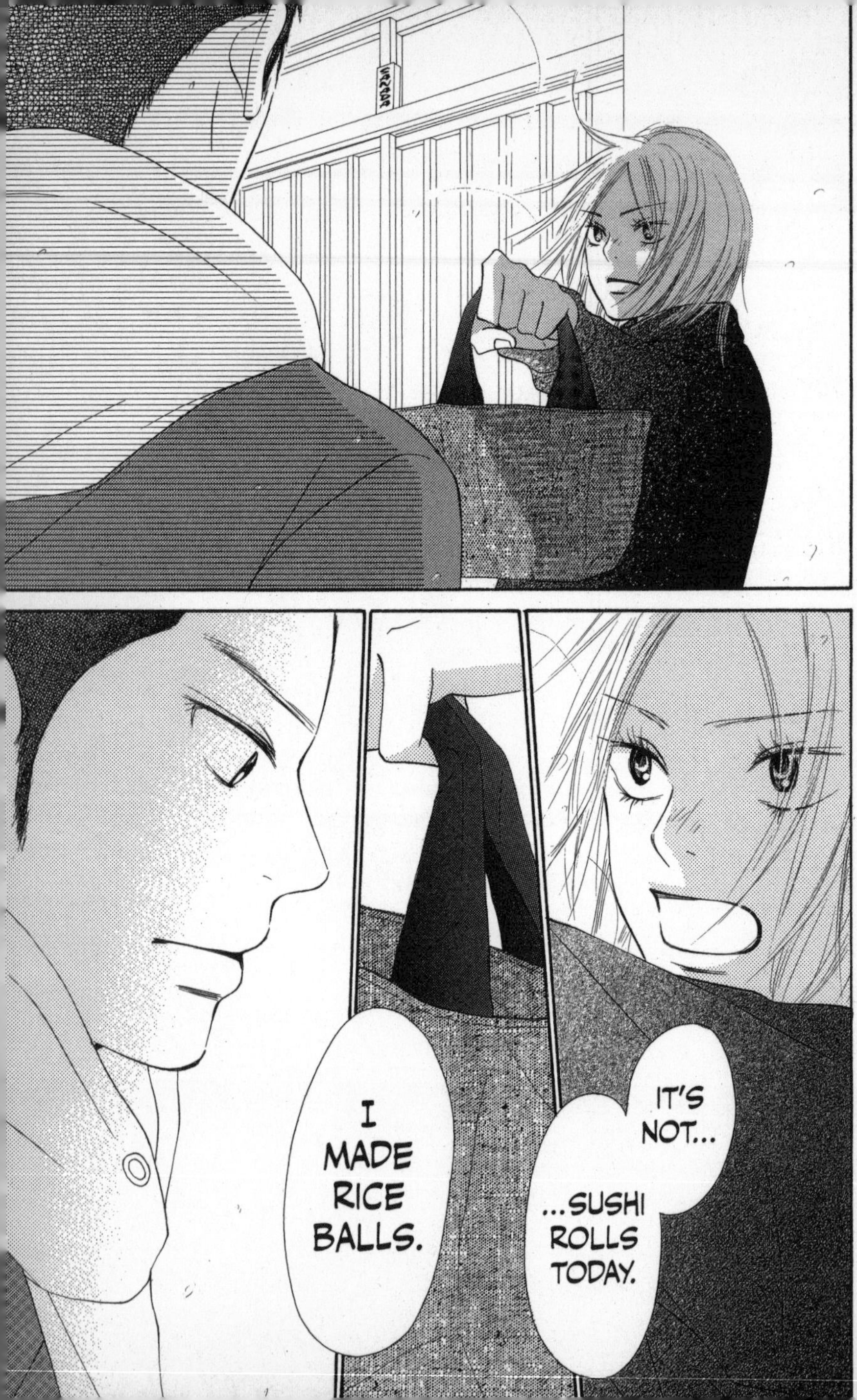
IT'S NOT... ...SUSHI ROLLS TODAY.
I MADE RICE BALLS.

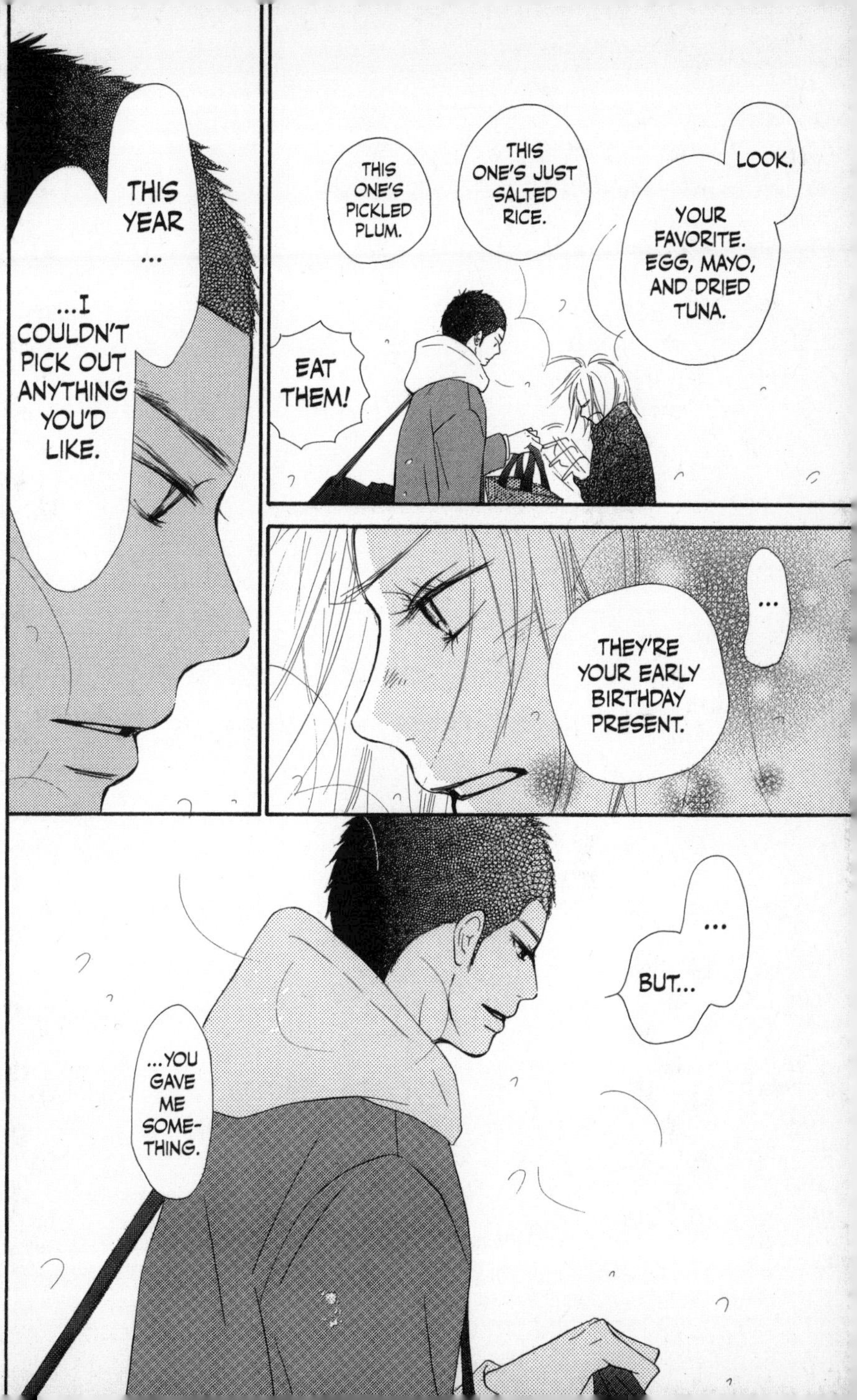
LOOK.
YOUR FAVORITE. EGG, MAYO, AND DRIED TUNA.
THIS ONE'S JUST SALTED RICE.
THIS ONE'S PICKLED PLUM.
EAT THEM!
...
THEY'RE YOUR EARLY BIRTHDAY PRESENT.
THIS YEAR ...
...I COULDN'T PICK OUT ANYTHING YOU'D LIKE.
... BUT...
...YOU GAVE ME SOMETHING.

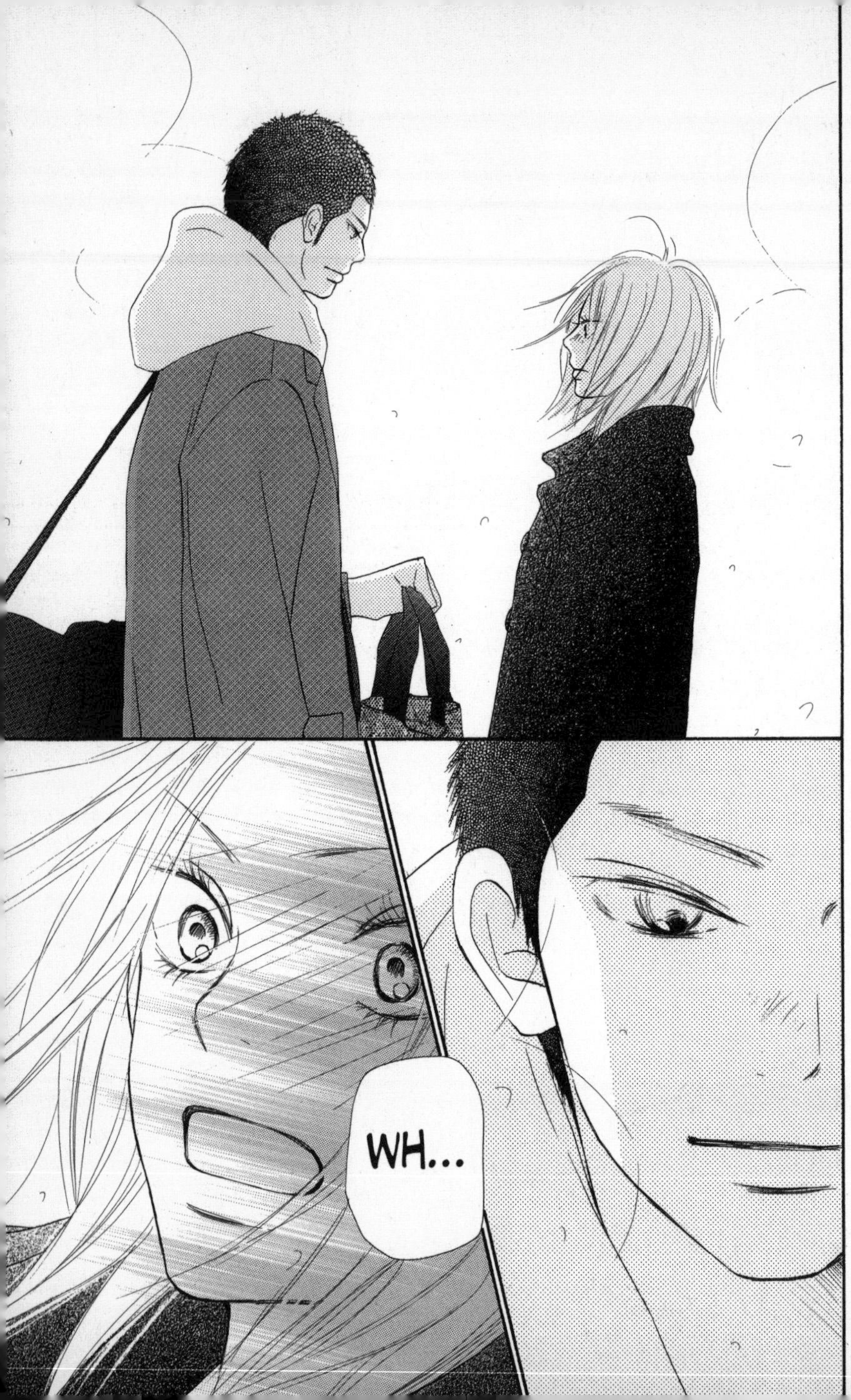
WH...

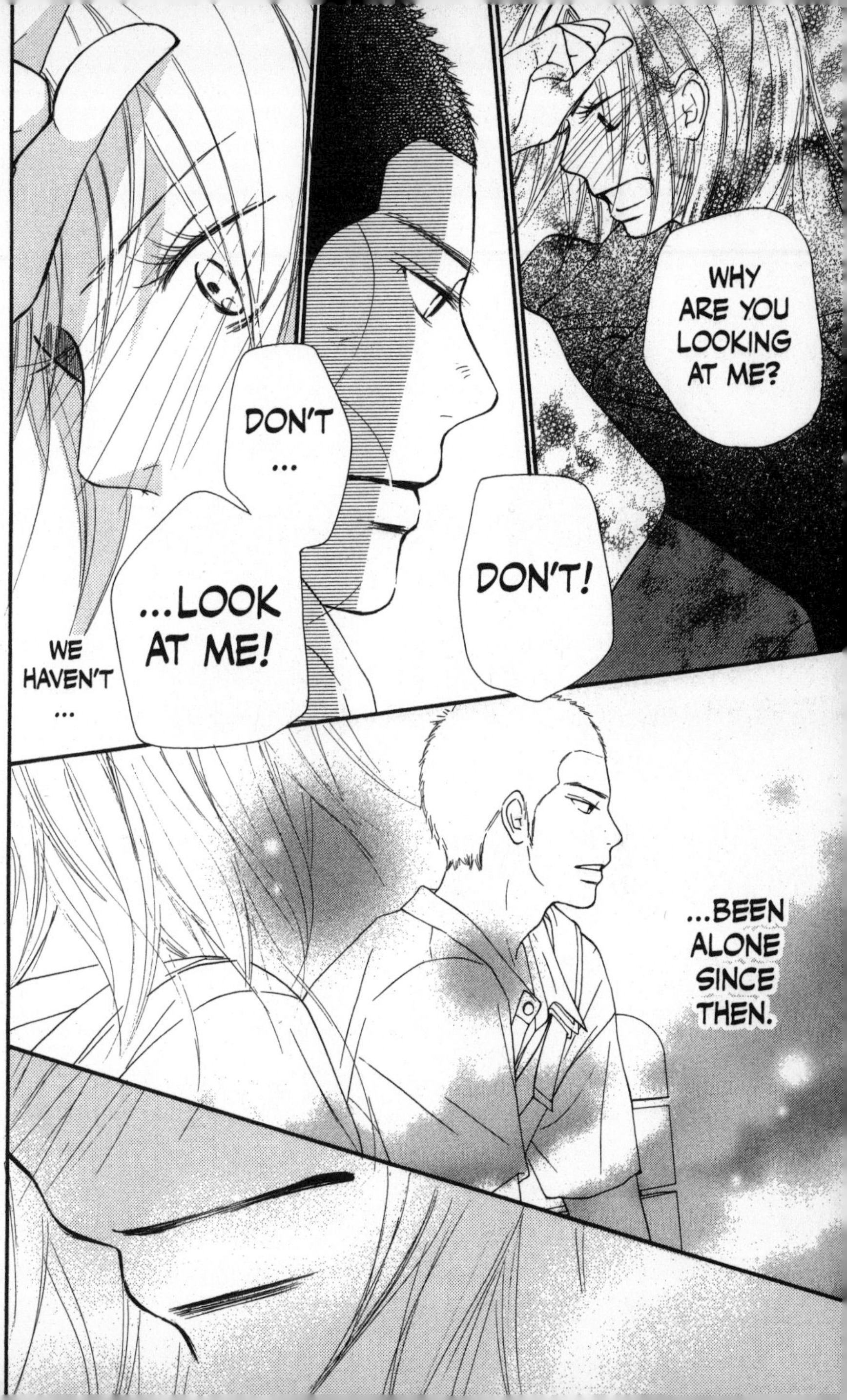
WHY ARE YOU LOOKING AT ME?
DON'T!
DON'T ...
...LOOK AT ME!
WE HAVEN'T ...
...BEEN ALONE SINCE THEN.

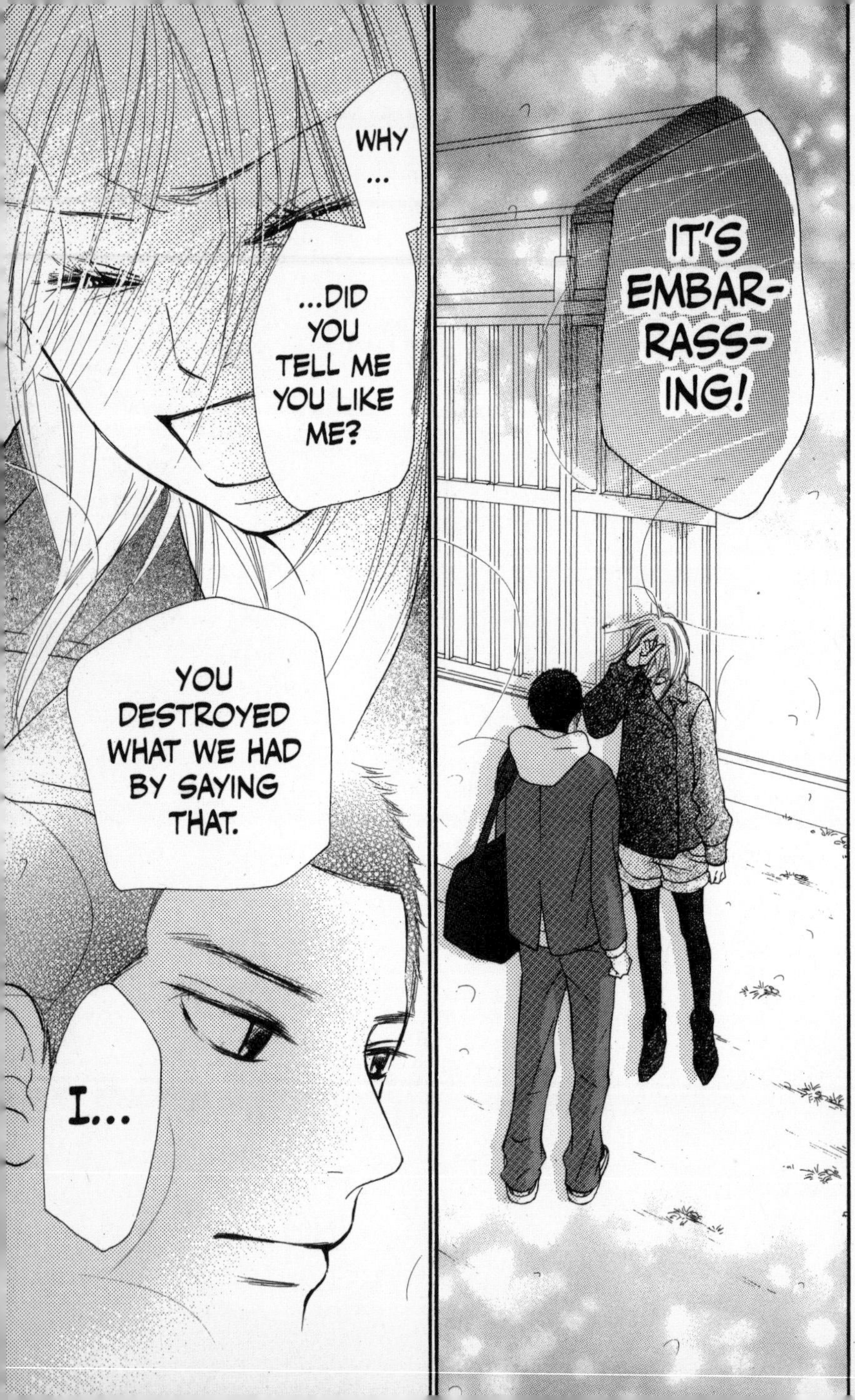
IT'S EMBARRASSING!
WHY...
...DID YOU TELL ME YOU LIKE ME?
YOU DESTROYED WHAT WE HAD BY SAYING THAT.
I...

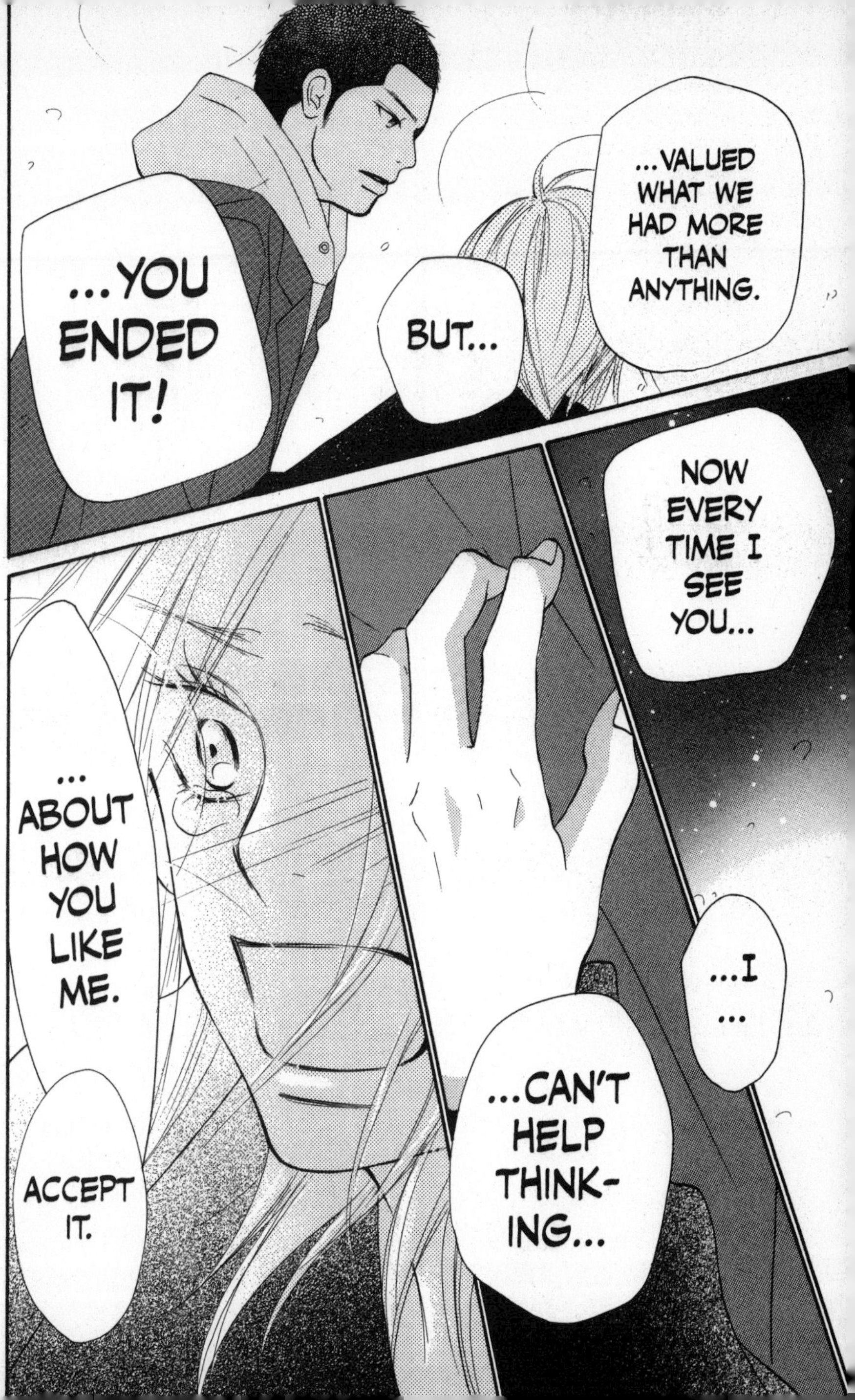
...VALUED WHAT WE HAD MORE THAN ANYTHING.
BUT...
...YOU ENDED IT!
NOW EVERY TIME I SEE YOU...
...I ...
...CAN'T HELP THINK-ING...
... ABOUT HOW YOU LIKE ME.
ACCEPT IT.

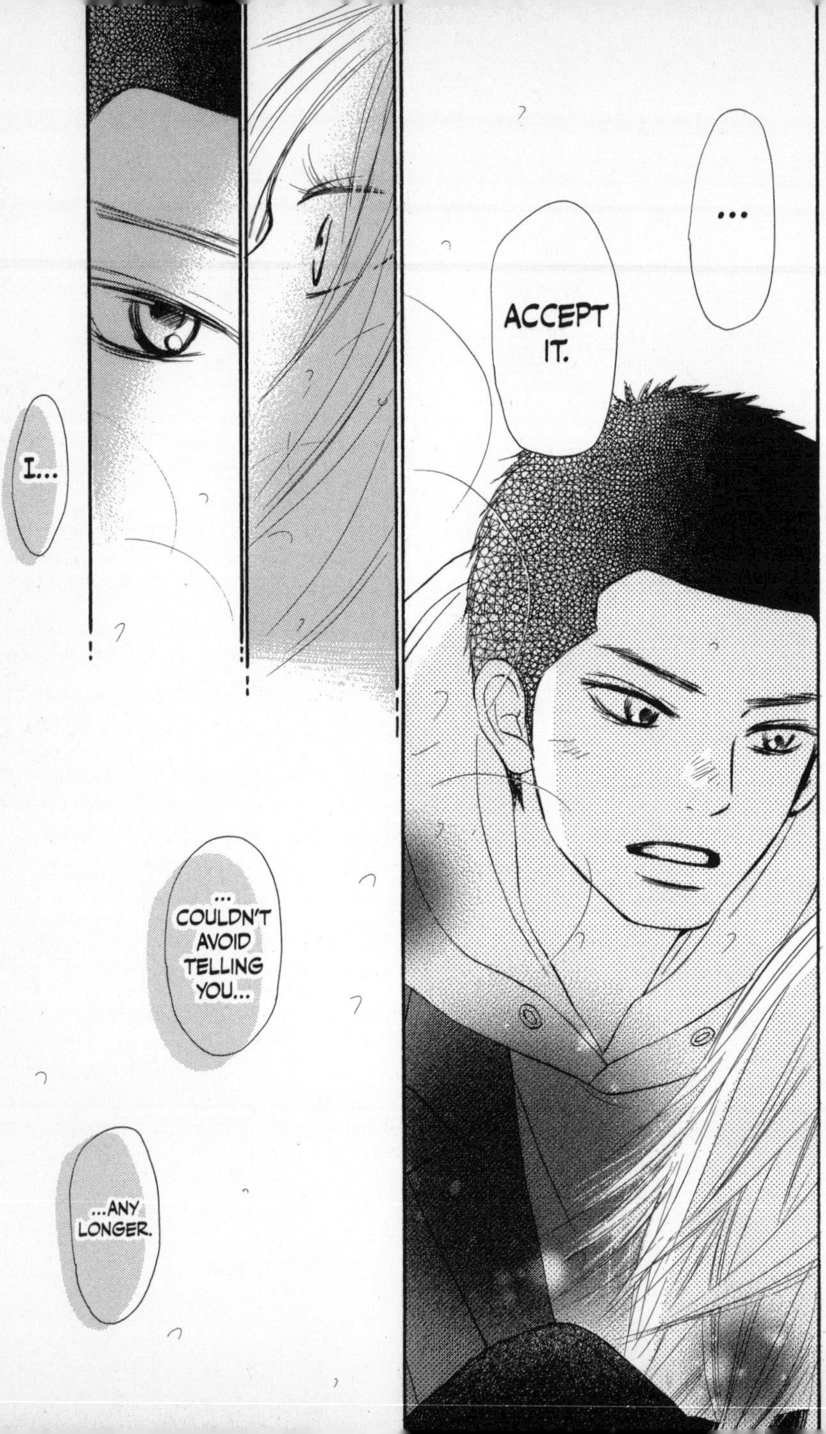
...
ACCEPT IT.
I...
...COULDN'T AVOID TELLING YOU...
...ANY LONGER.

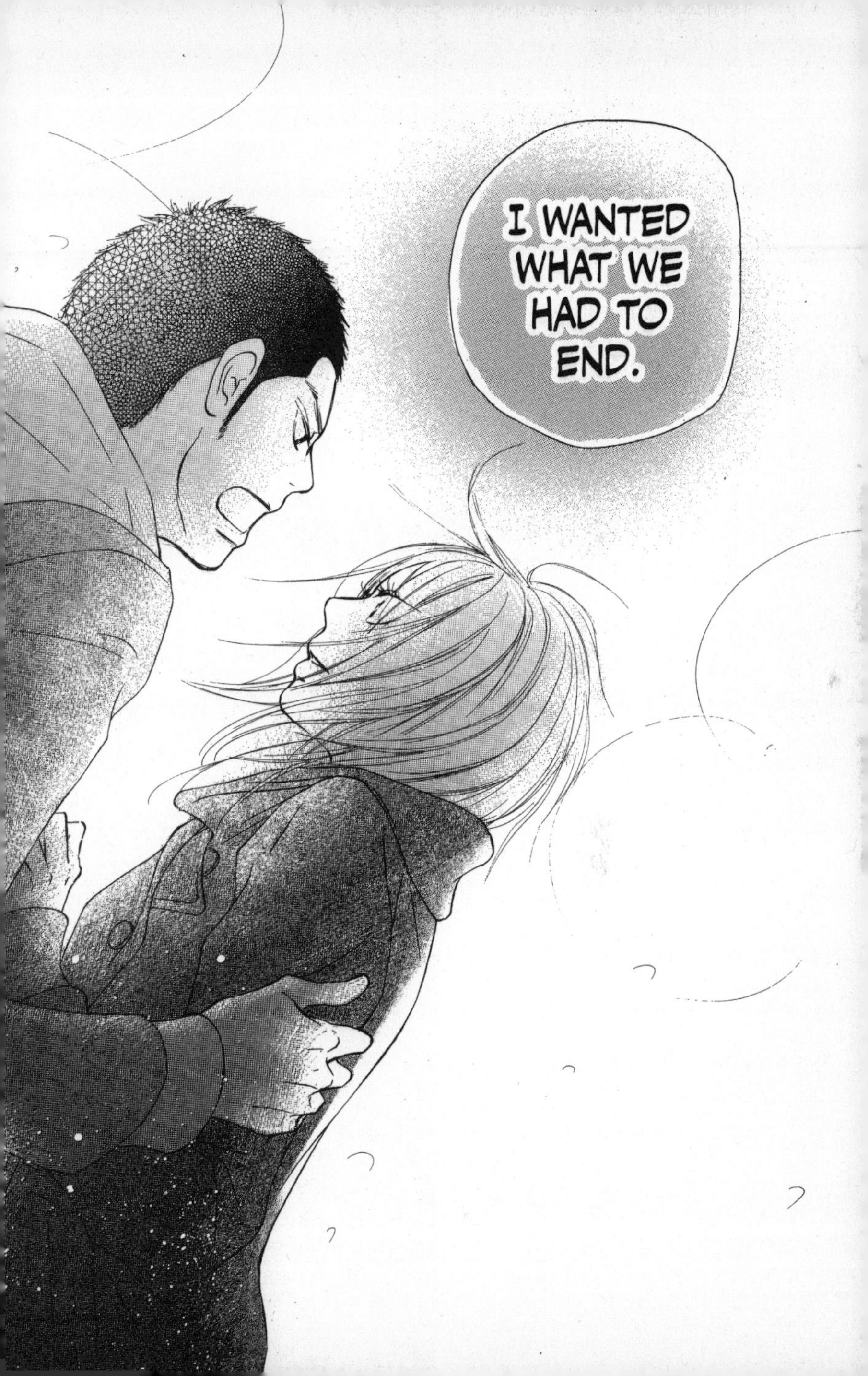
I WANTED WHAT WE HAD TO END.

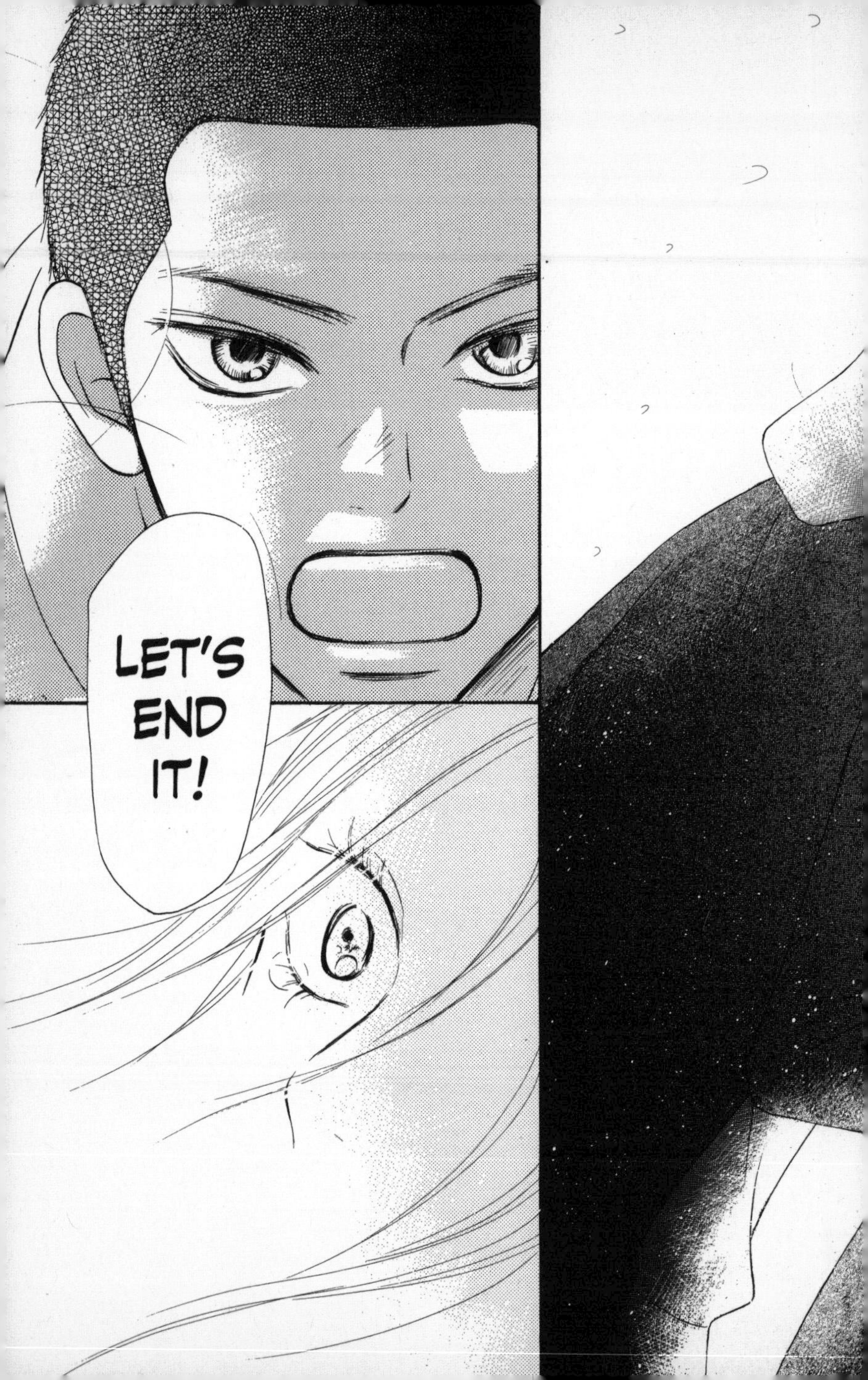
LET'S END IT!

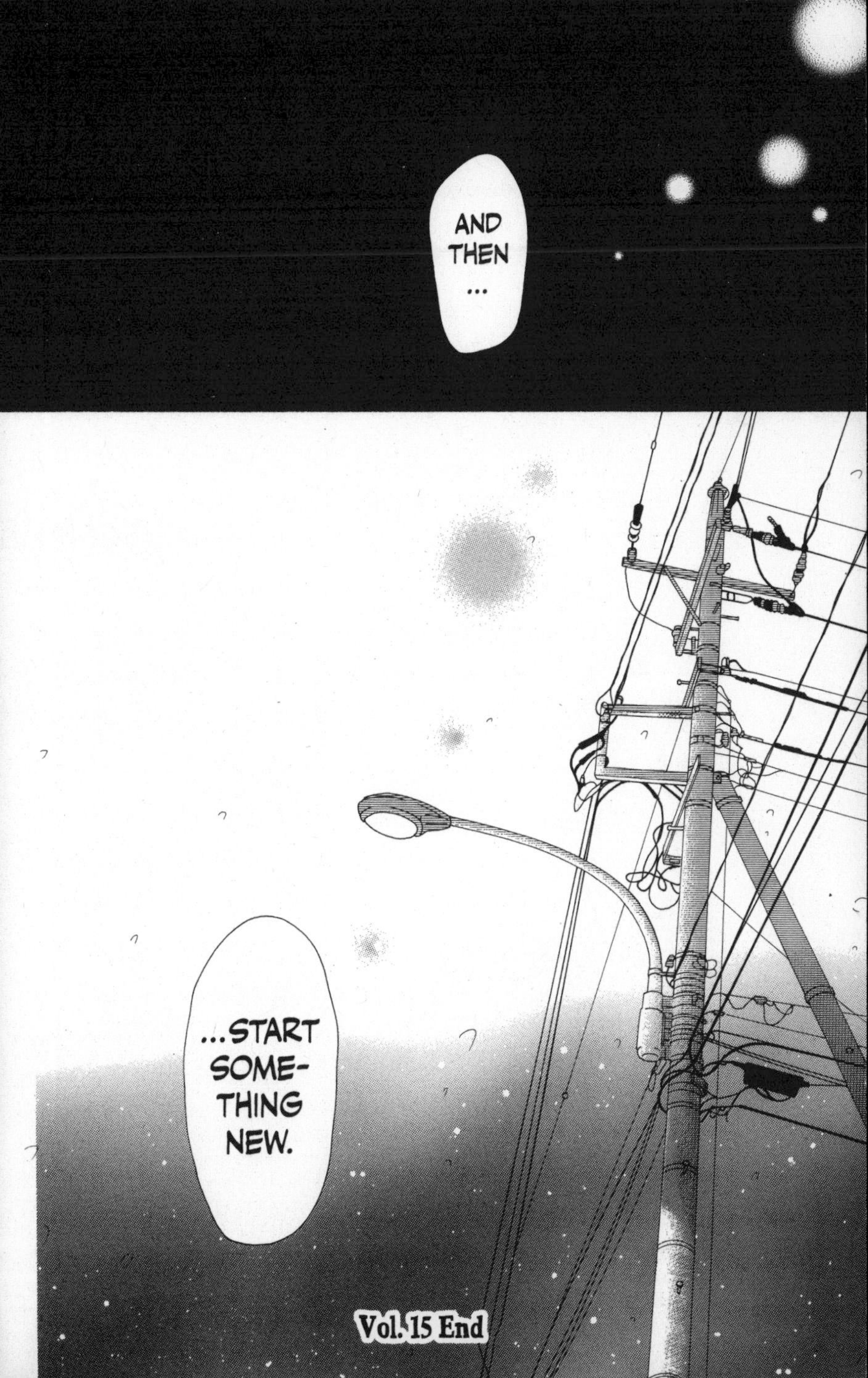
AND THEN ...
...START SOME-THING NEW.
Vol. 15 End

From me (the editor) to you (the reader).

Here are some Japanese culture explanations that will help you better understand the references in the *Kimi ni Todoke* world.

Honorifics:
When saying someone's name in Japanese, a suffix is often attached to indicate how familiar the speaker is with the person. Some are more polite and respectful, while others are endearing. Calling someone by just their first name is the most informal.
-kun is used for young men or boys, usually someone you are familiar with.
-chan is used for young women, girls or young children and can be used as a term of endearment.
-san is used for someone you respect or are not close to, or to be polite.

Page 27, rice ball:
An *onigiri* is a wedge of rice that can be wrapped in seaweed and stuffed with various fillings.

Page 44, sushi rolls:
Norimaki is an umbrella term for sushi rice and various ingredients rolled in seaweed. The California roll is a popular sushi roll in the U.S.

Page 109, goat:
Chizu's mom uses *yaki ireru* for "get mad" and Chizu repeats that phrase. Ryu doesn't understand and hears *yagi*, which means "goat," instead of *yaki*.

Page 120, Tanabata:
A Japanese festival celebrating the annual meeting of the stars Vega and Altair. According to myth, the stars are lovers separated by the Milky Way.

Page 121, red-bean bun:
A bun filled with sweetened *azuki* (red bean) paste.